MASCULINITIES

MASCULINITIES

R. W. Connell

Second Edition

University of California Press
Berkeley   Los Angeles

University of California Press
Berkeley and Los Angeles, California

Copyright © R. W. Connell 1995, 2005

Published by arrangement with Polity Press

Library of Congress Cataloging-in-Publication Data

Connell, R. W.
    Masculinities / R. W. Connell. — 2nd ed.
      p.   cm.
    Includes bibliographic references and index.
    ISBN 0-520-24698-5 (pbk. : alk. paper)
    1. Masculinity.   2. Sex role.   I. Title.
  HQ1088.C66   2005
  305.3—dc22

                                           2005050590

Typeset in Baskerville on 11/12 pt
by SNP Best-set Typesetter Ltd., Hong Kong
Printed and bound in the United States of America

13   12   11   10   09   08   07   06   05
10 9 8 7 6 5 4 3 2 1

The paper used in this publication meets the minimum requirements of
ANSI/NISO Z39.48-1992 (R 1997) (*Permanence of Paper*).

Contents

Acknowledgments

Even for a practised writer, this book has been difficult to write. The issues are explosive and tangled, the chances of going astray are good. The support I was given made the difference. The advice and love of Pam Benton and Kylie Benton-Connell were vital at the time of the first edition. Pam did not live to see the second; Kylie's support has continued, and has made my later work possible.

Norm Radican and Pip Martin worked as interviewers for the study reported in Part II. I am grateful to them and to all the men who participated in this project. Tim Carrigan and John Lee were research assistants on the project which provided the basis for Chapter 1, and I learnt a great deal from them. Mark Davis was research assistant on a later interview project that influenced my view of class and sexuality. I am grateful for the extensive typing done by Marie O'Brien, Yvonne Roberts and Alice Mellian. Major funding for the research was provided by the Australian Research Grants Committee, and supplementary funding by Macquarie University, Harvard University, and the University of California at Santa Cruz.

I would like to acknowledge the friendship and intellectual contribution of colleagues, especially Mike Donaldson, Gary Dowsett, Øystein Holter, Heinz Kindler, Ilse Lenz, Jim Messerschmidt, Mike Messner, Ulla Müller, Rosemary Pringle, Lynne Segal, Barrie Thorne, Steve Tomsen and Linley Walker. They are among the makers of the new era in gender research; I hope their work and mine contribute to a new era in practice.

Parts of this book have previously appeared in different formats. They are: the section on clinical knowledge in Chapter 1, in 'Psychoanalysis on masculinity', in Michael Kaufman and Harry Brod, eds, *Theorizing Masculinities*, Sage Publications, 1994;

Chapter 4 as 'Live fast and die young: the construction of masculinity among young working-class men on the margin of the
labour market', *Australian and New Zealand Journal of Sociology*
(now *Journal of Sociology*), 1991, vol. 27, no. 2; Chapter 5 as 'A
whole new world: remaking masculinity in the context of the environmental movement', *Gender and Society*, 1990, vol. 4, no. 4;
Chapter 6 as 'A very straight gay: masculinity, homosexual experience and the dynamics of gender', *American Sociological Review*,
1992, vol. 57, no. 6; parts of Chapter 8 as 'The big picture: masculinities in recent world history', *Theory and Society*, 1993, vol. 22,
no. 5; part of the Introduction in 'Masculinities, change and conflict in global society: thinking about the future of men's studies',
Journal of Men's Studies, 2003, vol. 11, no. 3; part of the Afterword
in 'Scrambling in the ruins of patriarchy: neo-liberalism and
men's divided interests in gender change', in Ursula Pasero, ed.,
Gender – from Costs to Benefits, Westdeutscher Verlag, 2003. I am
grateful to these publishers and journals for permission to repro-
duce this material.

Introduction to the Second Edition

Introducing *Masculinities*

It is now ten years since the first edition of *Masculinities* was published. In the meantime a great deal of research, public debate and policy-making has occurred. In the new edition, while keeping the original text unchanged, I also describe the new work and discuss the meaning of this field of knowledge as a whole. In this Introduction I sketch the origins of the book, and discuss in greater detail the research that has been done since it appeared. In the Afterword I trace recent debates about the politics of masculinities, and discuss the implications of masculinity research for understanding current world issues.

Masculinities tries to do five things within a single conceptual framework:

- trace the history of the modern Western investigation of masculinity (Chapter 1);
- present a theory of masculinities, embedded in a social theory of gender (Chapters 2–3);
- describe the lives of four groups of men caught up in processes of change (Chapters 4–7);
- synthesize the history of Western masculinities and their political expressions (Chapters 8–9);
- propose strategies for the politics of gender equality (Chapter 10).

The book had multiple origins, and rests, like all social science, on the contributions of many people besides the author. A debate about men and gender had taken off in the wake of the Women's Liberation movement; there was even a small Men's Liberation movement in the 1970s that attempted to reform the 'male sex role'. This gave rise to interesting political discussions about men, power and change. But it did not immediately produce much research about what men and boys actually do, and it suffered from deep conceptual confusions about gender.

In the late 1970s I was one of a research group making a study of inequalities in education. This involved an empirical study of social relations in secondary schools, in the course of which we identified multiple patterns of masculinity and femininity among teenagers (Connell, Ashenden, Kessler and Dowsett 1982). In the early 1980s I was involved in a conceptual project with two men who were both gay activists and theoreticians, which produced an outline for 'a new sociology of masculinity' (Carrigan, Connell and Lee 1985). I was soon also involved in a program of research on social dimensions of AIDS, mainly in the context of gay men's lives. This led to some hard thinking about theories of sexuality as well as the shape of connections among men (Connell and Dowsett 1992, Kippax, Connell, Dowsett and Crawford 1993).

In the mid-1980s I was concerned about the lack of empirical knowledge about masculinities, and so launched a study of the gender practices and consciousness of men in circumstances of change, using life-history interviews. I conducted this with the assistance of Norm Radican and Pip Martin, and in due course it became the basis of Chapters 4–7 of *Masculinities*.

In a broader sense, the book grew out of theoretical work on gender as a social structure. I had been trying for years to formulate an integrated social-scientific account of gender relations, and eventually got this together in *Gender and Power* (1987). This analysis showed there were bound to be multiple masculinities, and more or less demanded that I should fill in the blanks about them. In turn, this theoretical work on gender grew out of my encounter with feminism – especially in the life and work of my wife and partner Pam Benton. She made it clear that issues about gender were never just contemplative, but always had to do with social action.

So the threads came together. But I was reluctant to weave them into a book, because there was already a genre of 'books about men' that had become hugely popular. This was a mixture of pop psychology, amateur history and ill-tempered mythmaking, and I hated it. Backward-looking, self-centred stereotypes of masculinity were the last things we needed. I didn't want to reinforce the imaginary identity of 'men' that was created by the very existence of this genre of books.

Eventually I became persuaded that a book documenting and explaining the diversity of gender patterns among men was worthwhile. We might drive out some of the bad coin with good. It wasn't easy to write. I dated the preface June 1994, which was two months after Pam began her long battle with cancer. Since I started work on the book, our family had moved house internationally three times, I had taught in three universities in two countries, and our daughter Kylie had been in four different schools. For all the turbulence of its writing, however, there is a consistent approach running through all the sections, and that is perhaps what has given the book its impact.

In 1995, *Masculinities* was published simultaneously in Australia, Britain and the United States. It was widely reviewed, and has certainly had a role in creating an intellectual agenda and consolidating a field of study. A distinguished German reviewer generously called it '*the* fundamental study on masculinity as a formative factor of modern social inequality, and also one of the most important books in the social sciences in recent years'. In 2003 the book was voted, by members of the Australian Sociological Association, one of the ten most influential books in Australian sociology. I am very pleased that the book has also circulated in other language communities. There have been translations into Swedish (1996), Italian (1996), German (1999 and 2000), Spanish (2003) and Chinese (2003), with Japanese forthcoming.

One of the things I hoped to do in *Masculinities* was to show that studies of masculinities and men's gender practices formed a comprehensible field of knowledge (though not an autonomous science). I tried to show its history, its context, its conceptual dilemmas, and some of its practical consequences. This field has, of course, continued to develop. I have made some further contributions, including the papers on globalization, embodiment, education, health and change collected in my book *The Men and the Boys* (2000). Through the work of a growing number of researchers, the field of knowledge has developed in highly interesting ways, and I will now turn to this story.

Growth of the Field of Study

International diversity

The argument in *Masculinities* drew extensively on the empirical research that had built up in the 1980s and early 1990s, most of which described the construction of masculinities in specific settings. This included studies of workplaces and schools (e.g. Cockburn 1983, Heward 1988), studies of sexualities and athletic careers (e.g. Messner and Sabo 1990, Connell 1992a), and historical accounts of changing ideas of masculinity (Phillips 1987). These studies produced a much more detailed, specific and differentiated view of men in gender relations, and so allowed a decisive move beyond the abstract 'sex role' framework that had been dominant earlier.

This ethnographic moment appeared first in research from the English-speaking world, mainly in Australia, the United States and Britain. In central and northern Europe, feminist and gay research had also taken an early interest in the gender practices of men. In this region, however, a different approach was taken, with more emphasis on survey research, and on the way men are positioned in relation to the gender equity policies of the state (Metz-Göckel and Müller 1985, Bengtsson and Frykman 1988, Holter 1989). There were, nevertheless, common themes. Both groups of researchers were concerned with the way change among men was linked to contemporary feminism, and both had an interest in using masculinity research to understand and combat violence.

At the time *Masculinities* was published, research on men and masculinities was already diversifying internationally. In the years since, this trend has accelerated. A measure of the global growth of the field is the appearance, within the last few years, not just of individual monographs but of *collections* of research in many regions and countries. As well as a continuing output of volumes mainly concerned with the United States and Britain (among the best are Kimmel and Messner 2001, Whitehead and Barrett 2001), these include

- Japan (Roberson and Suzuki 2003)
- Australia (Tomsen and Donaldson 2003)
- New Zealand (Worth et al. 2002, Law et al. 1999)

- Southern Africa (Morrell 2001b)
- Latin America (Olavarría and Moletto 2002, Gutmann 2001)
- Scandinavia (Fronesis 2001, Kvinder Kon & Forskning 1999)
- the Middle East (Ghoussoub and Sinclair-Webb 2000)
- France (Welzer-Lang 2000)
- Germany (Bosse and King 2000, Widersprüche 1998)
- rural regions of developed countries (Campbell and Bell 2000)
- the post-colonial world (Ouzgane and Coleman 1998)
- Brazil (Arilha et al. 1998).

This work has tremendously diversified the ethnographic documentation of social constructions of masculinity. It has also brought into view new questions about global difference, integration and inequality, which I will discuss shortly. In 2000 the first large-scale multi-national research project on men and masculinity was launched, the 'CROME' project in Europe (Hearn et al. 2002a, 2002b), which has set a very important precedent for the future.

Applied research

Another important direction of change is the growth of applied research, policy work and professional practice. The new knowledge about constructions of masculinity is being put to work across a broad spectrum of issues. The major areas of recent applications are:

- *Education.* This work considers the making of masculinity in schools, identity formation in youth, issues of school discipline, harassment, etc.; and the learning problems of boys (Lingard and Douglas 1999, Martino and Pallotta-Chiarolli 2003).
- *Health.* The making of gender is relevant to the health and safety of men and boys, and men's role in reproductive and sexual health issues (Schofield et al. 2000, Hurrelmann and Kolip 2002).
- *Violence.* Knowledge about masculinity is relevant to the prevention of masculine violence, in contexts ranging from domestic and sexual assault to institutional violence and war (Breines et al. 2000, Kaufman 2001, Wölfl 2001).

- *Fathering.* This work considers men's relationship to children, especially as fathers; difficulties in traditional masculinities, and the development of new models of fathering and family relations (Olavarría 2001, McKeown et al. 1999, Kindler 2002).
- *Counselling.* Understanding the construction of masculinity is important for effective counselling and psychotherapy of men, both individual and group, in ways that pay attention to gender relations and gender specificity (Kupers 1993, Brandes and Bullinger 1996).

Intellectual applications

In some fields of knowledge, an understanding of the construction of masculinity has (sometimes suddenly) been seen as relevant to the understanding of another problem or theory. A good example is international diplomacy and power relations. This is documented in Zalewski and Parpart's (1998) book *The 'Man' Question in International Relations*. It had been taken for granted, in international relations practice and research, that all the leading players – diplomats, ministers, generals, corporate executives, etc. – were men. This has now come into focus as an issue. The reasons why the players in international power politics are mostly men, and the consequences that fact might have for diplomacy, war and peace, are now actively debated.

Another example is the recognition that there is a dimension of masculinity in the culture of imperialism (Gittings 1996) and in the construction of nationalism and national identities (Nagel 1998). It is specifically male heroism that is celebrated in the US national anthem 'The Star-Spangled Banner', in Australia's 'Anzac Day' ceremonies, in the Arc de Triomphe – and this tells us something important about the process of nation-building, and the kind of society being built.

Debates and Difficulties

Knowledge about masculinities has developed very rapidly over the past two decades and the accomplishments of researchers in the field are considerable, with new methods, new topics of investigation and new groups being studied. At the same time problems have emerged, and both practical and conceptual debates have sharpened.

The focus on men and masculinity

Not all applications of masculinity research are trouble-free. In particular, there have been sharp debates about a men-and-masculinity focus in two fields: domestic and sexual violence, and economic development in poor countries.

In both cases there is concern that a focus on men will result in resources being diverted from women – from particularly disadvantaged women, at that. White (2000), in a thoughtful critique of the masculinity literature, describes these hazards in relation to 'gender and development' policy in poor countries. Men and their practices are part of the problem of gender inequalities in aid, education and empowerment, and should be part of the solution. But there is a risk that letting men in on what is, at present, the only development agenda controlled by women, will open the door to backlash.

Problems of method

The descriptive research methods that flourished in the wave of masculinities research *c.* 1985–95 are being used in many new studies. These methods are still productive, as shown by recent monographs on youth (Olavarría 2001) and violence (e.g. Hearn 1998), as well as the collections of research listed above.

But these methods are yielding fewer new insights than before. We are getting an ever-growing library of descriptive studies, which provide important understandings of specific settings and problems. But we do not seem to be getting a corresponding growth of general ideas about men and masculinities.

Recent research has documented different forms of masculinity, but has not succeeded in showing how they are distributed across populations. For instance ethnographic studies (e.g. Poynting et al. 1998) strongly suggest that ethnic differences in masculinity construction are important in social conflict, in a context such as multi-cultural Western Sydney. But such studies are not in a position to measure difference. We need information about how different masculinities are distributed between social groups, such as ethnic communities, regions or social classes.

Cross-sectional surveys might provide this information. Such studies have been done in several countries, the most impressive series coming from Germany (Zulehner and Volz 1998). However with one exception, a Norwegian study (Holter and Aarseth 1993), these are essentially surveys of gender *attitudes*. They have not yet been integrated with the concept of masculinities as *configurations of practice*, as explained in this book. A novel kind of quantitative study seems to be required, based on a model of gender practices.

Understanding hegemony

The concept of 'hegemonic masculinity', introduced to the field in the 1980s and formalized in this book, has provided guidance for a large body of research. But it has now come under challenge from several directions (Petersen 1998, Demetriou 2001, Jefferson 2002). It is timely to reconsider the concept, since changes have been made to the theory of gender that framed it (Connell 2002), and much richer empirical material on men and masculinities is now available.

But whether to discard the concept of hegemonic masculinity, reconstruct it, or reaffirm it, is still sharply debated. In my view we still require a way of theorizing gendered power relations among men, and understanding the effectiveness of masculinities in the legitimation of the gender order. This is necessary if theories of masculinity are to connect with wider theories of gender and are to have any grip on practical issues such as the prevention of violence. Therefore I think the concept of hegemonic masculinity, as developed in this book, is still essential.

Discursive approaches

An influential approach has recently emerged that treats masculinity as a discursive construction. This is influenced by Foucauldian post-structuralism, postmodernism and discursive psychology (Petersen 1998, Wetherell and Edley 1999). Discursive studies suggest that men are not permanently committed to a particular pattern of masculinity. Rather, they make situationally specific choices from a cultural repertoire of masculine behaviour (Wetherell and Edley 1999).

In one of the best studies in this vein, Collier (1998) questions the recent 'masculinity turn' in criminology based on social-constructionist accounts of masculinity. He argues that a binary division between sex and gender, as well as other binaries (man/woman, hetero/homosexual, for instance) pervade research on masculinities, and need to be disrupted.

Discursive research on masculinity is already producing interesting empirical studies, such as the psychological work brought together in a recent issue of *Feminism and Psychology* (2001). Another example is the subtle cultural analysis undertaken by Buchbinder (1998), with its interesting account of the *absences* in representations of the masculine.

Yet discursive approaches have significant limits. They give no grip on issues about economic inequality and the state, which as Segal (1997) argues are crucial to change in masculinities. The idea of tactical choice from a repertoire is difficult to reconcile with studies of the development of gender identities through the life cycle, influenced by psychoanalysis (e.g. Chodorow 1994).

A theoretical impasse has thus developed, which is directly relevant to practical problems. This can be seen in the striking divergence between developmental/psychoanalytic approaches to men's crime (e.g. Hayslett-McCall & Bernard 2002) and the discursive approaches. It can also be seen in the difficulty of linking either of these theories of masculinity to issues about poverty, state power and global conflict, whose role in contemporary violence is incontestable in the era of al-Qaeda and the US invasion of Iraq.

New directions?

As Pease (2000) argues, masculinity research must be integrated with more general analyses of social change. Pease emphasizes theories of postmodernity. I would also emphasize analyses of commodification, neo-liberalism and market society.

Conceptualizations of masculinity must be confronted with *all* the relevant evidence. In *Masculinities* I tried to bring together the evidence from the whole field of study, and however difficult this now is, it is still important to try. Quantitative research on gender difference is rarely mentioned in the recent conceptual debates about masculinities. Yet meta-analyses of 'sex difference' studies point to the situationally specific production of gender differences (Connell 2002, ch. 3) which cannot be fully explained by either discursive or psychoanalytic models.

The issue of the situational specificity of masculinities needs close attention. Discursive psychology is right to address this question. Certain studies in criminology have also shown the power of a situational analysis of masculinities. Tomsen's (1997) research on drinking violence is exemplary. I think that a situational approach, connected with the conscious historicity of studies such as Gutmann's and Morrell's (discussed below), may be the way discursive and structural approaches to masculinity can be reconciled.

In thinking about how to develop research on men and masculinities, we should not treat this as an isolated field. These issues are strategic for other questions in the social sciences. For instance, men's predominant use of violence is only one facet of gendered power, which includes men's predominance in state authority and corporate management. This power is under challenge, especially from feminism and gender equity measures. But masculine authority is defended by 'backlash' politics, and perhaps reinstated by military confrontations. At the same time, the forms of social authority in general are changing with the global shift towards market society, and the social turbulence accompanying economic restructuring. An exploration of emergent masculinities and issues of violence should, therefore, throw light on central questions about power in 'new times'.

The Global Dimension

We now have studies of masculinities from many regions and countries; but we cannot simply add these together to arrive at a global understanding of masculinities. To understand masculinities on a world scale we must also grasp the global relationships involved.

The great strength of the recent empirical work on masculinity has been its local focus and rich detail. This is what took us beyond 'sex role' research. But, in an increasingly globalized world, local understandings are no longer enough. Large-scale social processes – global market relations, migration and ethnic/ cultural conflict – are increasingly important for understanding gender issues in general (Marchand and Runyan 2000).

In this respect, the work of Gutmann and Morrell point the way forward. Gutmann's (1996, 2002) nuanced descriptions of the lives of men and the shaping of masculinities in an urban-fringe working-class settlement in Mexico City are among the best ethnographies of masculinity we have. But Gutmann also weaves into the analysis the relations that this community, and these men, have to the broad economic and political processes which are re-shaping their worlds, and to which they make active, if not always successful, responses.

Morrell's (2001a) wonderfully detailed reconstruction of the masculinizing agendas of white boys' schools in Natal, South Africa, is a fine example of ethnographic social history. But it also is something more. Morrell firmly links the construction of a specific form of masculinity to the geo-political process of conquest and colonization, and the economic imperatives of a particular stage in the world economy.

To generalize this approach requires an understanding of the globalization of gender. Most theories of globalization have little or nothing to say about gender. But Sklair's (1995) concept of 'transnational practices' gives an indication of how the problem can be approached. As Smith (1998) argues in relation to international politics, the key is to shift our focus from individual-level gender differences to 'the patterns of socially constructed gender relations'. If we recognize that very large-scale institutions such as the state and corporations are gendered, and that international relations, international trade and global markets are inherently an arena of gender politics, then we can recognize the existence of a world gender order (Connell 2002).

The world gender order can be defined as the structure of relationships that interconnect the gender regimes of institutions, and the gender orders of local societies, on a world scale. This gender order is an aspect of a larger reality, global society. Current discussions of 'globalization', especially in the media of the rich countries, picture an all-conquering wave sweeping across the world. Driven by new technologies, this wave of change produces vast unfettered global markets, world music, global advertising and world news in which all participate on equal terms. In reality, however, the global economy is highly unequal, and the degree of economic and cultural homogenization is often exaggerated (IIirst and Thompson 1996, Bauman 1998).

The historical processes that produced global society were, from the start, gendered. This is argued in Chapter 8 of *Masculinities*, and the point has been amply confirmed by research since. Imperial conquest, neo-colonialism, and the current world systems of power, investment, trade and communication, have brought very diverse societies in contact with each other. The gender orders of those societies have consequently been brought into contact with each other. The gender systems that result are local patterns, but carry the impress of the forces that make a global society.

A striking example is provided by Morrell's (2001b) analysis of the situation of men in contemporary South Africa. The transition from Apartheid – itself a violent but doomed attempt to perpetuate colonial race relations – has created an extraordinary social landscape. In a context of reintegration into the global polity and economy, rising unemployment, continuing violence, and a growing HIV/AIDS epidemic, there are attempts to reconstitute rival patriarchies in different ethnic groups. These attempts clash with agendas for the modernization of masculinity, with South African feminism and the ANC government's 'human rights' discourse. Some of these ideas, in turn, are challenged by arguments for 'African philosophy' and for policies based in indigenous communal traditions, which would de-emphasize gender divisions.

The movement of populations and the interaction of cultures under colonialism and post-colonial globalization have linked the making of masculinity with the construction of racial and ethnic hierarchies. It seems that ethnic and racial conflict has been growing in importance in recent years in many parts of the world. As Klein (2000) argues in the case of Israel, and Tillner (2000) in the case of Austria, this is a fruitful context for producing masculinities oriented towards domination and violence. Poynting, Noble and Tabar (1998), interviewing male youth of the Lebanese immigrant community in Australia, find contradictory gender consciousness and a strategic use of stereotypes in the face of racism. Racist contempt from Anglo society is met by an assertion of dignity – but for Lebanese boys this is specifically a masculine dignity, in a context that implies the subordination of women.

The creation of a world gender order, however, involves something more than the interaction of existing gender systems. It also involves the creation of new arenas of gender relations beyond individual countries and regions. The most important seem to be: (1) Transnational and multi-national corporations, which typically have a strong gender division of labour, and a strongly masculinized management culture (Wajcman 1999). (2) The international state, including the institutions of diplomacy and UN agencies. These too are gendered, mainly run by men, though with more cultural complexity than multi-national corporations (Gierycz 1999). (3) International media, which have a strong gender division of labour and powerfully circulate gender meanings through entertainment, advertising and news. New media participate in the commodification of women in an international trade in wives and sexual partners (Cunneen and Stubbs 2000). (4) Global markets – in capital, commodities, services and labour – have an increasing reach into local economies. They are often strongly gender-structured (e.g. Chang and Ling 2000), and are now very weakly regulated, apart from border controls on migration.

This is the context in which we must now think about the lives of men and the construction and enactment of masculinities. A key question is what pattern of masculinity is dominant within these global arenas.

With the collapse of Soviet communism, the decline of post-colonial socialism, and the ascendancy of the new right in Europe and North America, world politics is now more and more organized around the needs of transnational capital and the creation of global markets. The neo-liberal market agenda has little to say, explicitly, about gender. But the world in which neo-liberalism is ascendant is still a gendered world, and neo-liberalism has an implicit gender politics. De-regulation of the economy places strategic power in the hands of particular groups of men – managers and entrepreneurs. I have suggested (Connell 1998) that these groups are the bearers of an emerging hegemonic form of masculinity in the contemporary global economy, which I call 'transnational business masculinity'.

Available research on business masculinities gives contradictory indications. Donaldson's unique (2003) study of 'the masculinity of the hegemonic', based on biographical sources about the very rich, emphasizes emotional isolation. Donaldson traces a deliberate toughening of boys in the course of growing up; and documents a sense of social distance from the masses, a life of material abundance combined with a sense of entitlement and superiority. Hooper's (2000) study of the language and imagery of masculinity in *The Economist* in the 1990s, a British business journal closely aligned with neo-liberalism, shows a distinct break from old-style patriarchal business masculinity. *The Economist* associates with the global a technocratic, new-frontier imagery; and emphasizes a cooperative, teamwork-based style of management.

A study of management textbooks by Gee, Hull and Lankshear (1996) gives a rather more individualistic picture. The executive in 'fast capitalism' is represented as a person with very limited loyalties, even to the corporation. His occupational world is characterized by a limited technical rationality, sharply graded hierarchies of rewards, and sudden career shifts or transfers between corporations. Wajcman's (1999) survey indicates a rather more stable managerial world, closer to traditional bourgeois masculinity, marked by long hours of work and both dependence on, and marginalization of, a domestic world run by wives.

A colleague and I have explored the idea of 'transnational business masculinity' in a small life-history study of Australian managers (Connell and Wood 2004). Their world is male-dominated but has a strong consciousness of change. An intense and stressful labour process creates a network of links among managers and subjects them to mutual scrutiny, a force for gender conservatism. In a context of affluence and anxiety, managers tend to treat their life as an enterprise and self-consciously 'manage' their bodies and emotions as well as their finances. Economic globalization has heightened their insecurity and changed older patterns of business. Managerial masculinity is still centrally related to power, but changes from older bourgeois masculinity can be detected: tolerance of diversity, and heightened uncertainty about one's place in the world and gender order.

The issue of globalization has only recently come into focus in studies of men (Pease and Pringle 2001). There are still only a handful of studies of masculinity formation in transnational arenas. This is, nevertheless, a crucial frontier of research – not least because of the light it could throw on global conflict and violence. I will return to these questions in the Afterword.

In Conclusion

The field of research, theory and practical debate that is mapped out in this book has continued to develop. In helping to guide this development, it seems that the intellectual framework offered by *Masculinities* has proved its value, and the empirical chapters have provided a point of reference for later research. Like every other contribution to knowledge, this is provisional and imperfect, open to debate and improvement. I think the book remains of value, both as a synthesis of ideas and as a source of empirical understanding. For that reason I am pleased to present this second English-language edition.

Part I

Knowledge and its Problems

1

The Science of Masculinity

Rival Knowledges

The concepts 'masculine' and 'feminine', Freud observed in a melancholy footnote, 'are among the most confused that occur in science'.[1] In many practical situations the language of 'masculine' and 'feminine' raises few doubts. We base a great deal of talk and action on this contrast. But the same terms, on logical examination, waver like the Danube mist. They prove remarkably elusive and difficult to define.

Why should this be? In the course of this book I will suggest that the underlying reason is the character of gender itself, historically changing and politically fraught. Everyday life is an arena of gender politics, not an escape from it.

Gender terms are contested because the right to account for gender is claimed by conflicting discourses and systems of knowledge. We can see this in everyday situations as well as in high theory.

On the desk in front of me is a clipping from a local newspaper in inner Sydney, *The Glebe*, headed:

Why women ask the way
Women are more likely to stop someone in the street and ask for directions than men – simply because the sexes think differently.

The story, by-lined Amanda Park, quotes a psychologist and counsellor, Mary Beth Longmore, explaining that the sexes have different purposes when they speak.

Women also don't understand that men view having information as a form of hierarchy – so people with more information are further up the hierarchy...Ms Longmore said it was for this reason that men tended not to ask a stranger for directions, because it was admitting that they were in some way inferior.

Readers wishing to understand the different languages men and women speak are invited to a workshop conducted by Ms Longmore on the following Friday.[2]

Local newspapers are always short of news. But this item struck me as exceptionally helpful, at least for clarifying types of knowledge about gender. In the first place it appeals to common-sense knowledge: men and women act differently ('women are more likely to stop someone'), and they act differently because they *are* different ('the sexes think differently'). Without this appeal to a commonly acknowledged polarity, the story would not work at all.

But the report also criticizes common sense. 'Men and women often don't understand each others' purpose [in speaking] ... Women also don't understand ...' The criticism is made from the standpoint of a science. Ms Longmore is identified as a psychologist, she refers to her knowledge as 'findings', and she enters a typical scientific caveat at the end of the item ('her findings were true of the majority but not all men and women'). Science thus revises common-sense knowledge of gender difference. The revision warrants a new practice, which will be explored in the workshop. The nature of the science is not specified, but it seems likely that Ms Longmore's claims are based on her stated experience as a counsellor.

In this short item we can see two forms of knowledge about masculinity and femininity – common sense and psychological science – partly reinforcing each other and partly at odds. We also get a glimpse of two practices in which psychological knowledge is produced and applied – individual counselling and group workshops.

In a more indirect fashion the story leads us to other forms of knowledge about masculinity and femininity. Workshops are widely used by therapists in the milieu that gave birth to the contemporary 'men's movement' (explored in Chapter 9). This movement claims a knowledge beyond both science and common sense, an intuitive knowledge of the 'deep masculine'.[3]

But if pressed on the question of sex differences, psychologist and journalist would more probably appeal to biology. They might recall research on sex differences in bodies and behaviour, brain sex, hormonal differences and genetic coding. These too have become staple media stories.

If *The Glebe* went in for investigative journalism and the writer stepped across Parramatta Road to Sydney University, she would find that these views of masculinity and femininity, uncontroversial in the biological sciences, are fiercely contested in the humanities and social sciences. On those parts of the campus, academics talk about 'sex roles' or 'gender relations', and speak of masculinity and femininity being 'socially constructed' or 'constituted in discourse'.

Biologists and social scientists alike, after leaving Sydney University and turning right down Parramatta Road, drive past a soot-stained church. The vicar of St Barnabas proclaims to the world, via a well-known billboard, that the gender order is ordained by God, and like other parts of the moral order is perilous to tamper with. The divine billboard, in turn, is answered on signs put up by the publican of the hotel on the opposite side of the highway. The publican frequently comments on the scriptural messages from the point of view of an earthy working-class hedonism.[4]

I could offer more examples, but these are perhaps enough. Our everyday knowledge of gender is subject to conflicting claims to know, explain and judge.

These forms of knowledge are, as the *Glebe* article showed, connected with particular social practices. This is generally true of knowledge, though intellectual debates are often conducted as if ideas fell from the sky. The sociology of knowledge showed, two generations ago, how major world-views are based on the interests and experiences of major social groups. Research on the sociology of science, giving fascinating glimpses of laboratory life and prestige hierarchies among scientists, has revealed the social relations underpinning knowledge in the natural sciences. The point is reinforced by Michel Foucault's celebrated researches on 'power-knowledge', the intimate interweaving of new sciences (such as medicine, criminology and sexology) with new institutions and forms of social control (clinics, prisons, factories, psychotherapy).[5]

So the conflicting forms of knowledge about gender betray the presence of different practices addressing gender. To understand both everyday and scientific accounts of masculinity we cannot remain at the level of pure ideas, but must look at their practical bases.

For instance, common-sense knowledge of gender is by no means fixed. It is, rather, the rationale of the changing practices through which gender is 'done' or 'accomplished' in everyday life – practices revealed in elegant research by ethnomethodologists.[6] The knowledge of gender deployed by Sigmund Freud and Mary Beth Longmore is intimately connected with a professional practice, the practice of psychotherapy. The knowledge offered by constructionists in the social sciences has a two-fold genealogy, stemming from the oppositional politics of feminism and gay liberation, and from the techniques of academic social research.

Accordingly, in discussing the main attempts to construct knowledge about masculinity, I will ask what practices enabled that knowledge to emerge. I will also ask how the practices shape and limit the forms that knowledge takes.

The different forms of knowledge do not stand on an equal footing. In most contexts, scientific claims have an undeniable edge. In the *Glebe* report, just a whiff of scientificity was enough to establish a right to criticize common-sense knowledge; common sense did not criticize science. Science has a definite hegemony in our education system and media.

This has shaped the development of ideas about masculinity through the twentieth century. All the leading discourses make some claim to be scientific, or to use scientific 'findings', however grotesque the claim may be. Even Robert Bly, in *Iron John*, uses scientific language for his gripping idea that one-third of our brain is a 'warrior brain' and that our DNA carries warrior instincts.

But the appeal to science plunges us into circularity. For it has been shown, in convincing historical detail, that natural science itself has a gendered character. Western science and technology are culturally masculinized. This is not just a question of personnel, though it is a fact that the great majority of scientists and technologists are men. The guiding metaphors of scientific research, the impersonality of its discourse, the structures of power and communication in science, the reproduction of its internal culture, all stem from the social position of dominant men in a gendered world. The dominance of science in discussions of masculinity thus reflects the position of masculinity (or specific masculinities) in the social relations of gender.[7]

In that case, what can be expected from a science of masculinity, being a form of knowledge created by the very power it claims to study? Any such knowledge will be as ethically compromised as a science of race created by imperialists, or a science of capitalism produced by capitalists. There are, indeed, forms of scientific talk about masculinity that have capitulated to the dominant interests in much the same way as scientific racism and neo-conservative economics.

Yet there are other potentials in science. Natural science arose as critique, from Copernicus's rejection of the idea that the sun revolved around the earth, to Darwin's rejection of the idea that species were created individually by divine providence. A heady mixture of critique, empirical information and imagination has been at work in each great scientific revolution. And in everyday scientific research the testing of hypotheses and the drive for generalization constantly push beyond the immediately given, and make science more than a simple reflection of what exists.[8]

Can we take another step, and connect this element of critique with the social critique involved in the analysis of masculinity? Or connect the drive for scientific generalization with the idea of generalizable interests in social life and thus with the concept of justice? These proposals are subject to the full weight of post-modern scepticism about 'grand narratives' and economic-rationalist scepticism about justice.[9] I will come back to the critique of masculinity in the final part of the book. Here I want merely to register the political ambiguities of scientific knowledge. Sciences of masculinity may be emancipatory or they may be controlling. They may even be both at once.

In the course of the twentieth century there have been three main projects for a science of masculinity. One was based in the clinical knowledge acquired by therapists, and its leading ideas came from Freudian theory. The second was based in social psychology and centred on the enormously popular idea of 'sex role'. The third involves recent developments in anthropology, history and sociology. In this chapter I will examine the character of knowledge about masculinity produced in each of these projects; then turn to the knowledge produced by movements of resistance in gender and sexual politics. The mis-matches among these projects raise the question of what, precisely, knowledge about masculinity is knowledge *of.* I will try to answer this question in the final section of the chapter.

Clinical Knowledge

The Oedipus complex

The first sustained attempt to build a scientific account of masculinity was made in the revolutionary depth psychology founded at the turn of the century by Freud. Psychoanalysis has had so tangled a development, and so vast an impact on modern culture, that its origins in medical practice are easily forgotten. The founder himself was always clear that psychoanalytic knowledge was based on clinical observation and was tested in a practice of healing.

This connection with medicine has linked psychoanalysis throughout its history to efforts at normalization and social control. Yet there have also been radical potentials in psychoanalysis from the start.[10] Freud's early work coincided with a ferment in the European intelligentsia that produced modernist literature, avant-garde painting and music, radical social ideas, spirited feminist and socialist movements, and the first homosexual rights movement. Freud was sufficiently open to this ferment to question – as his clinical practice levered him away from professional orthodoxy – almost everything European culture had taken for granted about gender.

This is what makes his work the starting-point of modern thought about masculinity, though most later masculinity researchers have known little and cared less about the detail of his ideas. It was Freud, more than anyone else, who let the cat out of the bag. He disrupted the apparently natural object 'masculinity', and made an enquiry into its composition both possible and, in a sense, necessary.

Freud nowhere wrote a systematic discussion of masculinity, but it is one of the continuing themes in his writing over thirty years. His ideas developed in three steps.

The first came in the initial statements of psychoanalytic principles: the idea of continuity between normal and neurotic mental life, the concepts of repression and the unconscious, and the method that allowed unconscious mental processes to be 'read' through dreams, jokes, slips of the tongue and symptoms. Freud understood that adult sexuality and gender were not fixed by nature but were constructed through a long and conflict-ridden process.

He increasingly saw the 'Oedipus complex', the emotional tangle of middle childhood involving desire for one parent and hatred for the other, as the key moment in this development. What precipitated the Oedipal crisis, for boys, was rivalry with the father and terror of castration. These ideas were documented in two famous case studies, 'Little Hans' and the 'Rat Man', in 1909. Here Freud identified a formative moment in masculinity and pictured the dynamics of a formative relationship.[11]

In his theoretical writing, however, Freud had already begun to complicate this picture. Homosexuality, he argued, is not a simple gender switch: 'a large proportion of male inverts retain the mental quality of masculinity.' Confronted with the facts of inversion, Freud offered the hypothesis that humans were constitutionally bisexual, that masculine and feminine currents coexisted in everyone.

This implied that adult masculinity had to be a complex, and in some ways precarious, construction. The second step in Freud's analysis of masculinity was the development of this architectural approach to gender. It was given full play in his longest case history, the 'Wolf Man', published during the Great War. Here Freud pushed behind the Oedipus complex to find a pre-Oedipal, narcissistic masculinity which underpinned castration anxiety. Tracking forward, Freud traced the interplay between this archaic emotion, the boy's desire for the father, his relationships with servants, his identification with women and jealousy of his mother. Freud used these contradictions to explain the change in the Wolf Man's adolescent and early adult life from a shallow heterosexual promiscuity to neurotic apathy.[12]

In this most brilliant of his case studies Freud demonstrated the power of the clinical method in separating layer after layer of emotion and mapping the shifting relationships between them. Nothing could be further from the one-dimensional formulae still commonly offered as the 'findings' of psychoanalysis. The Wolf Man study is a challenge to all later research on masculinity. No approach is adequate that has not absorbed this lesson about the tensions within masculine character and its vicissitudes through the course of a life.

In the years after the Great War, Freud developed his account of the structure of personality; in particular the concept of the super-ego, the unconscious agency that judges, censors, and presents ideals. This concept was the basis of a third step in analysing masculinity. The super-ego is formed in the aftermath of the Oedipus complex, by internalized prohibitions from the parents. Freud gradually came to see it as having a gendered character, being crucially a product of the child's relation with the father, and more distinct in the case of boys than of girls. In *Civilization and its Discontents* and other writings about culture, he also began to see a sociological dimension in the super-ego. He treated it as the means by which culture obtains mastery over individual desire, especially aggression.[13]

These lines of thought remained speculative and incomplete, but they have profound implications. Here was the germ of a theory of the patriarchal organization of culture, transmitted between generations through the construction of masculinity. To develop this theory would be to tilt further towards social analysis than Freud and his orthodox followers were ever willing to do. Radical psychoanalysis, however, moved in just that direction.

So Freud opened more doors than he walked through. But the openings he supplied for the analysis of masculinity were remarkable enough. He provided a method of research, 'psychoanalysis' itself; a guiding concept, the dynamic unconscious; a first map of the development of masculinity; and a warning about the necessary complexity and limits of the idea. The point he most insistently made about masculinity was that it never exists in a pure state. Layers of emotion coexist and contradict each other. Each personality is a shade-filled, complex structure, not a transparent unit. Though his theoretical language changed, Freud remained convinced of the empirical complexity of gender and the ways in which femininity is always part of a man's character. It was this critical and disturbing insight that was thrown out with the bathwater when later, more conservative, psychoanalysts abandoned the theory of bisexuality.

The potential in Freud's work for a science of masculinity was apparent very early. It was taken up even before the Great War by Alfred Adler, whose theory of the 'masculine protest' will be discussed shortly. In the 1920s and 1930s more orthodox psychoanalysts engaged in a vehement debate about femininity, which spun off a minor debate about masculinity. This focused on the earliest years of childhood. The first contributors were surprised to find clinical evidence of a pre-Oedipal *femininity* in boys, resulting from identification with the mother, though also marked by jealousy towards her.

The argument was given a more feminist turn by Karen Horney in a paper crisply titled 'The dread of woman' (1932). For Horney, fear of the mother is more deep-seated and more energetically repressed than fear of the castrating father. The vagina itself is the symbolic centre of the process. Boys' feelings of inadequacy lead them to withdraw emotional energy from the mother and focus it on themselves and their genitals – thus preparing the ground for castration anxiety. Later reactions among men are fuelled by these emotions. Among them are the tendency to choose socially inferior women as love objects, and the habit of actively undermining women's self-respect in order to support 'the ever precarious self-respect of the "average man"'.[14]

Horney's paper was the high point of the critique of masculinity in classical psychoanalysis. It crystallized two important points: the extent to which adult masculinity is built on over-reactions to femininity, and the connection of the making of masculinity with the subordination of women. But in terms of mainstream psychoanalysis, this was an end not a beginning.

Between 1930 and 1960 psychoanalysis moved far to the right on most issues, and the theory of gender was no exception. When psychoanalysts such as Theodor Reik became popular writers on gender issues in the 1950s, they no longer stressed the contradictory character of gender or the clash between social order and desire. Rather, their message identified mental health with gender orthodoxy, especially conventional heterosexuality and marriage. The course towards adult heterosexuality, which Freud had seen as a complex and fragile construction, was increasingly presented as an unproblematic, natural path of development. Anything else was viewed as a sign of pathology – especially homosexuality. This was declared inherently pathological, the product of 'disturbed parent–child relationships', as a team of New York psychoanalysts led by Irving Bieber announced in 1962. Psychoanalysis as a practice increasingly became a technique of normalization, attempting to adjust its patients to the gender order.[15]

As Kenneth Lewes's splendid history of psychoanalytic ideas about male homosexuality shows, this privileging of one healthy

path of development required a radical alteration in the concept
of the Oedipus complex.[16] To Freud and his early followers, the
Oedipus complex was necessarily traumatic, and its passing was
necessarily disruptive. That was basic to their sense of the fragility
of adult masculinity, founded on the tragic encounter between
desire and culture. The non-tragic, normalizing psychoanalysis of
the 1940s and after lost the capacity for a critique of masculinity
that classical theory had provided. It took a long detour for that
capacity to be recovered.

Archetype and identity

Clinical experience is so complex that it always allows a range of
interpretations. Different interpretations of cases suggest different theoretical frameworks, and the history of psychoanalysis is
rich in systems that offer alternative readings of emotional life.
Several have produced theories of masculinity, including the best
known, the work of Carl Jung.

Gender questions were central to the system Jung began to
develop after his break with Freud. Jung distinguished between
the self constructed in transactions with the social environment,
which he called the 'persona', and the self formed in the unconscious out of repressed elements, which he called the 'anima'.
These, he argued, tend to be opposites, and the opposition is to
a large extent a gendered one:

> the repression of feminine traits and inclinations causes these con-
> trasexual demands to accumulate in the unconscious.[17]

Like Freud and Klein, Jung was concerned with the presence of
femininity within men. But his account of it gradually took on a
different colour, focusing not on the process of repression but on
the resulting balance between a masculine persona and a feminine anima.

Further, Jung was increasingly prone to argue, the feminine
interior of masculine men was shaped not only by the life-history
of the particular man but also by inherited, 'archetypal' images
of women. The idea of archetypes in the collective unconscious
was originally introduced in such arguments to account for paradoxes of emotional life. In time the archetypes parted company

from clinical knowledge. They became the main theme of later Jungian argument about gender.

In Jung's hands, ideas such as the 'anima' could be put to subtle use. He developed an interesting theory of the emotional dynamics of patriarchal marriages. He used the idea of a masculine/feminine polarity to call for a gender balance in mental and social life, a progressive position in the 1920s. He even devised a kind of masculinity therapy, arguing that 'a certain type of modern man', accustomed to repress weakness, could no longer afford to do so. In a striking passage, foreshadowing techniques of therapy that became popular fifty years later, Jung suggested methods for talking to one's anima, as if to a separate personality, and educating it.[18]

But in other ways Jung's analysis became schematic and speculative in the extreme. While Freud was struggling to overcome the masculine/feminine polarity, Jung not only settled for it, but presented the familiar opposition as rooted in timeless truths about the human psyche.

In the absence of the discipline of clinical case studies, 'archetypes' are fatally easy to find. Jung's later books found them in esoteric arts and world religions, and his followers have scoured other mythological systems. This results in deeply confused texts such as Marshall Bethal's 'The mythic male', an erratic hunt through Greco-Roman myths, taken utterly out of context, for male gods who might personify modern 'modes of masculine consciousness'. *Iron John* is a Jungian work in exactly this vein, except that Robert Bly finds his archetypes in a folk tale recast by the Brothers Grimm rather than more conventionally in the pages of Ovid. Bly too ignores the cultural origins of his tale, and scrambles its interpretation with notions of 'Zeus energy' and even wilder borrowings from oral cultures.[19]

Jung's treatment of the masculine/feminine polarity as a universal structure of the psyche also leads to a quagmire. No historical change in their constitution is conceivable; all that can happen is a change in the balance between them.

In modern Jungian writing this yields an interpretation of feminism not as resistance to the oppression of women, but as the reassertion of the archetypal feminine. In past history it is not men who have dominated women, so much as the masculine that has dominated the feminine. One can see why Jungian theory has become central to the current backlash among formerly progressive men.[20] For this approach immediately yields the idea that modern feminism is tilting the balance too far the other way, and suppressing the masculine. Bly's influential criticism of 'soft men' who have caved in to feminism and thus have lost the 'deep masculine' is based precisely on this Jungian formula of archetypal balance.

Since Jung's original texts are now little studied, the roots of this argument in the early history of psychoanalysis are forgotten. It is worth recalling what has been lost. Jung based his analysis of gender on an abstract opposition of masculinity and femininity which Freud was gradually working his way past. Jung's formulations lost most of the complexity in Freud's map of psychosexual development. And by seeking the main determinant of gender in the racial unconscious, the supposed repository of the archetypes, Jung turned his back on the path towards a socially literate psychoanalysis that was pointed out by Adler and Horney.

In recent popular psychologies of masculinity the main alternative to the idea of gender archetypes has been the concept of 'gender identity'. This stems from the work of Erik Erikson, perhaps the most influential psychoanalyst of the generation after Freud and Jung. In *Childhood and Society* Erikson argued that the crucial issues in emotional development in the mid-twentieth century had to do with the establishment of ego-identity. 'Identity' became a catchword, and Erikson's model of stages in its development became immensely popular.[21]

The main application of identity concepts to gender came from the American psychiatrist Robert Stoller. Stoller's work centred on a remarkable development in gender practice, the invention of the transsexual. The creation of surgical techniques for 'gender reassignment' created a need to assess who should go under the knife, and this led to research on claims of gender membership.

Stoller made clinical studies of adult men who wanted to be women, and boys who seemed to be on a path towards femininity – a path he called 'male childhood transsexualism, a clear-cut, potentially malignant personality disorder'. This research did not lead him towards the classical Freudian view of gender as a contradictory structure. Rather he considered he had discovered a unitary 'core gender identity' laid down in the earliest years of life. Gender identity is established by emotional interaction between parents and children – Stoller has some harsh things to say about mothers – and is powerful enough to override the physical facts about the body. Transsexualism for men is thus defined not as the desire to be a woman, but as the belief that one already is. In the normal case, of course, a boy acquires a male gender identity and all is well. Gender identity theory has had wide circulation as an account of gender development. It has influenced recent psychoanalytic writing on child development and on homosexuality, as well as anthropological discussions of masculinity.[22]

Though built on the lurid contradictions of transsexual lives, this is unquestionably a normalizing theory. It locates identification with women not in the unconscious of all men, but in a specific deviant group. (It is not surprising that men wanting sex reassignment surgery take great care, as the sociologist Anne Bolin has shown, to conform to the *doctors'* beliefs about feminine dress and conduct.) In a biting critique, Robert May has questioned whether this is a psychoanalytic theory at all. May argues that Erikson's approach is really a meliorist ego psychology, and that Stoller's concept of 'core gender identity' has lost essential psychoanalytic insights about conflict, fantasy and the unconscious. It is hard to disagree. If Jung reduced the contradictions of gender to a universal dichotomy within the psyche, gender identity theory has gone one better, eliminating contradiction altogether.[23]

Thus, over the half-century that followed the Wolf Man case study, Freudian psychoanalysis and the two most influential alternatives to it developed conservative gender practices and normalizing theories of masculinity – theories that identified psychological health with a narrow orthodoxy in sexuality and emotion. But this was not the only direction Freud's ideas could be taken. Around the edges of the medical world, dissident versions and unexpected applications of psychoanalysis multiplied. A number of them produced original ideas about gender.

Radical psychoanalysis

The first dissident analyst was Alfred Adler, a socialist doctor convinced of the importance of social factors in disease. Adler was president of the Psychoanalytic Society in Vienna at the time of his split with Freud in 1911. The occasion of the conflict was a series of papers read to the Society by Adler, and it is a remarkable fact that their centrepiece was a theory of masculinity.

Adler's argument started from the familiar polarity between masculinity and femininity, but immediately emphasized the feminist point that one side of the polarity is devalued in culture and associated with weakness. Children of both sexes, being weak *vis-à-vis* adults, are thus forced to inhabit the feminine position. They develop a sense of femininity and doubts about their ability to achieve masculinity. The 'childish value judgements' about the masculine/feminine polarity persist as a motive in later life.

Submission and striving for independence occur together in the child's life, setting up an internal contradiction between masculinity and femininity. In normal development some kind of balance is struck. The adult personality is thus formed out of compromise and exists under tension.

But if there is weakness (and Adler had the idea that neurosis was often triggered by some physical weakness or inferiority), there will be anxiety which motivates an exaggerated emphasis on the masculine side of things. This 'masculine protest', in Adler's famous phrase, is central to neurosis. It means over-compensation in the direction of aggression and restless striving for triumphs.

Adler considered the masculine protest to be active in normal as well as neurotic mental life. It was not far from this idea to a critique of conventional masculinity. The masculine protest was a feature of women's psychology as well as men's, but over-determined by women's social subordination. In men it could become a public menace. Adler took a highly critical view of dominating masculinities, commenting on

> the arch evil of our culture, the excessive pre-eminence of manliness.

Adler worked in Austrian military hospitals during the Great War, and was left in no doubt about the connections between masculinity, power and public violence. His 1927 book *Understanding Human Nature* made a clearer statement of a psychoanalytic case for feminism than was found anywhere else until the 1970s.[24]

As an account of the sources of neurosis, this had moved far from Freud's libido theory. Adler criticized the theory of repression as mechanistic, and saw the Oedipus complex as only one form that might be taken by a larger dynamic, 'a stage of the masculine protest'. On both points he anticipated later theory. Freud rejected Adler's view as an unwarranted simplification of neurosis (and was certainly right in that). Judging that he no longer needed their support, Freud forced Adler and his followers out of the psychoanalytic movement.

The split was a loss for both sides. Adler lost touch with Freud's marvellous sense of the intricacies of mental life, and never did theorizing of such quality again. On the orthodox side, psychoanalysis became an increasingly closed system, resisting precisely the issues of social power that Adler had raised. Those issues were, however, taken up by other intellectual movements: Marxist psychoanalysis, existentialism and feminist psychoanalysis.

The many attempts to link Marxism and psychoanalysis circled around the issue of masculinity without directly addressing it. Wilhelm Reich, perhaps the most original mind in the Freudian left between the wars, developed a method of 'character analysis' which shifted attention from the individual symptom to the style of the entire personality. His attempt to synthesize Marxist economic analysis and Freudian sexual science led to a brilliant analysis of ideology. This highlighted the 'authoritarian family' as the site where the reproduction of class society and patriarchy is accomplished. Reich's *The Mass Psychology of Fascism*, published only three years after Freud's *Civilization and its Discontents*, is a world ahead in the sophistication of its social science. Reich's concept of a condensation of larger structures of authority in the psychodynamics of the family provided exactly the dimension of social realism that Freudian and Jungian speculation about masculinity lacked.[25]

But Reich lacked the appreciation of feminism that illuminated Adler's work. So he did not treat masculinity itself as a problem. Nor did the Frankfurt School theorists of the next two decades, who picked up Reich's idea of character analysis, his concern with authoritarianism and his project of reconciling Marx with Freud. In the work of Max Horkheimer, Erich Fromm and Theodor Adorno, 'authoritarianism' gradually emerged as a distinct character type – or, if looked at with feminist eyes, a type of masculinity.

The most famous psychological works of the Frankfurt School, Fromm's *The Fear of Freedom* (1942) and the collective work *The Authoritarian Personality* (1950), were, in effect, catalogues of masculinities and the conditions that produce them. Fromm suggested a broad historical succession of character types over several centuries. *The Authoritarian Personality* worked at much closer focus. It included two famous case studies, 'Mack' and 'Larry', which are the first detailed clinical pictures of masculinities carefully linked to the economic and cultural settings in which they emerged. The 'authoritarian' type was a masculinity particularly involved in the maintenance of patriarchy: marked by hatred for homosexuals and contempt for women, as well as a more general conformity to authority from above, and aggression towards the less powerful. These traits were traced back to rigid parenting, dominance of the family by the father, sexual repression and conservative morality. The 'democratic' character was less clearly drawn, but included markedly more tolerance and was linked to more relaxed and affectionate family relationships.[26]

Here was empirical evidence of diversity in psychosexual character within the same broad social setting. Anthropologists influenced by psychoanalysis, such as the great ethnographer Bronislaw Malinowski, had already shown the diversity between cultures in their handling of sexuality and their shaping of character.[27] It became increasingly clear that Freud's theory of the Oedipus complex cannot provide an analysis of masculinity in general. This is, rather, a map of *one* historically possible pattern, and it is necessary to think about this particular pattern in relation to the others. This conclusion has broad implications for a theory of masculinity, which I will explore in following chapters.

Neither Reich nor the Frankfurt School shared Adler's doubts about the theory of libido, but such doubts were proclaimed by Jean-Paul Sartre in *Being and Nothingness* (1943). Sartre saw 'empirical psychoanalysis', as he called the Freudian school, as too mechanical, taking one possible form of life (determined by sexual desire) for the condition of all lives. Sartre outlined a striking alternative which he called 'existential psychoanalysis'. He replaced the concept of the unconscious with an argument about the different ways our self-knowledge is organized. The 'mystery in broad daylight' could be unravelled by tracking back down the life-history to establish the primary commitments through which a person's life had been constituted.

Sartre himself applied the method only in literary biography. It was Simone de Beauvoir who applied existential psychoanalysis directly to gender, in *The Second Sex* (1949). Her best-known argument showed woman being constituted as 'other' to the male subject. But the book also included a series of essays on different types of femininity which gave a much more active place to the women's desires. Existential psychoanalysis allowed her to move beyond the static typologies familiar in psychology. Gender emerged in her treatment as an evolving engagement with situations and social structures. Different gender forms are different ways of life rather than fixed character types.[28]

As far as I know this approach has never been explicitly applied to the First Sex, as a theory of masculinity. But the potential for doing so is clear in the work of the Scottish psychiatrist R. D. Laing. Laing's studies of schizophrenia produced vivid pictures of men's activities in the emotional interior of families, and a few individual case studies of men. These included the case of 'David', a student whose studied eccentricity provided a clue to a whole life stuck together from discordant dramatic roles. The most powerful of these dramatic roles were women's, drawing their emotional impact from a family dynamic set up by his mother's death. David's 'schizophrenia' was a consequence of his grappling with unmanageable gender contradictions. In escaping his feminine identifications David set up a whole series of other personae, which now formed an elaborate false-self system.[29]

This is not a 'type' of masculinity; in existential psychoanalysis the contradictions of gender are not fixed and their result is not an identity. They are produced socially, but they become contradictions precisely by being taken up as incompatible courses of action. This approach to personality can connect to theories of social structure, but it does so by an emphasis on engagement and action, not social mechanism.[30]

Apart from Simone de Beauvoir there was little interaction between feminism and psychoanalysis between the early 1930s and the late 1960s. Yet the radical potentials of psychoanalysis gradually emerged in feminist thought, in two main forms.

The first stemmed from the work of Jacques Lacan. Feminists influenced by Lacan, such as Juliet Mitchell in Britain and Luce Irigaray in France, have been more concerned to theorize femininity than masculinity. Yet this work has an implicit account of masculinity. Lacanian theory focuses on symbolic processes in which Freud's models of the emotional relations of the family are writ large. The 'Law of the Father' *constitutes* culture and the possibility of communication. Here masculinity is not an empirical fact (as in classical psychoanalysis), still less an eternal archetype (as in Jung). It is, rather, the occupant of a *place* in symbolic and social relations. Oedipal repression creates a system of symbolic order in which the possessor of the phallus (a symbol, to be clearly distinguished from any empirical penis) is central.[31]

Treating gender as a system of symbolic relationships, not fixed facts about persons, makes acceptance of the phallic position a highly political act. It is always possible to refuse it – though the consequences of refusal are drastic. Gilles Deleuze and Felix Guattari explored rejection of the Oedipal structuring of desire in their obscure but influential *Anti-Oedipus*. This provided the basis for Guy Hocquenghem's dramatic reading of homosexuality for men as the rejection of phallic sexuality and Oedipal repression.[32]

While Lacanian feminism in Europe suggested a political, symbolic reading of masculinity, North American feminism turned to the mundane issue of family relationships, and crystallized an important shift in thinking about boys' psychosexual development. In classical psychoanalysis the drama had centred on the Oedipal entry into masculinity (whether the key agent was the father, as Freud thought, or the mother, as Horney thought). In the work of Nancy Chodorow and Dorothy Dinnerstein the drama centres on the pre-Oedipal separation from femininity, with the focus definitely on the mother.

Chodorow's account of this separation has had a large impact on recent writing about men. She proposed that boys are pushed to disrupt their primary identification with the mother, partly by the mother's own emotional investment in gender difference. This results in character structures that emphasize boundaries between people, and lack the need for relationship that is characteristic of women. Dinnerstein's argument gave greater emphasis to pre-Oedipal fear of the mother, and to men's violence as a consequence of the 'female monopoly of early child care'.[33]

Here the development of personality is connected firmly to the division of social labour. Child care is work; the workforce is gendered; this fact matters for emotional development. However we modify the details, this simple and powerful argument must be acknowledged in any future account of the formation of masculinities.

Looking back, it is clear that while Freud gave us an essential tool, it was radically incomplete; and psychoanalytic orthodoxy consists of defending this incompleteness. Ultimately the worth of psychoanalysis in understanding masculinity will depend on our ability to grasp the structuring of personality and the complexities of desire at the same time as the structuring of social relations, with their contradictions and dynamisms. That observation leads us directly towards the social sciences.

The Male Role

The first important attempt to create a social science of masculinity centred on the idea of a male sex role. Its origins go back to late nineteenth-century debates about sex difference, when resistance to women's emancipation was bolstered by a scientific doctrine of innate sex difference. Women's exclusion from universities, for instance, was justified by the claim that the feminine mind was too delicately poised to handle the rigours of academic work. The resulting mental disturbance would be bad for their capacities to be good wives and mothers. The first generation of women who did get into North American research universities not only violated this doctrine. They also questioned its presuppositions, by researching the differences in mental capacities between men and women. They found very few.[34]

This scandalous result triggered an enormous volume of follow-up research, which has flowed from the 1890s to the 1990s. It has covered not only mental abilities but also emotions, attitudes, personality traits, interests, indeed everything that psychologists thought they could measure. There is a remarkable amount of 'sex difference' research. It is technically fairly simple to do, and there is constant interest in its results.

That in itself is curious, for the results have not changed. Sex differences, on almost every psychological trait measured, are either non-existent or fairly small. Certainly they are much smaller than the differences in social situations that are commonly justified by the belief in psychological difference – such as unequal incomes, unequal responsibilities in child care and drastic differences in access to social power. When groups of studies are aggregated by the statistical technique of meta-analysis, it is more likely to be concluded that *some* sex differences in psychological characteristics do exist. But their modest size would hardly register them as important phenomena if we were not already culturally cued to exaggerate them – as in the newspaper report about men's and women's different languages discussed at the start of this chapter. Cynthia Epstein has aptly called her book about these issues *Deceptive Distinctions*.[35]

Around the mid-century, sex difference research met up with a concept that seemed to explain its subject-matter in an up-to-date way, the concept of 'social role'. The meeting gave birth to the term 'sex role', which in time passed into everyday speech.

The idea of a sex role is now so common that it is worth emphasizing its recent origin. The metaphor of human life as a drama is of course an old one – it was used by Shakespeare. But the use of 'role' as a technical concept in the social sciences, as a serious way of explaining social behaviour generally, dates only from the 1930s. It provided a handy way of linking the idea of a place in social structure with the idea of cultural norms. Through the efforts of a galaxy of anthropologists, sociologists and psychologists the concept, by the end of the 1950s, had joined the stock of conventional terms in social science.[36]

There are two ways in which the role concept can be applied to gender. In one, the roles are seen as specific to definite situations. For instance Mirra Komarovsky, in her classic study of American working-class families *Blue Collar Marriage* (1964), offered detailed descriptions of script-following in courtship and within marriage.

Much more common, however, is the second approach, in which being a man or a woman means enacting a *general* set of expectations which are attached to one's sex – the 'sex role'. In this approach there are always two sex roles in any cultural context, a male one and a female one. Masculinity and femininity are quite easily interpreted as internalized sex roles, the products of social learning or 'socialization'.

This concept connected smoothly to the idea of sex differences, which were so easily explained by sex roles that the two ideas have been persistently blurred since the 1940s. Research journals are still publishing papers in which findings of sex differences (usually slight) are simply *called* 'sex roles'.

Most often, sex roles are seen as the cultural elaboration of biological sex differences. But this is not necessary. The sophisticated statement of sex role theory made in the mid-1950s by Talcott Parsons in *Family, Socialization and Interaction Process* takes another approach. Here the distinction between male and female sex roles is treated as a distinction between 'instrumental' and 'expressive' roles in the family considered as a small group. Thus gender is deduced from a general sociological law of the differentiation of functions in social groups.[37]

The idea that masculinity is the internalized male sex role allows for social change, and that was sometimes seen as role theory's advantage over psychoanalysis. Since the role norms are social facts, they can be changed by social processes. This will happen whenever the agencies of socialization – family, school, mass media, etc. – transmit new expectations.

Change was a central theme in the first detailed discussions of the 'male sex role', which appeared in American social science journals in the 1950s. The most notable was a paper by Helen Hacker called 'The new burdens of masculinity', which suggested that expressive functions were now being added to instrumental functions. Men were thus expected to show interpersonal skills as well as being 'sturdy oaks' – an idea that was to become a cliché in the 1970s. Such role theory could even admit the idea of conflict within masculinity, derived from conflicting or unmanageable social expectations rather than from repression.[38]

For the most part, however, the first generation of sex role theorists assumed that the roles were well defined, that socialization went ahead harmoniously, and that sex role learning was a thoroughly good thing. Internalized sex roles contributed to social stability, mental health and the performance of necessary social functions. To put it formally, functionalist theory assumed a concordance among social institutions, sex role norms and actual personalities.

It was the political complacency of this framework, rather than the 'sex role' concept itself, that was disrupted by feminism in the 1970s. Indeed, sex role research bloomed as never before with the growth of academic feminism. But it was now generally assumed that the female sex role was oppressive and that role internalization was a means of fixing girls and women in a subordinate position. Role research became a political tool, defining a problem and suggesting strategies for reform. Sex roles could be changed by changing expectations in classrooms, setting up new role models, and so on. Starting in the United States, these strategies of sex role reform were soon being followed internationally, as illustrated by the remarkable 1975 Australian government report *Girls, School and Society*, and by the United Nations global Decade for Women.[39]

The ferment among the women in the Western intelligentsia gradually had an impact on the men. By the mid-1970s there was a small but much-discussed Men's Liberation movement in the

United States, and a small network of men's consciousness-raising groups in other countries as well. Authors such as Warren Farrell in *The Liberated Man,* and Jack Nichols in *Men's Liberation,* argued that the male sex role was oppressive and ought to be changed or abandoned. A minor boom developed in a new genre of Books About Men, and in papers in counselling and social science journals. Their flavour is given by two titles: 'The inexpressive male: a tragedy of American society' and 'Warning: the male sex role may be dangerous to your health'. The idea of 'men's studies', to go with the feminist project of women's studies, was floated.[40]

The picture of the male sex role painted in most of this literature was quite conventional, which is not surprising as little new research was being done. Rather, the male sex role literature assembled familiar items such as feminist criticisms of men, media images of masculinity, paper-and-pencil tests of attitudes, findings of sex differences and autobiographical anecdotes about sport – and called the assembly a 'role'.

There was little attempt to investigate the effects of expectations or norms in social life. They were simply assumed to exist and to be effective. There was some attempt to outline a process of change. The American psychologist Joseph Pleck, one of the most prolific writers in this field, contrasted a 'traditional' with a 'modern' male role. Much of the writing of the 1970s encouraged men towards the modern version, using therapy, consciousness-raising groups, political discussion, role-sharing in marriage or self-help.

These discussions began with Women's Liberation, and for a time remained sympathetic to feminism. Some statements were very clear about the power dimension in gender, such as Pleck's 1977 essay 'Men's power with women, other men, and society: a men's movement analysis', and Jon Snodgrass's lively anthology *For Men Against Sexism.* These texts made a connection between the subordination of women and the hierarchy of power among men, particularly the oppression of black men and gay men. But in other parts of the male role genre there was an ambivalence about women and a willingness to mute the commitment to feminism. Some writers equated the oppression of men with the oppression of women, and denied that there was any 'hierarchy of oppressions'.[41]

This ambivalence was inherent in the 'sex role' framework. For the logical presupposition of sex role analysis is that the two roles are reciprocal. Roles are defined by expectations and norms, sex roles by expectations attaching to biological status. There is nothing here that positively requires an analysis of power. On the contrary there is a basic tendency in sex role theory to understand men's and women's positions as complementary – the point made explicit by Parsons's theory of instrumental (masculine) and expressive (feminine) orientations.

To the extent oppression appears in a role system, it appears as the constricting pressure placed by the role upon the self. This can happen in the male role as readily as in the female. This pressure was indeed a central theme of the 1970s Books About Men. Their authors offered anecdote after anecdote about the python-like grip of sports broadcasters, inarticulate fathers and boastful peer groups upon the youth of the land.

When Pleck in 1981 published a comprehensive re-examination of the male role literature, *The Myth of Masculinity*, this relation between role and self was central. He criticized the 'Male Sex Role Identity' paradigm (his name for functionalist sex role theory) above all for its assumption of concordance between norm and personality – the idea that conformity to sex role norms is what promotes psychological adjustment.

This criticism was highly effective. Pleck demonstrated how much is taken for granted by functionalist sex role discourse, and how little empirical support there is for its key ideas. Even more interesting, Pleck offered an almost Foucaultian argument that the rise of normative sex role theory was itself a form of gender politics. Historical changes in gender relations required a shift in the form of social control over men, from external to internal controls.

> The concept of sex role identity prevents individuals who violate the traditional role for their sex from challenging it; instead, they feel personally inadequate and insecure.[42]

Normative sex role theory thus helps dampen social change.

What Pleck proposed instead was a non-normative sex role theory, one that disconnected the role from the self. He wanted a model of the male sex role which allowed that sex role conformity might be psychologically dysfunctional; that the role norms might change, and at times ought to; and that many people did violate norms, and might suffer retribution, so many people also overconformed. This would make the theory of the male role more internally consistent, shaking off the bits of biological determinism and identity theory that clung to it; but it would not break out of the intellectual limits of the role perspective.

These limits have repeatedly been shown.[43] Because role theorists almost unanimously ignore this critique, and because the term 'male role' is still widely used, I will risk overkill and recite the main points.

Role theory in general is logically vague. The same term is used to describe an occupation, a political status, a momentary transaction, a hobby, a stage in life and a gender. Because of the shifting bases on which 'roles' are defined, role theory leads to major incoherence in the analysis of social life. Role theory exaggerates the degree to which people's social behaviour is prescribed. But at the same time, by assuming that the prescriptions are reciprocal, it underplays social inequality and power. For all these reasons 'role' has proved unworkable as a general framework for social analysis.

This is not to say the dramaturgical metaphor of role is entirely useless in understanding social situations. It is apt for situations where (a) there are well-defined scripts to perform, (b) there are clear audiences to perform to, and (c) the stakes are not too high (so it is feasible that some kind of performing is the main social activity going on). None of these conditions, as a rule, applies to gender relations. 'Sex role' is basically an inappropriate metaphor for gender interactions. (One can, of course, think of specific situations in gender interaction where roles are definitely played. Ballroom dancing competitions spring to mind – as in the charming film *Strictly Ballroom.*)

In sex role theory, action (the role enactment) is linked to a structure defined by biological difference, the dichotomy of male and female – not to a structure defined by social relations. This leads to categoricalism, the reduction of gender to two homogeneous categories, betrayed by the persistent blurring of sex differences with sex roles. Sex roles are defined as reciprocal; polarization is a necessary part of the concept. This leads to a misperception of social reality, exaggerating differences between men and women, while obscuring the structures of race, class and sexuality. It is telling that discussions of 'the male sex role' have mostly ignored gay men and have had little to say about race and ethnicity.

The distinction between behaviour and expectation is basic to the role metaphor. But the male sex role literature fails to document them separately, and takes either as evidence of the other. The result is an inability to understand resistance in sexual politics. People contesting power (for instance, using a stigmatized identity to assert solidarity and mobilize resistance, as Gay Liberation did) simply cannot be represented in the role categories of 'norm' and 'deviance'.

Sex role theory has a fundamental difficulty in grasping issues of power. To explain differences in the situation of men and women by appeal to role differentiation is to play down violence, and suppress the issue of coercion by making a broad assumption of consent. Even Pleck, sensitive to power and sceptical about consent, could not hold these ideas about men consistently with the rest of the sex role framework. In consequence these issues slipped out of his writing.

This difficulty with power is part of a wider difficulty with social dynamics. The male sex role literature, though aware of change and often enthusiastic about it, persistently sees change as impinging on the role from elsewhere (as a result of technological change, for instance). It does not have a way of understanding change as a dialectic *within* gender relations.

The male sex role approach, then, is fundamentally reactive. It does not generate a strategic politics of masculinity. I think this is an underlying reason why men who had worked hard for sex role change in the 1970s could make no effective resistance in the 1980s to ideologues who rejected their modernity as 'softness', and instituted a cult of an imaginary past.

The New Social Science

Histories

The elements of a new approach to masculinity have been emerging in several social science disciplines, stimulated by Men's Liberation and sex role psychology but not limited by role theory. A key element is the evidence of diversity and transformation in masculinities provided by history and ethnography.

Academic historical writing has, of course, always been about men – at least, about rich and famous men. This was pointed out by feminists, and in the 1970s a strong movement developed to write 'women's history' and redress the balance. Given the assumption of reciprocal sex roles, it could not be long before someone concluded that there was need for a reciprocal 'men's history'. This was announced, and began to be practised, towards the end of the 1970s.[44]

But there already was a men's history. The central theme of a new men's history, then, could only be what was missing from the non-gendered history of men – the *idea* of masculinity. This was often called a history of the male role, and the first wave of American work in the genre overlapped the male sex role literature just discussed. It was marked by the same vagueness of scope, and was often written at a high level of generality.

Though broad surveys of cultural norms for manhood continue to be produced, a more incisive approach to the issue has emerged, taking its cue from the wealth of local studies in women's history. Some of this writing continues to use sex role language, though it entertainingly shows that expectations are more varied, and more contested, than used to be thought. But the best of this work has gone beyond norms to the institutions in which they are embedded.

Such a study is Christine Heward's *Making a Man of Him*, which traces change and difference in an English private school. She shows not only how the school's practices of discipline, dress, academic hierarchy and team games constructed respectable masculinities, but also how the institution responded to the gender and class strategies of the boys' families. Another case is Michael Grossberg's study of the practice of law in the nineteenth-century United States. This shows how the boundaries of the profession were policed against women while its internal organization (such as the 'circuit' of court hearings) sustained a particular version of masculinity – and finally transformed it, when the rise of the law firm changed the gender dynamics and made women's entry possible.[45]

The same logic applies to larger institutions such as labour markets. The male role literature took it for granted that being a breadwinner was a core part of being masculine. But where did this connection come from? Wally Seccombe has shown that the male 'breadwinner' wage is a recent creation and was far from universally accepted. It was produced in Britain around the middle of the nineteenth century in the course of a broad realignment of social forces. Both capitalists and workers were deeply divided over the issue. Trade unions gradually adopted the 'breadwinner' wage objective, at the price of driving divisions between male and female workers, and between craftsmen and unskilled labourers.[46]

It is clear from such studies that definitions of masculinity are deeply enmeshed in the history of institutions and of economic structures. Masculinity is not just an idea in the head, or a personal identity. It is also extended in the world, merged in organized social relations. To understand masculinity historically we must study changes in those social relations. As Michael Gilding's recent book *The Making and Breaking of the Australian Family* shows, this requires us to open up a unit such as 'the family' into the different relationships that compose it – in this case child-rearing, employment, sexual relations and the division of labour. They may change at different rhythms, with resulting tensions in masculinity and femininity.[47]

Social relations on the widest possible scale, the global expansion of European power, are the theme of the most remarkable historical study of masculinity that has yet appeared. It is worth looking in a little detail at Jock Phillips's research on colonial and twentieth-century New Zealand.[48]

Phillips starts with the demography and economics of settlement, which created both a surplus of men among the white settlers and niches for all-male work groups on the frontier. A turbulent masculine subculture resulted, which posed serious problems of social order. The colonial state tried to impose control, partly by promoting agricultural settlement based on family farms. This tied masculinity into marriage and a more orderly way of life.

By the turn of the century, with more balanced sex ratios and increasing urbanization, and conquest of the Maori people virtually complete, the demands of social control were changing. The state now reversed course and set about the incitement of a violent masculinity. First for the Boer War, then for the two World Wars, white New Zealand men were mobilized for the British imperial armies. In fascinating case studies of public rituals around arrival and departure, Phillips shows how politicians and press fabricated a public account of New Zealand manhood. This linked a farmer-settler ethos with racist notions of imperial solidarity. Maori men, at the same time, were mobilized for Maori battalions with appeals to a separate warrior myth.

The device bridging the contradictions around masculine violence and social control was organized sport, especially rugby football. The premier of the country met the national football team when their ship returned from the 1905 tour of England, amid well-orchestrated mass enthusiasm. Team sport was being developed at this time, across the English-speaking world, as a heavily convention-bound arena. The exemplary status of sport as a test of masculinity, which we now take for granted, is in no sense natural. It was produced historically, and in this case we can see it produced deliberately as a political strategy.

The details of this story are specific to New Zealand, but the approach has much wider implications. Phillips shows an exemplary masculinity being produced as a cultural form. (To some effect: it sent men to their deaths.) It was produced in an interplay between the changing social relations of a settler population, the local state, the British imperial system and the global rivalry of imperialist powers. The gender pattern was not a mechanical effect of these forces; it was nurtured as a strategic response to a given situation. And it was not the only pattern that could have emerged in that situation. Labour or pacifism could have become stronger, football could have been discredited, Maori/white relations could have taken a different turn. The production of a particular exemplary masculinity required political struggle, and it meant the defeat of historical alternatives.

Thus historical research on masculinity leads via institutions to questions of agency and social struggle. A similar logic has emerged in anthropology.

Ethnography of the other

The core subject-matter of anthropology is the small-scale societies encountered by Europeans and North Americans in the course of their colonial expansion. In the early twentieth century ethnography became the characteristic research method: the immensely detailed description of a way of life in which the researcher had participated, based on personal observation and talking with informants in their native language.

What ethnography tried to grasp was the way colonized cultures differed from the secular, market-based and state-controlled societies of Europe and North America. This led to a focus on religion and myth, and on the kinship systems that were generally thought to provide the structure of 'primitive' societies. Both of these enquiries are rich sources of information about gender. So ethnographic reports, accumulating in the libraries of the imperial powers, were a mine of information about the very issues debated by feminism, psychoanalysis and sex role theory.

Accordingly, anthropology became an important source for these controversies. I have mentioned the debate over the universality of the Oedipus complex which Malinowski launched, on the basis of his ethnography in the Trobriand Islands. Margaret Mead's *Sex and Temperament in Three Primitive Societies*, written in the 1930s, was a powerful demonstration of the cultural diversity of meanings for masculinity and femininity – though Mead never quite overcame a conviction that a natural heterosexuality underpinned it all.[49] In the 1970s second-wave feminism gave rise to fresh work on the anthropology of gender. As in history, most of the new work was done by women and tried to document women's lives. And as in history, this was followed by research on masculinity.

Some of this focuses on the cultural imagery of masculinity. An example is Michael Herzfeld's elegant and entertaining *The Poetics of Manhood*, which tells about sheep-stealing in Cretan mountain villages as an occasion for masculine performance. An ethnographic debate about 'machismo' in Latin America has also given a lot of attention to the ideology – a masculine ideal stressing domination of women, competition between men, aggressive display, predatory sexuality and a double standard.[50]

Ideology is more firmly embedded in practice in Gilbert Herdt's *Guardians of the Flutes*, the most spectacular piece of recent ethnographic work on masculinity. The book is a conventional, even conservative, ethnography of a culture in the eastern highlands of Papua New Guinea, the 'Sambia'. It describes a gardening and gathering economy, a small-scale village political order, a cosmology and set of myths, and a system of ritual. The culture is marked by chronic warfare, a sharp gender division of labour, and a strongly emphasised, aggressive masculinity.

The core of Herdt's account concerns the men's cult and its initiation rituals. Initiation involves sustained sexual relationships between boy initiates and young adult men, in which the penis is sucked and semen swallowed. Semen is considered an essence of masculinity that must be transmitted between generations of men to ensure the survival of the society. This belief is supported by a whole system of story and ritual, embracing the natural environment, the social order of the Sambia, and the sacred flutes whose music is a feature of the men's cult.

It is the sexual component that has made Herdt's ethnography scandalous. He presents the spectacle of a violent, aggressive masculinity, apparently like the exaggerated masculinity familiar in our own culture, but based on homosexual relationships – which our culture believes produce effeminacy. The ethnography further violates our culture's strong assumption (often expressed by scientists as well as politicians) that homosexuality is confined to a small minority. Among the Sambia *all* the men, more or less, become homosexual at a certain stage of life. Herdt dubbed this pattern 'ritualized homosexuality' and assembled studies of similar practices in other Melanesian societies.[51]

What kind of science does such research produce? In the positivist model of social science, multiple cases are put together in attempts to arrive at cross-cultural generalizations and overall laws about human society. This is exactly the approach of David Gilmore's *Manhood in the Making*, the most ambitious recent attempt to state what anthropological science says about masculinity.

Gilmore noted correctly that anthropology is a mine of information about men and masculinity. On the wings of a good library he ranged across the world, summarizing ethnographies from Spain, the Truk Islands, Brazil, Kenya, Papua New Guinea, Polynesia and Malaysia, as well as bits and pieces from 'East and South Asia' and elsewhere. His purpose was to find a broad basis for generalizations about manhood and its achievement, to answer the questions: 'Is there a deep structure of manhood? Is there a global archetype of manliness?'.

Gilmore's broad answer was that manhood is difficult to achieve, and that it involves striving in a distinctively masculine realm, so its achievement needs to be marked by rites of entry. The cultural function of masculine ideology is to motivate men to work:

> So long as there are battles to be fought, wars to be won, heights to be scaled, hard work to be done, some of us will have to 'act like men.'

Psychologically masculinity is a defence against regression to pre-Oedipal identification with the mother. All this is true across most cultures, in Gilmore's view, but there are a few exceptions, more relaxed and 'passive' patterns of masculinity, in Tahiti and among the Semai in Malaysia.[52]

That a world-wide search of the ethnographic evidence should produce results of such stunning banality is cause for a certain wonder. Has something gone wrong with the ethnographies? I think not; the problem is the way they are put to use. Gilmore's framework is sex role theory, and his work embodies the confusions and foreshortenings discussed above. At a deeper level, his book shows the futility of the attempt to produce a positivist science of masculinity by cross-cultural generalization.

The positivist method presupposes a stable object of knowledge which is constant across all the cases. Is 'manhood' or masculinity' such an object? Other ethnography suggests it is not. Marilyn Strathern's complex analysis of what she calls the achievement of sex, among the people of Hagen in the New Guinea highlands shows gender as metaphor, not as sex role. When someone at Hagen says (meaningfully) 'our clan is a clan of men', they are not saying that there are no women in the clan, nor that the women adopt a male sex role. They are saying something about the capacity and power of the clan as a collective. The idiom contradicts the idea of sex difference and disrupts a positivist definition of masculinity.[53]

Strathern's ethnography forces us to think our way into a very different universe of meaning about gender. So did Herdt's original account of the Sambia, a moving ethnography that conveys to a Western reader something genuinely alien, an experience and a practice profoundly unlike ours. A science that attempts to grasp this experience through concepts that reflect the distinctive social relations of modern European/American society – as conventional concepts of masculinity do (see Chapter 3) – must go awry.

How, then, can ethnography be part of a social science of gender? Only by recognizing the social relations that are the condition for producing ethnographic knowledge.

When Herdt assembled his comparative volume *Rituals of Manhood* in 1982, he included E. L. Schieffelin's work on the *bau a* ceremonial men's hunting lodge among the Kaluli people of the Papuan plateau. Schieffelin gave a detailed ethnography of this periodic retreat by older and younger men from mundane society. The event involved a changed relationship with the spirit world, a ritual avoidance of women, a period of peace in the endemic conflicts of local society, and rising excitement culminating in the ceremonial distribution of the smoked meat collected through hunting.

Schieffelin, it turns out, never witnessed a *bau a*. In 1958 the Australian colonial government had begun regular police patrols to the area. In 1964 the missionaries arrived, with a party of workers, and began to build a mission station and an airstrip. Two Kaluli communities happened to be sponsoring *bau a* at that time, and their youth were in the forest hunting. For a variety of reasons it would have been ritually disastrous if the new arrivals walked in on the *bau a*. On the basis of their experience with previous patrols the Kaluli especially feared the theft of the smoked meat. So they hastily terminated the *bau a* and distributed the meat; and have never held one again.[54]

Ethnography has always worked at the point of contact between indigenous societies and the expansion of Western economic and political empires. Recent rethinking of ethnography as a method has emphasized the presence of the ethnographers and the charged social relations they bear: the colonist's gaze on the colonized, the power relations defining who is the knower and who the known.[55]

Positivist science works by suppressing this historical dimension. It invites us to forget those who steal the smoked meat. But we need not accept this amnesia. I would argue that ethnographic knowledge about masculinity is valuable precisely to the extent we understand it as part of a global history, a history marked by dispossession, struggle and transformation. As indigenous people increasingly claim the right to tell their own stories, our knowledge of *Western* masculinity will certainly change profoundly.

Social construction and gender dynamics

Sociology, the academic home of some of the earliest sex role work on masculinity, is the site of the sharpest break from the sex role framework. In the last ten years field studies in the industrial countries have multiplied and new theoretical languages have been proposed. There is no settled paradigm for this new work, but some common themes are clear: the construction of masculinity in everyday life, the importance of economic and institutional structures, the significance of differences among masculinities and the contradictory and dynamic character of gender.

That gender is not fixed in advance of social interaction, but is constructed in interaction, is an important theme in the modern sociology of gender – from fine-grained ethnomethodological studies of conversations, to organizational research on discrimination by managers. It is a key concern of recent work on masculinity, such as Michael Messner's interview study of professional athletes, *Power at Play*, and Alan Klein's participant-observation study of body-building gyms, *Little Big Men*.[56]

Like sex role research, this is concerned with public conventions about masculinity. But rather than treat these as pre-existing norms which are passively internalized and enacted, the new research explores the making and remaking of conventions in social practice itself. On the one hand this leads to an interest in the politics of norms: the interests that are mobilized and the techniques used to construct them. Richard Gruneau and David Whitson's *Hockey Night in Canada* shows in great detail how business and political interests constructed the aggressively masculinized world of professional ice hockey. On the other hand, this approach leads to an interest in the forces that counterbalance or limit the production of a particular kind of masculinity. The role of injuries in limiting athletic careers, and the sexual contradictions around body-building, are examples from Messner's and Klein's research.

The construction of masculinity in sport also illustrates the importance of the institutional setting. Messner emphasizes that when boys start playing competitive sport they are not just learning a game, they are entering an organized institution. Only a tiny minority reach the top as professional athletes; yet the production of masculinity throughout the sports world is marked by the hierarchical, competitive structure of the institution. And this structure is not produced by accident. As Gary Fine notes, not only corporations but the American state itself became involved in organizing boys' leisure through 'Little League' baseball. One member of the governing body was J. Edgar Hoover.[57]

What is true of sport is true of workplaces in general. Economic circumstance and organizational structure enter into the making of masculinity at the most intimate level. As Mike Donaldson observes in *Time of Our Lives*, hard labour in factories and mines literally uses up the workers' bodies; and that destruction, a proof of the toughness of the work and the worker, can be a method of demonstrating masculinity. This happens not because manual work is necessarily destructive, but because it is done in a destructive way under economic pressure and management control.[58]

The making of working-class masculinity on the factory floor has different dynamics from the making of middle-class masculinity in the air-conditioned office – though, as Collinson, Knights and Collinson's *Managing to Discriminate* shows, the creation and defence of masculinized white-collar occupations may be just as conscious a process. Class differences in masculinities have been a theme of British research since Andrew Tolson's pioneering book *The Limits of Masculinity* assembled the evidence in the 1970s. Class difference in the United States is a theme of James Messerschmidt's *Masculinities and Crime*, which shows how white-collar and street crimes become resources in the construction of class-specific masculinities. Economics and ideology were equally emphasized in Robert Staples's *Black Masculinity*, a pioneering study of ethnic difference. Staples connected the social situation of black men within American racism to the dynamic of colonialism in the third world, an insight which has rarely been followed up.[59]

Difference between class or race settings is important to recognize, but it is not the only pattern of difference that has emerged. It has become increasingly clear that different masculinities are produced in the same cultural or institutional setting. This first emerged in research on schools, such as Paul Willis's *Learning to Labour*, on a working-class secondary school in England. Willis showed the rough 'lads' developing an oppositional masculinity which led them towards the factory floor, and marked them off from the 'ear'oles', the boys from the same milieu who conformed to the school's requirements and competed through academic work. Surprisingly similar patterns emerged in an Australian ruling-class school, and in other school studies.[60]

Such observations, together with the psychoanalytic work on character discussed above, and gay-liberation ideas discussed below, led to the idea of hegemonic masculinity. To recognize diversity in masculinities is not enough. We must also recognize the *relations* between the different kinds of masculinity: relations of alliance, dominance and subordination. These relationships are constructed through practices that exclude and include, that intimidate, exploit, and so on. There is a gender politics within masculinity.[61]

School studies show patterns of hegemony vividly. In certain schools the masculinity exalted through competitive sport is hegemonic; this means that sporting prowess is a test of masculinity even for boys who detest the locker room. Those who reject the hegemonic pattern have to fight or negotiate their way out. James Walker's ethnography of an Australian inner-city boys' school, *Louts and Legends*, provides an elegant example. He describes the case of the 'three friends', who scorned the school's cult of football. But they could not freely walk away from it; they had to establish some other claim to respect – which they made by taking over the school newspaper.[62]

Hegemony, then, does not mean total control. It is not automatic, and may be disrupted – or even disrupt itself. There can, for instance, be too much sporting prowess. Messner cites the troublesome cases of American football players whose 'legal' violence became too severe. When other players were badly injured, the enactment of masculine aggression risked discrediting the sport as a whole.

Such observations show that the relationships constructing masculinity are dialectical; they do not correspond to the one-way causation of a socialization model. The masculinity of the 'lads' described in *Learning to Labour* was certainly not intentionally produced by the school. Rather, school authority served as a foil *against* which the boys constructed an oppositional masculinity. Contradictions of another kind abound in Klein's study of bodybuilding. Some committed body-builders need to support themselves by selling sexual and other services to middle-class gay men who admire and desire them. But homosexual practice, in a homophobic culture, discredits the masculinity these men literally embody. So those who 'hustle' find marvellous ways of reinterpreting what they are up to, and denying their own homosexual engagement.[63]

In recognizing different types of masculinity, then, we must not take them as fixed categories. Here the psychoanalytic theory of character types can be misleading. It is essential to recognize the dynamism of the relationships in which gender is constituted. Cynthia Cockburn's splendid study of the collective construction of masculinity in London print shops, *Brothers*, speaks of

> the break-up of old structures within the working class, and the dissolution of some of the patriarchal forms of relationship that governed the craft tradition. The authority of old men, the subservience of the 'lads', the manhood rituals of chapel life and, above all, the exclusion of women, are melting away.

Cockburn emphasizes the political character of the construction of masculinity, and of change in masculinity. The same point is made by a Canadian research team in *Recasting Steel Labour*, the first important study of masculinity to combine survey research with ethnography. In the Hamilton steelworks a dramatic shift in the acceptability of women as co-workers, and some rethinking of masculine ideologies, accompanied the union's drive to break down gender discrimination. But this ran up against a management strategy of downsizing in pursuit of profitability; the result was less gender change than might have occurred.[64]

Despite the emphasis on multiple masculinities and on contradiction, few researchers have doubted that the social construction of masculinities is a systematic process. This has been emphasized in Britain, in the main attempts so far to develop a general theory of masculinity. The work has come from the political left and reflects a profound questioning of traditional forms of left politics among men. Jeff Hearn, in *The Gender of Oppression*, transforms Marxist analysis to analyse men's appropriation of women's labour and more generally of women's 'human value'. He builds an ambitious (though somewhat arbitrary) model of patriarchy, as an impersonal and complex structure of relations among men which manages the exploitation of women – a considerable advance on dichotomous theories of patriarchy. Victor Seidler's *Rediscovering Masculinity* does for culture what Hearn does for social structure, locating men's everyday experiences in a broad framework of patriarchy. Seidler emphasizes the control of emotions and the denial of sexuality in the construction of masculinity, and connects this to the exaltation of abstract reason in Western intellectual traditions. This theoretical work is still in progress. It has, nevertheless, convincingly shown that masculinity must be understood as an aspect of large-scale social structures and processes.[65]

Hearn's work apart, the new sociology of masculinity does not offer deterministic models. To use Sartre's term, it studies various projects of masculinity, the conditions under which they arise and the conditions they produce. Such knowledge will not support a positivist science of masculinity. It will, however, illuminate social practice; and in that respect has much in common with the knowledge of masculinity coming from social movements.

Political Knowledge

We have now examined the main forms of organized knowledge about masculinity produced in clinical practice and academic research. These, however, are not the only ways of knowing masculinity. Many kinds of practice, perhaps all, produce knowledge. Social struggles on gender issues have certainly generated highly significant information and understanding about masculinity.

This is knowledge organized in a different way from clinical and academic knowledge. It does not lie around in bodies, but is found, often in very summary form, in programmes, polemics and debates over strategy. While academic knowledge mostly takes the form of description, concerned with what is or has been, political knowledge mostly takes an active form, concerned with what can be done and what must be suffered.

Political knowledge of masculinity has developed in several contexts. There has been constant debate in the anti-sexist Men's Liberation movement and its successors (such as the current National Organization for Men Against Sexism in the United States). There is a discourse of masculinity in conservative parties and fundamentalist churches, struggling to restore what they take to be the 'traditional' (regrettably quite modern) family.[66] Much the most important, in terms of originality and intellectual power, are the analyses of masculinity made by two oppositional movements, Gay Liberation and Women's Liberation.

Gay men mobilizing for civil rights, safety and cultural space have acted on the basis of a long experience of rejection and abuse by heterosexual men. The term 'homophobia' was coined in the early 1970s to describe this experience. A central insight of Gay Liberation is the depth and pervasiveness of homophobia, and how closely it is connected with dominant forms of masculinity.[67]

Yet gay men have also noticed a fascination with homosexuality on the part of straight men. Some have seen homophobia as the expression of a secret desire, driven out of consciousness and converted into hatred. This view is especially found among gay writers influenced by Freud, such as Mario Mieli in *Homosexuality and Liberation*. Others have noticed a curious willingness of straight men to be seduced, given the right time and a secluded place; or have noted how widespread homosexual sex becomes in all-male institutions such as armies and prisons. This knowledge was behind the slogan 'Every Straight Man is a Target for Gay Liberation!'. It points to the widespread but mostly unspoken sexualization of men's social worlds, rarely acknowledged in academic research.[68]

Homophobia is not just an attitude. Straight men's hostility to gay men involves real social practice, ranging from job discrimination through media vilification to imprisonment and sometimes murder – the spectrum of what Gay Liberation called oppression'. The point of these practices is not just to abuse individuals. It is also to draw social boundaries, defining 'real' masculinity by its distance from the rejected. Early Gay Liberation saw the oppression of homosexuals as part of a larger enterprise of maintaining an authoritarian social order, and often understood it to be connected with the oppression of women.[69]

In homophobic ideology the boundary between straight and gay is blurred with the boundary between masculine and feminine, gay men being imagined as feminized men and lesbians as masculinized women. Yet gay men also know the prevalence of homosexual desire among the apparently highly masculine (the gay jock, the warder who rapes, the army 'buddies'). Gay Liberation tactics included direct assault on gender conventions (radical drag, public kiss-ins), now brought up to date by Queer Nation. Styles in the gay communities of Western cities have shifted from camp to butch, and may be shifting again with queer. Gay men's collective knowledge, thus, includes gender ambiguity, tension between bodies and identities, and contradictions in and around masculinity.

Women's Liberation shared the concept of 'oppression' with the gay movement (and with the black power movement in the United States), but gave it a different emphasis. Feminist analyses stressed the structural position of men. Feminist researchers documented men's control of governments, corporations, media; men's better jobs, incomes and command of wealth; men's control of the means of violence; and the entrenched ideologies that pushed women into the home and dismissed their claims for equality. Straight men appeared to feminists more like a ruling class than a target for liberation. The term 'patriarchy' came into widespread use around 1970 to describe this system of gender domination.[70]

There is of course a personal level to patriarchy. Early Women's Liberation writing emphasized the family as the site of women's oppression. Theorists and activists documented wives' unpaid labour for husbands, mothers' imprisonment in the house and men's prerogatives in daily life. Lee Comer wrote of *Wedlocked Women*, Selma James and the Power of Women Collective demanded Wages for Housework. Many feminists experimented with new family arrangements, often trying to negotiate with men a new division of labour and a new system of child care.[71]

In time, however, Western feminism's picture of men shifted from the domestic patriarch consuming unpaid labour to focus on men's aggression against women. Women's shelters spread awareness of domestic violence, and campaigns against rape argued that every man is a potential rapist. Anti-pornography feminism in the 1980s carried this further, seeing men's sexuality as pervasively violent, and pornography as an attack upon women. The view that it is mainstream masculinity that is violent, not just a deviant group, also spread in feminist peace movements and the environmental movement.[72]

Feminists have differed sharply over heterosexual men's potential for change: whether better relationships can be negotiated, or misogyny is so entrenched that separation or compulsion is required for change. Economic advantage alone suggests that most men have a limited interest in reform. Barbara Ehrenreich in *The Hearts of Men* crystallized these doubts in the thesis of a 'flight from commitment' by men in the United States since the 1940s. Men's Liberation has often been seen by feminists as a way for men to extract benefits from feminism without giving up their basic privileges, a modernization of patriarchy, not an attack on it. There is widespread feminist scepticism about the 'new father', the 'new sensitive man', and other images of a kinder, gentler masculinity.[73]

At the same time, many feminists welcome signs of progress among men, and have noted differences among men and complexities in their relationships with women. Phyllis Chesler, for instance, wrote a vivid essay *About Men* that explored the variety of emotional ties between women and men. The most systematic and penetrating feminist analysis of masculinity, Lynne Segal's *Slow Motion*, has a great deal to say on divisions among men and their implications for feminist politics. Segal emphasizes that the pace of reform is not determined by men's psychology alone. It is also strongly influenced by their objective circumstances, such as the economic resources available to support full-time fathering of young children. Here feminist political argument converges with the social science research emphasizing the institutional dimension of masculinity.[74]

Gay theory and feminist theory share a perception of mainstream masculinity as being (in the advanced capitalist countries at least) fundamentally linked to power, organized for domination, and resistant to change because of power relations. In some formulations, masculinity is virtually equated with the exercise of power in its most naked forms.

This critique has been hard for many heterosexual men to take. The connection of masculinity with power is the point most persistently denied in the anti-feminist turn in the men's movement, a denial reinforced by pop psychology and neo-Jungian theories of masculinity (as will be seen in detail in Chapter 9). But the insight is of Fundamental importance. I will explore its relationships with both psychoanalytic and sociological research in the course of the book.

The Object of Knowledge

Once we recognize the institutional dimension of gender it is difficult to avoid the question: is it actually masculinity that is a problem in gender politics? Or is it rather the institutional arrangements that produce inequality, and thus generate the tensions that have brought 'masculinity' under scrutiny?

It is certainly important to acknowledge a social dynamic in its own right, and not try to read it off from men's psychology. Yet it is difficult to deny gay men's experiences of the personal emotion in homophobia, women's experiences of misogyny, or feminist arguments about the importance of desire and motive in the reproduction of patriarchy. Whatever is significant in issues about masculinity involves both personality and social relations; centrally, it involves the interplay between the two.

But is there a stable object of knowledge in this interplay? Can there be literally a science of masculinity?

In discussing ethnography I mentioned Strathern's evidence that gender categories work differently at Hagen from the way their analogues work in European/American culture. If a man, a woman or a clan can all be 'like a man' but need not be, depending on their achievements; and if 'it is an insult for a woman to be singled out as exemplifying feminine traits'; then it is clear that the world is being handled in a different way by Hagen gender concepts than by Western gender concepts. Conversely, applying Western concepts of gender identity would misrepresent Hagen social processes.

Such discontinuities logically rule out a positivist science of masculinity. There is no masculine entity whose occurrences in all societies we can generalize about. The things designated by the term in different cases are logically incommensurable.

Positivism has one line of escape from this difficulty. What is more or less constant, through the shifts of culture, is the anatomy and physiology of male bodies. We could pursue a science of *men*, defining 'masculinity' as the character of anyone who possessed a penis, a Y chromosome and a certain supply of testosterone. A recent French book about masculinity, one of the better popular books about men, is simply called *XY*. This is, perhaps, what is ultimately implied by the idea of 'men's studies'.[75]

This solves the logical problem, but it is not likely to lead to a science worth having. It is unmanageably vague: what action of any man in the world would *not* be an instance of masculinity? It would be impossible in such a framework to explore one of the main issues raised by psychoanalysis, the masculinity within women and the femininity within men. To believe that we can understand the social world through a biological demarcation is to misunderstand the relation between bodies and social processes (as will be shown in Chapter 2).

Masculinity and femininity are inherently relational concepts, which have meaning in relation to each other, as a social demarcation and a cultural opposition. This holds regardless of the changing content of the demarcation in different societies and periods of history. Masculinity as an object of knowledge is always masculinity-in-relation.

To put the point in another and perhaps clearer way, it is *gender relations* that constitute a coherent object of knowledge for science. Knowledge of masculinity arises within the project of knowing gender relations. To anticipate the definitions in Chapter 3, masculinities are configurations of practice structured by gender relations. They are inherently historical; and their making and remaking is a political process affecting the balance of interests in society and the direction of social change.

We can have systematic knowledge of such objects, but this knowledge does not follow the model of positivist science. Studies of a historical, political reality must work with the category of possibility. They grasp the world that is brought into being through social action in the light of the possibilities not realized, as well as those that are realized. Such knowledge is based on a critique of the real, not just a reflection of it.

Critical social science requires an ethical baseline empirically grounded in the situations under study. The baseline for the analysis in this book is social justice: the objective possibility of justice in gender relations, a possibility sometimes realized and sometimes not. To adopt such a baseline is not to propose an arbitrary value preference that is separate from the act of knowing. Rather, it is to acknowledge the inherently political character of our knowledge of masculinity. We can treat that as an epistemological asset, not an embarrassment.[76]

In this sense we can have a meaningful science of masculinity. It is part of the critical science of gender relations and their trajectory in history. That, in turn, is part of the larger exploration of human possibility, and its negations, which both social science and practical politics require.

2

Men's Bodies

True Masculinity

Arguments that masculinity should change often come to grief, not on counter-arguments against reform, but on the belief that men *cannot* change, so it is futile or even dangerous to try. Mass culture generally assumes there is a fixed, true masculinity beneath the ebb and flow of daily life. We hear of 'real men', 'natural man', the 'deep masculine'. This idea is now shared across an impressive spectrum including the mythopoetic men's movement, Jungian psychoanalysts, Christian fundamentalists, sociobiologists and the essentialist school of feminism.

True masculinity is almost always thought to proceed from men's bodies – to be inherent in a male body or to express something about a male body. Either the body drives and directs action (e.g., men are naturally more aggressive than women; rape results from uncontrollable lust or an innate urge to violence), or the body sets limits to action (e.g., men naturally do not take care of infants; homosexuality is unnatural and therefore confined to a perverse minority).

These beliefs are a strategic part of modern gender ideology, in the English-speaking world at least. So the first task of a social analysis is to arrive at an understanding of men's bodies and their relation to masculinity.

Two opposing conceptions of the body have dominated discussion of this issue in recent decades. In one, which basically translates the dominant ideology into the language of biological science, the body is a natural machine which produces gender difference – through genetic programming, hormonal difference, or the different role of the sexes in reproduction. In the other approach, which has swept the humanities and social sciences, the body is a more or less neutral surface or landscape on which a social symbolism is imprinted. Reading these arguments as a new version of the old 'nature vs. nurture' controversy, other voices have proposed a common-sense compromise: both biology and social influence combine to produce gender differences in behaviour.

In this chapter I will argue that all three views are mistaken. We can arrive at a better understanding of the relation between men's bodies and masculinity. But this cannot be done by abstract argument alone. So I will introduce, a little out of order, some evidence from the life-history study presented more fully in Part II.

Machine, Landscape and Compromise

Since religion's capacity to justify gender ideology collapsed, biology has been called in to fill the gap. The need may be gauged from the enormous appetite of the conservative mass media for stories of scientific discoveries about supposed sex differences. My favourite is the story that women's difficulty in parking cars is due to sex differences in brain function. (There is no actual evidence of the sex difference in parking, to start with.)

Speculation about masculinity and femininity is a mainstay of sociobiology, the revived attempt at an evolutionary explanation of human society that became fashionable in the 1970s. An early example of this genre, Lionel Tiger's *Men in Groups*, offered a complete biological-reductionist theory of masculinity based on the idea that we are descended from a hunting species. One of Tiger's phrases, 'male bonding', even passed into popular use.

According to these theorists, men's bodies are the bearers of a natural masculinity produced by the evolutionary pressures that have borne down upon the human stock. We inherit with our masculine genes tendencies to aggression, family life, competitiveness, political power, hierarchy, territoriality, promiscuity and forming men's clubs. The list varies somewhat from theorist to theorist, but the flavour remains the same. According to Edward Wilson, the doyen of sociobiologists, 'the physical and temperamental differences between men and women have been amplified by culture into universal male dominance.' More specifically, others claim that current social arrangements are an outgrowth of the endocrine system: for instance, that patriarchy is based in a hormonal 'aggression advantage' which men hold over women.[1]

The endocrine theory of masculinity, like the brain-sex theory, has also passed into journalistic common sense. Here, for instance, is the opening of a recent newspaper article on snowboarding safety:

> The most delusional, risk-inducing cocktail in the world is not a Zombie, a Harvey Wallbanger, or even the infamous Singapore Sling. It's the red-hot blend of testosterone and adrenaline that squirts through the arteries of teenagers and young men. That is why more than 95 per cent of the injuries in snowboarding are experienced by males under the age of 30, and the average age at injury is 21.[2]

The account of natural masculinity that has been built up in sociobiology is almost entirely fictional. It presupposes broad differences in the character traits and behaviours of women and men. As I noted in Chapter 1, a great deal of research has now been done on this issue. The usual finding, on intellect, temperament and other personal traits, is that there are no measurable differences at all. Where differences appear, they are small compared to variation within either sex, and very small compared to differences in the social positioning of women and men. The natural-masculinity thesis requires strong biological determination of group differences in complex social behaviours (such as creating families and armies). There is no evidence at all of strong determination in this sense. There is little evidence even of weak biological determination of group differences in simple individual behaviours. And the evidence of cross-cultural and historical diversity in gender is overwhelming. For instance, there are cultures and historical situations where rape is absent, or extremely rare; where homosexual behaviour is majority practice (at a given point in the life-cycle); where mothers do not predominate in child care (e.g., this work is done by old people, other children or servants); and where men are not normally aggressive.

The power of biological determination is not in its appeal to evidence. Careful examinations of the evidence, such as Theodore Kemper's *Social Structure and Testosterone*, show that nothing like one-way determination of the social by the biological can be sustained; the situation is far more complex. As Kemper bluntly concludes, 'When racist and sexist ideologies sanction certain hierarchical social arrangements on the basis of biology, the biology is usually false.'[3]

Rather, the power of this perspective lies in its *metaphor* of the body as machine. The body 'functions' and 'operates'. Researchers discover biological 'mechanisms' in behaviour. Brains are 'hardwired' to produce masculinity; men are genetically 'programmed' for dominance; aggression is in our 'biogram'. Both academic and journalistic texts are rich in these metaphors. For instance, few American readers of the snowboarding article just quoted would have missed the metaphor of the fuel-injected engine that has got mixed up with the cocktail metaphor. This neatly assimilates the exotic snowboard injuries to the all-too-familiar case of motor accidents caused by reckless young men – which in turn are commonly assumed to have a biological explanation.

When a metaphor becomes established it pre-empts discussion and shapes the way evidence is read. This has certainly happened with the metaphor of biological mechanism, and it affects even careful and well-documented research (which most sociobiology is not). A good example is a widely discussed study by Julianne Imperato-McGinley and others. A rare enzyme deficiency, of which 18 cases were found in two villages in the Dominican Republic, led to genetic-male infants having genitals that looked female, so they were raised as girls. This is analogous to the situations in the early lives of transsexuals described by Stoller in the United States, and on his argument should lead to a female 'core gender identity'. But in the Dominican Republic cases, the situation changed at puberty. At this point, normal testosterone levels masculinized the adolescents physically. The authors reported that 17 of the 18 then shifted to a male 'gender identity' and 16 to a male 'gender role'. The researchers saw this as proof that physiological mechanisms could override social conditioning.[4]

Closely examined, the paper shows something very different. McGinley and her colleagues describe a village society with a strong gender division of labour and a marked cultural opposition between masculine and feminine – both of which are social facts. The authors trace a gradual recognition by the children and their parents that a social error had been made, the children had been wrongly assigned. This error was socially corrected. The bodily changes of puberty clearly triggered a powerful *social* process of re-evaluation and reassignment. What the study refutes is not a social account of gender, but the particular thesis that core gender identity formed in early childhood always pre-empts later social development.

The Dominican Republic study inadvertently shows something more. The authors observe that, since the medical researchers arrived in the community, 5-alpha-reductase deficiency is now identified at birth, and the children are mostly raised as boys. Medicine thus has stepped in to normalize gender: to make sure that adult men will have masculine childhoods, and a consistent gender dichotomy will be preserved. Ironically, Stoller's work with transsexuals in the United States does the same. Gender reassignment surgery (now a routine procedure, though not a common one) eliminates the inconsistency of feminine social presence and male genitals. The medical practice pulls bodies into line with a social ideology of dichotomous gender.

This is what would be predicted by a semiotic analysis of gender. Approaches that treat women's bodies as the object of social symbolism have flourished at the meeting-point of cultural studies and feminism. Studies of the imagery of bodies and the production of femininity in film, photography and other visual arts now number in the hundreds. Closer to everyday practice, feminist studies of fashion and beauty, such as Elizabeth Wilson's *Adorned in Dreams* and Wendy Chapkis's *Beauty Secrets*, trace complex but powerful systems of imagery through which bodies are defined as beautiful or ugly, slender or fat. Through this imagery, a whole series of body-related needs has been created: for diet, cosmetics, fashionable clothing, slimming programmes and the like.

This research is supported, and often directly inspired, by the post-structuralist turn in social theory. Michel Foucault's analysis of the 'disciplining' of bodies is a corollary of his account of the production of truth within discourses; bodies became the objects of new disciplinary sciences as new technologies of power brought them under control in finer and finer detail. The sociology of the body developed by Bryan Turner moves in the same direction at a somewhat more material level. Observing that 'bodies are objects over which we labour – eating, sleeping, cleaning, dieting, exercising', Turner proposes the idea of 'body practices', both individual and collective, to include the range of ways in which social labour addresses the body.

These practices can be institutionally elaborated on a very large scale. This is demonstrated, and connected to the production of gender, in recent work on the sociology of sport. Nancy Theberge's 'Reflections on the body in the sociology of sport' convincingly shows how the different regimes of exercise for women and men, the disciplinary practices that both teach and constitute sport, are designed to produce gendered bodies. And if social discipline cannot produce adequately gendered bodies, surgery can. Cosmetic surgery now offers the affluent an extraordinary range of ways of producing a more socially desirable body, from the old 'face-lifts' and breast implants to the newer surgical slimming, height alterations, and so on. As Diana Dull and Candace West found by interviewing cosmetic surgeons and their patients in the United States, cosmetic surgery is now thought natural for a woman, though not for a man. Nevertheless the technology now extends to the surgical production of masculinity, with penile implants, both inflatable and rigid, to the fore.[5]

Though work on the semiotics of gender has overwhelmingly focused on femininity, at times the approach has been extended to masculinity. Anthony Easthope in *What a Man's Gotta Do* surveys the issues and is easily able to demonstrate how men's bodies are being defined as masculine in the imagery of advertising, film and news reports. There are studies at closer focus, of which perhaps the most remarkable is Susan Jeffords's *The Remasculinization of America*, which traces the reconstitution and celebration of masculinity in films and novels about the Vietnam war after the American defeat. There has also been a recent interest in gender ambiguity. Marjorie Garber's encyclopaedic account of literary, stage and filmic cross-dressing, *Vested Interests*, takes the semiotic approach to gender about as far as it will go in claiming that the mismatch of body and clothing is an 'instatement of metaphor itself'.[6]

Social constructionist approaches to gender and sexuality underpinned by a semiotic approach to the body provide an almost complete antithesis to sociobiology. Rather than social arrangements being the effects of the body-machine, the body is a field on which social determination runs riot. This approach too has its leading metaphors, which tend to be metaphors of art rather than engineering: the body is a canvas to be painted, a surface to be imprinted, a landscape to be marked out.

This approach also – though it has been wonderfully productive – runs into difficulty. With so much emphasis on the signifier, the signified tends to vanish. The problem is particularly striking for that unavoidably bodily activity, sex. Social constructionist accounts were certainly an improvement on the positivist sexology of Kinsey and Masters and Johnson. But social constructionist discussions had the odd effect of disembodying sex. As Carole Vance ruefully put it,

> to the extent that social construction theory grants that sexual acts, identities and even desire are mediated by cultural and historical factors, the object of the study – sexuality – becomes evanescent and threatens to disappear.[7]

Gender is hardly in better case, when it becomes just a subject-position in discourse, the place from which one speaks; when gender is seen as, above all, a performance; or when the rending contradictions within gendered lives become 'an instatement of metaphor'. As Rosemary Pringle argues in 'Absolute sex?', her recent review of the sexuality/gender relationship, a wholly semiotic or cultural account of gender is no more tenable than a biological reductionist one.[8] The surface on which cultural meanings are inscribed is not featureless, and it does not stay still.

Bodies, in their own right as bodies, do matter. They age, get sick, enjoy, engender, give birth. There is an irreducible bodily dimension in experience and practice; the sweat cannot be excluded. On this point we can learn even from the sex role literature. One of the few compelling things the male role literature and Books About Men did was to catalogue Problems with Male Bodies, from impotence and ageing to occupational health hazards, violent injury, loss of sporting prowess and early death. Warning: the male sex role may be dangerous to your health.[9]

Can we, then, settle for a common-sense compromise, asserting both biology and culture in a composite model of gender? This is, essentially, the formula of sex role theory, which, as shown in Chapter 1, adds a social script to a biological dichotomy. Moderate statements of sociobiology often acknowledge a cultural elaboration of the biological imperative. A similar position was argued in the 1980s by Alice Rossi, who had been one of the feminist pioneers in sociology:

> Gender differentiation is not simply a function of socialization, capitalist production, or patriarchy. It is grounded in a sex dimorphism that serves the fundamental purpose of reproducing the species.[10]

Masculinity, it would follow, is the social elaboration of the biological function of fatherhood.

If biological determinism is wrong, and social determinism is wrong, then it is unlikely that a combination of the two will be right. There are reasons to think these two 'levels of analysis' cannot be satisfactorily added. For one thing, they are not commensurate. Biology is always seen as the *more* real, the *more* basic of the pair; even the sociologist Rossi speaks of the social process being 'grounded' in sex dimorphism, the reproductive purpose being 'fundamental'. And that is taken for granted in sociobiology. (These metaphors, I would argue, express an entirely mistaken idea of the relationship between history and organic evolution.)

Nor does the pattern of difference at the two levels correspond – though this is constantly assumed, and sometimes made explicit in statements about 'sex dimorphism in behaviour'. Social process may, it is true, elaborate on bodily difference (the padded bra, the penis-sheath, the cod-piece). Social process may also distort, contradict, complicate, deny, minimize or modify bodily difference. Social process may define one gender ('unisex' fashion, gender-neutral labour), two genders (Hollywood), three (many North American native cultures), four (European urban culture once homosexuals began to be sorted out, after the eighteenth century), or a whole spectrum of fragments, variations and trajectories. Social process has recast our very perception of sexed bodies, as shown by Thomas Laqueur's remarkable history of the transition in medical and popular thought from a one-sex model to a two-sex model.[11]

However we look at it, a compromise between biological determination and social determination will not do as the basis for an account of gender. Yet we cannot ignore either the radically cultural character of gender or the bodily presence. It seems that we need other ways of thinking about the matter.

The Body Inescapable

A rethinking may start by acknowledging that, in our culture at least, the physical sense of maleness and femaleness is central to the cultural interpretation of gender. Masculine gender is (among other things) a certain feel to the skin, certain muscular shapes and tensions, certain postures and ways of moving, certain possibilities in sex. Bodily experience is often central in memories of our own lives, and thus in our understanding of who and what we are. Here is an example, from a life-history interview in which sexuality was a major theme.

* * *

Hugh Trelawney is a heterosexual journalist aged about thirty, who remembers his earliest sexual experience at age 14. Very unusually, Hugh claims to have fucked before he masturbated. The well-crafted memory is set in a magical week with perfect waves, Hugh's first drink in a hotel, and 'the beginning of my life':

> *The girl was an 18-year-old Maroubra beach chick. What the hell she wanted to have anything to do with me I don't know. She must have been slightly retarded, emotionally if not intellectually. I suppose she just went to it for the image, you know, I was already the long-haired surfie rat. I recall getting on top of her and not knowing where to put it and thinking, gee, it's a long way down . . . and when I sort of finally got it in, it only went in a little way, and I thought this isn't much. Then she must have moved her leg a little way, and then it went further and I thought oh! gee, that's all right. And then I must have come in about five or six strokes, and I thought the feeling was outrageous because I thought I was going to die . . . And then during that week I had a whole new sense of myself. I expected – I don't know what I expected, to start growing more pubic hair, or expected my dick to get bigger. But it was that sort of week, you know. Then after that I was on my way.*

* * *

This is a tale of a familiar kind, recounting a sexual coming-of-age. In almost every detail it shows the intricate interplay of the body with social process. Choice and arousal, as Hugh reconstructs it, are social (the 'beach chick', the 'surfie rat'). The required performance is physical, 'getting it in'. The young Hugh lacks the knowledge and skill required. But his skill is improved interactively, by his partner's bodily response ('she must have moved her leg a little bit'). The *physical* feeling of climax is immediately an interpretation ('I thought I was going to die'). It triggers off a familiar symbolic sequence – death, rebirth, new growth. Conversely the *social* transition Hugh has accomplished, entering into sexual adulthood, immediately translates as bodily fantasy ('more pubic hair', 'dick to get bigger').

Hugh jokingly invokes the metonymy by which the penis stands for masculinity – the basis of castration anxiety and the classical psychoanalytic theory of masculinity discussed in Chapter 1 – but his memory also points beyond it. The first fuck is set in a context of sport: the week of perfect waves and the culture of surfing. In historically recent times, sport has come to be the leading definer of masculinity in mass culture. Sport provides a continuous display of men's bodies in motion. Elaborate and carefully monitored rules bring these bodies into stylized contests with each other. In these contests a combination of superior force (provided by size, fitness, teamwork) and superior skill (provided by planning, practice and intuition) will enable one side to win.[12]

The embodiment of masculinity in sport involves a whole pattern of body development and use, not just one organ. Highly specific skills are of course involved. For instance, bowling a googly in cricket – an off-break ball delivered deceptively with a leg-break action out of the back of the hand with the elbow held straight – must be among the most exotic physical performances in the entire human repertoire. But players who can do only one thing are regarded as freaks. It is the integrated performance of the whole body, the capacity to do a range of things wonderfully well, that is admired in the greatest exemplars of competitive sport – figures such as Babe Ruth in baseball, Garfield Sobers in cricket or Muhammad Ali in boxing.

The institutional organization of sport embeds definite social relations: competition and hierarchy among men, exclusion or domination of women. These social relations of gender are both realized and symbolized in the bodily performances. Thus men's greater sporting prowess has become a theme of backlash against feminism. It serves as symbolic proof of men's superiority and right to rule.

At the same time, the bodily performances are called into existence by these structures. Running, throwing, jumping or hitting outside these structures is not sport at all. The performance is symbolic and kinetic, social and bodily, at one and the same time, *and these aspects depend on each other.*

The constitution of masculinity through bodily performance means that gender is vulnerable when the performance cannot be sustained – for instance, as a result of physical disability. Thomas Gerschick and Adam Miller have conducted a small but remarkably interesting study of American men trying to deal with this situation after disabling accidents or illness. They distinguish three responses. One is to redouble efforts to meet the hegemonic standards, overcoming the physical difficulty – for instance, finding proof of continued sexual potency by trying to exhaust one's partner. Another is to reformulate the definition of masculinity, bringing it closer to what is now possible, though still pursuing masculine themes such as independence and control. The third is to reject hegemonic masculinity as a package – criticizing the physical stereotypes, and moving towards a counter-sexist politics, a project of the kind explored in Chapter 5 below. So a wide range of responses can be made to the undermining of the bodily sense of masculinity. The one thing none of these men can do is ignore it.[13]

Nor can the manual workers whose vulnerability comes from the very situation that allows them to define masculinity through labour. Heavy manual work calls for strength, endurance, a degree of insensitivity and toughness, and group solidarity. Emphasizing the masculinity of industrial labour has been both a means of survival, in exploitative class relations, and a means of asserting superiority over women.

This emphasis reflects an economic reality. Mike Donaldson, collecting accounts of factory labour, notes that working men's bodily capacities *are* their economic asset, are what they put on the labour market. But this asset changes. Industrial labour under the regime of profit uses up the workers' bodies, through fatigue, injury and mechanical wear and tear. The decline of strength, threatening loss of income or the job itself, can be offset by the growth of skill – up to a point. 'It is at that point, unless he is very lucky, that a man's labouring days are over.

The combination of force and skill is thus open to change. Where work is altered by deskilling and casualization, working-class men are increasingly defined as possessing force alone. The process is virulent where class exclusion combines with racism, as in South Africa under apartheid. (The apartheid economy literally 'reserved' skilled jobs for white men, and casualized black labour on a massive scale.) Middle-class men, conversely, are increasingly defined as the bearers of skill. This definition is supported by a powerful historical change in labour markets, the growth of credentialism, linked to a higher education system that selects and promotes along class lines.[14]

This class process alters the familiar connection between masculinity and machinery. The new information technology requires much sedentary keyboard work, which was initially classified as women's work (key-punch operators). The marketing of personal computers, however, has redefined some of this work as an arena of competition and power – masculine, technical, but not working-class. These revised meanings are promoted in the text and graphics of computer magazines, in manufacturers' advertising that emphasizes 'power' (Apple Computer named its laptop the 'PowerBook'), and in the booming industry of violent computer games. Middle-class male bodies, separated by an old class division from physical force, now find their powers spectacularly amplified in the man/machine systems (the gendered language is entirely appropriate) of modern cybernetics.

The body, I would conclude, is inescapable in the construction of masculinity; but what is inescapable is not fixed. The bodily process, entering into the social process, becomes part of history (both personal and collective) and a possible object of politics. Yet this does not return us to the idea of bodies as landscape. They have various forms of recalcitrance to social symbolism and control, and I will now turn to this issue.

Complexities of Mire or Blood

W. B. Yeats's wonderful poem 'Byzantium' imagines a golden mechanical bird, symbol of the artifice of an ageing civilization, scorning 'all complexities of mire or blood'. Images of remoteness and abstraction contrast with 'mere complexities, The fury and the mire of human veins'.[15] The 'mere' is deeply ironic. It is precisely the plurality and recalcitrance of bodies that gives force to Yeats's irony.

Philosophy and social theory often speak of 'the body'. But bodies are plural (about 5.4 thousand million in 1994) and are very diverse. There are large bodies and small bodies; bodies permanently stained with soil or grease, bodies permanently stooped from bending over a desk, and other bodies with spotless, manicured hands. Every one of these bodies has its trajectory through time. Each one must change as it grows and ages. The social processes that engulf it and sustain it are also certain to change.

What is true of 'bodies' in general is true of men's bodies in particular. They are diverse to start with, and they get more diverse as they grow and age. In an earlier essay on 'men's bodies',

I wrote poetically of bodily masculinity as centring on the combination of force and skill symbolized by sport; and remarked that

> To be an adult male is distinctly to occupy space, to have a physi-
> cal presence in the world. Walking down the street, I square my
> shoulders and covertly measure myself against other men. Walking
> past a group of punk youths late at night, I wonder if I look for-
> midable enough. At a demonstration I size up the policemen and
> wonder if I am bigger and stronger than them if it comes to the
> crunch – a ludicrous consideration, given the actual techniques
> of mass action and crowd control, but an automatic reaction
> nevertheless.[16]

That was ten years ago. Ten years later, rising fifty, the body concerned is a bit balder, significantly more stooped, decidedly less
space-occupying, and much less likely to be in dodgy situations
on the street.

Not only are men's bodies diverse and changing, they can be
positively recalcitrant. Ways are proposed for bodies to participate
in social life, and the bodies often refuse. Here are two examples
from the life-history interviews.

*   *   *

*Hugh Trelawney, whose sexual initiation story was quoted above, launched as a
student on a familiar path. Determined to be a 'legend', Hugh became 'animal
of the year' at his university, on a spree of booze, drugs and sex. A couple of years
out, working as a teacher, he was becoming alcoholic and seriously ill. He left his
job, wound up in a drug-induced emotional crisis and a detoxification unit. The
blow to his pride was as much about the body as about the social humiliation:
'This is all wrong, I'm a first grade footballer.'*

*   *   *

*Tip Southern, starting from a position of greater class advantage, partied even
harder. His private-school peer group called itself the 'Sick Patrol,' dressed out-
landishly, crashed parties and took them over, smoked lots of dope.*

> *We were pretty radical, rebellious, angry young men. Men with a mission
> but partying full on all the time. Towards the end it was just one big blur.
> Binge after binge after binge . . . It was just full on, we were getting pissed
> all the time; really, really drunk but handling it because we were so full of
> energy. You don't get hangovers when you are that young and that much
> on the go.*

Off to university, things got heavier again: 'really heavy wild parties', punch made with industrial alcohol, hash and hallucinogens. In due course both Tip's family and his body stopped coming through.

I tried to get jobs. 'What are you qualified for?' Nothing. I didn't have any good clothes with me because I had been roughing it for a long time . . . So I never got jobs. I don't think I looked like the most respect – I mean, I was very undernourished in a general way, I was taking a lot of drugs, a lot of acid, drinking a lot. I have got this picture of me in my room, hidden away, of myself in the worst state that you can imagine: big stoned swollen red eyes, a huge stye in this eye, and just the most pallid face. I was drinking far too much, taking really nasty drugs, really dirty acid, eech! And just got real bogged down with it all. And finally I just knew I had to do something drastic.

*　　*　　*

Crisis stories such as these show bodies under pressure reaching limits. Michael Messner, interviewing former athletes in the United States, heard parallel stories. The pressure of high-level competitive sport obliges professional players to treat their bodies as instruments, even as weapons. As Messner puts it, 'the body-as-weapon ultimately results in violence against one's own body.' Playing hurt, accidents, drug use and constant stress wear down even the fittest and strongest. Timothy Curry's recent case study of an American wrestler shows how sports injuries become a normal career expectation. The body is virtually assaulted in the name of masculinity and achievement. Ex-athletes often live with damaged bodies and chronic pain, and die early.[17]

These are extreme cases; but the principle applies in much more routine situations, such as the industrial workplaces discussed above. Bodies cannot be understood as a neutral medium of social practice. Their materiality matters. They will do certain things and not others. Bodies are *substantively* in play in social practices such as sport, labour and sex.

Some bodies are more than recalcitrant, they disrupt and subvert the social arrangements into which they are invited. Homosexual desire, as Guy Hocquenghem argued, is not the product of a different kind of body. But it is certainly a bodily fact, and one that disrupts hegemonic masculinity.[18]

Even more striking is the case of gender-switching, where bodies pass the most fundamental of boundaries set for them by the modern gender order. The very language for talking about this issue has been captured by medicine, freezing desperation and carnival into conditions and syndromes: 'transvestite' and 'transsexual'. This freezing has been aptly criticized by social scientists and postmodern theorists; 'Queer Theory' celebrates the symbolic disruptions of gender categories. Yet the medical ideology and the critique collude in reading culture as the active term and bodies as passive, as landscape. Gender-switching can even be seen as the ultimate triumph of symbol over flesh, with transsexuals' having their bodies literally carved to the shape of the symbolic identity they have adopted.

Accounts by people doing gender switches do not show the body under the rule of the symbol. The autobiography of Katherine Cummings, a level-headed and witty Australian gender traveller, speaks of an incomprehensible but undeniable material need, to which symbolic self and social relations had to give ground. Gary Kates, re-examining the classic gender-switching story of the Chevalier d'Eon in the late eighteenth century, observes that d'Eon, though convinced of being a woman, disliked the symbolism and practicalities of women's clothes. D'Eon only put them on, under protest, when obliged to by the French political authorities.

These are not unique cases. At the boundaries of gender categories, bodies may travel in their own right. The momentum may be so strong that proprioceptive consciousness is transformed, with hallucinations of the other-sexed body – some temporary, some permanent. In the case of 'David', mentioned in Chapter 1, Laing wrote of 'the woman who was inside him, and always seemed to be coming out of him'. I suggest this is a bodily, not just a mental, experience. Two differently gendered bodily experiences emerge in the same place. Bodies, it seems, are not only subversives. They can be jokers too.[19]

Banquo's Ghost: Body-Reflexive Practices

How can we understand the situation when bodies, like Banquo's ghost, refuse to stay outdoors in the realm of nature and reappear uninvited in the realm of the social? Mainstream social science gives little help. As Turner observed in *The Body and Society*, bodies went missing a long time ago from social theory. Social theory for the most part still operates in the universe created by Descartes, with a sharp split between the knowing, reasoning mind and the mechanical, unreasoning body. Theories of discourse have not overcome this split: they have made bodies the objects of symbolic practice and power but not participants.

To break out of this universe it is not enough to assert the significance of bodily difference, important as this has been in recent feminist theory. We need to assert the activity, literally the *agency*, of bodies in social processes. The crisis stories earlier in this chapter showed the rebellion of bodies against certain kinds of pressure. This is a kind of effectiveness, but not full-blown agency. I want to argue for a stronger theoretical position, where bodies are seen as sharing in social agency, in generating and shaping courses of social conduct.[20]

*   *   *

Don Meredith, a great storyteller, offered a long comic tale of his youthful search for the First Fuck. After a series of fiascos he reached the goal, formed a relationship and then found himself unable to ejaculate. In time, however, he became more sophisticated:

> I am very anal oriented. And I discovered this in a relationship with a young woman quite accidentally, I really enjoyed it. She was inserting her finger into my anus and I thought 'My god this is fantastic.' And like even with masturbation I sort of generally touched round that area but never really gone into it. But I guess that was like a trigger for it. When this young woman was doing it, it was just really electrifying me, and I never found it difficult to ejaculate with her. She really touched a spot well and truly. So I thought now what I would really like is to have a relationship with a man where I would be inserted into. And that really excited me, the whole idea of it.

*   *   *

Here the bodily arousal and action is woven into the social action. Don experienced his body and its capacities through interaction. In a strong sense one can say that he discovered his body in interaction. He was virtually led to his anus by a partner. The climax of his first fuck was simultaneously a physical sensation and the high-point of the longer narration of the Tale of Don's Virginity – 'wow, I've never had this before'.

The socialness of the physical performance is not a matter of social framing around a physiological event. It is a more intimate connection that operates especially in the dimension of fantasy – both in nuances of Don's virginity story, and more directly in the fantasy of a new social relation 'where I would be inserted into'.

This fantasy started from the experience of being finger-fucked. It arose in a social interaction, but it was wholly a bodily experience too. The body's response then had a directing influence on Don's sexual conduct. 'Agency' does not seem too strong a word for what Don's sphincter, prostate gland and erectile tissues here managed between them.

Research on sport that has emphasized the disciplinary practices producing gender does not capture this side of things. Jogging, for instance, is certainly a socially disciplined activity. I tell myself this every second morning while struggling out of bed and tying on the running shoes. Yet each August in Sydney, 40,000 pairs of feet *willingly* set off down William Street towards Bondi in the 'City to Surf' run. A crowd run is a striking illustration of the pleasure of sociability through shared bodily performance.

Nor does the idea of 'resistance' to disciplinary practices cover what happens when the iron cage of discipline clunks down on the ground and gets bent. Two days ago, in the bus going up to the university, I sat opposite a young woman who was wearing running shoes, running socks, running shorts, a silk blouse, long silver earrings, full make-up and blow-dried hair with combs. Was she being simultaneously controlled by *two* disciplinary regimes, sport and fashion, each of which gave up somewhere about the waist? At the least she was doing something witty with them, she was able to manoeuvre.

With bodies both objects and agents of practice, and the practice itself forming the structures within which bodies are appropriated and defined, we face a pattern beyond the formulae of current social theory. This pattern might be termed body-reflexive practice.

Don Meredith's electrification illustrates the circuits involved. The bodily pleasure of being finger-fucked, which results in stimulation of the prostate gland as well as the anal sphincters and rectal lining, had social effects. It led directly to the fantasy of a new social relation, one with a man, 'where I would be inserted into. And that really excited me.'

This excitement was transgressive. Don thought of himself as heterosexual. He had rejected advances from a gay man while on the great quest to lose his virginity, 'beat him off with a tent peg'. But now the bodily experience of being penetrated led to the fantasy of a homosexual relationship, and in due course to real homosexual encounters. (Don had no luck. In his exploratory gay fuck the partner lost his erection.)

There is nothing about sphincter relaxation and prostate stimulation that demands a relationship with a man. A woman can do the job perfectly well. It is the social equation between anal penetration and a male partner that provides the structure of Don's bodily fantasy. Anal sex is a key symbol of Western male homosexuality, though AIDS research shows it is done less often than its symbolic importance might suggest.[21]

The circuit in this case goes from bodily interaction and bodily experience, via socially structured bodily fantasy (involving the cultural construction of hegemonic and oppressed sexualities), to the construction of fresh sexual relationships centring on new bodily interactions. This is not simply a matter of social meanings or categories being imposed on Don's body, though these meanings and categories are vital to what happens. The body-reflexive practice calls them into play, while the bodily experience – a startling joy – energizes the circuit.

* * *

Adam Singer recalled a moment of trauma with his father:

> *He bought my brother a cricket bat for Christmas and he wouldn't buy me one. He'd say I couldn't play cricket. And things like throwing a ball. How a man throws a ball is different to how a woman throws a ball. I didn't want to throw a ball in front of my Dad because I knew it wouldn't look right, it wouldn't be like the way a good strong boy should throw it. And once, I remember, I was brave enough to throw it. And he made fun of me and said I threw it like a girl.*

* * *

Here the circuit is condensed in time. The public gender meanings are instantaneously fused with the bodily activity and the emotions of the relationship. Even so, there is a split perception. Adam has learned how to be both in his body (throwing), and outside his body watching its gendered performance ('I knew it wouldn't look right').

In Adam's story the body-reflexive practice of sport called out a declaration of difference ('he made fun of me and said . . .'), with all the emotional charge of the father–son relationship behind it. In time, Adam collected more evidences of being different. Finally he deliberately began a relationship with a man to find out whether he was gay – that is, to find out where in the gender order this 'brave enough' body belonged.

* * *

Steve Donoghue had no doubts about his location. He was a national champion in surf sport, making a rich living from prizes, sponsorships and commercials. He had a superb physique, cultivated with four to five hours' training every day. Steve's body was capable of astonishing feats of precision as well as endurance:

> *I can spread my energy over a four-hour race to not die, to not have to start up slowly. I can start at a pace and finish at a pace every time. When I swam, I used to do 200 metres, which is four fifty-metre laps. I can start off, and any fifty is pretty well to the tenth of a second the same time each lap, and I wouldn't even be looking at a watch . . .*

Like others skilled at sports, Steve had a detailed and exact knowledge of his body, its capabilities, its needs, and its limits.

* * *

The body-reflexive practice here is familiar; its gender consequences perhaps less so. Steve Donoghue, young-man-about-beach, was trapped in the practices required to sustain Steve Donoghue, famous-exemplar-of-masculinity. He could not drink-drive, nor get into fights when pushed around (for fear of bad publicity). He could not go boozing (because of training), nor 'have much of a sex life' (his coach was against it, and women had to fit in with his training schedule). In other words, much of what was defined in his peer culture as masculine was forbidden him.

Indeed, the body-reflexive practice that constructed Steve's hegemonic masculinity also undermined hegemonic masculinity. Steve's social and psychological life was focused on his body. The competitiveness essential to the making of a champion was turned inwards. Though encouraged by the coach to hate his

competitors, Steve did not. Rather, he talked of 'mental toughness' and his ability to 'control the pain', to 'make my body
believe that I am not hurting as much as I am'.

In short, Steve was driven towards narcissism – while the hegemonic construction of masculinity in contemporary Australian
culture is outward-turned and plays down all private emotion.
Yet the narcissism could not rest in self-admiration and bodily
pleasure. This would have destroyed the performance on
which Steve's life trajectory depended.

In his version of competition, the decisive triumph was over
one's body. Steve's magnificent physique had meaning only when
deployed in winning. The will to win did not arise from personal
'drive', a familiar word in sports talk that Steve did not use at all.
It was given to him by the social structure of sporting competition; it was his meaning, as a champion.

The circuit of Steve's body-reflexive practice was thus a complex
one, moving through the institutionalized system of commercial-
ized sport, beach product manufacturing and advertising, and
mass media, to the personal practices of training and competition. This system is far from coherent. Indeed it contains substantial contradictions, betrayed by the contradictory masculinity
produced in Steve's life. And if this is true for an exemplary masculinity such as Steve's, there is little reason to think the circuits
of body-reflexive practice for the majority of men are markedly
more coherent.

Body-reflexive practices, as we see in all these instances, are not
internal to the individual. They involve social relations and symbolism; they may well involve large-scale social institutions. Particular versions of masculinity are constituted in their circuits as
meaningful bodies and embodied meanings. Through body-
reflexive practices, more than individual lives are formed: a social
world is formed.

Forming the World

Through body-reflexive practices, bodies are addressed by social
process and drawn into history, without ceasing to be bodies. They
do not turn into symbols, signs or positions in discourse. Their
materiality (including material capacities to engender, to give
birth, to give milk, to menstruate, to open, to penetrate, to ejac-

ulate) is not erased, it continues to matter. The *social* process of gender includes childbirth and child care, youth and ageing, the pleasures of sport and sex, labour, injury, death from AIDS.

The social semiotics of gender, with its emphasis on the endless play of signification, the multiplicity of discourses and the diversity of subject positions, has been important in escaping the rigidities of biological determinism. But it should not give the impression that gender is an autumn leaf, wafted about by light breezes. Body-reflexive practices form – and are formed by – structures which have historical weight and solidity. The social has its own reality.

When feminism around 1970 spoke of 'patriarchy' as the master pattern in human history, the argument was overgeneralized. But the idea well captured the power and intractability of a massive structure of social relations: a structure that involved the state, the economy, culture and communications as well as kinship, child-rearing and sexuality.

Practice never occurs in a vacuum. It always responds to a situation, and situations are structured in ways that admit certain possibilities and not others. Practice does not proceed into a vacuum either. Practice makes a world. In acting, we convert initial situations into new situations. Practice constitutes and re-constitutes structures. Human practice is, in the evocative if awkward term of the Czech philosopher Karel Kosík, onto-formative. It makes the reality we live in.[22]

The practices that construct masculinity are onto-formative in this sense. As body-reflexive practices they constitute a world which has a bodily dimension, but is not biologically determined. Not being fixed by the physical logic of the body, this new-made world may be hostile to bodies' physical well-being. Tip Southern's and Hugh Trelawney's enactments of hegemonic masculinity were hostile in this way – examples of 'self-inflicted wounds', as Australian slang calls a hangover. The practice of unsafe sex, in the context of the HIV epidemic, is a more sinister case in point.

Both Tip Southern and Hugh Trelawney, as it happens, undertook reform of their masculinity – bodily reform as well as change in relationships. Hugh went into a detoxification unit, and decided to make 'fundamental changes' in his conduct. He determined to be less competitive, more open to others, and to treat women as people not as objects in a sexual game. Where this reform led will be seen in Chapter 7. Tip got off the drugs and found an outdoor job doing physical labour, which helped return him to health. He formed, for the first time, a lasting relationship with a young woman.

Of course no two stories could represent all attempts by men to change. Different trajectories will be found in Chapter 5. What these two stories illustrate, nevertheless, is an inescapable fact about any project of change. For men, as for women, the world formed by the body-reflexive practices of gender is a domain of politics – the struggle of interests in a context of inequality. Gender politics is an embodied-social politics. The shapes taken by an embodied politics of masculinity will be a principal theme of the rest of this book.

3

The Social Organization of Masculinity

Chapter 1 traced the main currents of twentieth-century research and showed that they had failed to produce a coherent science of masculinity. This does not reveal the failure of the scientists so much as the impossibility of the task. 'Masculinity' is not a coherent object about which a generalizing science can be produced. Yet we can have coherent knowledge about the issues raised in these attempts. If we broaden the angle of vision, we can see masculinity, not as an isolated object, but as an aspect of a larger structure.

This demands an account of the larger structure and how masculinities are located in it. The task of this chapter is to set out a framework based on contemporary analyses of gender relations. This framework will provide a way of distinguishing types of masculinity, and of understanding the dynamics of change.

First, however, there is some ground to clear. The definition of the basic term in the discussion has never been wonderfully clear.

Defining Masculinity

All societies have cultural accounts of gender, but not all have the concept 'masculinity'. In its modern usage the term assumes that one's behaviour results from the type of person one is. That is to say, an unmasculine person would behave differently: being peaceable rather than violent, conciliatory rather than dominating, hardly able to kick a football, uninterested in sexual conquest, and so forth.

This conception presupposes a belief in individual difference and personal agency. In that sense it is built on the conception of individuality that developed in early-modern Europe with the growth of colonial empires and capitalist economic relations (an issue I will explore further in Chapter 8).

But the concept is also inherently relational. 'Masculinity' does not exist except in contrast with 'femininity'. A culture which does not treat women and men as bearers of polarized character types, at least in principle, does not have a concept of masculinity in the sense of modern European/American culture.

Historical research suggests that this was true of European culture itself before the eighteenth century. Women were certainly regarded as different from men, but different in the sense of being incomplete or inferior examples of the same character (for instance, having less of the faculty of reason). Women and men were not seen as bearers of qualitatively different characters; this conception accompanied the bourgeois ideology of 'separate spheres' in the nineteenth century.[1]

In both respects our concept of masculinity seems to be a fairly recent historical product, a few hundred years old at most. In speaking of masculinity at all, then, we are 'doing gender' in a culturally specific way. This should be borne in mind with any claim to have discovered transhistorical truths about manhood and the masculine.

Definitions of masculinity have mostly taken our cultural standpoint for granted, but have followed different strategies to characterize the type of person who is masculine. Four main strategies have been followed; they are easily distinguished in terms of their logic, though often combined in practice.

Essentialist definitions usually pick a feature that defines the core of the masculine, and hang an account of men's lives on that. Freud flirted with an essentialist definition when he equated masculinity with activity in contrast to feminine passivity – though he came to see that equation as oversimplified. Later authors' attempts to capture an essence of masculinity have been colourfully varied: risk-taking, responsibility, irresponsibility, aggression, Zeus energy . . . Perhaps the finest is the sociobiologist Lionel Tiger's idea that true maleness, underlying male bonding and war, is elicited by 'hard and heavy phenomena'.[2] Many heavy-metal rock fans would agree.

The weakness in the essentialist approach is obvious: the choice of the essence is quite arbitrary. Nothing obliges different essentialists to agree, and in fact they often do not. Claims about a universal basis of masculinity tell us more about the ethos of the claimant than about anything else.

Positivist social science, whose ethos emphasizes finding the facts, yields a simple definition of masculinity: what men actually are. This definition is the logical basis of masculinity/femininity (M/F) scales in psychology, whose items are validated by showing that they discriminate statistically between groups of men and women. It is also the basis of those ethnographic discussions of masculinity which describe the pattern of men's lives in a given culture and, whatever it is, call the pattern masculinity.[3]

There are three difficulties here. First, as modern epistemology recognizes, there is no description without a standpoint. The apparently neutral descriptions on which these definitions rest are themselves underpinned by assumptions about gender. Obviously enough, to start compiling an M/F scale one must have some idea of what to count or list when making up the items.

Second, to list what men and women do requires that people be already sorted into the categories 'men' and 'women'. This, as Suzanne Kessler and Wendy McKenna showed in their classic ethnomethodological study of gender research, is unavoidably a process of social attribution using common-sense typologies of gender. Positivist procedure thus rests on the very typifications that are supposedly under investigation in gender research.

Third, to define masculinity as what-men-empirically-are is to rule out the usage in which we call some women 'masculine' and some men 'feminine', or some actions or attitudes 'masculine' or 'feminine' regardless of who displays them. This is not a trivial use of the terms. It is crucial, for instance, to psychoanalytic thinking about contradictions within personality.

Indeed, this usage is fundamental to gender analysis. If we spoke only of differences between men as a bloc and women as a bloc, we would not need the terms 'masculine' and 'feminine' at all. We could just speak of 'men's' and 'women's', or 'male' and 'female'. The terms 'masculine' and 'feminine' point beyond categorical sex difference to the ways men differ among themselves, and women differ among themselves, in matters of gender.[4]

Normative definitions recognize these differences and offer a standard: masculinity is what men ought to be. This definition is often found in media studies, in discussions of exemplars such as John Wayne or of genres such as the thriller, Strict sex role theory treats masculinity precisely as a social norm for the behaviour of men. In practice, male sex role texts often blend normative with essentialist definitions, as in Robert Brannon's widely quoted account of 'our culture's blueprint of manhood': No Sissy Stuff, The Big Wheel, The Sturdy Oak and Give 'em Hell.[5]

Normative definitions allow that different men approach the standards to different degrees. But this soon produces paradoxes, some of which were recognized in the early Men's Liberation writings. Few men actually match the 'blueprint' or display the toughness and independence acted by Wayne, Bogart or Eastwood. (This point is picked up by film itself, in spoofs such as *Blazing Saddles* and *Play it Again, Sam.*) What is 'normative' about a norm hardly anyone meets? Are we to say the majority of men are unmasculine? How do we assay the toughness needed to resist the norm of toughness, or the heroism needed to come out as gay?

A more subtle difficulty is that a purely normative definition gives no grip on masculinity at the level of personality. Joseph Pleck correctly identified the unwarranted assumption that role and identity correspond. This assumption is, I think, why sex role theorists often drift towards essentialism.

Semiotic approaches abandon the level of personality and define masculinity through a system of symbolic difference in which masculine and feminine places are contrasted. Masculinity is, in effect, defined as not-femininity.

This follows the formulae of structural linguistics, where elements of speech are defined by their differences from each other. The approach has been widely used in feminist and post-structuralist cultural analyses of gender and in Lacanian psychoanalysis and studies of symbolism. It yields more than an abstract contrast of masculinity and femininity, of the kind found in M/F scales. In the semiotic opposition of masculinity and femininity, masculinity is the unmarked term, the place of symbolic authority. The phallus is master-signifier, and femininity is symbolically defined by lack.

This definition of masculinity has been very effective in cultural analysis. It escapes the arbitrariness of essentialism and the paradoxes of positivist and normative definitions. It is, however, limited in its scope – unless one assumes, as some postmodern theorists do, that discourse is all we can talk about in social analysis. To grapple with the full range of issues about masculinity we need ways of talking about relationships of other kinds too: about gendered places in production and consumption, places in institution and in natural environments, places in social and military struggles.[6]

What can be generalized is the principle of connection. The idea that one symbol can only be understood within a connected system of symbols applies equally well in other spheres. No masculinity arises except in a system of gender relations.

Rather than attempting to define masculinity as an object (a natural character type, a behavioural average, a norm), we need to focus on the processes and relationships through which men and women conduct gendered lives. 'Masculinity', to the extent the term can be briefly defined at all, is simultaneously a place in gender relations, the practices through which men and women engage that place in gender, and the effects of these practices in bodily experience, personality and culture.

Gender as a Structure of Social Practice

In this section I will set out, as briefly as possible, the analysis of gender that underpins the argument of the book.

Gender is a way in which social practice is ordered. In gender processes, the everyday conduct of life is organized in relation to a reproductive arena, defined by the bodily structures and processes of human reproduction. This arena includes sexual arousal and intercourse, childbirth and infant care, bodily sex difference and similarity.

I call this a 'reproductive arena' not a 'biological base' to emphasize the point made in Chapter 2, that we are talking about a historical process involving the body, not a fixed set of biological determinants. Gender is social practice that constantly refers to bodies and what bodies do, it is not social practice reduced to the body. Indeed reductionism presents the exact reverse of the real situation. Gender exists precisely to the extent that biology does *not* determine the social. It marks one of those points of transition where historical process supersedes biological evolution as the form of change. Gender is a scandal, an outrage, from the point of view of essentialism. Sociobiologists are constantly trying to abolish it, by proving that human social arrangements are a reflex of evolutionary imperatives.

Social practice is creative and inventive, but not inchoate. It responds to particular situations and is generated within definite structures of social relations. Gender relations, the relations among people and groups organized through the reproductive arena, form one of the major structures of all documented societies.

Practice that relates to this structure, generated as people and groups grapple with their historical situations, does not consist of isolated acts. Actions are configured in larger units, and when we speak of masculinity and femininity we are naming configurations of gender practice.

'Configuration' is perhaps too static a term. The important thing is the *process* of configuring practice. (Jean-Paul Sartre speaks in *Search for a Method* of the 'unification of the means in action'.) Taking a dynamic view of the organization of practice, we arrive at an understanding of masculinity and femininity as *gender projects*. These are processes of configuring practice through time, which transform their starting-points in gender structures. In the case studies in Part II, I will analyse the lives of several groups of men as gender projects in this sense.[7]

We find the gender configuring of practice however we slice the social world, whatever unit of analysis we choose. The most familiar is the individual life course, the basis of the common-sense notions of masculinity and femininity. The configuration of practice here is what psychologists have traditionally called 'personality' or 'character'. The psychoanalytic arguments discussed in Chapter 1 focus almost exclusively on this site.

Such a focus is liable to exaggerate the coherence of practice that can be achieved at any one site. It is thus not surprising that psychoanalysis, originally stressing contradiction, drifted towards the concept of 'identity'. Post-structuralist critics of psychology such as Wendy Hollway have emphasized that gender identities are fractured and shifting, because multiple discourses intersect in any individual life.[8] This argument highlights another site, that of discourse, ideology or culture. Here gender is organized in symbolic practices that may continue much longer than the individual life (for instance: the construction of heroic masculinities in epics; the construction of 'gender dysphorias' or 'perversions' in medical theory).

Chapter 1 noted how social science had come to recognize a third site of gender configuration, institutions such as the state, the workplace and the school. Many find it difficult to accept that institutions are substantively, not just metaphorically, gendered. This is, nevertheless, a key point.

The state, for instance, is a masculine institution. To say this is not to imply that the personalities of top male office-holders somehow seep through and stain the institution. It is to say something much stronger: that state organizational practices are structured in relation to the reproductive arena. The overwhelming majority of top office-holders are men because there is a gender configuring of recruitment and promotion, a gender configuring of the internal division of labour and systems of control, a gender configuring of policymaking, practical routines, and ways of mobilizing pleasure and consent.[9]

The gender structuring of practice need have nothing biologically to do with reproduction. The link with the reproductive arena is social. This becomes clear when it is challenged. An example is the recent struggle within the state over 'gays in the military', i.e., the rules excluding soldiers and sailors because of the gender of their sexual object-choice. In the United States, where this struggle was most severe, critics made the case for change in terms of civil liberties and military efficiency, arguing in effect that object-choice has little to do with the capacity to kill. The admirals and generals defended the status quo on a variety of spurious grounds. The unadmitted reason was the cultural importance of a particular definition of masculinity in maintaining the fragile cohesion of modern armed forces.

It has been clear since the work of Juliet Mitchell and Gayle Rubin in the 1970s that gender is an internally complex structure, where a number of different logics are superimposed. This is a fact of great importance for the analysis of masculinities. Any one masculinity, as a configuration of practice, is simultaneously positioned in a number of structures of relationship, which may be following different historical trajectories. Accordingly masculinity, like femininity, is always liable to internal contradiction and historical disruption.

We need at least a three-fold model of the structure of gender, distinguishing relations of (a) power, (b) production and (c) cathexis (emotional attachment). This is a provisional model, but it gives some purchase on issues about masculinity.[10]

(a) *Power relations* The main axis of power in the contemporary European/American gender order is the overall subordination of women and dominance of men – the structure Women's Liberation named 'patriarchy'. This general structure exists despite many local reversals (e.g., woman-headed households, female teachers with male students). It persists despite resistance of many kinds, now articulated in feminism. These reversals and resistances mean continuing difficulties for patriarchal power. They define a problem of legitimacy which has great importance for the politics of masculinity.

(b) *Production relations* Gender divisions of labour are familiar in the form of the allocation of tasks, sometimes reaching extraordinarily fine detail. (In the English village studied by the sociologist Pauline Hunt, for instance, it was customary for women to wash the inside of windows, men to wash the outside.) Equal attention should be paid to the economic consequences of gender divisions of labour, the dividend accruing to men from unequal shares of the products of social labour. This is most often discussed in terms of unequal wage rates, but the gendered character of capital should also be noted. A capitalist economy working through a gender division of labour is, necessarily, a gendered accumulation process. So it is not a statistical accident, but a part of the social construction of masculinity, that men and not women control the major corporations and the great private fortunes. Implausible as it sounds, the accumulation of wealth has become firmly linked to the reproductive arena, through the social relations of gender.[11]

(c) *Cathexis* As I noted in Chapter 2, sexual desire is so often seen as natural that it is commonly excluded from social theory. Yet when we consider desire in Freudian terms, as emotional energy being attached to an object, its gendered character is clear. This is true both for heterosexual and homosexual desire. (It is striking that in our culture the non-gendered object choice, 'bisexual' desire, is ill-defined and unstable.) The practices that shape and realize desire are thus an aspect of the gender order. Accordingly we can ask political questions about the relationships involved: whether they are consensual or coercive, whether pleasure is equally given and received. In feminist analyses of sexuality these have become sharp questions about the connection of heterosexuality with men's position of social dominance.[12]

Because gender is a way of structuring social practice in general, not a special type of practice, it is unavoidably involved with other social structures. It is now common to say that gender 'intersects' – better, interacts – with race and class. We might add that it constantly interacts with nationality or position in the world order.

This fact also has strong implications for the analysis of masculinity. White men's masculinities, for instance, are constructed not only in relation to white women but also in relation to black men. Paul Hoch in *White Hero, Black Beast* more than a decade ago pointed to the pervasiveness of racial imagery in Western discourses of masculinity. White fears of black men's violence have a long history in colonial and post-colonial situations. Black fears of white men's terrorism, founded in the history of colonialism, have a continuing basis in white men's control of police, courts and prisons in metropolitan countries. African-American men are massively over-represented in American prisons, as Aboriginal men are in Australian prisons. This situation is strikingly condensed in the American black expression 'The Man', fusing white masculinity and institutional power. As the black rap singer Ice-T put it,

> It makes no difference whether you're in or out. The ghetto, the Pen, it's all institutionalized. It's being controlled by the Man . . . Ever since 1976, they stop trying to rehabilitate Brothers. Now it's strictly punishment. The Man's answer to the problem is not more education – it's more prisons. They're saying let's not educate them, let's lock them the fuck up. So when you come outta there you're all braindead, so yeah it's a cycle.[13]

Similarly, it is impossible to understand the shaping of working-class masculinities without giving full weight to their class as well as their gender politics. This is vividly shown in historical work such as Sonya Rose's *Limited Livelihoods*, on industrial England in the nineteenth century. An ideal of working-class manliness and self-respect was constructed in response to class deprivation and paternalist strategies of management, at the same time and through the same gestures as it was defined against working-class women. The strategy of the 'family wage', which long depressed women's wages in twentieth-century economies, grew out of this interplay.[14]

To understand gender, then, we must constantly go beyond gender. The same applies in reverse. We cannot understand class, rice or global inequality without constantly moving towards gender. Gender relations are a major component of social structure as a whole, and gender politics are among the main determinants of our collective fate.

Relations among Masculinities: Hegemony, Subordination, Complicity, Marginalization

With growing recognition of the interplay between gender, race and class it has become common to recognize multiple masculinities: black as well as white, working-class as well as middle-class. This is welcome, but it risks another kind of oversimplification. It is easy in this framework to think that there is *a* black masculinity or *a* working-class masculinity.

To recognize more than one kind of masculinity is only a first step. We have to examine the relations between them. Further, we have to unpack the milieux of class and race and scrutinize the gender relations operating within them. There are, after all, gay black men and effeminate factory hands, not to mention middle-class rapists and cross-dressing bourgeois.

A focus on the gender relations among men is necessary to keep the analysis dynamic, to prevent the acknowledgement of multiple masculinities collapsing into a character typology, as happened with Fromm and the *Authoritarian Personality* research. 'Hegemonic masculinity' is not a fixed character type, always and everywhere the same. It is, rather, the masculinity that occupies the hegemonic position in a given pattern of gender relations, a position always contestable.

A focus on relations also offers a gain in realism. Recognizing multiple masculinities, especially in an individualist culture such as the United States, risks taking them for alternative lifestyles, a matter of consumer choice. A relational approach makes it easier to recognize the hard compulsions under which gender configurations are formed, the bitterness as well as the pleasure in gendered experience.

With these guidelines, let us consider the practices and relations that construct the main patterns of masculinity in the current Western gender order. *[and femininity]*

Hegemony

The concept of 'hegemony', deriving from Antonio Gramsci's analysis of class relations, refers to the cultural dynamic by which a group claims and sustains a leading position in social life. At any given time, one form of masculinity rather than others is culturally exalted. Hegemonic masculinity can be defined as the configuration of gender practice which embodies the currently accepted answer to the problem of the legitimacy of patriarchy, which guarantees (or is taken to guarantee) the dominant position of men and the subordination of women.[15]

This is not to say that the most visible bearers of hegemonic masculinity are always the most powerful people. They may be exemplars, such as film actors, or even fantasy figures, such as film characters. Individual holders of institutional power or great wealth may be far from the hegemonic pattern in their personal lives. (Thus a male member of a prominent business dynasty was a key figure in the gay/transvestite social scene in Sydney in the 1950s, because of his wealth and the protection this gave in the cold-war climate of political and police harassment.)[16]

Nevertheless, hegemony is likely to be established only if there is some correspondence between cultural ideal and institutional power, collective if not individual. So the top levels of business, the military and government provide a fairly convincing *corporate* display of masculinity, still very little shaken by feminist women or dissenting men. It is the successful claim to authority, more than direct violence, that is the mark of hegemony (though violence often underpins or supports authority).

I stress that hegemonic masculinity embodies a 'currently accepted' strategy. When conditions for the defence of patriarchy change, the bases for the dominance of a particular masculinity are eroded. New groups may challenge old solutions and construct a new hegemony. The dominance of *any* group of men may be challenged by women. Hegemony, then, is a historically mobile relation. Its ebb and flow is a key element of the picture of masculinity proposed in this book. I will examine its long-term history in Chapter 8 and recent contestations in Chapters 9 and 10.

Subordination

Hegemony relates to cultural dominance in the society as a whole. Within that overall framework there are specific gender relations of dominance and subordination between groups of men.

The most important case in contemporary European/ American society is the dominance of heterosexual men and the subordination of homosexual men. This is much more than a cultural stigmatization of homosexuality or gay identity. Gay men are subordinated to straight men by an array of quite material practices.

These practices were listed in early Gay Liberation texts such as Dennis Altman's *Homosexual: Oppression and Liberation.* They have been documented at length in studies such as the NSW Anti-Discrimination Board's 1982 report *Discrimination and Homosexuality.* They are still a matter of everyday experience for homosexual men. They include political and cultural exclusion, cultural abuse (in the United States gay men have now become the main symbolic target of the religious right), legal violence (such as imprisonment under sodomy statutes), street violence (ranging from intimidation to murder), economic discrimination and personal boycotts. It is not surprising that an Australian working-class man, reflecting on his experience of coming out in a homophobic culture, would remark:

> You know, I didn't totally realize what it was to be gay. I mean it's a bastard of a life.[17]

Oppression positions homosexual masculinities at the bottom of a gender hierarchy among men. Gayness, in patriarchal ideology, is the repository of whatever is symbolically expelled from hegemonic masculinity, the items ranging from fastidious taste in home decoration to receptive anal pleasure. Hence, from the point of view of hegemonic masculinity, gayness is easily assimilated to femininity. And hence – in the view of some gay theorists – the ferocity of homophobic attacks.

Gay masculinity is the most conspicuous, but it is not the only subordinated masculinity. Some heterosexual men and boys too are expelled from the circle of legitimacy. The process is marked by a rich vocabulary of abuse: wimp, milksop, nerd, turkey, sissy, lily liver, jellyfish, yellowbelly, candy ass, ladyfinger, pushover, cookie pusher, cream puff, motherfucker, pantywaist, mother's boy, four-eyes, ear-'ole, dweeb, geek, Milquetoast, Cedric, and so on. Here too the symbolic blurring with femininity is obvious.

Complicity

Normative definitions of masculinity, as I have noted, face the problem that not many men actually meet the normative standards. This point applies to hegemonic masculinity. The number of men rigorously practising the hegemonic pattern in its entirety may be quite small. Yet the majority of men gain from its hegemony, since they benefit from the patriarchal dividend, the advantage men in general gain from the overall subordination of women.

As Chapter 1 showed, accounts of masculinity have generally concerned themselves with syndromes and types, not with numbers. Yet in thinking about the dynamics of society as a whole, numbers matter. Sexual politics is mass politics, and strategic thinking needs to be concerned with where the masses of people are. If a large number of men have some connection with the hegemonic project but do not embody hegemonic masculinity, we need a way of theorizing their specific situation.

This can be done by recognizing another relationship among groups of men, the relationship of complicity with the hegemonic project. Masculinities constructed in ways that realize the patriarchal dividend, without the tensions or risks of being the frontline troops of patriarchy, are complicit in this sense.

It is tempting to treat them simply as slacker versions of hegemonic masculinity – the difference between the men who cheer football matches on TV and those who run out into the mud and the tackles themselves. But there is often something more definite and carefully crafted than that. Marriage, fatherhood and community life often involve extensive compromises with women rather than naked domination or an uncontested display of authority.[18] A great many men who draw the patriarchal dividend also respect their wives and mothers, are never violent towards women, do their accustomed share of the housework, bring home the family wage, and can easily convince themselves that feminists must be bra-burning extremists.

Marginalization

Hegemony, subordination and complicity, as just defined, are relations internal to the gender order. The interplay of gender with other structures such as class and race creates further relationships between masculinities.

In Chapter 2 I noted how new information technology became a vehicle for redefining middle-class masculinities at a time when the meaning of labour for working-class men was in contention. This is not a question of a fixed middle-class masculinity confronting a fixed working-class masculinity. Both are being reshaped, by a social dynamic in which class and gender relations are simultaneously in play.

Race relations may also become an integral part of the dynamic between masculinities. In a white-supremacist context, black masculinities play symbolic roles for white gender construction. For instance, black sporting stars become exemplars of masculine toughness, while the fantasy figure of the black rapist plays an important role in sexual politics among whites, a role much exploited by right-wing politics in the United States. Conversely, hegemonic masculinity among whites sustains the institutional oppression and physical terror that have framed the making of masculinities in black communities.

Robert Staples's discussion of internal colonialism in *Black Masculinity* shows the effect of class and race relations at the same time. As he argues, the level of violence among black men in the United States can only be understood through the changing place of the black labour force in American capitalism and the violent means used to control it. Massive unemployment and urban poverty now powerfully interact with institutional racism in the shaping of black masculinity.[19]

Though the term is not ideal, I cannot improve on 'marginalization' to refer to the relations between the masculinities in dominant and subordinated classes or ethnic groups. Marginalization is always relative to the *authorization* of the hegemonic masculinity of the dominant group. Thus, in the United States, particular black athletes may be exemplars for hegemonic masculinity. But the fame and wealth of individual stars has no trickle-down effect; it does not yield social authority to black men generally.

The relation of marginalization and authorization may also exist between subordinated masculinities. A striking example is the arrest and conviction of Oscar Wilde, one of the first men caught in the net of modern anti-homosexual legislation. Wilde was trapped because of his connections with homosexual working-class youths, a practice unchallenged until his legal battle with a wealthy aristocrat, the Marquess of Queensberry, made him vulnerable.[20]

These two types of relationship – hegemony, domination/subordination and complicity on the one hand, marginalization/authorization on the other – provide a framework in which we can analyse specific masculinities. (This is a sparse framework, but social theory should be hardworking.) I emphasize that terms such as 'hegemonic masculinity' and 'marginalized masculinities' name not fixed character types but configurations of practice generated in particular situations in a changing structure of relationships. Any theory of masculinity worth having must give an account of this process of change.

Historical Dynamics, Violence and Crisis Tendencies

To recognize gender as a social pattern requires us to see it as a product of history, and also as a *producer* of history. In Chapter 2 I defined gender practice as onto-formative, as constituting reality, and it is a crucial part of this idea that social reality is dynamic in time. We habitually think of the social as less real than the biological, what changes as less real than what stays the same. But there is a colossal reality to history. It is the modality of human life, precisely what defines us as human. No other species produces and lives in history, replacing organic evolution with radically new determinants of change.

To recognize masculinity and femininity as historical, then, is not to suggest they are flimsy or trivial. It is to locate them firmly in the world of social agency. And it raises a string of questions about their historicity.

The structures of gender relations are formed and transformed over time. It has been common in historical writing to see this change as coming from outside gender – from technology or class dynamics, most often. But change is also generated from within gender relations. The dynamic is as old as gender relations. It has, however, become more clearly defined in the last two centuries with the emergence of a public politics of gender and sexuality.

With the women's suffrage movement and the early homophile movement, the conflict of interests embedded in gender relations became visible. Interests are formed in any structure of inequality, which necessarily defines groups that will gain and lose differently by sustaining or by changing the structure. A gender order where men dominate women cannot avoid constituting men as an interest group concerned with defence, and women as an interest group concerned with change. This is a structural fact, independent of whether men as individuals love or hate women, or believe in equality or abjection, and independent of whether women are currently pursuing change.

To speak of a patriarchal dividend is to raise exactly this question of interest. Men gain a dividend from patriarchy in terms of honour, prestige and the right to command. They also gain a material dividend. In the rich capitalist countries, men's average incomes are approximately *double* women's average incomes. (The more familiar comparisons, of wage rates for full-time employment, greatly understate gender differences in actual incomes.) Men are vastly more likely to control a major block of capital as chief executive of a major corporation, or as direct owner. For instance, of 55 US fortunes above $1 billion in 1992, only five were mainly in the hands of women – and all but one of those as a result of inheritance from men.

Men are much more likely to hold state power: for instance, men are ten times more likely than women to hold office as a member of parliament (an average across all countries of the world). Perhaps men do most of the work? No: in the rich countries, time-budget studies show women and men work on average about the same number of hours in the year. (The major difference is in how much of this work gets paid.)[21]

Given these facts, the 'battle of the sexes' is no joke. Social struggle must result from inequalities on such a scale. It follows that the politics of masculinity cannot concern only questions of personal life and identity. It must also concern questions of social justice.

A structure of inequality on this scale, involving a massive dispossession of social resources, is hard to imagine without violence. It is, overwhelmingly, the dominant gender who hold and use the means of violence. Men are armed far more often than women. Indeed under many gender regimes women have been forbidden to bear or use arms (a rule applied, astonishingly, even within armies). Patriarchal definition of femininity (dependence fearfulness) amount to a cultural disarmament that may be quite as effective as the physical kind. Domestic violence cases often find abused women, physically able to look after themselves, who have accepted the abusers' definitions of themselves as incompetent and helpless.[22]

Two patterns of violence follow from this situation. First, many members of the privileged group use violence to sustain their dominance. Intimidation of women ranges across the spectrum from wolf-whistling in the street, to office harassment, to rape and domestic assault, to murder by a woman's patriarchal 'owner', such as a separated husband. Physical attacks are commonly accompanied by verbal abuse of women (whores and bitches, in recent popular music that recommends beating women). Most men do not attack or harass women; but those who do are unlikely to think themselves deviant. On the contrary they usually feel they are entirely justified, that they are exercising a right. They are authorized by an ideology of supremacy.

Second, violence becomes important in gender politics among men. Most episodes of major violence (counting military combat, homicide and armed assault) are transactions among men. Terror is used as a means of drawing boundaries and making exclusions, for example, in heterosexual violence against gay men. Violence can become a way of claiming or asserting masculinity in group struggles. This is an explosive process when an oppressed group gains the means of violence – as witness the levels of violence among black men in contemporary South Africa and the United States. The youth gang violence of inner-city streets is a striking example of the assertion of marginalized masculinities against other men, continuous with the assertion of masculinity in sexual violence against women.[23]

Violence can be used to enforce a reactionary gender politics, as in the recent firebombings and murders of abortion service providers in the United States. It must also be said that collective violence among men can open possibilities for progress in gender relations. The two global wars this century produced important transitions in women's employment, shook up gender ideology, and accelerated the making of homosexual communities.

Violence is part of a system of domination, but is at the same time a measure of its imperfection. A thoroughly legitimate hierarchy would have less need to intimidate. The scale of contemporary violence points to crisis tendencies (to borrow a term from Jürgen Habermas) in the modern gender order.

The concept of crisis tendencies needs to be distinguished from the colloquial sense in which people speak of a 'crisis of masculinity'. As a theoretical term 'crisis' presupposes a coherent system of some kind, which is destroyed or restored by the outcome of the crisis. Masculinity, as the argument so far has shown, is not a system in that sense. It is, rather, a configuration of practice *within* a system of gender relations. We cannot logically speak of the crisis of a configuration; rather we might speak of its disruption or its transformation. We can, however, logically speak of the crisis of a gender order as a whole, and of its tendencies towards crisis.[24]

Such crisis tendencies will always implicate masculinities, though not necessarily by disrupting them. Crisis tendencies may, for instance, provoke attempts to restore a dominant masculinity. Michael Kimmel has pointed to this dynamic in turn-of-the-century United States society, where fear of the women's suffrage movement played into the cult of the outdoorsman. Klaus Theweleit in *Male Fantasies* traced the more savage process that produced the sexual politics of fascism in the aftermath of the suffrage movement and German defeat in the Great War. More recently, Women's Liberation and defeat in Vietnam have stirred new cults of true masculinity in the United States, from violent 'adventure' movies such as the *Rambo* series, to the expansion of the gun cult and what William Gibson in a frightening recent study has called 'paramilitary culture'.[25]

To understand the making of contemporary masculinities, then, we need to map the crisis tendencies of the gender order. This is no light task! But it is possible to make a start, using as a framework the three structures of gender relations defined earlier in this chapter.

Power relations show the most visible evidence of crisis tendencies: a historic collapse of the legitimacy of patriarchal power, and a global movement for the emancipation of women. This is fuelled by an underlying contradiction between the inequality of women and men, on the one hand, and the universalizing logics of modern state structures and market relations, on the other.

The incapacity of the institutions of civil society, notably the family, to resolve this tension provokes broad but incoherent state action (from family law to population policy) which itself becomes the focus of political turbulence. Masculinities are reconfigured around this crisis tendency both through conflict over strategies of legitimation, and through men's divergent responses to feminism (see Chapter 5). While the tension leads some men to the cults of masculinity just mentioned, it leads others to support feminist reforms.[26]

Production relations have also been the site of massive institutional changes. Most notable are the vast postwar growth in married women's employment in rich countries, and the even vaster incorporation of women's labour into the money economy in poor countries.

There is a basic contradiction between men's and women's equal contribution to production, and the gendered appropriation of the products of social labour. Patriarchal control of wealth is sustained by inheritance mechanisms, which, however, insert some women into the property system as owners. The turbulence of the gendered accumulation process creates a series of tensions and inequalities in men's chances of benefiting from it. Some men, for instance, are excluded from its benefits by unemployment (see Chapter 4); others are advantaged by their connection with new physical or social technologies (see Chapter 7).

Relations of cathexis have visibly changed with the stabilization of lesbian and gay sexuality as a public alternative within the heterosexual order (see Chapter 6). This change was supported by the broad claim by women for sexual pleasure and control of their own bodies, which has affected heterosexual practice as well as homosexual.

The patriarchal order prohibits forms of emotion, attachment and pleasure that patriarchal society itself produces. Tensions develop around sexual inequality and men's rights in marriage, around the prohibition on homosexual affection (given that patriarchy constantly produces homo-social institutions) and around the threat to social order symbolized by sexual freedoms.

This sketch of crisis tendencies is a very brief account of a vast subject, but it is perhaps enough to show changes in masculinities in something like their true perspective. The canvas is much broader than images of a modern male sex role, or renewal of the deep masculine, imply. Economy, state and global relationships are involved as well as households and personal relationships.

The vast changes in gender relations around the globe produce ferociously complex changes in the conditions of practice with which men as well as women have to grapple. No one is an innocent bystander in this arena of change. We are all engaged in constructing a world of gender relations. How it is made, what strategies different groups pursue, and with what effects, are political questions. Men no more than women are chained to the gender patterns they have inherited. Men too can make political choices for a new world of gender relations. Yet those choices are always made in concrete social circumstances, which limit what can be attempted; and the outcomes are not easily controlled.

To understand a historical process of this depth and complexity is not a task for *a priori* theorizing. It requires concrete study; more exactly, a range of studies that can illuminate the larger dynamic. That is the project attempted in Part II.

Part II

Four Studies of the
Dynamics of Masculinity

Introduction

Chapter 3 spelt out a framework for thinking about masculinity, and the next four chapters will put it to work. They report a life-history study of four groups of Australian men chosen to explore different possibilities of change in masculinity.

Collecting life histories is one of the oldest research methods in the social sciences. Life histories give rich documentation of personal experience, ideology and subjectivity. This is the usual justification of the method, set out in detail in Ken Plummer's *Documents of Life*. But life histories also, paradoxically, document social structures, social movements and institutions. That is to say, they give rich evidence about impersonal and collective processes as well as about subjectivity.

The philosophical argument in *Search for a Method* by Jean-Paul Sartre helps explain this paradox. A life-history is a project, a unification of practice through time (see the discussion of existential psychoanalysis in Chapter 1 above). The project that is documented in a life-history story is itself the relation between the social conditions that determine practice and the future social world that practice brings into being. That is to say, life-history method always concerns the making of social life through time. It is literally history.

This makes life-history a first-class method for the study of social change. It was used that way in an early classic of empirical sociology, William Thomas and Florian Znaniecki's *The Polish Peasant in Europe and America*; and is still used that way, for instance in Bob Blauner's unique three-decade study of race relations in the United States, *Black Lives, White Lives*. This capacity, however, comes at a cost. Life-history, as well as being one of the richest methods in social science, is also one of the most time-consuming. Using it to study large-scale social changes requires a trade-off between depth and scope. A life-history study of masculinity, for instance, cannot sample a broad population of men while gaining any depth of understanding of particular situations.[1]

Rather than spread the research thin, I decided to concentrate on a few situations where the theoretical yield should be high. Using the analysis of crisis tendencies in the gender order (Chapter 3), I tried to identify groups of men for whom the construction or integration of masculinity was under pressure.[2] Four groups in particular are the focus of this project, chosen by the following reasoning.

Crisis tendencies in power relations threaten hegemonic masculinity directly. These tendencies are highlighted in the lives of men who live and work with feminists in settings where gender hierarchy has lost all legitimacy. The radical environmental movement is such a setting. Men in this movement must be dealing, in one way or another, with demands for the reconstruction of masculinity.

In the established gender order, relations of cathexis are organized mainly through the heterosexual couple. This is the taken for granted meaning of 'love' in popular culture and it has massive institutional support. Masculinity is necessarily in question in the lives of men whose sexual interest is in other men. Men in gay and bisexual networks will be dealing with issues about gender quite as serious as environmentalists', though differently structured.

In relation to production, masculinity has come to be associated with being a breadwinner. This definition will come under pressure when it becomes impossible for men to win the bread. Structural unemployment is now a reality for considerable parts of the working class, especially youth. Young working-class men without regular jobs were therefore chosen as a third group.

Other crisis tendencies surface among the affluent. Hegemonic masculinity is culturally linked to both authority and rationality, key themes in the legitimation of patriarchy. But authority and rationality can be pushed apart, given changing economic relations and technologies. Men in middle-class occupations based on technical knowledge, but lacking the social authority of capital and the old professions – men of the 'new class' as some theorists put it – should give us insight into changes in the pattern of hegemony.

The interviews followed the same overall plan, with a great deal of flexibility in each conversation. The interviewers asked for a narrative ('story of your life'). We kept the focus on the practices in which relationships were constructed, i.e., on what people actually did in the various settings of their lives. We used transitions between institutions (e.g., entry to high school) as pegs for memory; but we also asked for accounts of relationships within institutions such as families and workplaces. We sought evidence about each of the structures of gender (power, labour and cathexis) from different periods of life. In a field interview it was not possible to explore unconscious motives. Nevertheless we sought clues to emotional dynamics by asking about early memories, family constellations, relationship crises and wishes for the future.

Packing that agenda into a tape-recorded interview session yielded, in most cases, rich and fascinating narratives. There is a tendency, in recent discussions of method, to treat any story as a fiction; to 'read' it for the figures of speech, motivated silences and narrative devices by which the teller as author constructs a meaningful tale. Any serious researcher using life-histories must be aware of these features of stories. But if the language is all we can see, then we are missing the point of a life-history – and spurning the effort that the respondents themselves make to speak the truth. An autobiographical story is evidence for a great deal beyond its own language. This evidence is not necessarily easy to use; it takes time and effort to examine the story from different angles and compare it with other evidence. My work on these stories went through the following steps.

In the first phase of analysis I listened to tapes, read transcripts, indexed, and wrote up each interview as a case study. In each case study the interview as a whole was examined from three points of view: (a) the narrative sequence of events; (b) a structural analysis, using a grid provided by the three structures of gender relations; (c) a dynamic analysis, tracing the making and unmaking of masculinity, trying to grasp the gender project involved. Writing up each case study was both an attempt at a portrait of a person, and a reflection on the portrait's meaning as evidence about social change.

In the second phase I reanalysed the case studies in groups. Here the goal was to explore the similarities and differences in the trajectories of men in a certain social location, and to understand their collective location in large-scale change. Again I used a grid derived from gender theory to make these comparisons systematic. I abstracted and reindexed the cases so that, as each topic came to be analysed, the whole group was in view, while the narrative shape of each life was preserved. I wrote this analysis for each group separately, making each report an attempt at a collective portrait of men caught up in a certain process of change. These reports are the bases of the following chapters.

I have spelt out this rather laborious procedure,[3] instead of jumping directly into the interviews, to emphasize that there is a systematic basis to the arguments that follow. Life-histories are wonderfully varied, and it is easy to get swept away by vivid characters and striking episodes. The procedure I followed puts the emphasis back on the common ground and the practical routines of social life. This is sometimes boring, but it is essential if we are to understand large-scale change.

These four studies are not intended in themselves as a map of large-scale change. Their purpose is to illuminate particular situations – which, for the reasons already given, might be strategic. On this basis I use their findings when discussing broader issues in Part III. The studies have of course also fed back into the theoretical arguments of Part I.

Not all of this project was illuminating; research cannot guarantee its results in advance. Some people believe that knowledge on this topic is not worth seeking in the first place, as this research also proved. The fieldwork was financed by the Australian Research Grants Committee, the national research funding body at the time. Before any findings were published, this project was attacked by the federal parliamentary 'Wastewatch Committee' of the Liberal and National Parties (the conservative coalition), as a conspicuous waste of public funds.

I am happy to let readers decide if they were right.

4

Live Fast and Die Young

Recent discussion of change in masculinity has focused on middle-class professional men. In much of this discussion working-class or 'blue-collar' men are presumed to be conservative in sexual politics, if not outright reactionary.

Yet working-class people, Judith Stacey notes of the United States, have pioneered new family forms. Working-class and labour parties, as Lynne Segal observes, have generally been more progressive in gender politics than parties drawing their bloc votes from the affluent.[1] In line with these observations, more discriminating accounts of working-class masculinity have been offered by writers influenced by socialist analyses of class relations.

Their arguments have emphasized manual labour, workplace relations and the wage. Andrew Tolson, for instance, argued that 'in our society the main focus of masculinity is the wage.' A little inconsistently, he made shop-floor struggle the centre of his analysis of masculine emotion and politics. Paul Willis connected masculinity to shop-floor culture and the wage form. Mike Donaldson more recently has argued that 'the consciousness of male labourers is crucially formed in the experience of the family-household and work-place', with masculinity both created and undermined in the interplay between the two.[2]

Conditions in the capitalist workplace certainly affect the construction of masculinity for the men employed there. But capitalist economies do not guarantee employment. In the wake of the economic downturn in the 1970s, it was estimated that thirty million people were out of work in the OECD countries. Unemployment or under-employment is chronic in less developed economies. Large numbers of youth are now growing up without any expectation of the stable employment around which familiar models of working-class masculinity were organized. Instead they face intermittent employment and economic marginality in the long term, and often severe deprivation in the short term. In such conditions, what happens to the making of masculinity?

Group and Context

The focus of the discussion is five young men who were contacted through staff of an agency working mainly with unemployed youth: Jack Harley (22), 'Eel' (c. 21), Patrick Vincent (17), Alan Rubin (29), Mal Walton (21). All are on the dole and have at best a spasmodic experience of employment. They left school at age 15 or 16, one being expelled and two others after much truanting. One is illiterate and another almost illiterate. They are, collectively, on the fringe of the labour market.

They have also been in conflict with the state. Most of them hated school and had antagonistic, sometimes violent, interactions with teachers. Four of the five have been arrested and two spent at least a year in custody. Though of Anglo-Australian background, in personal style as well as past history they are outside the 'respectable' working class. Three ride motorbikes and for two of them biking is a major passion.

I will compare their experiences with three men of similar age and very similar class backgrounds who now have a different position in the labour market. Stewart Hardy (24) is a computer trainee in a bank; Danny Taylor (23) is an office worker in an environmental organization; Paul Gray (26) is a temporary office worker in a welfare agency.

All eight are children of manual workers, and several grew up in very poor households. In such settings the breadwinner/homemaker division becomes an irrelevance. In most cases the boys' mothers had jobs while the boys were still young. In several cases, at various times – modest ups and sharp downs punctuate life at this end of the labour market – mothers were the main income earner for the household. This is easily accepted; only one of the eight expresses any discomfort about women earning an income.

There is little sense, either, of an instrumental/expressive division in gender. Like the working-class girls discussed by Linley Walker, these young men do not consider women as emotional specialists or as being expressive or person-oriented in a way that men are not.[3]

The families in which they grew up had two contrasting economic patterns. In one, the family operated as a tightly-knit cooperative. Stewart Hardy's father was a jack-of-all-trades outback manual worker, travelling from property to property to get jobs. His wife travelled with him and expanded his labour-power, for instance by doing the washing on farms where he was working. When Stewart was in high school his parents were working together as contract cleaners, with Stewart working on their contracts too.

Mal Walton's parents showed the other pattern starkly. He never saw his father, who left his mother when she was pregnant with Mal. His mother supported her mother and her child on her wage as a factory worker, and later at a caravan park.

Like the American working-class families discussed by Stacey, these families seem to have been postmodern before the middle class was. Not that these patterns were consciously chosen as alternative family forms. Few doubt that two earners are better, but sometimes one earner is all that a household can manage to have. The two-earner pattern was in fact re-created in Mrs Walton's family when her lover moved in, leaving his wife and children. Mal refused to accept him as a substitute father, though he would accept discipline from his grandmother.

Abstract Labour

The interviews document quite fully the group's encounters with each of the structures of gender relations. Let us start with production relations. The crucial point the life-histories reveal is that masculinity is shaped, not in relation to a specific *workplace*, but in relation to the *labour market as a whole*, which shapes their experience as an alternation of work and unemployment. This is best seen through specific histories.

Alan Rubin, the oldest of the group, has more work experience than most. He left school at 15, against his parents' wishes, having been truanting systematically before. He got a job in a book-binding shop, possibly arranged by his mother. Then he got a job as a labourer for the local council, because he knew someone in the council office. Then he travelled to New Zealand surfing. He ran out of money, took a job in a car assembly plant and loathed it – not that he minded manual work, he says, but the place was run like a concentration camp, managed by cretins and manned by 'robot ants'. Back in Australia he travelled round with professional gamblers for a while, then worked as a mail sorter; that was 'my intellectual job', he remarks sarcastically. After that he held down a job painting containers for two years, and saved enough to travel to Europe. Back in Australia he settled into a rut, doing 'nothing out of the ordinary', on the dole most of the time, with occasional jobs but none lasting long. He lives with his parents to save money.

Though this is the longest work history, its content is characteristic. Alan has no saleable skills, no qualifications or positional power, therefore no leverage in the labour market. All he has to sell is precisely described by Marx's concept of abstract labour, the lowest common denominator, the capacity to do what almost anyone can do:

> He becomes transformed into a simple, monotonous productive force that does not have to use intense bodily or intellectual faculties. His labour becomes a labour that anyone can perform. Hence, competitors crowd upon him on all sides.[4]

From the employer's point of view, Alan is interchangeable with any other worker. From Alan's point of view, any job is interchangeable with any other – at least so far as the work is concerned. The human relations can make a difference. He has done quite a range of indoor and outdoor jobs. His account of them gives off an odour of total boredom, an alienation you could cut with a knife.

Such a reaction is not surprising when the capacity to earn a living is vulnerable to an impersonal labour market and to employers who have no interest whatever in the individual workers. Livelihood is a prime issue for working-class teenagers, as Bruce Wilson and Johanna Wyn have shown in their Melbourne research.[5] This experience on entering the workforce must have a strong effect. 'Labour market vulnerability' is a genteel phrase, but it is a gut-level reality for these young men and the others in their lives.

Jack Harley, for instance, has worked as a shearer, a labourer, a printer, a barman and a truck driver. He is not trying to broaden his skills, because he has little sense of being skilled in the first place. All of the jobs have been short term; he simply takes what he can get. His *de facto* wife Ilsa worked as a telegraphist in a country town. Telecom automated the exchange and she was laid off. She got a job in a shop. After three months, business got slow and she was laid off again.

Jack's friend Eel did try to break out of the world of abstract labour by starting an apprenticeship. His first employer, at the end of the low-paid three-month trial period, sacked all but one of the apprentices. Eel was not the lucky one. He got a start with another small employer, and this time was kept on. Three years into his apprenticeship, the firm closed down. Unable to get a similar job in the six weeks allowed by the apprenticeship rules, Eel was out of the course.

In such a situation one does not develop trusting, optimistic views of the economy. Jack Harley has never had a job that lasted and does not expect to get one. He does expect to live on the dole and pick up jobs on the side. He finds the Commonwealth Employment Service unhelpful, its staff 'piggy' and not interested in young unskilled people. More help comes from family and friends.

People survive in an impersonal labour market by mobilizing personal links. Alan Rubin's first two jobs, as noted, came through connections. Jack has worked for his wife's aunt as a barman, and for her father in a family group travelling round the countryside doing contract shearing. His own father took him on a motorbike trip round Australia and organized a temporary job for him as a labourer in the Pilbara mining district. Almost every work history in the group shows the importance of personal links, especially family links, in negotiating the labour market.

Beyond that, Jack has developed what one might politely call a radical pragmatism in his approach to earning a living. He does not care in the least if his wife can get a better job than he can. In exactly the same tone of voice he observes that, if he can get another job while on the dole, it will be in another name (an offence, if he is caught). His approach to unions is at best manipulative. He liked the transport union, but lost his driver's licence so was out of that job. He disliked the shearers' union because it was constantly in disputes and he lost work. He took a strike-breaking job in a print shop because he 'needed the money', and is now banned by the union from jobs in the printing industry.

None of the five has any commitment to unionism. Given that unionism normally relies on grassroots solidarity in an industry, developed over time, it is not hard to see why. As a form of working-class mobilization, mainstream unionism is essentially irrelevant to people so marginal to the labour market.

For several of the group, radical pragmatism extends to crime. There is an element of excitement and entertainment in this, especially car theft by the younger men. But for the most part it is a kind of work. Mal Walton describes his early experience, and the ruinous rate of exchange:

> I used to run round pinching milk money. We'd break into cars and pinch their – I was into a real era of pinching stereos and selling them. And we used to be like that because what – well I didn't get into drugs until I left school. That's because I was probably bored with nothing to do. I wasn't working – sorry I was working, I was, but I lost that job a couple of weeks later. But we used to look around for stereos, good stereos, and like they would be worth $500 or something. And we would just take them to our local drug dealer, say 'have this, give us a stick', or 'give us two sticks' or something. We used to always do that. We were lucky we didn't get busted. Been chased a few times, but always got away, never got caught. The only time I got caught I stole a cook book.

It is obviously a better proposition to be the dealer. At least one of the group is a dealer, and claims to make $300 a week at it. (The figure seems high, given his standard of living; it may represent his best week.) Two others probably deal in a smaller way. Drug dealing does not stand out in their thinking. It is basically another way to make a dollar, as episodic and chancy as employment. The moral outrage of the government's Drug Offensive (the militaristic title of a national programme begun in 1986, imitated from the US anti-drug campaign) is a complete irrelevance. We might as well have an offensive against second-hand furniture dealers.

Violence and the State

The outstanding feature of this group's experience of power relations is violence, To a sheltered academic observer, there seems a great deal of violence in these lives. The interviews mention bullying and outrageous canings at school, assaulting a teacher, fights with siblings and parents, brawls in playgrounds and at parties, being arrested, assaults in reform school and gaol, bashings of women and gay men, individual fist fights and pulling a knife. Speeding in cars or trucks or on bikes is another form of intimidation, with at least one police chase and roadblock and one serious crash as results.

Pat Vincent's memories of violence begin with his family. His father gave him hidings, which he does not resent though he is still frightened of 'the old man coming down heavy'. His big sister treated him the same way: 'if you give any trouble I'll punch you in the head'. Perhaps by way of a pre-emptive strike, Pat took an aggressive stance towards his teachers, 'gave them heaps' [of abuse], apart from a couple whom he liked. Eventually he threw a chair at a teacher and was expelled from school.

By his own account he was violent with his peers – a fight a day in his first year at a Catholic high school when about 12 years old. He felt the school did not care about him, and he 'wanted to be someone, school write-off is better than being nothing.' 'I wasn't a nobody.' There was even some positive prestige to be gained among other boys: 'If you have a fight and you win, you're a hero.'

But there were limits to this prestige. Pat does not seem to have been a peer group leader. He perhaps seemed too violent, especially as the peer group grew a little older. The number of fights declined, and eventually he 'got out of the habit of fighting'. Now he would avoid it, especially if up against someone who will 'smash shit out of you'. But when sent to a juvenile institution after an arrest for car theft he had two fights where he 'smashes shit out of him', perhaps trying to establish a reputation there as a dangerous man.

Pat Vincent, Jack Harley and Eel state a belief about fighting in such similar terms that it is obviously an ideological theme in their networks. Violence is OK when it is justified, and it *is* always justified when the other man starts it. Eel almost drafts it as law:

> Unnecessary violence I am against. Violence that has been provoked, if someone has brought it on themselves – they deserve every bit they get.

There is an ethic here, a positive obligation to reciprocate violence. But they are divided on violence towards women. Eel tells with some relish how his biker group got rid of an assertive woman:

There weren't many, no very few. There's my missus, her sister, a couple of the young blokes had girlfriends, and that's about it. All the birds are virtually taken, you know. Most of them are pretty quiet anyway. One loud-mouth bitch, she got a smack in the mouth one night, we haven't seen her since. She pushed one of my mates too far. He said if you don't shut up I'm going to smack you in the head. She kept going, so he did. She got all huffy about it, a bugger came up to hit him from behind type thing, all the rest of it. So we got rid of them quick smart.

It is clear why there are not many women in the group. Similar treatment of women is documented in male-supremacist biker groups in the United States.[6]

Pat Vincent, however, would disapprove. To him, men who bash women are 'wimps', a term of severe disapproval, because 'if guys hit chicks' they cannot defend themselves. Women are presumed unable to compete in the masculine world of violence and are not legitimate participants in the exchange of physical aggression. Physical fights in the family, or with girlfriends and *de facto* wives, happen often enough. But no pride is taken in them.

Institutional power and organized violence are encountered in the form of the state. The flavour of this relationship is encapsulated in Paul Gray's earliest memory. His family used to take boys from orphanages for a Christmas treat. One time when Paul was six or seven they were driving on the highway:

And there was copper on a motor bike in the bush. And he [the orphan] saw him, and bellowed out at the top of his lungs 'Hey Pig!'. And so we all [were] followed and we pulled into like a motel for the rich – and the copper went straight past, you know.

But the times when poor people can successfully pretend to be rich are few, and the coercive arm of the state weighs heavily on them.

Above all, these young men encounter the state in the form of the school. The dynamic that results is a key to their course in life and to the failure of the public education system.

For most of them, schooling is far from being an empowering experience. They encounter school authority as an alien power and start to define their masculinity against it. In some circumstances (e.g., assault on a teacher) this leads directly to the police and courts. In other circumstances they drop out, or are expelled or 'exploded' from school, as Linley Walker puts it for working-class young women, with no qualifications worth having. The pattern is all too familiar in schools dealing with disadvantaged youth, such as the New York high school studied by Michelle Fine.[7]

Pat Vincent, as a result of his career of schoolboy violence, was thrown out of two schools and ended his education at Year 10. Unemployed, he went onto drugs, and quarrelled with his parents over the curfew they imposed. His father, a back-hoe operator, eventually organized an apprenticeship. (Since it was in an occupation without a regular apprenticeship scheme, this probably meant an informal training arrangement.) Pat sketches what happened next:

How long was that?
    Seven weeks.
What happened?
    I got locked up so I lost it.
What did you get locked up for?
    Pinched a few cars and B & E [breaking and entering] and got busted.
Where did you get sent?
    Alpha [juvenile detention centre], I was there for a week and a half and I escaped from there. Then I got busted and I got caught and went to Beta [higher-security institution] for four or five weeks and then got out on CSO [community service order, an alternative sentence].
Was that because of your age?
    No, it was – a few times I have been busted, but I went up on about 16 charges . . . Walked off [i.e., escaped] which was three months [sentence] providing . . . I asked for CSO and I got it. I haven't been in any trouble since then. Keeping out.

This laconically covers a year in and out of custody, two arrests, breaches of bail conditions, surveillance, legal bargaining, and a rapid education in the technicalities of the juvenile justice system and the folkways of detention centres.

Pat bears no grudge against the police. When first arrested, after a chase in a stolen car, he thought: 'Shit, I'm gone! I thought they would kill me.' But the police were not as hard as he expected. Nor were the staff of the detention centres. He experienced none of the rapes or bashings of rumour. In fact he claims about Centre Beta, 'A holiday, chicks in there every night just about.' This is face-work – or, to put it in simple English, boasting – about being tough, a frequent move in Pat's personal style. He is learning to moderate the masculine display. He will shortly have his eighteenth birthday, and from now on he faces the big people's prison, a different proposition. So for the moment he is keeping out of trouble.

But in the course of these manoeuvres Pat has lost something already. From the detention centre he wrote a hurtful letter home, and his mother now will not speak to him. Pat's mother is a factory worker, the family's regular wage earner, a charge hand and possibly (Pat's language is vague) a union delegate. It seems that she has been trying to keep the kids in line and lift the family out of poverty. Pat's bull-headed fight with the law, and complaints against his family, on top of the school expulsions, got too much for her. His older brother has given him a bed.

The others' experiences differ in detail but not in character. Jack Harley did graduate from juvenile institution to gaol. Mal Walton was arrested for theft but got off with a bond. Eel has been locked up at least once and has had police as regular visitors to his drunken parties. Of the unemployed, only Alan Rubin does not mention being arrested; on other counts, too, he seems the best tactician. Among the employed, Paul Gray had a similar career to Jack Harley, graduating from juvenile institution to gaol on a drug charge.

In this class setting, state power is no abstraction. It is a material presence in young men's lives. The state's force cannot be incorporated into the peer-group exchange of violence, though Pat Vincent at first responded to it that way. The police are the Great Power in street politics, and one cannot get back at the state by personal confrontation, however tough one is. The tactic to learn is the one Paul Gray's parents neatly improvised on the highway – evasion. So the boys learn to dodge the police, to manipulate the welfare system, to find the soft legal options, as far as they can without turning into wimps themselves.

None of the five unemployed has found the state an asset in any substantial way, but one of the employed group did. Stewart Hardy, after leaving school and coming to the city, decided that his parents had been right about the need for qualifications. He took himself to technical college, got the Higher School Certificate, and has gone on to tertiary training.

The decisive thing here was Stewart's capacity to use the education system rather than fight against it. That approach had roots in high school. Stewart had spent some time as a 'hood' but did not go very far down that track. In middle adolescence he constructed a more peaceable relationship with his teachers. In fits and starts, Stewart got himself onto a career track and a masculinity organized more around knowledge and calculation than around confrontation.

Compulsory Heterosexuality for Men

Pat Vincent's sexual awakening came when he was about 11; 'kid stuff' he now thinks. He cannot remember how he learned about it, he just seemed to know, but he remembers his first fuck about 13: 'Just got onto a chick and ended up going all over her. Then I just kept it up.' Sex seems casual and easy, something that is always on tap. It is very important to Pat as part of his self-image, markedly less so to Alan Rubin, who satirizes the breathless boy-talk about 'Have-you-done-this-have-you-done-that-have-you-done-this?' and recalls his first fuck about 15:

> Do you want to hear what my opinion of it was?
> *Yes.*
> *So what!* . . . Turned out to be a bit of a bore.

This is a minority view. Eel shares Pat's stick-it-up-them enthusiasm, though he started later, at 17. His first fuck was with an older woman, who 'taught me a hell of a lot'. Then he started relationships with women his own age:

> I was going out with another bird, and she moved to Gamma [another city]. We were still going out while she was living there, with each other sort of thing. And I planned a trip to go and visit her, you know, to spend a month there, see how she had been doing and the rest of it. And in the meantime I got onto this other bird that I am with now. Just bedwarmer type thing, you know. And about a week before I went to leave for Gamma she turned around and told me she was pregnant. I just went absolutely berko on her. Well I took off to Gamma and I wasn't going to come back. Ended

up coming back anyway and about two months later I split up with the bird that I had in Gamma. I have always just kept her around because of the kid.

Eel's antagonism to women is naked. He lashes out at his mother, 'she gives me the shits and I give her the shits'; at his father's new woman, 'a bitch'; at his wife's mother, 'a real bitch'; and at his wife too:

> Well, she's me missus but, first chance I can see to get rid of her, she's gone.
> *Why is that?*
> Oh, I can't live with her. I've lived with her for what, three years now, she is just driving me up the wall.
> *What does she do?*
> Oh . . . the things she says, the way she does things, the way she carries on over stupid shit . . . always whingeing because I never take her out anywhere.

Why do the women put up with this kind of treatment? There is excitement and pleasure in sex, doubtless. But probably the key is lack of alternative. Gayle Rubin wrote of 'obligatory heterosexuality' and Adrienne Rich of 'compulsory heterosexuality', naming the cultural and social pressures on women to make themselves sexually available to men, on whatever terms they can get. What needs to be added is the fact, made very clear in these life-histories, that compulsory heterosexuality is also enforced on men.[8]

This works even at the level of their relationship to their own bodies. Mal Walton accidentally learnt how to masturbate, and rather enjoyed it:

> After that I started masturbating a lot – too much in fact. It catches up with you. It does. I read in a book that if you masturbate too much, it's because your hand's harder than a vagina, you get used to it being hard. And then when you start to go with a girl you just don't, you just don't enjoy it.
> *Did that happen for you?*
> Yeah. That's why I stopped completely. I don't need to now anyway. No more, that's it, as soon as I found that out. It freaked me out.

So the male body has to be disciplined to heterosexuality. That means other bodies as well as one's own. Eel has a friend Gary who is 'more or less like a brother . . . everything we did together: we got locked up together, we got beat up, partied together.' Gary nearly killed Eel one night with a .22 rifle in a drunken argument when Eel insulted an ex-girlfriend of Gary's. But they are united on policing male sexuality:

> Gays I have trouble putting up with . . . we used to go poofter-bashing up the Cross and all the rest of it, me and Gary, a few of the other blokes. [King's Cross is near the centre of gay men's social life in Sydney.]

Eel ran into trouble on this front, because his older brother 'turned queer'. Eel, who has a keen sense of humour, acknowledges his brother's skill at handling a homophobic milieu:

> All his mates are trendies and yuppies, fags. He comes out to visit me and Mum. And all my mates are over – they're all like me. He feels as awkward at Mum's place when they're around as I do at his place. But he copes with it all right, he copes well. He sort of tries to, when he comes down, he plays both sides of the fence. And when the guys aren't there he is his normal self. And when the guys come over he's not as bad as what he is. Just, so they don't, so he doesn't get a hassle, or hassle me or Mum.

The brother grew up in the same school of aggression as Eel, but grew bigger and stronger: 'Picks me up and bash lands me. If I give him any shit – *pain!*' So Eel does not make his trips to King's Cross any more. 'So long as they stay out of my way I don't give a shit what they do. As long as they don't cross my path.'

The acknowledged sexuality of the five is exclusively heterosexual. But there are many homosexual possibilities in working-class life too, as AIDS prevention research has found.[9] Paul Gray met these possibilities early on, sharing sex play with a boy friend in primary school. His first fuck and first relationship were with a girl, crude and unsatisfying: 'in, out, in, out, and off, kind of thing'. Then he discovered beats, places where men meet for anonymous homosexual contact:

> I found out about toilets after that so, sex was – toilets. I saw the writing on the wall if you like. OK, then explored that side of it. It was fine, I enjoyed it all the time. But when it was over I wanted to go, I didn't ever want to hang around and spend the night.

It is quite possible he was making money from it. Despite a number of relationships with men he never settled into a gay social identity. At the same time he could not settle into a heterosexual masculinity. He eventually found a more radical solution, which will be discussed below.

Masculinity as Collective Practice

Responses to the circumstances of these men's lives are collective as much as they are individual. This can be seen in Eel's discussion of his motorbike fraternity:

> It wasn't really a gang so much.
> *You mean you weren't like Hell's Angels?*
> No, it's nothing like that. I mean we partied just as hard as them but, we didn't have the reputation, you know. Kept it quiet. We used to go away for weekend rallies, day rides, night rides, and parties and all those sort of things.
> *Everyone gets ripped and pissed?*
> Yes, yes, we had some good parties. We used to get a couple of ounces, put them in the bowl, couple of grams of speed or something. Occasionally someone would bring some hammer [heroin] or something around, snowcap and throw it on top of the cone, smoke ourselves stupid. Demolished a house that I was renting, totally demolished that place. All the parties, there was a party every night. I'd moved out of home, with a bloke at work, and we could – one other bloke and a couple of birds moved in with us. And we got kicked out of the place we were in so we moved up the Delta Road. There was parties there every night. There was always someone coming over with some booze, or some snow or something. Yes, we had, we used to, cops sitting out front taking down rego numbers. Something like 20 bikes parked outside the front of this house every night of the week, seven days a week. Just one big party, because a lot of us were out of work at the time too so nothing better to do.

The parties often turned into violence. I have already quoted Eel's description of a violent put-down of a 'loud-mouth bitch' at one of them. More often it was brawls among the men.

This is not uncontrolled, psychotic violence. It is socially defined and even managed. Eel and his mates dumped people who were too aggressive, to maintain good feeling in the group:

How do people get on in the group?
> Generally excellent, normally it was fantastic. You get the occasional person that climbs up the wall every time they open their mouth, type thing. You sort of edge them out real quick. Otherwise we all got on superbly. We still do.

Most of the actual violence is confined within the group, where it will not attract police action. Violence directed outwards is mainly symbolic, as Eel acknowledges:

Did you get into many fights?
> No not really, very few. Most people would take one look at us and move. No big drama. Anyone who has got any guts to stand up they ended up backing down anyway most times.

Was it just from sheer numbers or people or . . . ?
> No, I think a lot of it's to do with appearance. About they, the way we look and the fact that we have got earrings and tattoos, we ride bikes. That's enough to scare shit out of most straight people. So that a lot of the real fights are between us personally – disagreements, you know.

The exceptions were expeditions to bash homosexuals, and possibly Asian immigrants.

Eel accurately remarks that his group is not Hell's Angels, not even the Comancheros or Bandidos, the two clubs involved in the 1984 'Father's Day massacre' at Milperra in Sydney's outer suburbs. But it is certainly part of the same milieu, a network of 'outlaw' motorbike clubs which developed in the postwar decades in Australia as in the United States. Chris Cunneen and Rob Lynch trace the growing conflict between these groups and the police which culminated in annual riots at the Bathurst motorcycle races. Their analysis of the role of state power in producing these conflicts has close parallels in the life-histories.[10]

As Chapter 1 noted, social science has increasingly recognized a collective dimension of masculinity, and the evidence here supports this concept. Of course individual practice is required. Eel wears earrings, has cropped hair long in the back, has tattoos on both arms, keeps a bike. On his own, this would mean little. It is the *group* that is the bearer of masculinity, in a basic way. In a different milieu, Eel is at a loss. He is currently doing a short course at a technical college, and his experience there is a telling example of the importance of milieu.

Well, I sort of find it hard to talk to women, you know, especially those in the Tech class. There's one I wouldn't mind getting myself into. I don't like to say the wrong thing, you know, because I don't know . . . Totally different class of birds . . . Drives me up the wall sometimes. Because I give her and this other bird and [a friend] a lift home, drop the others home and then she's the last one I drop off on my way to work, kind of thing. We can sit in the car for 15 minutes and not say a word. Because I just can't think of what to say and what not to say.

A different proposition from picking up a 'bedwarmer' in a setting where he feels comfortable.

In other cases there is not such a tight-knit peer group. Pat Vincent, for instance, is not a biker and has a loose network of friends. He and his best friend get along well, go surfing together, go out 'raging' and spend time talking – though, Pat specifies, 'not heaps of personal stuff'. It seems a ritualized relationship in which an acceptable masculinity is sustained. Pat is homophobic ('should be shot'). Accordingly he and his mate are careful not to let their friendship spill over into homoeroticism.

Across the broader milieu where these young men have grown up, the interviews suggest significant tensions in sexual ideology. A thin, contemptuous misogyny, in which women are treated basically as disposable receptacles for semen, coexists with a much more respectful, even admiring view of women's strength. Sometimes these views coexist in the same head. Homophobia is common but not universal. Some of the young men reach easily for live-and-let-live formulae. Fatherhood is feared, because it means commitment, but also desired, especially if the child is a boy. Anger at girlfriends for getting pregnant – the boys never blame themselves – battles with a practical willingness to live together and share child care. The ritual denunciation of feminist extremists that we came to expect from most men we interviewed sits beside straightforward and unselfconscious statements supporting sex equality. Pat Vincent, for instance, did not know what 'feminism' meant; but when the interviewer explained the term, Pat was wholeheartedly in agreement:

I reckon women should have equal rights. I think they have. Still a lot of prejudiced blokes around, who say women can't do this or that. I think they can do what we can do.

These ideological tensions get sorted out in different ways by different men, with no obvious connection to social position. No collective process seems to be going on that is likely to resolve them.

Protest Masculinity

Turning now to the level of personality, I explored the life-histories at some length for patterns of emotion. Orthodox psychoanalytic ideas gave little help. There seems less prospect of primary identification with the mother than in the conventional bourgeois family, given the economic arrangements; but also there is no clear-cut pattern of identification with fathers.

More strikingly, there is little indication of the emotional investment in gender differences we have come to expect in analyses of masculinity.

For instance, Jack Harley, a biker with a history of violence and a criminal record, feels no unease about staying home to do the child care if his wife can get a better-paying job than he can. Several of his mates do just that. He hopes to get trained to do bar work. What he likes in it is the human dimension, the chance to meet people and hear their troubles. Not exactly super-masculine; indeed this could easily be seen as women's work, the classic function of a barmaid.

What emerges here is a combination of a sharply marked gender boundary and a remarkable (from a bourgeois point of view) indifference to its psychological content. Difference is confined to sexuality and violence, both being immediate functions of the body. Jack is homophobic, worried that there are more gays and lesbians than before, but he has a solution. Sex with men is OK if a man wants to become a woman (implying transsexual surgery), but it is wrong the way men are.

This view of difference, in the context of poverty, does make psychodynamic sense along another theoretical track. Let us consider one personal trajectory in a little more detail.

Mal Walton was an only child, deserted by his father before he was born. He has lived with his mother and grandmother until very recently:

What was it like growing up with your Mum and your Nan?
>   Hard.
Why was it hard?
>   Two women – never had a man there to, you know, give me a good
>   tan about the arse. Because I've, I've pretty well had it my way, you
>   know, but – that's why I wished that I had a Dad, so, you know, he
>   would kick me up the bum and say 'you've done wrong'. Because I
>   have always done the opposite. I've kicked Mum up the bum and
>   said, 'No, I want to do that.'

But he rejected his mother's attempt to make him respect a
stepfather's authority. The only person he listened to was his
grandmother. By early adolescence he was uncontrollable
from his mother's point of view, out all night and fucking girls.
His school had no more success, despite savage canings. Mal
refused to learn, was treated as disruptive, and was placed in
the bottom stream and in a special class. Increasingly he did not
turn up to school at all. He left school as soon as he was legally
able to, without having learned to read. This puts him at a
desperate disadvantage in the labour market. He tries to conceal
his inability to read from the employment service as well as from
bosses.

Mal got into minor crime as a teenager. After leaving school he
got into more serious theft to finance dope purchases. Arrested
at 15, he got off with a bond and managed to keep out of the
courts from then on. After drifting for three years, mainly on the
dole, he decided to take himself in hand and found a number of
short-term labouring jobs, including some 'black money'. This
went to finance a motorbike and elaborate tattoos. Speeding on
the bike, he had a crash and was seriously injured. He is currently
living with a girlfriend, the first household away from his
mother's, and is making heavy weather of it. They are $2,000 in
debt and he is trying to work out how to get an illicit job to pay
it off.

The gender practice here is essentially the same as with Pat
Vincent, Jack Harley, Eel and Paul Gray (up to middle adolescence): violence, school resistance, minor crime, heavy
drug/alcohol use, occasional manual labour, motorbikes or cars,
short heterosexual liaisons. There is something frenzied and
showy about it. It is *not* simply adopting the conventional stereotype of masculinity, as Paul Willis perceptively noted in his case

study of bike boys in Britain.[11] Mal, for instance, does not care for sport, which he finds 'boring'. This opinion is shared by Pat Vincent, though not by Eel – so dubbed because in childhood he was a fanatical supporter of the Parramatta Rugby League team 'the Eels'.

This practice has a good deal in common with what Alfred Adler called the 'masculine protest'. Adler's concept (discussed in Chapter 1 above) defined a pattern of motives arising from the childhood experience of powerlessness, and resulting in an exaggerated claim to the potency that European culture attaches to masculinity. Among these young men too there is a response to powerlessness, a claim to the gendered position of power, a pressured exaggeration (bashing gays, wild riding) of masculine conventions.

The difference is that this is a collective practice and not something inside the person. Very similar patterns appear in the collective practice of working-class, especially ethnic minority, street gangs in the United States.[12] There seems to be no standard developmental path into it, apart from the level of tension created by poverty and an ambience of violence. Through interaction in this milieu, the growing boy puts together a tense, freaky facade, making a claim to power where there are no real resources for power.

There is a lot of concern with face, a lot of work put into keeping up a front. With Patrick Vincent, I have a sense of a false-self system, an apparently rigid personality compliant to the demands of the milieu, behind which there is no organized character at all. He scares me. Both Eel and Mal Walton talked about going on massive binges when they had a little money saved up. Eel scared himself:

> I ended up going through three grand in two months, on speed alone. It was straight up my nose. Wasted two months. Didn't know whether I was coming or going.
>
> *Did you enjoy it?*
>
> I enjoyed it yes, I still do enjoy it, but I wouldn't get as heavily involved as I was.
>
> *Why the change?*
>
> By the end of the two months I noticed the change in myself. Really hot tempered – one wrong word and I was right off the deep end. Hitting people and breaking things in the house, breaking walls, punch out, breaking windows and stuff, so . . .

Protest masculinity in this sense is not simply observance of a stereotyped male role. It is compatible with respect and attention to women (Mal Walton – in contrast to Eel's misogyny), egalitarian views about the sexes (Pat Vincent), affection for children (Jack Harley), and a sense of display which in conventional role terms is decidedly feminine. Mal Walton is a living work of art. His body is bejewelled with tattoos, which he has planned and financed over the years with as much care as any *Vogue* wardrobe.

Other Trajectories

Alan Rubin ran out of control as a child, truanted and left school at 15. He has stayed in the same social milieu and economic circumstances as the men just discussed. But he has constructed a laid-back, ironic, intellectual, 'bohemian' (his word) personal style. He is scathing about 'yobbos' and 'ockers', and has no antagonism to gays. He has, I think, recognized protest masculinity and has consciously distanced himself from it.

Stewart Hardy's interrupted educational career has been outlined already. His father, a 'battler', had little communication with Stewart, except when the boy went to get money off him in the pub. Stewart was closer to his mother, but also fought with her, especially when his father was drunk and Stewart had clashed with him.

Stewart found little to value here, and has built his life into another space, socially and geographically. He distanced himself from the tough gangs at school, after a flirtation with their aggressive style. His next way out was provided by religion. He became involved, via a couple of young women, with a fundamentalist church which absorbed his energies for several years and decisively separated him from his rough school mates. His final way out was coming to the big city. Here he acquired a white-collar job, lost his religion, got into computing, went to technical college, and is now lining up for university. He has become involved with a girl six years younger, but more sexually experienced. He is disconcerted by the sophistication of her peer group and wonders darkly what they say about him behind his back.

Paul Gray and Danny Taylor also started close to the masculine-protest trajectory. Paul was right on track with family violence, theft, a juvenile institution and gaol. Danny was a little more conventional in his masculinity, aligned with a 'football mad' brother and father. They, like Stewart Hardy, moved away from this trajectory, but at much sharper angles, attempting to negate hegemonic masculinity and expel themselves from the ranks. Danny's path is discussed in Chapters 5, so I will be very brief here. He realigned himself with his mother, later found himself very dependent in a love affair, sought healing, and became involved with 'green' politics. He was offered work by an environmental organization, and has tried to accept at a personal level the feminist critique of men's misogyny.

Paul Gray's path is even more surprising. His early exit from school, his involvement in minor crime, his arrest and institutionalization, his aggression towards mother and sister and his first sex with a girl are very like the stories of Jack Harley, Patrick Vincent and Mal Walton. But Paul was also encountering gay men at the beats. In late adolescence he was at the same time on the fringe of the gay world, secretly cross-dressing, and nostalgic for a heterosexual relationship. He travelled around Australia, did time for possession of drugs and was nearly raped in gaol; eventually he formed a relationship with a woman, which lasted for a couple of years, and travelled overseas.

When he came back to Australia, Paul began cross-dressing regularly and is now trying to live as a woman. This resolved his 'confusion', as he puts it. Cross-dressing gives him relief from 'tension', but it is clear that considerable effort goes into it too:

Have you yet gone out in public?
Yes, in the last year and half, that's, when I go out I mainly go out as a woman.
And is that different for you?
Yes, it is. Because it is, I become more aware of people around me. It's still quite hard to do. But it is a matter of forcing myself to do it. And I have, a rule I suppose that once I leave the front door there is no going back in, so, until the course is run and the night is finished. Yes, but I mean, I mainly go to gay bars and that sort of thing. I see a lot of movies, go to a lot of restaurants and that sort of thing. The majority of my friends, a large majority, know about it now. The guy I work with knows about it. He has only just in the last week or so knew about it, that was really quite funny telling him.

There are major costs. Given that he does not completely pass (few cross-dressers do), there is physical and social risk. Further, the process broke up his longest relationship, as his partner could not accept what he was doing.

The psychiatric literature on transvestism and transsexualism treats them as pathological syndromes, to be explained by some abnormality in early development.[13] Paul Gray certainly had a distant father. But so did half the other men in the group. His childhood situation was well within the normal range in this milieu. And far from having a feminine core identity, he was, by mid-adolescence, engaged in violence, petty crime and fucking girls. The conventional psychopathology of gender misses both the structural issues and the agency involved in such a story. The outcome of the contradictory relationships and affects in Paul's life can hardly have been predetermined. Paul constructed an outcome *as a practice*, and he still has to work at it, and pay the price.

Divergent Masculinities and Gender Politics

The life-histories show diverging trajectories from substantially similar starting-points. The masculinities constructed mostly represent two of the positions defined in Chapter 3. Protest masculinity is a marginalized masculinity, which picks up themes of hegemonic masculinity in the society at large but reworks them in a context of poverty. Stewart Hardy and Alan Rubin, in different fashions, have constructed complicit masculinities, distancing themselves from the direct display of power but accepting the privilege of their gender.

Danny Taylor and Paul Gray reject this privilege. Paul, it is worth noting, has not gone straight for a sex change. He does not want 'the operation'; what he wants to do is 'live as a woman' on an everyday basis. His practice is above all a path out of a masculine identity. In that respect – though spectacularly different in appearance – it is logically very similar to Danny's attempt to fight free from his masculine consciousness. These two cases break the boundaries of a classification of masculinities. We cannot define their personalities as types of masculinity. But we can certainly understand what they are doing in terms of the politics of masculinity.

An active process of grappling with a situation, and constructing ways of living in it, is central to the making of gender. The political character of the process emerges as a key to the differences among these men.

All their projects are shaped by the fact of class deprivation. They have constructed gender from a starting-point in poverty, and with little access to cultural or economic resources. The bikers' anger at 'straight people' is a class resentment as well as a display of collective masculinity. Stewart Hardy's rejection of protest masculinity is intimately connected with his hard-won upward mobility, his discovery of a class practice that attempts to gain leverage in education, in religion and in employment.

Alan Rubin, who does not participate in the displays of protest masculinity, is even more bitter than the bikers against convention and authority. He regards the political and economic system as 'totally corrupt' and religion as 'mumbo jumbo'. He is scathing about 'plastic people' who 'just exist' and don't know what is really going on. Alan objects to jobs where he is 'taking orders from a load of people whom I consider to be cretins', and making profits for owners who are millionaires already. The code of revenge – 'if anyone gives me a hard time I give them a hard time back' – takes on extra depth here as a class statement. Yet Alan in practice is not fighting back. In a classic piece of research Richard Sennett and Jonathan Cobb wrote of 'the hidden injuries of class' among American men.[14] There is a good deal of class injury here too, a sense of limited options and constricted practice, as well as class anger.

Stewart Hardy, despite his expanding education, remains homophobic and misogynist. His treatment of women in actual relationships is manipulative. His responses to questions about feminism are long, confused and mostly angry. And, in stark contrast to Pat Vincent and Jack Harley, he has a conventional hostility to the idea of his wife earning more than he, because it would damage his self-esteem.

But though they want the benefits of male supremacy, Stewart and Alan do not care to pay the full price. They opt out of the physical confrontations, the emotional labour, the maintenance of peer life. They look down with contempt on the naively masculine 'ockers' and the 'little shits' – people like Eel or Patrick – who do the dirty work of sexual politics for them.

So, though Alan and Stewart are genuinely distanced from hegemonic masculinity, it is difficult to see them as engaged in resistance. Rather, their masculinity is complicit in the collective project of patriarchy. Indeed, since these men pay less of the price of sustaining patriarchy, their practice may be less likely to generate resistance and change than protest masculinity is.

The project of protest masculinity also develops in a marginal class situation, where the claim to power that is central in hegemonic masculinity is constantly negated by economic and cultural weakness. Mal Walton may be strong and his tattoos scary, but he cannot even read. Eel may be the toughest brawler among his mates, but the police as an institution are tougher than the lot of them put together, and they know it.

By virtue of class situation and practice (e.g., in school), these men have lost most of the patriarchal dividend. For instance, they have missed out on the economic gain over women that accrues to men in employment, the better chances of promotion, the better job classifications. If they accept this loss they are accepting the justice of their own deprivation. If they try to make it good by direct action, state power stands in their way.

One way to resolve this contradiction is a spectacular display, embracing the marginality and stigma and turning them to account. At the personal level, this translates as a constant concern with front or credibility. This is not necessarily defence of a traditional working-class masculinity. Jack Harley, as already mentioned, is not concerned if his woman earns more than he does. But he is very upset if another man's child is foisted on him as his own, or if his woman is fucking someone else. He is concerned to be a credible revenge threat, to ward off injury by being known as someone who injures back. Through the interview he repeats formulae like 'they pull a knife on me I'll pull a knife on them'.

At the group level, the collective practice of masculinity becomes a performance too. Eel's parties have witnesses – the silenced women, the cops outside – just as the bikers out riding together are witnessed by straight people. Whatever one thinks of the script, it has to be acknowledged as a skilled, finely pitched production mounted on a shoestring.

The trouble is that the performance is not leading anywhere. None of the five has much sense of an individual or a shared future, except more of the same. Eel is doing a short computer course, and imagines doing well at it, but the image is immediately cut off:

I don't really think much about the future, I just take things day to day. Hopefully one day I might end up as a systems analyst with computers. And if everything works out with this training course, managed to get a start after that, work myself up to an operator, programmer, and then a systems analyst. Either that or I'll be dead by the time I'm forty.

From what?

I don't know. But well, live fast and die young sort of thing . . . I love my bikes. I'll be on my bike till the day I die. I'll die on the bike. I'm not going to stop partying. It's a way of life isn't it? Called Rastafarians. I'm a believer in that religion.

These remarks are not as casual as they sound. Death, especially death on the bike, is a powerful theme in motorbike culture internationally.[15]

The interviews with Pat Vincent and Mal Walton, normally less eloquent than Eel, have haunting passages about what they can pass on to their children. Pat has imagined only a boy, and his vision is of teaching him boxing and weight-training, so that by the time the boy is 18 he will be able to kick the shit out of anyone who hassles him. Mal also wants a boy to carry on his name, as well as a girl ('because you can dress them up and make them look really cute'). He wants the boy to be what he could not. He also wants to pass on his own most valuable knowledge. This is what it is:

Like if he wants to smoke pot, sure, as long as he smokes it with me. Or if I'm not smoking then as long as he smokes it around me. And I don't, like I don't want his first experience with drugs to be a real – like someone, say he goes and gets some speed and gets it cut with glass, which some people do, and he shoots it up without filtering it, then he would really fuck himself up. I want him to come to me and say, 'look Dad I want to try speed' or 'I want to try some smoke', or 'I want to get pissed'. As long as he comes to me and does it and then I'll know, like, I'll know that he knows what he is getting and what it's all about.

Protest masculinity looks like a cul-de-sac. It is certainly an active response to the situation, and it builds on a working-class masculine ethic of solidarity. But this is a solidarity that divides the group from the rest of the working class. The loss of the

economic basis of masculine authority leads to a divided consciousness – egalitarianism *and* misogyny – not to a new political
direction.

The tracks away from hegemonic masculinity taken by Danny
Taylor and Paul Gray are, in their own ways, as dramatic as the
bikers' display. They differ in being strongly individualized.
Danny is engaged in a direct negation of hegemonic masculinity
by way of a personal quest, as a remaking of the self, not as a
shared project.

Paul is even more deeply self-absorbed. He is in the throes of
coming out in women's clothes to friends and to family, and has
just come out at his workplace. He is learning to negotiate public
spaces while dressed, trying to work out what living as a woman
means for his sex life, reinterpreting his past. He is not a conventional transsexual[16] and does not make the classic claim that
he is 'really a woman'. In his life a contradiction developed which
has split, but not overwhelmed, the sense of masculinity. At best
he feels himself to be a woman-under-construction, and has clash-
ing fantasies of his future as a man and as a woman-with-male-
genitals. However it turns out, at the moment the project is
completely individualized.

Paul's gender practice elaborates, where the bikers attenuate,
the cultural dimension of gender. There are political possibilities
here, difficult to crystallize but implicit in Paul's multiple loca-
tions in gender relations over the past few years. Gender politics
might seek to complicate and cross-fertilize, rather than to shrink,
the sphere in which gender is expressed or represented.

Yet it is hardly likely that either Danny's green activism or Paul's
high-heeled shoes are the forerunners of a mass movement
among working-class youth. The wider prospects lie in aspects of
the situation that are overshadowed by protest masculinity but are
still present in the unemployed men's life-histories. These are the
economic logic that underpins egalitarian households, the personal experience of women's strength, and the interest that
several of the men have in children (an interest which few of them
experienced from their own fathers). These details suggest a
domestic gender equality which contradicts the hyper-masculine
display of the road and the party scene.

There are intriguing and perhaps important possibilities here.
Whether they are realized depends on a more explicitly political
response to gender issues emerging among working-class men. As

the United Steelworkers of America (in Canada) and the Builders Labourers Federation (in Australia) have shown, such a response *can* come from male-dominated unions.[17] But in an age of union decline, and mostly defensive battles to prevent job losses, it is difficult to see how a wider response will develop.

5

A Whole New World

This chapter will discuss an experience radically different from protest masculinity. It concerns a group of men who have attempted to reform their masculinity, in part because of feminist criticism. They are exactly the kind of 'soft' men scorned by the mythopoetic men's movement and other masculine revivalists. Looked at closely, their project is more difficult, and their story more interesting, than such dismissals suggest.

Chapter 4 emphasized the divergence of gender projects coming out of the same situation. This chapter will analyse just one project, since the gender trajectories of the men concerned are fundamentally similar. But it will do so in greater depth and with more attention to the project's internal contradictions.

First, it is necessary to describe the setting of the encounter with feminism. As in the United States, an Australian counter-culture developed in the wake of the student movement. By the later 1970s a back-to-earth movement had created a network of rural communes and counter-cultural households scattered across the eastern states. The bulk of the counter-culture, however, remained urban.

With the decline of political radicalism in the mid-1970s, the focus of counter-cultural life shifted towards introspection and personal relationships. By the early 1980 there was a well-developed therapeutic milieu devoted to personal growth and healing. An interest in meditation often connected, through vegetarianism and holistic philosophies, to a concern with nature.[1]

At the same time a new activism was growing around environmental issues. Groups such as the Movement Against Uranium Mining, Friends of the Earth, Greenpeace, and various *ad hoc* campaign groups became vehicles of youth activism. They stirred established groups such as the Australian Conservation Founda-

tion to more militant action. By the early 1980s this movement was strong enough to mount a long blockade of hydro-electric dam construction in Tasmania on the remote Franklin River. This highly publicized and very popular wilderness, defence action helped defeat the conservative federal government in the 1983 election.[2]

A Women's liberation movement emerged from campus radicalism at the end of the 1960s, displacing established women's organizations and rapidly growing in scale and visibility. By International Women's Year in 1975, the new feminism was a major topic of media attention. In the later 1970s feminism was consolidating in women's services, in the bureaucracy, in academic life, among students and in the counter-culture.[3]

Its impact on the environmental movement by the early 1980s was strong. Eco-feminism had emerged internationally as a major current of feminist thought, resonating with Green critiques of destructive development. Some conflicts with the men running environmental action groups occurred, yet many of the men were receptive to feminist ideas. In Australian politics there are few areas where feminist pressure has been more successful. Men engaged with environmental politics cannot avoid gender politics as defined by feminism, whatever their personal histories.

The six men discussed in this chapter were all involved in the environmental movement and most had a wider experience of the counter-culture. They are: Barry Ryan (22), a trainee nurse, Danny Taylor (23), an office worker for an environmental action group, Bill Lindeman (28), an occasionally employed photographer, Nigel Roberts (31), unemployed, Tim Marnier (33), a public servant, and Peter Geddes (50), an occasionally employed journalist.

All are heterosexual; two have children. All come from urban backgrounds, but as a result of their environmental or counter-cultural politics most have lived for some period on farms or in the bush. Three were directly involved in the Franklin Dam action. All have been involved in environmental campaigns in other parts of the country, such as rainforest protection actions.

The Moment of Engagement

What we learn from the men's earliest memories, and their accounts of family relationships, shows conventional childhood experiences. In all six cases primary parenting was done by the mother, For five out of six, the mother was a full-time housewife while the boy was young. The conditions for pre-Oedipal identification with the mother were more clearly present than for most of the men discussed in Chapter 4, and this certainly reflects the more comfortable incomes of most of these families.

Feminist object-relations theory (Chapter 1) alerts us to the pressures for separation from this relationship, and these pressures can be traced in the childhood memories of most of the group. They are sometimes directly linked to fathers, and here a classic post-Oedipal pattern of identification with the powerful and distant father can be found. Barry Ryan is the most obviously identified with his father, Tim Marnier next. Both fathers were professionals, carrying a recognized social authority, and are presented by their sons as somewhat distant. But even here, identification is not all that is going on. The Ryans separated when Barry was about 12. Unlike his older siblings, Barry chose to live with his father, not his mother, and the circumstances suggest a current of Oedipal desire underlying the identification.

Other histories show that we need to go beyond a narrow focus on the Oedipal triangle of mother/father/son. The father is not the only bearer of masculinity in a small boy's field of vision. He may indeed be less visible, in some family configurations, than an older brother. Thus Danny Taylor's brother was the one who took him in hand and taught him about sex, who was 'best friend' in Danny's late childhood and early adolescence. 'We'd go out together, play together all the time, we used to have the same room, and we shared a lot of things.' The brother was thus a model for developing masculinity. And a model of hegemonic masculinity, since he was a football star, egged on by their father who was 'football mad'. So Danny took up football too.

Here, on the face of it, are two versions of the social reproduction of hegemonic masculinity: father to son, older brother to younger brother. These events could be read in psychoanalytic terms as identification, or in sex role terms as successful social learning. But these readings are too mechanical. There was also an active appropriation of what was offered, a purposeful construction of a way of being in the world.

I will define this appropriation as the *moment of engagement* with hegemonic masculinity, the moment in which the boy takes up the project of hegemonic masculinity as his own. This moment appears in each of the six life-histories. 'None of these men was, so to speak, born feminist. Each made a substantial commitment of the developing person towards hegemonic masculinity. The life-histories show such familiar items as competitiveness, career orientation, suppression of emotions, homophobia.

As I argued in Chapter 2, the bodily sense of masculinity is central to the social process. A key part of the moment of engagement, then, is developing a particular experience of the body and a particular physical sensibility. Barry Ryan, now in training as a nurse, said he came to value 'feminine' traits such as sensitivity, expressiveness and caring, and came to reject the 'masculine' things he was taught at school. But at the same time:

> I'm still really masculine, and I feel definitely male and I like that too. I like some aspects of being male, the physical strength I really like, I really like my body; that sort of mental strength that men learn to have whereby they can choose to put aside their feelings for the moment, which I think, is great.

This process of masculinization extends into perception and sexual arousal. It foregrounds experiences of the body that define females as other, and shapes desire as desire for the other. The obligatory heterosexuality discussed in Chapter 4 thus takes shape at the level of bodily experience, as a pattern of sensation or a capacity for sensation (for instance, sexual arousal in response to women only). I will call this pattern 'heterosexual sensibility', an awkward term but an important concept.

A heterosexual sensibility may be present as a contradictory layer of awareness within a social practice constructing femininity. This is illustrated by Barry Ryan's sense of himself as a male nurse. More commonly for men, it underlies social practices constructing masculinity. It is the principal reason why heterosexual desire is felt to be natural, seamlessly connected with a body experienced as male.

By adolescence, the construction of heterosexuality was a collective practice usually undertaken in peer groups. This is familiar in youth studies, and needs little comment. Peter Geddes wryly recalls a familiar social technique of Australian men:

> As a teenager you went out and got drunk so that you wouldn't feel intimidated or shy or nervous. And you got hold of any, virtually any one, particularly the prettiest one, but if not it really didn't

matter as long as she would get laid . . . My teenage sex life and most of my married life had been on that basis: where I usually was pretty pissed, and I got my end in, and I had an orgasm . . . and I said 'thank you, that was lovely, goodnight', and you went home or fell asleep.

Family and peer group between them provided plenty of support for the boys' engagement with hegemonic masculinity amid its structuring of desire.

Distancing

Yet the same relationships held tensions that could lead in other directions. Danny Taylor's path into adulthood, for instance, was not as straightforward as its starting-point might suggest. A dialectic developed from his attempts to imitate his older brother and appropriate masculinity.

He took up football to impress his father, but the move did not work. The solidarity between his brother and his father proved too close. Danny became acutely jealous of his brother, and came to resent being dominated by him. He turned to his mother, who saw what was going on and gave him extra 'loving attention'. By the time he reached middle adolescence – Danny dates it 'precisely at age 15 – the emotional links had been reconfigured and the family was factionalized and angry.

> Just a couple of months ago I had an argument with my brother, and he said – just out of the blue, it had nothing to do with it – 'Oh, Mum thinks the sun shines out of your arse'. And it brought back all those feelings. We had this rift, my father and my brother, my mother and me, and there was this huge gap. There was real bitterness between my mother and my brother. . . . And my father and myself, our relationship was horrible. I used to really groan at him, and if he was aggressive or angry against my mother, then I'd feel it was aimed at me as well. And in turn, if I got picked on for anything by my father – which may have been justified sometimes too – my mother would rush to my defence.

It appears, then, that an Oedipal separation of boy from mother can be renegotiated, and to some degree reversed, in later practice. This was not a shallow change. Danny went on from this reworked solidarity with his mother to solidarity, even identification, with other women. The shape of Danny's life-history strongly suggests that the reconfiguration of family relationships in his adolescence was the emotional basis of his dissident gender politics in early adulthood.

Such distancing can be found in other lives, if less dramatically. Bill Lindeman, who was quite warm about his father, nevertheless pitied him and spoke of his 'tragic' life course, 'a whole chunk of his life eaten out by spending 35 years, or whatever, working for money'. Nigel Roberts was more bitter about his father, describing him as a pale, defeated person who 'never did become a man'. Though Nigel's career as a student activist led to physical confrontation with police and arrest, he did not sustain such militancy. Indeed, he described himself as unable to relate to girls in late adolescence because he was *not* macho but did not know another way of presenting himself.

None of these episodes was a positive move towards an alternative form of masculinity. The moment here was one of negation, at most a distancing within an accepted gender framework. Consider Nigel Roberts's complaint that his father was not man enough.

Yet the gender order itself is contradictory, and practical experience can undermine patriarchal conventions. Five of the six described a close encounter with a woman's strength in the course of their personal formation. For instance, Peter Geddes's father, unable to find his feet after the Second World War, seems to have been pushed along by his wife. Peter resented his mother's snobbishness but acknowledged her as the force in the family. Nigel Roberts, at a loss after leaving school, clung to a relationship with his girlfriend as a mainstay while drifting around the rural counter-culture. When they met feminism later, feminist images of women's strength could resonate with something in their own experience.

The Environmental Movement

The six came towards Green politics along different paths. Nigel Roberts's environmental activism was an aspect of youthful radicalism. For Peter Geddes it was the end-point of an odyssey started by the crisis of his career in journalism. For Bill Lindeman, interest in the environment started with his family's liking for the bush and practice of camping out on holidays.

Tim Marnier came to environmental issues from the managerial rather than the movement side, though his family was part of the progressive liberalism of the 1960s and 1970s and he lived in a communal household with a group of feminist women. He became 'fed up with taxi driving, mostly picking up drunk males at night'. A friend offered him a part-time job on an environmental research project, which developed into a full-time job which has now 'changed my life'.

Danny Taylor came to environmental issues as part of his exploration of the counter-culture, in a search for healing after a crisis of his sexual life. For Barry Ryan, like Bill Lindeman, environmentalist sympathies were probably part of a background of progressive social thought in family and school. When the chance for action at the Franklin River came along, in the course of a motorbike tour of Australia with a male friend, it was a simple decision to join in.

In the environmental movement the men found a potent combination of personal relationships and cultural ideals. Green politics engaged their lives at more than one level and met a variety of needs – for solidarity with others, for moral charity, for a sense of personal worth. This engagement was important in producing a gender politics. The movement had leverage, so to speak, on its participants' emotional life.

This can be seen in Barry Ryan's account of his initiation:

> So we travelled around, and I ended up in Tasmania. The Franklin River blockade was on down there. I was just going there for a couple of weeks; and I got there and I discovered all these wonderful people being extremely nice to each other, and having a good time, and doing something valuable, and learning so much. And I thought this is too good an opportunity to be missed, so I just stayed there . . .
>
> I stayed in Tasmania for about six months. Spent a lot of time in the bush, taking photos of dam works, did a bit of blockading [i.e., confronting construction workers and transport for the dam], a bit of work in the office, and it was just great. It was just the best time in my life . . .
>
> Discovered some really good ways of working in groups and having relationships. I had my first, what I thought were valuable, relationships with women there . . . Really nice relationships

because they were fairly self-aware people I think, and fairly confident in themselves – you had to be, to be involved in something
like that – and mostly they were older than me. . . . And after that
six months I'd had some really, really good friendships with women
as well as sexual relationships with women. And I started to discover
that most of my friendships were actually with women, and I was
less interested in friendships with men.

Of course other forms of political activism also engage emotions and meet a range of personal needs. The environmental
movement, however, did this in a way that posed a challenge to
hegemonic masculinity through its own ethos and organizational
practices.

This challenge was implicit in several of the movement's
themes, as they came out in the interviews:

(1) *A practice and ideology of equality*   The common sense of the
movement includes these principles: no one is supposed to be
boss; workplaces are run democratically; no group has rights over
others; decisions are made by consensus. There is a sharp critique
of hierarchy and authoritarianism.

(2) *Emphasis on collectivity and solidarity*   What Barry Ryan
called 'good ways of working in groups' at the Franklin River were
no accident. Bill Lindeman recalls how they were fostered:

I was working as a trainer on the non-violence workshops and that
meant that I was doing a lot of work with people in small groups.
And that was wonderful, it just opened up so much in terms of relat-
ing and feeling good about meeting people . . . creating the type
of workshops that we wanted. and just learning as a group, so fast.
There was nothing that we could take it from. We read all the
Gandhi books and the Movement for a New Society books from the
States, and we used that as a basis. But we had to adapt and develop
exercises and ways of working with people, facilitating people to
be effective individually and in groups for the situation, for the
blockade.

(3) *A practice and ideology of personal growth*   All six men saw
their involvement with environmental politics as part of their
growth towards being better, wiser people. With Peter Geddes and
Danny Taylor the search for personal growth was primary and
environmentalism grew out of it. The wider counter-culture pro-

vided techniques of meditation and personal development. An important technique is what Bill Lindeman called 'working on social relationships', through mutual critique and attempts to reform existing sexual, friendship and work relationships. Outside the furnace of environmental activism, this work merges into the group therapy, conferences and workshops that are the bread and butter of the growth movement.

(4) *An ideology of organic wholeness* This theme is widespread in the counter-culture, linked to its critique of alienating, mechanical Western civilization. For environmentalists it centres on the connection with nature. To Peter Geddes and Bill Lindeman especially, time spent by oneself in the bush means a transcendental experience. As Bill Lindeman put it:

> That experience of being alone, wandering round and doing things and appreciating things and enjoying a beautiful place can really give me a wonderfully clear, pure feeling.

Drugs would only cloud such an experience. Though all these men have used psychoactive drugs, most have given them up. Diet is an important part of the relationship with nature. Peter Geddes set up a health food shop; Danny Taylor certainly and others probably are vegetarian.

Even without feminism, these themes of Green politics and culture would provide some challenge to hegemonic masculinity, at least at the level of ideas. Dominance is contested by the commitment to equality and participatory democracy. Competitive individualism is contested by collective ways of working. Organic ideologies are not necessarily counter-sexist, as many counter-cultural women can testify, having been defined as Earth-Mothers and left with the babies and the washing-up. But the emphasis on personal growth tends to undermine the defensive style of hegemonic masculinity, especially its tight control over emotions.

The environmental movement, then, is fertile ground for a politics of masculinity. But it does not make an issue of gender, and produce an explicit masculinity politics, unaided. That requires the impact of feminism.

Encounters with Feminism

Most of the group first met feminism directly in the counter-culture or in environmental action groups. Barry Ryan was the exception. He learned about gender politics from a feminist mother and an anti-sexist course at school, which undermined his participation in adolescent peer masculinity. Nevertheless, even for him, it was environmental politics which produced the key encounter with feminist practice.

Given initial engagement with hegemonic masculinity, the encounter with feminism had to be stressful. Barry Ryan recalled reading feminist books:

> After university I was at the stage where I could understand academic literature, and I read some pretty heavy stuff, which made me feel terrible about being male for a long time. And I remember I found it really hard, because there was these conflicting needs. I needed sex and I needed relationships, and then again I needed to set aside my ideals [i.e., wishes] and my own sexism, and I couldn't reconcile those. And so I went through lots and lots of guilt.

Guilt is a key theme. Barry took feminism aboard as an accusation. The language for gender politics that he learned centred on the term 'sexism', by which he understood men's personal attitudes towards women. His task, in responding to feminism, was therefore to change his head, to adopt more supportive attitudes towards women, and to criticize other men's attitudes.

Barry's view of feminism was broadly shared by the other men in the group. Bill Lindeman, for instance, spoke of 'women feeling their strength' as feminists, becoming 'strong, independent, active'. Their attitude to feminism was highly positive, in contrast to the other groups in this research. Yet their understanding of feminism was limited.

This can be seen in Nigel Roberts's account of his experience of feminism. It was not very real, he recalls, until he started living with a feminist woman:

> Although I was conscious of it before that, just from doing a bit of reading, and thinking about it. Logically it just didn't seem reasonable that women who were human beings also had this role that was different and so less validated. It just didn't make sense. And so Kathy and I did things like swapping roles – she went out to work quite a lot of the time while I stayed home . . . and I'd do all the domestic things, which I really like doing. And so I learned it on a practical level. I just learned it through talking to people and through just common sense. You know, like I never accepted the

normal precepts of this society so I didn't have to fight them away.
. . . I learned feminism through practice, not through reading
about it, which probably makes it a lot more real and a lot more
relevant. And for me it was a big change to come in contact with
it because it made me realize there was another side to life. The
female side to life that I hadn't been experiencing, or taking into
account. [Which involves] giving to people, looking after people,
those sort of things.

This passage is typical of the men's talk about feminism and
sexual politics. They focus on expectations and attitudes, on personal styles and face-to-face interactions, with little attention to
economic inequality or institutionalized patriarchy, or to feminism as a political movement.

The Moment of Separation

Within its own sphere, however, this understanding of feminism
was a potent force. In combination with the ethos of environmental radicalism, and a variety of personal events, it was suffi-
cient to launch these men on a project of reform. The project
was to separate themselves from the mainstream masculinity
with which they were familiar, and to reconstruct personality to
produce a new, non-sexist self

Their sexual politics, with its theme of guilt about masculinity,
was part of a larger agenda of personal change. The idea of a new
self is not simply rhetoric. Three of the six were assailed by a sense
of personal crisis or worthlessness. Nigel Roberts, for instance, at
the age of twenty had a strong 'sense of failure in everything', in
education, family relationships, sex and politics. There was a
broad need to change a way of life.

This project is highly compatible with general ideas about
growth and personal change in the counter-culture, which often
require one to renounce straight society. In many parts of the
counter-culture the core of the new self is spiritual. There is often
an important relationship with a healer – for instance, a teacher
of yoga or an acupuncturist – a large number of whom are
women. The reform is totalizing; the new self is revealed in every
sphere of life. Everyday practice is expected to express an inner
reality, as Bill Lindeman explains:

I've changed in moral codes and ways of doing things and social attitudes and diet and things like that. As much as possible I want those changes to be coming from things that I feel. . . . I think it's important to be in touch with how my body – through diet, and exercises and clean air and that sort of stuff – What my body says to me about that.

What happens when this approach is used to reconstruct masculinity? The theme of renunciation is central. Peter Geddes gave up a successful career and pressured lifestyle at the age of thirty:

We walked out of the hotel at 9 o'clock in the morning and at 4 o'clock in the afternoon we were standing on a beach watching the plane taxi away. And my wife was wearing high heels and a suit, and we waved. We had a truck, and climbed into that, and drove to our little shack. We didn't have any electricity. And that was the beginning of a whole new world.

Less dramatic but also serious were renunciations of professional training or career openings by Bill Lindeman and Tim Marnier, and of qualifying for university by Nigel Roberts.

This has practical as well as symbolic consequences. Renouncing a career separates men from the masculinizing practices of conventional workplaces, discussed in Chapter 1. It results in a lower income, on which it is difficult to support a conventional family. Survival then depends on income-sharing practices in collective households. Renunciation also means giving up everyday masculine privileges and styles of interaction, for instance, by consciously trying not to dominate discussions and decisions.

Renunciation also has important consequences for sexuality and emotional expression. With the core of patriarchy perceived to be sexist attitudes and behaviours towards women, the main contribution a man can make is to hold back from any sexist action or utterance. Barry Ryan saw holding back as the core of his gender politics. It led to unexpected trials, when he found himself unable to establish sexual relationships at all.

Within a relationship, the strategy of renunciation means that men are likely to feel guilty about taking the initiative sexually, i.e., making another male demand upon a woman. Both Nigel Roberts and Barry Ryan were uncomfortable in sexual relationships until they met up with heterosexual feminist women who took the initiative and effectively controlled the relationship.

Nigel moved in with a woman all 'fire and energy' who managed to transmit a bit of decisiveness to him, giving him two days to decide whether to be involved in bringing up a baby.

The moment of separation from hegemonic masculinity basically involves choosing passivity. Since all these men were initially engaged with a masculinity defined by dominance and assertiveness, this choice is likely to be difficult. Danny Taylor, remarking about the 'long haul' of changing his own sexism, said, 'It's hard not to be aggressive sometimes'. At the same time, renunciation may express a deep-seated *wish* for passivity, normally repressed (indeed, furiously denied) in hegemonic masculinity, now surfacing again. There is something deeply problematic here, expressed in ambiguities of the actions. Peter Geddes's renunciation of his masculine career was a highly masculine act. Among other things, he did not tell his wife about it until after he had bought their farm. Renunciation can be conducted as an act of individual willpower, and this presupposes the masculine ego that the act is intended to deny.

Still, renunciation and denial are not the crux of the matter. They are intended to provide the space in which new personal qualities can grow. The six men were in close agreement about the qualities they admired and wished to develop.

Two are central. The first is the capacity to be expressive, to tell the truth, especially about feelings. Danny Taylor told a story to illustrate his openness:

> I'm much more open, and really very very honest. People are always telling me, 'you're very open, you're very disarming' . . . [About a new worker, an 'extrovert'] When she first came in I was a bit taken aback by this and I kept my distance. Everyone else got really sort of very chummy with her, and I didn't. And then I started to talk to her after she'd settled in a bit. And I was just really honest about how I felt that day, and what troubled me, and my problems and stuff like that – and my joys, too [laugh]. And, Jesus, she just came out with all her things, too. And it was really disarming for her because, like, I just cut through all this superficiality of mannerisms and stuff, and just went straight to the core, the soul. And now we have this relationship, she's closer to me than anybody else there.

The other quality most admired is the capacity to have feelings worth expressing: to be sensitive, to have depth in emotion, to care for people and for nature. The experience of solitude in the bush is one dimension of this. Caring about partners in political action, in households, in workplaces or in sex is another. The men's sharpest criticisms were of people who failed in this caring; who, for example, manipulated the collective processes of a workplace or a household to their own advantage.

These qualities of openness and caring are supposed to be put to work in new-model personal relationships. In the case of sexual and domestic relationships with women, this means being 'very careful' not to act oppressively, not to dominate the talk nor use sexist language. There was a common assumption in the interviews that men should adopt feminist good manners and tread cautiously when among women – which meant, given this milieu, most of the time.

More obviously troubling was the project of new-model relationships with men. Most of the six expressed a desire for better relationships with men, and most recorded difficulty in getting them. Bill Lindeman described some progress:

> I've always found it much easier to relate to women than to men. I couldn't just say 'OK, I'll start relating to men', because it just wasn't happening. So it meant a process for me, making choices to spend time, even though the time was initially less satisfactory. That's gone on over six months or a year. That has helped to change quite a lot, and I've got a lot more from my friendships with other men. Now my friendships with men are more important with me than friendships I have with women.
> *How have you changed your relationships with men?*
> Being able to be more – more open, more close, more trusting, more caring, more physically caring, touching and cuddling.

The classic barrier to friendships among heterosexual men is homophobia. All of the six were heterosexual, and a standard part of hegemonic heterosexuality in Australian culture is antagonism to gay men and fear of being called homosexual. Chapter 4 showed this playing out among working-class youth. Of the Green activists, three mentioned brief homosexual encounters, none with any enthusiasm and one with some distaste. Their political line was pro-gay and some described warm friendships with gay men, but several also showed a touch of homophobia. They had learned a feminism that directly challenged 'sexism' but gave no clear line on homosexuality among men. Their practice of change did not bring into question the heterosexual sensibility of their bodies. So they had no way of bringing into focus the difficulties involved in new-model relationships among men.

To the extent their project addressed the body, it was along the lines described by Bill Lindeman: allowing messages from the body to be heard, or treating the body better with healthy food and less stress. Though their attempt to reconstruct relationships could easily be seen as acquiring a kind of femininity, no side of their project addressed the issues explored in Chapter 2, the practices through which masculinity becomes embedded in the body.

Rather, the body was treated as a natural object and thought of as ideally harmonious with other parts of nature. The trick of speech which Bill Lindeman used, talking about 'my body' and 'me' as if two separate people were talking over a telephone line, is very significant. The reformed self is not understood as being embodied. At the same time, masculinity is separated out into social conventions, which can be discarded, and natural features of the body, which can not. The men were operating with a kind of sex role theory, which simply could not carry them very far.

The themes of openness and honesty involve yet another problem for men who adopt a principled passivity in relation to women. Honesty requires speaking bitterness at times, and anger is often generated by workplace relationships, sexual relations and tensions in the movement. No amount of feminist principle or communal feeling can prevent that. A double bind results, with the men pressed on one principle to express emotions and on another to suppress them.

The sense of impasse here is reinforced by the frozen time perspective in most of these interviews. Though the men were clear about the personal qualities they wished to develop, they had no comparable clarity about the future to which their reconstruction led. Renouncing straight careers had rubbed out conventional images of the life course, and nothing yet seemed to have taken their place.

The Annihilation of Masculinity

The moment of separation sometimes appears an act of pure will. The project of remaking the masculine self certainly, requires a good deal of willpower in the face of derision from other men, half-shared homophobia and ambivalence from feminists. More than willpower is involved, however. The project is embroiled with the relationships and emotions through which masculinity was initially formed. In these relationships and emotions are motives that support the new emotional work, and some reasons for its shape and limits.

In early childhood, all six men were mothered within a conventional gender division of labour, and we may infer a primal identification with the mother. All then went through (in different configurations) a process of Oedipal masculinization under the influence of fathers, brothers or symbolic patriarchy. In several cases there followed some distancing from hegemonic masculinity, through realliance with the mother or a recognition and admiration of women's strength. But in general, by late adolescence, most of these men seemed well on track for the production of hegemonic or at least complicit masculinities.

Instead, they all went through a project of reforming the self that was directed at undoing the effects of Oedipal masculinization. It seems likely that this project was supported by emotional currents from pre-Oedipal relationships: centrally, the prima relationship with the mother.

Direct evidence of such archaic levels in personality is difficult to obtain, but there were some very interesting indications in our interviews. For example, in the early stages of Peter Geddes's interview he gave a clear journalistic narrative, responding to questions and setting out a vivid, chronologically arranged story. In the second half of the interview, when he talked about his counter-cultural life and moved into an account of the reconstruction of the self, his style of speech changed. His talk now was unpunctuated with questions, unstructured by chronology, pursuing themes and associations in no obvious order, with ideas, events and commentary tumbling out together. If one follows Julia Kristeva's argument that separation from the mother and the advent of Oedipal castration awareness are connected with a particular phase in language, where subject and object are separated and propositions or judgements arise (the 'thetic' phase), Peter's shift in speech would make sense as the sign of an attempt to undo Oedipal masculinity.[4]

Most of the men embrace holistic philosophies as part of their counter-cultural or environmental outlook. An emphasis on undifferentiated wholeness, especially where it is linked to a passive-receptive attitude towards an embracing Nature, is so strongly reminiscent of primal relationships with the mother that the point is noted in counter-cultural literature itself. Bill Lindeman's 'wonderfully clear, pure feeling' of communion with nature is reminiscent of the 'oceanic' feeling that Freud suggested was derived from the earliest period of life.[5] A desire for passivity expressed in renunciation of masculine striving is also likely to be based in the pleasures of this relationship.

Similarly, the goal of openness, total honesty and emotional vulnerability is precisely about removing barriers, reversing separation and differentiation, re-establishing raw connection – that is, backtracking on steps by which Oedipal masculinity was formed. The urge to resolve the tensions of power and sexuality by forming a relationship with a strong woman who takes the initiative and supplies the energy also has unmistakable overtones of early relations with a mother.

In pointing to these links, I am emphatically not suggesting that environmental activism, or the project of reconstructing masculinity, means psychological regression. If anything, such connections are a measure of the seriousness of the project. These men are not day-trippers playing at being the Sensitive New Man. They are committed to a real and far-reaching politics of personality. What I am suggesting is that the specific form their project takes is supported by emotional responses deriving from archaic levels in personality.

These emotions, in adulthood, involve considerable risk. The project of having an open, non-assertive self risks having no self at all; it courts annihilation. 'I felt like I was losing my centre', said Nigel Roberts about his relationship with a feminist woman. Danny Taylor constructed a passive-dependent relationship with an admired woman that placed him in a position feminists have long criticized for women:

> I was really amazed that she liked me, and I guess I was like a bit of a lap dog for a while . . . I sort of identified myself with her, and all her achievements were my achievements, and her successes were all mine. I had none myself. I felt that I would just shrivel up and blow away once the relationship ended.

The relationship did indeed end with a messy separation, and lasting self-disgust on Danny's part.

The annihilation of masculinity was both a goal and a fear for these men. Oedipal masculinization structured the world and the self for them in gendered terms, as it does for most men. To undo masculinity is to court a loss of personality structure that may be quite terrifying: a kind of gender vertigo.

There are consequently strong motives to set limits to the loss of structure. Such limits are visible in the paradoxical assertion of the masculine self in the act of renunciation. They are also visible in the maintenance of a heterosexual sensibility and heterosexual object-choice.

Alternatively, gender vertigo may impel men to reach for other ways of structuring the world. Here, one of Freud's subtler points about Oedipal relationships is important. He observed that the 'complete' Oedipus complex involved the superimposition of two patterns of erotic attraction and fear. One led to identification with the father, the other to choice of the father as erotic object and to rivalry and identification with the mother.

We need not accept Freud's pan-sexualism to agree that power relations and emotional dependencies in the patriarchal family create the possibility of Oedipal identification with the mother, a pattern distinct from primal identification and playing a different role in gender politics. This is a gendered relationship, a highly structured one – and hence a possible answer to vertigo. It is likely to involve an experience of shared vulnerability rather than a sense of the mother's omnipotence, as emphasized in Karen Horney's and Dorothy Dinnerstein's accounts of primal identification.[6] It may mean rivalry with the mother for the father's affections rather than an easy solidarity with her. I observed earlier that Barry Ryan, in a crisis of family separation, went back to live with his father. In adulthood, Barry still sought his father's affection more than most men in the research.

Where it is present, Oedipal identification with the mother provides an emotional basis for handling the loss of structure in demasculinization. One can assert, with some conviction, solidarity with women and distance from men, especially from conventionally masculine men. These emotions were common in the interviews.

The evidence in these six cases is clear that this solidarity with women need not modulate into full-scale feminization. They are not on a transsexual track. Rather, Oedipal identification with the mother appears to coexist with Oedipal masculinization at an unconscious level as a contradiction within personality.

Adult gender politics activates this contradiction, especially around the theme of guilt. In classical psychoanalysis, guilt in men is thought to be closely connected with Oedipal masculinization, and identification with the father is the basis of the super-ego. In terms of this model, the material from at least two of our cases was paradoxical. There was plenty of guilt, but it was attached to fulfilling rather than transgressing the law of the father, Barry Ryan felt guilty simply about 'being male'. Bill Lindeman felt guilty about a particular episode of unequal attachment ('I used her', he said, in a phrase with a double meaning) and also about masculine aggression in general.

A major strand in feminist literature, which both Barry and Bill had been carefully reading in the early 1980s, presented a harsh view of men in its focus on sexual violence, pornography and war. I think that the wave of guilt each felt had to do with the contradiction between Oedipal masculinization and Oedipal identification with the mother, freshly activated by this political context.

Not all of the group reported massive feelings of guilt. Nigel Roberts, exposed to the same literature, responded more coolly. Indeed he criticized the effeminist reaction triggered by guilt:

> I think a lot of pro-feminist men are still into judging other men, the things they say and the way they behave, just like feminists do. When you find out about feminism, you tend to go through a period of not wanting to be a man and not liking other men, and just listening to women and wanting to be around them. And in a sense you still feel threatened by other men, and you sort of don't want them to be, as good at being a feminist as you are, kind of thing.

There is perhaps a specific reason why Nigel did not respond to feminism with guilt. His family, and his sex life in adolescence, muted the theme of gender difference. Any contradiction of identifications in his personality, therefore, would probably be weaker than for the others.

Rather, Nigel seemed disconcerted by feminism, as if he were somehow placed at a disadvantage. He acknowledged the facts of gender inequality and accepted the principle of gender equality. He went beyond that to a revalorization of 'the female side of life'. But he could not turn this response into a livable project. He fell out of control ('losing my centre'), or was in danger of it, so he avoided risk with feminist women. The annihilation of structure involved in the project of feminism for men (in which he had been engaged longer than any other in this group) seemed to have left him adrift or out of focus. He had not found a way of refocusing through identification either with women or with feminist men.

To sum up, the project of remaking masculinity can be emotionally configured in a number of ways. None of them appears well resolved or particularly stable. I think the reason is that these emotional dilemmas have no resolution at the level of personality alone. To pursue the reconstruction of gender any further requires a move to a new terrain, where the structural sources of emotional contradiction can be addressed directly. It requires a move towards collective practice.

The Moment of Contestation

There is a mis-match between the social character of gender issues and the individualized practices with which the counter-culture generally handles them. Therapeutic methods of reforming personality treat the individual as the unit to be reformed and propose more individuality as the way forward, searching for a 'trueself' or a 'real me'.

Given this focus, the project of remaking the self may represent containment, not revolution, in relation to the patriarchal gender order. Danny Taylor, for instance, was not ignorant of the facts of social and economic structure. He described them clearly, talking of women as 'the slaves of the slaves'. But it was change inside his head that he was working on, and nothing in that project must lead to a slave revolt. Danny might succeed in finding his new self, might create a masculinity that incorporated the considerateness for women, emotional openness and sexual passivity he sought. This masculinity could slot into a reconstituted patriarchal order, admittedly not as the hegemonic form, but in a well-recognized and secure subaltern position.

The political risk run by an individualized project of reforming masculinity is that it will ultimately help modernize patriarchy rather than abolish it. The Sensitive New Man is already a media figure, used by first-world advertisers in marketing clothes made by third-world women at rock-bottom wages.[7] A sense that the reform is just window-dressing has made many feminist women sceptical of feminist men.

Another stance seems to align men more closely with feminism: guilt, antagonism to men and complete subordination to the women's movement, a stance dubbed 'effeminism' in the 1970s.[8] This accepts the individualizing logic that locates the source of oppression in men's personal sexism, and offers a moral rather than a practical reform. Nigel Roberts's critique of effeminism was quoted above. He repeats the now conventional joke about how masculine it is to compete to be the best feminist. More profoundly, his comment points to the antagonism among men that undermines their response, where men's relationship to feminism is built on a moralized individualism.

Two of the six men took their political practice beyond remaking the self and blaming men. Barry Ryan was training as a nurse. In the hospital he met, as might be expected in an institution so emphatic about gender, a good deal of patriarchal ideology and practice.[9] He took some pleasure in subverting masculine convention just by being there. More important, he went on to some deliberate consciousness-raising in the workplace:

> My role very much at the moment, as a mature-age student, is that I'm organizing students and doing some teaching stuff there as well as you know, informal teaching. And I do things like point out to people the fact that men are talking more in the groups, and wonder why this is happening.

Barry felt that this collective work required him to halt the project of radical personal reconstruction. He was therefore willing to settle for a more moderate, livable feminism.

Bill Lindeman also put energy into reshaping his relationships with men, in a way that moved beyond individualism. He described his practice:

> Feeling a really strong energy to become involved with other men who were trying to change in the same way, so becoming involved in men's CR [consciousness-raising] groups and that sort of thing. Reading. There are a small number of books written by men for men, men with 'changing' issues. Reading a lot of feminist literature. I see feminism – and how I've encountered it with my relationships – as being a really powerful catalyst for me to change. [Pause] I've read lots and gained lots.

Bill attempted to combine a role in men's counter-sexist groups with environmental activism. He was trying to find other men with a similar combination of commitments, and get them to work with him on projects that would use photography and other art forms in the cause of change. But this was not easy:

> To get men from that sort of sentiment [i.e., wishing to change masculinity] who are also involved in Green issues . . . It's a really small pool of people that I feel really good about working with. So it feels a lot slower, there's a lot more blocks.

These two projects are obviously limited in scope. At the time of the interview, Barry Ryan was still in training for his job. Trying to influence a training programme from the position of a student, even a mature-age student, does not have great prospects. Bill Lindeman was trying something with larger possibilities, but he defined the people he could work with as those who were already members of two political movements at the same time. In consequence, his immediate field of action was narrow indeed.

But although these two initiatives were tentative and small-scale, they represented, in terms of their logic, a new moment in the project of change. Individualizing gestures, in which a man tries to separate himself from the project of masculinization, are transcended in the direction of political mobilization, a process in which a patriarchal social order is contested.

In later chapters I will look at other forms of contestation. These two cases are obviously a slender base on which to build. Yet I want to underline their conceptual importance, the transition they mark. Collective projects of transformation operate at the level of the social. They address the institutional order of society as well as the social organization of personality. They involve the creation of units larger than the individual life (from face-to-face work groups to social movements). In these respects, the moment of contestation is very different from the project of reconstructing the self.

I would also re-emphasize the way in which the environmental movement serves as midwife to gender politics. In this movement, substantial numbers of men commit themselves to collective processes that, partly because of the feminist presence in environmental action, provide social leverage' on conventional masculinities. These processes also offer highly relevant models of political practice, as shown in the Franklin Dam action.

Yet the cultural history of the environmental movement limits this transformation of masculinity even as it makes it possible. For the most part the environmental movement, like the counter-culture generally, tries to work on a non-gendered basis. It even tries to be degendering, to undo gender differentiation. Its commonest ideal is a fusion of feminine and masculine principles. Each of the six men in this study saw some kind of androgyny as their goal.

The problem is that a degendering practice in a still-patriarchal society can be demobilizing as well as progressive. A response that simply negates mainstream masculinity, that remains in the moment of rejection, does not necessarily move towards social transformation. To move further, in the face of the gender vertigo documented in this chapter, would seem to require a gendered counter-sexist politics for men who reject hegemonic masculinity. What this involves will be considered in Chapter 10.

6

A Very Straight Gay

No relationship among men in the contemporary Western world carries more symbolic freight than the one between straight and gay. This is a collective, not just a personal, relationship. It affects gender on a society-wide scale. This chapter explores its consequences for the formation of masculinity.

Patriarchal culture has a simple interpretation of gay men: they lack masculinity. This idea is expressed in an extraordinary variety of ways, ranging from stale humour of the limp-wrist, panty-waist variety, to sophisticated psychiatric investigations of the 'aetiology' of homosexuality in childhood. The interpretation is obviously linked to the assumption our culture generally makes about the mystery of sexuality, that opposites attract. If someone is attracted to the masculine, then that person must be feminine – if not in the body, then somehow in the mind.

These beliefs are not particularly coherent (for instance, they have difficulty with the fact that gay men are attracted to each other) but they are pervasive. Accordingly they create a dilemma about masculinity for men who are attracted to other men.

This dilemma has grown increasingly public with the emergence of gay communities in the rich countries during the 1970s and 1980s. Research in Britain, the United States, Canada and Australia has shown the historical roots of these communities, the more or less underground networks in earlier generations that provided support for some homosexual men. In the 1960s and early 1970s a dramatic change occurred. There was greater sexualization of the general culture; open challenges to orthodoxy by the Civil Rights movement in the United States, the New Left and the counter-culture; the advent of Women's Liberation; and the political mobilization of gay men and women in Gay Liberation.[1]

In the space opened by these movements, the gay settlements in certain urban areas (the most famous being those around Castro Street in San Francisco and Christopher Street in New York) grew and became institutionalized. They acquired a range of businesses (bars, shops, nightclubs, saunas) as well as political groupings (Gay Liberation, gay cultural politics, AIDS action groups). Being a homosexual man now could mean, and increasingly did mean, being affiliated with one of these gay communities.

It is not surprising that the social-scientific view of male homosexuality also changed. It moved away from the psychiatrists' preoccupation with aetiology and treatment, and from the sociologists' view of homosexuality as a form of 'deviance' to be listed alongside stuttering, alcoholism and cheque-forging. A social psychology now developed in the United States which saw homosexuality as an 'identity', and traced the steps by which this identity was built up and integrated into the self. This merged with a new approach in sociology which treated homosexuality as a 'subculture , sustained (like others in a pluralistic society) by socializing new members, and negotiating boundary relationships with mainstream society.[2]

These trends produced a more respectful account of male homosexuality than the hostile picture of twisted minds and furtive deviance that passed for science only thirty years ago. But the American focus on identity and subculture has drawn attention away from the politics of sexuality and gender. Whether the gay community is a site of subversion and cultural change, or gender conservatism, has been more debated in Britain. Gregg Blachford has argued that gay communities provide a certain resistance, but not a significant challenge, to the culture of male dominance in the society as a whole. Jeffrey Weeks, taking a post-structuralist view of social order, sees sexual subcultures as more diverse and having greater potential for change.[3]

These issues are far from settled, partly because of the HIV epidemic. For people simultaneously fending off a new wave of prejudice, dealing with AIDS illness and deaths, and mobilizing resources for care, treatment and prevention, theoretical questions about gender have not been high on the list. Yet these questions have not gone away; they are, indeed, very relevant to understanding the society's reponses to AIDS.

This chapter is based on interviews with eight men connected with the gay community in Sydney. Some other men in the research have had homosexual experience (including three of the men discussed in Chapter 5 and at least two of those in Chapter 4), but none of those were recruited from gay networks and only one has any connection to those networks (Paul Gray, who uses gay venues for safety when cross-dressing).

The eight are: Mark Richards (early 20s), a trainee nurse; Dean Carrington (mid-20s), a heavy vehicle driver; Alan Andrews (late 20s), a technician in an outdoor trade; Jonathan Hampden (late 20s), a tradesman's assistant; Damien Outhwaite (early 30s), unemployed, occasionally working as a taxi driver; Adam Singer (early 30s), professional in the city office of a large organization; Gordon Anderson (early 40s), a company manager; Gerry Lamont (late 40s), a professional in private practice.

Most have had some sexual relationships with women, though all but one currently focus on sex with men. Two have children, others think they might. Three come from the country (one from overseas), and their migration to the big city was connected with their entry into gay social networks. Most come from working-class backgrounds, and several have been upwardly mobile. One began in the world of privilege and went to an elite private school.

The Moment of Engagement

The older discourses of homosexuality were preoccupied with its origin. Richard von Krafft-Ebing, the founder of modern sexology, defined it as 'a sexual instinct . . . the exact opposite of that characteristic of the sex to which the individual belongs', and saw its main cause as hereditary degeneracy. Psychiatry in this century has presumed some abnormality in development as the cause, though debate has raged about what exactly the abnormality is. Orthodox psychoanalysts in the past blamed family pathology, distant fathers and seductive mothers. Recent opinion has been influenced by a San Francisco study by the Kinsey Institute which found little support for the seductive-mother/weak-father thesis, but found stories of gender nonconformity in childhood to be common among homosexual men.[4]

Neither view of origins throws light on the life-histories in this study. All the men in the group grew up in families with a conventional division of labour and a conventional power structure. Dean Carrington jokingly refers to his father as a 'Victorian male';

half the fathers took dominance as far as violence towards their wives. The mothers worked as housewives and child carers, a few having paid jobs from time to time. The family constellations, in brief, fell within the range of what was numerically normal or socially conventional in Australia in the 1950s and 1960s.[5]

Nor was there much gender nonconformity for the boys. These conventional family settings were the sites of masculinizing practices exactly parallel to those in the heterosexual life-histories. Their mothers put them in pants rather than skirts, their fathers taught them football, they learned sexual difference. Moving out of the family they were inducted into the usual sex-typed peer groups, received the usual sexist informal sex education, and were subjected to the gender dichotomies that pervade school life. Mark Richards got mixed up with a tough peer group and minor crime, Jonathan Hampden became a football player, Gerry Lamont faced down his drunken father when he was roughing up Gerry's mother.

Moving into the workforce, most remained socially masculinized. Jonathan Hampden, for instance, is working comfortably in a male-dominated manual trade. Dean Carrington, whose affectionate joke about his 'Victorian male' father was quoted above, works as a driver of heavy vehicles. Regardless of his sexual preference for men, he continues to define masculinity as sexual agency, as taking an active and directing part. Gordon Anderson runs his office on conventional boss/secretary lines and shows the controlled, authoritative manner that goes with the well-cut mid-grey suit he was wearing when interviewed. Gordon is a skilful business tactician and a knowledgeable commentator on politics.

There is, then, a moment of engagement with hegemonic masculinity in these lives, as there was for the environmentalists discussed in Chapter 5. That is, after all, to be expected from the hegemony of the dominant pattern: it impacts on all others.

But as we saw with some of the family dynamics in Chapter 5, the relationships through which gender is constructed contain other possibilities. Families are not fixed, mechanical systems. They are fields of relationship within which gender is negotiated. Their configurations often change over time, as alliances form and dissolve and people enter and leave.

Given households with a conventional division of labour, boys' relations with mothers and sisters are both their primary means of marking sexual difference, *and* sources of alternatives to identification with the father. The conventional structure of the patriarchal household necessarily opens up a range of possibilities in emotional relations and in the construction of gender.

So we find, in Jonathan Hampden's case, a powerful identification with his father, but also a distinct identification with his elder sister. This relationship developed as his father's affection was withdrawn. At a later stage again, Jonathan's relation with his sister was vehemently repudiated. Alan Andrews, a country boy like Damien Outhwaite, was always closer to his mother, had mainly girls as friends in childhood, and has generally admired and felt close to women. Alan had to be pushed out of the nest by his mother. Damien dodged his mother's control and escaped to the city; but he too has kept emotionally linked with her.

On a wider stage, the insistently masculinized public culture – in peer groups, schools, workplaces, sporting organizations, media – sustains conventional definitions of gender. But its very insistence cues young people to use gender as an issue for resistance to adults and established authority.

Resistance may mean seizing on a hyper-masculine persona, which Jonathan Hampden did as a teenager: smoking, fighting and resisting his ruling-class school like several of the working-class youth discussed in Chapter 4. But resistance may equally mean doing something outrageously unmasculine. Two of the group at the end of adolescence did just that. Damien Outhwaite, moving from a stifling rural background to college in the city, broke out by dyeing his hair, wearing hipster jeans, putting on nail-polish and taking up knitting. Mark Richards, uncontrollable and hostile as a teenager, reversed gears as a young adult and became a nurse.

The moment of engagement, then, has its complexities. Some engagement with hegemonic masculinity is found in each of these lives. It ranges from heavy commitment to wistful fantasy, but it is always there. In no sense is their homosexuality built on a lack, a gender vacuum. Yet the construction of masculinity occurs through relationships that are far from monolithic. The gender dynamic is both powerful and sufficiently complex and contradictory to be inflected in different ways. In these men's lives, the decisive inflection generally followed from a sexual experience – the discovery of sexuality, or a discovery in sexuality.

The Grain of Sand: Sexuality

For more than half the group, their first major sexual relationships were heterosexual. Two have been married and have children, others have been close to marriage. Dean Carrington's first
was 'a beautiful relationship and we're still good friends', with
good sex and mutual caring. The couple, he reflects, could easily
have got married. For Alan Andrews, growing up in the country,
sexuality was effectively defined as relationship with a girl. His
mother and his peer group put pressure on him to find a girlfriend. His mates tried to organize one for him. He tells a comic
tale about being pushed into the girls' tent, one night when the
peer group was out in the bush camping, and grabbing the wrong
girl. Compulsory heterosexuality was, as we have seen in other
groups, a taken-for-granted part of growing up.

> There was a lot of pressure on boys at the age of 16 or 17 to not
> be virgins, and I was a virgin. So I always thought it will be really
> good when I meet the right girl. But it happened to be a boy.

As Alan implies, public discourse takes heterosexuality for
granted. But compulsory heterosexuality was not necessarily
realized in practice. The narratives describe childhoods with
both cross-gender and same-gender experiences.

Adam Singer recalls being 'very sexual from as young as I can
remember'. He gives circumstantial detail of sex games with peers
of both genders in primary and secondary school, including a
delightful vignette of the 'nudist colony' set up by primary school
boys in the bush just beyond the school fence. Jonathan
Hampden likewise recalls childhood sex play with both genders,
though less idyllic. He was caught playing with the girl next door,
aged seven. Later, into 'gang bangs' (probably meaning mutual
masturbation) with boys, he became aware of the prohibition on
homosexuality and developed guilt feelings. In one case sexual
initiation in childhood was with an adult woman, a relative, with
great emotional turmoil resulting.

Such experience of childhood sex with partners of both
genders is found in life-histories of heterosexual as well as homosexual adults. Early sexual contact with boys or men does not in
itself prevent heterosexuality. There is survey evidence from other
countries that many more men have had same-sex contact in their

A lesson in imagery. The contemporary mythopoetic men's movement honours the 'hairy man' as an archetype of the deep masculine. In other parts of the world this image has a very different significance. This is a Chinese image of a European sailor, from the 1850s, during the long and painful process by which Western commerce and culture, not to mention opium, were forced on the Chinese. It is called 'Old Hairy One'. (Source: Hulton Deutsch Collection, London)

Masculinity as cultural process. Without mentioning gender, this advertisement calls on the imagery of a masculinized 'sport' (drag racing) to sell its hardware. In doing so, it defines personal computing as a domain of masculine power, linking unheroic office work to a remembered/imagined world of danger, speed and noise. (Source: Seiko Epson Corporation © 1992 Epson America Inc.)

bring out the male
in your man

THE ROYAL ARCADE
SYDNEY'S LEADING
MENSWEAR CENTRE

between
Pitt and George Streets,
under
the Sydney Hilton Hotel

STYLE IS NEVER OUT OF FASHION

BOSS
HUGO BOSS

Semiotics of masculinity. Creation of advertising images of hegemonic masculinity runs into a contradiction: narcissistic pleasure in display violates the code being appealed to. These advertisements show two solutions. Left, forbidding, self-contained power is emphasized by a literal multiplication of the images. Right, the code is gently spoofed, and the artificiality of the image emphasized. (Sources: advertisements in Air Canada in-flight magazine and advertising supplement to *Sydney Morning Herald*, 1987)

The masculine state. The public arena is symbolically defined as a space for hegemonic masculinity; real spaces are occupied by real men. This occasion is a moment of patriarchal succession, 20 January 1953. The former general Dwight Eisenhower is sworn in as US President, in the presence (among other men) of Harry Truman and Richard Nixon. (Source: Associated Press Ltd. London)

Girls love it

They love it because Plessey make it enjoyable. The very latest in up-market, high-tech, advanced business telephone systems make the telephone receptionist's job a dream.

Are you ready for tomorrow's telephone system? They are. Talk about the future and you're talking about Plessey. Be connected to the future with a tailor-made system, call Plessey NOW.
Syd: 808 3322, Melb: 320 4333, Bris: 854 1300, Adel: 42 6241, Perth: 368 2966.

PLESSEY
Connecting the future
WOSD120·IS

Available now

Constructing difference. The two office workers shown are doing the same thing, speaking on the telephone; but they are presented very differently. Apart from clothing, make-up, moustache, hair-do and lack of nose, the female worker is called a 'girl', and the male worker is shown holding the phone with a firm, regular grip. There is no doubt which is in control. (Source: advertisement in *Sydney Morning Herald*, 21 August 1986)

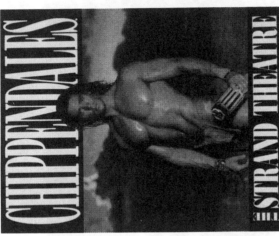

Hegemonic masculinity as object of desire. Advertisement for a male striptease show, aimed at heterosexual women, but the image is close to many in gay men's erotica also. The accessories are meant to suggest primitivism, but it is clearly understood that this is the controlled kind familiar in tourist packages. (Source: Chippendales World Theatre Show, for ladies only)

Working-class masculinity as exemplary. The toughness and bravery of the linemen is used as a symbol of the corporation's commitment to service. (Source: *Collier's*, 15 January 1949)

C. v. d. Haardt
Der Marsch
ins
Dritte Reich

Masculinity politics from the right. One of a genre of propaganda images from the Nazis' rise to power presenting fascism as an exemplary form of hegemonic masculinity. The anonymous and almost identical stormtroopers are presented as warriors, some already injured in the battle. Hitler (who was in fact a highly decorated war veteran) is part warrior, part prophet. The bottom right-hand corner shows hegemony at work, as sinister figures representing cowardice and corruption (Jews, communists, etc.) cringe. (Source: Weimar Archive)

Frontier imagery. Curious that 'the way ahead' for the Australian bicentennial should be an image so firmly located in the colonial past, the white stockman on his working horse. The checked shirt is an American improvement, however – just as 'country' music in Australia now draws its inspiration from Nashville, not Oodnadatta. (Source: Australian Bicentennial Authority, *Bicentenary '88*, October 1986)

Hegemonic masculinity and the military. Fantasy image of the soldier from a Great War recruiting poster. (Source: postcard published by Schellmark Inc., reproduced from a collection of Meehan military posters, New York)

Playing with the elements of gender. Halloween on Haight Street, San Francisco. The conventions of femininity combine with male bodies in a way that spoofs gender distinction itself. (Source: postcard published by The Bowler Hat, San Francisco)

Recomposing gender. An example of the images emphasizing the pleasure of men with babies. It seems that this father has not been wholly swept up in the oceanic feeling, however; he still wears his watch. (Source: © Noel Butcher 1985/*Melbourne Herald*/'Hot day, cool dip')

youth than the number who become wholly or mainly homosexual. Young people's sexuality is a field of possibilities, not a deterministic system. Freud pointed to free-form childhood sexuality (his famous joke about the 'polymorphously perverse disposition' of the child), but located it only in early childhood. Cases such as Adam Singer and Jonathan Hampden show polymorphous sexuality extending up to, and well into, adolescence.[6]

Adult homosexuality, like adult heterosexuality, is a closure of this field. It is something that happens, that is produced by specific practices, not something predetermined. The sexual closure involves choice of an object. This focusing can be traced in some, though not all, of the interviews.

With Mark Richards, a period of severe early-adolescent unhappiness and rejection of authority was resolved, when he was sent to an all-boys boarding school, by falling in love with a classmate. He calls it 'a classic boarding-house story . . . a very close friendship and on top of that . . . quite a strong sexual relationship as well.' It was furtive, but full on:

> We didn't get caught – and where we didn't do it! I mean, under the Assembly Hall, and under the stairs. He took up music lessons just because I was taking music lessons, we'd go out on the same days . . .
>
> *Did people in the school know about it?*
> Oh God no. No. Absolutely not. I don't know how, but no.

From then on, Mark's choice of men as erotic objects has never been in doubt.

This is not a fetishistic fixation on a particular feature of the object. Rather it is a consolidation of Mark's sexual practice around the relationship, creating a structure which Mark transferred as a whole to later attachments. Mark's sex life has, accordingly, been conducted through several relatively long-term relationships. He rejects fast-lane sexuality and speaks with heavy irony of the 'wonderful' effects of AIDS, 'stop everyone fucking around everywhere'.

Sexual closure can happen, and in Mark's case did, without any reference to homosexual identity or any social definition as gay. The relationship itself was the basis. Adam Singer's sexuality, free-form to an extreme in childhood, also consolidated around emotional relationships, not excluding relations with women but placing much more emphasis on men. In high school Adam became sexually aware of the masculine aura of senior students: 'they were students just like me, but their maleness was very, very strong'. As an adult he can express his desire, facetiously but effectively: 'A big muscley man who I feel I can cuddle up to, and I love being nurtured.' The choice of an object here is defined through a contradictory gender imagery ('muscley'/'nurtured'), and this contradiction is not abstract hut embodied. By comparison the image of the 'right woman', with whom Adam intends some day to have children, is shadowy.

The social process here cannot be captured by notions of 'homosexual identity' or a 'homosexual role'. As in the heterosexual cases discussed in Chapter 2, both sexual practice and sexual imagery concern gendered bodies. What happens is the giving and receiving of bodily pleasures. The social process is conducted mainly through touch. Yet it is unquestionably a *social* process, an interpersonal practice governed by the large-scale structure of gender.

A similar pattern is evoked by Dean Carrington, who has also had relationships with both men and women. When asked about the difference he gave a notable answer focused on bodily sensation, worth examining in detail:

> In the traditional sense it's been the same. I mean anal sex, or anything else: kissing, touching, sucking, licking, the whole works has been the same physically. But I've decided to think perhaps how much more exciting it is with a man. Because I know I can stimulate a man. I know how I like to be stimulated. And that's good, it's fantastic, I'm actually relating more. Whereas my lover Betty never would say. She loved everything but she wouldn't point out one thing and say 'I'd like you to do it this way, I'd like you to put pressure on, or do a certain thing, or wear certain clothes' . . .
>
> I feel I can relate more to a man because his body's the same as mine . . . having sex with a man, I'm able to find out how I feel better . . . I'm actually finding out more about my body . . . I've developed two breasts, I know what they're like, these two tits there: they're not very big, they're very flat, but they're beautiful. And I've missed out on so many things. Such a shame, such a bloody waste.

Dean's answer rocks back and forth across the terrain of similarity and difference. It is plain that he experiences no categorical difference between the sexes in their erotic qualities, and does not engage in different practices with them. His answer accords with survey findings about the sexual repertoire among gay and bisexual men in Sydney.[7] The commonest practices in male-to-male sex in this culture (kissing, erotic hugging, etc.) are also common in female-to-male sex. What is different with a man, Dean makes clear, is the *Gestalt* of the body: a configuration whose similarity is both disturbing and reassuring. The similarity allows exploration of another's body to be a means of exploring one's own.

Being Gay: Identity and Relationships

A gendered sexuality, such evidence implies, is likely to be a gradual and provisional construction. But the social identity of being gay is another matter. The category is now so well formed and readily available that it can be imposed on people whether they like it or not. Damien Outhwaite as a late-adolescent rebel experienced this at a time when he was still actively interested in women:

> There was one guy at college that immediately identified me as being gay, and he used to give me a bit of a hassle about it . . . used to identify things I would do to being gay. One of the things was that I was one of the first to wear hipster jeans when they came in – he thought of that as being gay. And the other thing that I did was that I used to carry my books around in a shoulder bag – he thought that was particularly gay too.

In due course Damien embraced this definition of himself, and was confirmed in it by oppression – losing two jobs – and by his increasing involvement in gay social networks.

Gayness is now so reified that it is easy for men to experience the process of adopting this social definition as discovering a truth about themselves. Gordon Anderson speaks of having 'realized' he was gay; Alan Andrews uses the same word.

Alan offers a classic coming-out narrative passing through six stages. *Prehistory*: growing up in a country town; a relaxed, conservative family; no particular tensions. *Preparation*: adolescent uncertainties – liking to be with girls, but not getting a girlfriend; sex play with a boy friend, who backs off. *Contact*: aged 19, he stumbles across a beat (a venue for semi-public encounters, like the American 'tea-room') and has sex with men. Then he goes looking for beats, gets better at it, has a 'wonderful' sex-laden beach holiday. *Acknowledgement*: aged twenty, 'I finally came to the conclusion I was gay, and I went to my first gay dance.' *Immersion*: does the bars under his own steam, has multiple relationships. *Consolidation*: aged 22, meets Mr Right, and settles into a couple relationship; gets more gay male friends, joins some gay organizations and comes out to his parents.

It all sounds very neat, and rather like the stage models of 'homosexual identity formation' devised by social psychologists. But the neatness of the sequence is deceptive, and the outcome is not the homogeneous identity implied by the ego-psychology on which those stage models depend.

Alan's first sexual experiences on the beat were disappointing. It took time for him to become skilled and gain much pleasure. When he hit the bar scene in Sydney – 'notoriously antisocial . . . very cold places' – he was exploited. A big, handsome, slow-talking country boy, he must have been something of a phenomenon around the Sydney bars, and did not lack partners. He was looking for love and affection but his partners wanted sex. He feels he was 'raped' by a couple, 'I was forced into anal sex by them.' He became critical of gay studs, interpreting their sexual expertise as over-compensation for insecurity. He learned to dissemble in heterosexual groups, to flirt surreptitiously. Coming out to his parents was hard, and not a success. His mother was upset and his father refused to talk. Both did their best to keep Alan's younger brother away from him, lest the corruption be passed on. Alan is not so hostile to them that this can pass without hurt.

In a story like this, 'coming out' actually means coming *in* to an already-constituted gay milieu. There has been debate among gay theoreticians, especially those influenced by Foucault, about the collective identity sustained in this milieu: whether it is a means of social regulation and thus, ultimately, oppression.[8] Certainly Damien Outhwaite's experience, accused of gayness because of his jeans and his bag, could be read that way. So, more subtly, could Alan Andrews's passage through beats and bars. Mark Richards distances himself from the fast-track lifestyle and the gay subculture, from effeminates and leathermen alike. This too could be read as a critique of the internal conformities of the gay world.

But there is no doubt that Damien, Alan and Mark also experienced their gay sexuality as freedom, as die capacity to do what they really wanted to do. This cannot be dismissed as false consciousness. Dean Carrington most vividly expresses the element of festival in coming out:

> Rage, rage, rage! Let's do everything you've denied yourself for 25 years. Let's get into it and have a good time sexually. And go out partying and dancing and drinking.

This was a key part of the original experience of Gay Liberation. It remains a post-AIDS presence, as shown by the continuing success of the Lesbian and Gay Mardi Gras festival – always one of the largest popular gatherings in Sydney's year. For Gordon Anderson, who remains closeted for powerful reasons (he would certainly lose his job, and probably lose access to his children, if he came out), gay sexuality and friendship networks are less flamboyant. But they are still experienced as a realm of freedom and pleasure outside the severe constraints of the other departments of his life.

Sexual freedom, 'partying' or 'kicking up one's heels' (Gordon Anderson's phrase), important as it is, does not define the kind of connection most wished for. Adam Singer calls his first sexual experience with a man 'not a relationship, but a sexual encounter'. Most of the others subscribe to this distinction and agree with Adam that they value the 'relationship' far more.

Their shared ideal is a long-term couple relationship, perhaps open to casual sex as well, but with emphasis on a primary commitment. What they value in it is both the sexual pleasure and the 'honesty . . . caring and sharing and learning from each other', in Alan Andrew's words. Others mention mutual involvement of emotions, common interests and just sitting down and listening as components of relationships that work.

How does the wish translate into practice? This is the most difficult part of the interview material to report, as it was the most difficult for some participants to talk about. Three of the group are currently living with male lovers in long-term relationships, which in one case has been going 11 years. Of these relationships the most troubled seems to be the one with the largest age difference, where mutuality is perhaps the hardest to achieve.

Three others are consciously in search of long-term relationships, whether rekindling an old flame or finding a new partner. In the meantime they are making do with 'encounters' or just waiting, as one of them put it, for the drought to break. Another has been involved mainly in short-term encounters with men (longer-term with women) and is now worrying about the ethics of such encounters. For only one of the eight is the emotional emphasis definitely on casual encounters. He is trying to weave together a mainly gay erotic life with a continuing domestic relationship with the mother of his children.

The preferred pattern, as in the heterosexual world these men know, is a committed long-term couple relationship. But such relationships are not easily come by. Casual encounters at beats or bars remain an important part of total experience. All the eight have had short-term encounters. For some this was the path into gay sexuality, and 'encounters' remain a significant possibility even after couple relationships are established.

Most of these men have had sexual relations with women as well as men. They are technically bisexual. But only Jonathan Hampden claims that as his sexual identity, and he immediately qualifies it: 'bisexual with a preference' [for men]. Gerry Lamont toys with the term 'bisexual', but for him it is mainly a way of refusing an identity as gay, from which he has always held back. He equates being gay with being out of control.

At this time and place there is do positive social category of the bisexual, no well-defined intermediate identity that the men can take up. Rather, bisexuality is experienced as an alternation between heterosexual and homosexual connections, or as a standing arrangement that fits them together by subordinating one to the other. In other cultures there are better-defined intermediate positions.[9] But it seems broadly true of contemporary European/American society that sexual preference is dichotomized and bisexuality is unstable.

Relations between Masculinities

As Chapter 3 argued, a specific masculinity is constituted in relation to other masculinities and to the structure of gender relations as a whole. These relations are not just definitions of difference, but involve material practices. Historically the relation between hegemonic and homosexual masculinity has involved the criminalization of male-to-male sex, as well as intimidation and violence outside the law.

At the time and place I wrote the first draft of this chapter (Sydney, 1991) a group of high school youths had recently been convicted for battering a gay man to death in an inner-city park, after luring him there by telephone. As David McMaster points out in his analysis of this attack, to beat someone to death is not easy; in this case it involved stomping on the head, jumping on the genitals, and snapping the ribs by dropping on the torso with the full weight of the attacker's body. Attacks on gays are common enough to have become an issue in Sydney's urban politics. The depth of homophobia in this inner-city youth culture is documented in James Walker's ethnographic research.[10]

None of the men interviewed in this study had been bashed, but some had been intimidated. Their conversation takes for granted that they live in a homophobic environment. Damien Outhwaite lost jobs. Adam Singer stuck with a career that did not much interest him, partly because it was a safe milieu for a gay man. Gordon Anderson stays in the closet for fear of losing job and children:

> I don't want to stop what I am doing, I don't want to stop being a good father, I can never see myself being very prominent about my lifestyle. That's the price I suppose.

Gordon gives a nice description of how the illusion of heterosexual masculinity is sustained when visiting businessmen have to be entertained. He has female friends who will come to his apartment and act as hostess, though the illusion wears thin when they have to ask where the pepper is kept.

Heterosexual masculinity, then, is encountered in the form of everyday relations with straight men that often have an undercurrent of threat. Wariness, controlled disclosure and turning inward to a gay network are familiar responses. But this does not necessarily mean conceding legitimacy. Straight men may also be seen as the pathetic bearers of outmoded ideas and a boring way of life. Dean Carrington went back to the country town of his childhood:

> I've seen friends, like a chap I went to school with . . . He's now 25, third child, and he's stuck in a rut, I went back to see him. I did

one of those terrible things of going back to your home town; and God, what an eye-opener! There's all these people grown up, and I hadn't got married and they had. They'd 'done the right thing', in inverted commas.

Alan Andrews had the same kind of reaction, watching his heterosexual brother's evolution into a drunken boor. Compared with this image, gay masculinity is all sophistication and modernity. Negotiating the relation with heterosexuality is then a question of establishing cultural, and often physical, distance.

Personal relationships do not exhaust the relation between masculinities. Hegemonic masculinity is also encountered as an institutional and cultural presence in collective practices. The football cult in Jonathan Hampden's school is a clear example, sustained by school policy and institutionalizing bodily confrontation and aggression. Masculinized authority in workplaces was a source of friction for Damien Outhwaite and Mark Richards. Adam Singer and Gerry Lamont distanced themselves from their masculinized professions.

Yet hegemonic masculinity has social authority, and is not easy to challenge openly. One of the effects of hegemony is to shape perceptions of gayness. Gordon Anderson, committed to his strategy of evasion, is critical of men who 'flaunt' their gayness – which he sees as characteristic of Australian gays. (But the same criticism is made by 'suburban homosexuals' in the United States.)[11] Adam Singer, Damien Outhwaite and Mark Richards all reject hyper-masculinity, but also express distaste for queens, i.e., effeminate gays. Mark puts the issue succinctly:

If you're a guy why don't you just act like a guy? You're not a female, don't act like one. That's a fairly strong point. And leather and all this other jazz, I just don't understand it I suppose. That's all there is to it. I am a very straight gay.

The sexual/cultural dynamic Mark names here is important. The choice of a man as sexual object is not just the choice of a-body-with-penis, it is the choice of embodied-masculinity. The cultural meanings of masculinity are, generally, part of the package. Most gays are in this sense 'very straight'. It is not just a question of middle-class respectability. Similar positions were taken by working-class men outside the gay community, in a study in the same state done shortly after this one.[12]

But from the point of view of hegemonic masculinity, the straightness is completely subverted by the wrong object-choice. Hence the common heterosexual stereotype of gays as all limp-wristed queens. This subversion is a structural feature of homo-sexuality in a patriarchal society; it is independent of the personal style or identity of gays like Mark. Hence those gay theorists who see a necessary effeminacy in homosexuality also have a point, if not quite in the way they intend. And if so, the accomplishment of a gay masculinity on Mark Richards's lines, which is at least common and perhaps predominant among urban gay men at present, cannot be stable.[13]

Facing Change

Change is a central theme of the life stories, in the specific form of movement between milieux. For several the big shift was from country conservatism to city lights. Dean Carrington's story of his boyhood friends who had 'done the right thing' is about small-town life as well as masculinity. Dean moved to Sydney and imme-diately began to have sex with men, to come out as gay, and to rage' around the bars and nightclubs. For others, the movement was within the city, but between milieux still quite distinct – the bour-geois school vs. the radical household (Mark Richards), the busi-ness workplace vs. the gay social network (Gordon Anderson), the professional career vs. the growth movement (Gerry Lamont).

The process of coming out, of establishing oneself as homo-sexual in a homophobic world, almost necessarily gives this struc-ture to the narratives. The life-history is experienced as migration, as a journey from another place to where one now is. Contrary to the arguments that see homosexual identity as regulation, I would emphasize the agency involved in this journeying. Dean Carrington pictures it as both escape and self-exploration:

> And this is one of the big things that led to me coming [to Sydney], to be able to get away from my parents, to think, and to find out who I really am, and what I really want, and why I was doing these things over the years, why I was changing, what was I hiding from.

Contrary to the traditional psychiatric belief in disordered rela-tions with parents, the majority of these cases show a firm ego-development which allows separation without rejection. Most have maintained as good relations with their parents as the parents would allow.

The desire for personal change that is clear in Dean Carrington's statement may lead to a deliberate reform of masculinity, of the kind discussed in Chapter 5. Damien Outhwaite has gone farthest down this track. He is working to overcome his 'competitiveness' and dominance. He has been to a counter-sexist men's movement event, and wants to pursue the issue of non-sexual physical closeness between men. Jonathan Hampden, despite an uncontrollable distaste for vagan coffee, has been living in a vegetarian household, has done 'rebirthing' therapy, and now has the 'dream' of setting up a centre for workshops on sexuality.

A demand for change in masculinity does not require the counter-culture to support it. One of the most dramatic moments in Jonathan Hampden's story was when his father, the high-powered professional whose emotional withdrawal from the family had influenced Jonathan's development, called a family conference:

> He sat down and said, 'What have I been doing wrong?' He was open to it for the first time, he actually really exposed himself and said, 'What have I been doing wrong? I obviously haven't been doing the right thing. I thought by working hard and supplying everything you would get everything that you need.' And my sisters and my mother just went [for him]. I just had to get out, because I knew the man, and I knew what he was feeling. And he was such a proud man and I couldn't watch it, just being torn to pieces you know. And they just laid it on straight and said, 'Look, for years we have been telling you, we don't want your money, all we want is you.' And finally it gelled, it got to him . . . and he just said he felt so bad about it, he just wanted to give it away, we couldn't believe it.

A year later he died of a heart attack. Jonathan thinks it may have been the first intimations of heart trouble that brought on the crisis about masculinity.

If Jonathan is right, then it took the threat of death, plus heavy pressure from women (not from Jonathan, who 'had to get out'), to crack the defences of hegemonic masculinity in Mr Hampden's life. In most men's lives that combination is not available, and there is less sense of urgency. Nevertheless many feel some need for change, and it is widely believed that sexual difference is in any case being reduced, that men are getting closer to women or more like them.

Damien Outhwaite suggests such a change within gay masculinity too, through the story of a party held by a young gay man in a provincial city. He invited some women, and when they arrived, the older gay men at the party left. Their social network excluded women and their outlook was misogynist – but this was not true for the younger men. Consistent with this, the three youngest among the group interviewed, Mark Richards, Dean Carrington and Alan Andrews, are those who most value and put most energy into their friendships with women.

Yet this consciousness of change has few political effects. The watering down of Gay Liberation politics into an affirmation of gay identity and a consolidation of gay communities, as Dennis Altman argued for the United States, has had a containing effect.[14] The men in this group have little sense of being connected to a broad movement of reform. So far as they have any commitment to a practice beyond the self, it is a therapeutic practice (Gerry Lamont's workshops, Jonathan Hampden's sexuality centre) assisting other men to pursue individualized projects of reform.

The absence of political consciousness is well shown by the group's stance towards feminism. Their usual position is to express some support for feminism, but to qualify it by disapproving of Those Who Go Too Far:

> I can't stand the butch dykes [who think] that males are shits. (Mark Richards)

> I have never had a personal conflict about it. I don't like extremisms of anything – the burn-bra thing sort of went over my head. (Gordon Anderson)

The attitude – and the level of ignorance about feminism – matches the most common view of feminism among the heterosexual men interviewed.

Gay Masculinity as Project and History

Familiar interpretations of homosexuality, both the traditional schema of 'normal/deviant' and the newer schema of 'dominant

culture/subculture', appear monolithic when confronted with
the realities of these men's lives. Their sexualities emerged from
many-sided negotiations in multiple arenas: emotional relations
in home and sexual marketplace; economic and workplace relations; authority relations and friendships. The pressures in these
relationships often pushed in different directions; and they are
linked in varying sequences.

To emphasize this complexity is not to deny the significance of
social structure, nor to say we cannot see a shape in what is hap-
pening. The same logical moments appear, despite the variety of
detail, in all these narratives. They are (a) an engagement with
hegemonic masculinity, (b) a closure of sexuality around relationships with men, (c) participation in the collective practices of
a gay community.

I am not offering these points as a new general model of homosexual identity formation. There is no general homosexual identity, any more than there is a general heterosexual identity. Many
men who have sex with men never enter a gay community. Some
men who do, have significant further moments in the construction of their sexuality – such as the 'leather and all this other jazz'
mentioned by Mark Richards.[15]

Rather, these moments define the project that can be documented in this specific setting, the making of a homosexual
masculinity as a historically realized configuration of practice.
They are comparable with the moments in the reconstruction of
heterosexual masculinities explored in Chapter 5, and indeed
share the same starting-point.

It is not any one of these three moments that defines the
project, but their interconnection. The closure of the sexual field
around relationships with other men has the character it does
because of their prior engagement, however limited, with hegemonic masculinity. Gay men are not free to invent new objects of
desire any more than heterosexual men are. Their desire is structured by the existing gender order. Adam Singer cathects not
a male body but a masculine body doing feminine things. Dean
Carrington's eroticism revolves around bodily similarity read in
gender terms (i.e., not in any of the other ways one could read
bodily difference and similarity; note his attention to breasts, a
major gender symbol in our culture). This gendered eroticism
has underpinned the making of the urban gay community with
which these men have to deal – sometimes with difficulty, as in

Alan Andrews's experience of the bars, and sometimes with relief – as the main definition here and now of what it is to be a gay man.

Given a project structured in this way, what is its historical direction? What possibilities does it open up, or close off?

One more easily sees these men as products than producers of history. Their privatized politics gives little leverage on the state of gender relations. The life-course shaped as a journey between milieux, illustrated by Dean Carrington's literal migration to the gay community, presupposes the history in which those milieux have been formed. The men are in a position to adopt, negotiate or reject a gay identity, a gay commercial scene and gay sexual and social networks, all of which they encounter ready formed. A decade on, they are the inheritors of the world made by the gay liberationists and 'pink capitalists' of the 1970s, the generation now devastated by AIDS. And they have very little sense of, or commitment to, this history.

In these respects the picture does resemble the controlled space theorized by Blachford, who sees the social change accomplished by gay politics as severely limited. The gendered eroticism of these men, the masculine social presence most of them maintain, their focus on privatized couple relationships and their lack of solidarity with feminism point in the same direction. There is no open challenge to the gender order here.

But this is not the whole story. In two other ways the project opens possibilities of change. First, the very reification of homosexuality that is usually theorized as a form of social control is for these men a condition of freedom. It is the counterbalance they need to the obligatory heterosexuality that surrounds them and constantly invades their lives. It makes possible the realization of forbidden pleasure, the element of festival in their sexuality and the building of long-term relationships with other gay men. (It is notable that the longest-established couple relationship in the group began at a beat, the classic site for casual encounters.)

Though most of these men have also had sexual experience with women, as we have seen they neither take nor receive a social position as bisexuals. Their point of reference for both personality and object-choice is masculinity.

The dominant culture defines homosexual men as effeminate. This definition is obviously wrong as a description of the men interviewed here, who mostly do 'act like a man'. But it is not wrong in sensing the outrage they do to hegemonic masculinity.

The masculinity of their object-choice subverts the masculinity of their character and social presence. This subversion is a structural feature of homosexuality in a patriarchal society where hegemonic masculinity is defined as exclusively heterosexual, and its hegemony extends to the rearing of boys. One cannot become homosexual without shattering this hegemony somehow. So it is not surprising to find, jammed in beside the elements of mainstream masculinity, such items as Damien Outhwaite's flamboyant fingernails, Mark Richards's nursing, Alan Andrews's and Jonathan Hampden's identifications with women.

Homosexual masculinity is a contradiction for a gender order structured as modern Western systems are. The evidence of these life-histories (and others like them) demonstrates that the possible contradiction has been realized, has even become routine. The apolitical outlook of the group itself demonstrates the stabilization of a public alternative to hegemonic masculinity. They do not have to fight for their very existence as gay men, as earlier generations did. This is all the more significant because they started out within the framework of hegemonic masculinity.

Sexuality is the point of rupture in this project, and sexual relations are where it takes a potentially radical turn. Relative to the mainstream in heterosexual relations, gay men's sexual relations show a notable degree of reciprocity.[16] There are exceptions, but reciprocity is emphasized as an ideal and is to a large extent practised.

The conditions for reciprocity are complex. They include the relatively equal ages of most partners, shared class position (both conditions were lacking in Alan Andrews's bar-scene experiences) and shared position in the overall structure of gender. Ironically, the difficulty of establishing the most valued kind of relationship, long-term couples, may also be a pressure towards reciprocity in the sexual culture. Finally there is the specific way the body is implicated in sexual practice: that mirroring of lover and loved naively but vigorously expressed by Dean Carrington, where the exploration of another's body becomes the exploration of one's own.

We are certainly not dealing with a bunch of revolutionaries here. But neither are we dealing with complete containment. The 'very straight gay' is a contradictory position in the politics of gender. The friendly, peaceable relationships with young women that the younger men are constructing in their workplaces and households, along with the reciprocity in their own sexuality, are indicators of the change these contradictions can produce.

7

Men of Reason

Chapters 4 and 6 discussed marginalized and subordinated masculinities. This chapter will focus on hegemonic and complicit masculinities, specifically on potentials for change connected with the issue of rationality.

A familiar theme in patriarchal ideology is that men are rational while women are emotional. This is a deep-seated assumption in European philosophy. It is one of the leading ideas in sex role theory, in the form of the instrumental/expressive dichotomy, and it is widespread in popular culture too. Science and technology, seen by the dominant ideology as the motors of progress, are culturally defined as a masculine realm. Hegemonic masculinity establishes its hegemony partly by its claim to embody the power of reason, and thus represent the interests of the whole society; it is a mistake to identify hegemonic masculinity purely with physical aggression. Victor Seidler's account of patriarchal culture emphasizes the mind/body split, and the way masculine authority is connected with disembodied reason – overcoming the contradictions of embodiment discussed in Chapter 2.[1]

In a pathbreaking article Michael Winter and Ellen Robert suggested that the connection between masculinity and rationality was a key site of change. Advanced capitalism meant increased rationalization not only of business, but of culture as a whole – increasingly dominated by technical reason, that is, reason focused on efficiency about means rather than ultimate ends. (The television industry in the United States is a striking example, with stunning technical virtuosity and enormous resources devoted to broadcasting junk.)

Winter and Robert argue that men's domination of women is now legitimated by the technical organization of production, rather than legitimated by religion or imposed by force. As boys grow up, their masculinity is shaped to fit the needs of corporate work. Masculinity as a whole is reshaped to fit the corporate economy and its tamed culture:

> Increasingly one finds masculinity identified with the traits that represent the individual internalisation of the forms of technical reason, for it is technical reason itself that constitutes the major form of repression in contemporary society.[2]

There is no doubt about the importance of these issues. Rationalization is a central theme of modern cultural history, and its connection with the social construction of gender is increasingly recognized. Winter and Robert's strategy of looking at the occupational world dominated by technical reason is sound.

But their argument is overgeneralized; this is a more limited occupational world than they imply. Historically there has been an important division between forms of masculinity organized around direct domination (e.g., corporate management, military command) and forms organized around technical knowledge (e.g., professions, science). The latter have challenged the former for hegemony in the gender order of advanced capitalist societies, without complete success. They currently coexist as inflections or alternative emphases within hegemonic masculinity.

There are specific settings where masculinities organized around technical knowledge predominate, particularly in the occupational world of the 'new middle class' – or the new class, intellectually trained workers, technostructure or new petty bourgeoisie, in rival theories. Common threads in these theories are the rise of knowledge-based industries, the growth of higher education and the multiplication of credentials, the influence of expertise, and the occupational culture of professional and technical work.[3] I propose to explore crisis tendencies around rationality by focusing on men working in such settings, who have a claim to expertise but who lack the social authority given by wealth, the status of the old professions or corporate power.

The account that follows draws on nine life-histories collected from men in this position. Their ages range from mid-20s to mid-40s. Their occupations are: accountant, architect, computer technician, journalist, librarian, pilot, psychologist, teacher and welfare administrator. Four are living with wives or lovers; one is about to marry; two are recently separated; two have long been single.

This is a more diverse group than those discussed in the previous chapters. Case-study material is always difficult to summarize; I am conscious of being even more selective here, but I hope there is enough detail to open up the issues.

Constructing Masculinity

For most of this group, like the men in Chapters 5 and 6, the childhood home was organized conventionally. An employed father claimed authority in the family, and a housebound mother did the child care and managed the family's emotional life. (Don Meredith's case was an exception, his mother leaving her husband and supporting the children on her own.) Few of the parents' marriages seem to have been warm or mutually supportive.

Chris Argyris's family is near the centre of the range. 'Dad was king', big (though not violent), authoritative in manner, the kind of person who 'rules your life'. Mother was 'soft, quiet, warm, wonderful'. She was in the background, with delegated authority – 'I'll tell your father!'. That, at least, was the appearance. Chris has increasingly seen her as a 'cunning' and successful manipulator; and has increasingly seen a 'soft' interior to his father. But as a child Chris could not have been in doubt about the masculine/feminine polarity.

He threw himself to the masculine side, becoming an enthusiastic and successful high school footballer and putting on a display with booze and bravado in the peer group. He notes that he simply was not around women very much. He had several brothers, he went to a boys' school, and he played football for recreation. He is still keen on football as an adult, though in principle is opposed to violence in every sphere outside sport.

Paul Nikolaou saw that kind of peer group from the outside. He was the only child of working-class immigrants, hard-working and poor. He paints a picture of a cold and hierarchical family with husband dominating wife, and mother dominating child. He acquired his father's contempt for his mother.

His parents sought a better life for him through education, and forced him to study long hours. In a sport-dominated school this had the effect of isolating him. He found some support in an ethnic enclave, where they derided the Anglo boys' 'conscious effort to be masculine . . . show off in front of girls and things like that'. Contradicting the Anglo stereotype about Mediterranean men, Paul insists this 'is not so dominant in a European lifestyle'. But if he is critical of the dominant culture's definition of masculinity, he is far from critical of his own. He is about to marry a young women of his own ethnic community, and expects her to stay at home with the babies while he earns a living. He will give some help with the nappies. This in his view flows from the natural difference between men and women:

> I believe that a female is more adept physically and psychologically to endure the trials and tribulations of bringing up a home, controlling a home and a family. While a male may not necessarily be physically stronger . . . but . . . in a sort of majority basis more, not ambitious, but greedy for the work; and feel that they need the responsibility to bring home the bread, for example.

Paul's comment about the Anglo peer group illustrates another theme, the importance of negative examples. About half of the group volunteered comments about the men or masculinities they felt repelled by or distanced themselves from. Hugh Trelawney has a whole battery of negative exemplars in his narrative. They include 'nerds' in the A class at school, a homosexual weight-lifter at school, 'wimps' who parade problems in their personal lives, 'sharpies' (when he was a surfie), gays, at least effeminate ones – but also the dim-witted footballers he played with at university:

> I was never fully accepted by the football club type, because they were the strong silent type but wild – but they had a very strong sense of how you behaved, what you said about yourself and what you said about other people and so forth. I had an affinity for non-footballers who were stoned all the time, witty and satirical all the time, who put shit on the footballers and said they were a pack of meatheads. So again an outsider, someone a bit different. But there were other guys like me who played football, you know, who weren't totally in the meathead set. So I did at least have some people who I felt some affinity for.

Hugh's well-crafted set of images brilliantly illustrates the relational character of definitions of masculinity. Paul Nikolaou's commentary shows this, and also shows how the definition of masculinity is not the construction of an isolated individual, but is the collective work of a group. In his case it is the ethnic peer group in his adolescence, and the whole ethnic network in relation to his approaching marriage.

Don Meredith shows the construction of gender in an occupational group, the inhabitants of a school staffroom:

> Well, the staff generally is very pro-sport. I mean, we've got a First Grade footballer, well he is the sort of guy who is very friendly and affable and people enjoy his company, but he is extremely sexist. People seem to feed on that . . . I think he influences the general atmosphere in the staffroom. Well they like to joke, they like to have a good time which is fine too . . . But to talk about the cultural side of the country, they don't really want to know. It's mainly women, and they're very – well they are sexist too in a way. They love to have somebody flirt with them and play little games with them . . . They don't look on me as somebody that they can do that with.

The hegemonic masculinity of the First Grade footballer can rely on routine support, even from the women. Don's dissent from sexism is read as being 'too serious'.

The narratives show a fair range of outcomes from these masculinizing processes. Charles Lawrence, upwardly mobile in a high-technology industry, reproduces his father's personal style and domestic arrangements. He takes a completely conventional view of gender dichotomy: 'I can never understand a female, that's for sure, and how they think.' This makes one a little cautious about his equally confident assertion that his wife is 'an extremely dedicated wife and dedicated mother'.

Other narratives show more trouble about the reproduction of hegemonic masculinity. Peter Blake recalls his reaction to a new school:

> The expectations were that you were to be the Leaders of Men and all this sort of nonsense. We were told that quite explicitly. The Great Hall where the assemblies were held was festooned with flags about dated bloody colonies and states. Memorial plaques to the lads who had died in whatever war it was. To the Captains of the First XI and the First XV, the great debaters and the great talkers. It was a classic Australian model of what they thought an English public school should be. I really disliked that.

Peter was nevertheless a footballer. His dissent fed on political radicalism – this was the time of the Vietnam war – and used a technique of emotional distancing he had developed in his conflict-ridden family. He has remained, in adulthood, unsettled except for a period of engagement in student activism.

Constructing Rationality

Discussions of the new middle class have emphasized the growing weight of formal education as a cultural and institutional system. All of the men in this group had post-secondary training, most at universities. Given the selectiveness of the Australian education system, this means they had all been relatively successful in school, some highly successful. There were, however, two rather different ways in which their expertise was defined.

Greg Brook, now a computer technician, recalls doing well in primary school, being 'a sponge' soaking up knowledge, 'always topped my class'. He was selected for opportunity class, a selective strand at upper primary level, and went easily through high school to university. This was a considerable social promotion. His mother worked as a barmaid, and his father, who had only primary schooling, sold produce off a truck because he lacked the capital to buy a shop.

That is how the story of Greg Brook's entry to his occupational world would be seen from the personal side. Seen from the institutional side, it reveals a system of education already organized to select and promote an 'intelligent' minority. That is what opportunity classes and selective entry to university are all about. Greg's formation as a skilled worker, and as a person, was structured by this broad institutional definition of him as being talented. He carries this principle into his sexual relations, insisting that he is 'picky and choosy' about women, that he likes intelligent girls best, that being clever is a form of attractiveness. In Greg's eyes, people are tested and valued in a relational marketplace:

> Personally, I think I'm a little above the average as such, and I look for something a little above the average as well. I probably look – strive – higher and higher all the time.

Charles Lawrence did adequately but not brilliantly at school, with plenty of sport. He developed a strong ambition to be a pilot. He applied for an airline cadetship, did not have the grades and was knocked back. Urged by the family to go to university, he went fruit-picking instead and saved some money to go to flying school. He became a qualified pilot, but was immediately unemployed in a period of recession. He reluctantly agreed to go to university, spent an unhappy few months as a student, then: 'in the end I decided if I'm going to fly, I'm going to fly.' He made the big jump and went into the Air Force, insisting on pilot training.

Here he found a different kind of education, a vehement regime intended to bind the trainee to the institution as well as to give technical skills. You were 'living and breathing flying and Air Force'. He makes a cool appraisal of the method of instruction, disliked but effective. The trainees' previous knowledge was ignored. There was a lot of stress, a lot of negative feedback, and a sense of being selected as an elite – only one in five got through. At the same time the trainees were required to socialize with each other and with officers, to display keenness, to work long hours and conform to Air Force custom. They were expected to marry, to live close to the base and to run a patriarchal household with wives married to the job.

Charles resisted being overwhelmed by the Air Force to this extent. He took his distance from the shallow friendships involved, and as soon as possible left for a job in civil aviation. He is now working up the ranks of air crew, getting on-the-job training and heading for promotion to captain.

These two cases show the different ways expertise is defined and sustained. Greg Brook was the beneficiary of a generalized definition of intellectual talent embodied in mainstream curriculum and educational assessment. With his school record he could have gone into any of a wide range of training programmes or jobs. Which particular one was not important; in the interview he showed no interest in explaining it, no commitment to a career.

Charles Lawrence by contrast has a strong sense of vocation. The whole person is engaged in the work. Yet this too is social. A family practice was involved: his mother found him a flying school, his father helped pay its fees. Once inside the world of flying, especially once in the Air Force, he was picked up by a vigorous induction process designed to press him into an institutional mould.

This specialized expertise differs from generalized expertise not only in its content but also in its institutional base. Unusually for our respondents, Charles expresses open scepticism about formal education. He distinguishes himself from the 'really smart fellows' at school, and insists that 'intelligence' like his father s is a matter of common sense and conduct, not qualifications.

But Charles is scrupulous about the importance of experience and skill in flying, about becoming 'very efficient at your own game'. The group of Air Force pilots live and breathe their flying. The Air Force cultivates this peer network, to sustain enthusiasm and develop skill. It is heavily masculinized and deliberately heterosexual (up to 1992 gay men were thrown out of the Australian military if discovered). Though Charles resisted complete absorption into this milieu, it is notable that his involvement in a technical peer group survived the shift to civil aviation. He is now happily identified with the 'tech crew' on his flights, who socialize together and are sharply distinguished from the 'cabin crew'. This distinction is, in its turn, gendered. The cabin crew in Charles's eyes is made up of women and gay men, and he takes his distance from them.

The pattern of a technical peer group sustaining a strongly masculinized definition of expertise has been found in other industries, for instance, by Cynthia Cockburn on the engineering side of new technologies in Britain.[4] Charles Lawrence's occupational world is an almost archetypal embodiment of instrumental reason, and there is little here that suggests pressure to reconstruct masculinity. Indeed the instrumental focus on means/end relations serves to limit the impact of training in rational analysis, and thus protects gender relations from critique.

Occupational knowledge, however, is not static. Techniques get reconstructed and new kinds of 'expertise' get created. Peter Streckfuss, for instance, is working as a counselling psychologist, having retrained from his first profession. He is well towards the humanist end of psychology, where a good deal of innovation and experimentation occurs. He is involved with growth-movement ideas and activities like those mentioned in Chapters 5 and 6.

The growth movement provides a technical peer group for workers like Peter, with its own specialized language. It has a characteristic institution, the workshop, in which ideas and techniques are disseminated. This peer group is not masculinized like Charles Lawrence's. Many therapists are women, and the usual ideology is pro-feminist. More, there is reflexivity about gender. Sexuality and gender relations are major topics in therapy and workshops, amid attempts are made to apply the techniques to the reform of masculinity. Technical rationality *can* thus be enlisted in a project of change.

Career and Workplace

Jürgen Habermas has argued that the rationalization of culture produces a motivation crisis for capitalism, undermining the cultural reasons for economic performance and political consent.[5] Hegemonic and complicit masculinities provide a possible solution to this problem, through gender motivation. About half the men in the group have careers that are emotionally engaging. Charles Lawrence and Peter Streckfuss are examples, Peter being the more typical in having changed direction during his occupational life.

The other half have careers that are, by comparison, emotionally empty. Peter Blake explains that his job is not so much a vocation as a last resort:

> I knew I didn't like teaching, I knew I didn't want a career in private enterprise, I knew I didn't necessarily want a career climbing up ludicrous ladders in the public service.

So he became a librarian. Clyde Watson hardly 'chose' a career in accounting, he simply followed where his father had made money. Clyde is currently doing a degree in business studies. It gives him no intellectual challenge and no ethic, but does give him some management jargon about 'achieving personal goals'. Clyde uses this to explain why he has no close relationships with women (their personal goals are incompatible) and why his brother is useless (he doesn't motivate himself). It's a wasteland out there.

If this is any sample of business education, one might conclude the motivation crisis was in full swing. But Habermas's argument underestimates the capacity of institutions to organize practice at the collective level. Rationality can be accomplished without much reference to individual motives, through the structure of the workplace. The interviews show this in two different forms.

Charles Lawrence is happy enough in a workplace with a sharp division of labour and clear-cut hierarchy: tech crew vs. cabin crew, second officer/first officer/captain. Peter Blake, who worked for a while on the other side of the cockpit door, recalls the shock when he came to airline work direct from the counterculture:

> From a world of long hair and beards and dope smoking, mushroom eating and God knows what, to a conservative plastic world where your moustache can't go down beyond the corners of your mouth and you had to be polite 24 hours a day. It was a real strain.

In hierarchically organized workplaces of this kind, superior knowledge is supposed to be concentrated at the top. The rationality of the organization is guaranteed by formal authority and tight social control.

In the second kind of workplace the focus is on common goals, not on formal lines of command. Chris Argyris started in the public service being bored out of his mind in the Taxation Office. The small welfare-sector office that he now runs emphasizes informality, equality and sharing among the staff. This is expected to produce better decision-making and service. It is similar to the style of environmental movement offices mentioned in Chapter 5. Chris learned the style in a collective household and it is reinforced in the welfare-agency milieu. But it is being undermined by sheer pressure of work (Chris was 'going mad' and had to cut back to a four-day week) and by accountability rules which required a formal role for a supervisory committee.

This workplace style is by no means confined to progressive groups. Clyde Watson keeps the books for a small firm on the fringe of the finance industry. In the interview he gave a detailed account of this workplace, painting it as freewheeling, fluid, 'relaxed'. There is little formal organization and minimal division of labour; each task or arrangement is negotiated on the run. Clyde probably exaggerates the fluidity, to emphasize his own importance; it is clear from some of his stories that there are bosses and that he is not one of them. But the main claims ring true. There is an anti-bureaucratic style in the business, instructions are vague and status negotiable. This was probably common in the whiz-kid end of the finance industry during the speculative boom of the 1980s. Clyde's story resembles accounts of the early days at Apple Computer, and – on a different scale – the famous junk bond operation run by Michael Milken.[6]

Thus there are very different experiences of workplace control. It is therefore a little surprising to find that, for almost all this group, the issue of expertise vs. authority takes the same shape. Whether Charles Lawrence resisting the heavy pressure from his Air Force superiors, or Chris Argyris fighting Living Death in the Taxation Office, it is a question of fending off authority, holding it at a distance. The general stance towards authority is critical, and some respondents have well-crafted horror stories about arrogant or rigid bosses.

But these are mostly men in career-structured jobs. Short of death or bankruptcy, they will in time move up and have authority over other workers. Several do already. While this is straightforward in a hierarchically organized workplace like Charles Lawrence's, it is not necessarily easy elsewhere.

Peter Blake, a conscious nonconformist, 'student radical and beard-wearer, could get by as a flight attendant with a little acting. As a librarian he is now responsible for a group of staff. He is uneasy with the division of labour, and dislikes using secretaries because of the hierarchical relationships involved. He is wrestling with how to supervise other staff and reconcile his actual authority with his belief in equality. So far the result is a draw; he is laying emphasis on 'communication'.

We may argue, 'then, that the relation between expertise and hierarchy in the workplace is a characteristic difficulty encountered by this group of men. Technical rationality, it would appear, is *not* completely integrated into a hierarchical social order. Uneasy compromises like Peter Blake's are likely results.

Another likely consequence is that intellectually trained heterosexual men as a group will split over issues where masculine authority and technical rationality in the workplace are at odds. Equal Employment Opportunity for women is such an issue. This is a rational management strategy in terms of expertise, as it gets the best-qualified person for the job. But at the same time it corrodes the masculine culture of technical workplaces, bringing women into what used to be men's clubs. The political possibilities opened by such divisions among men are significant.

The Irrational

The rationality of the workplace, then, is at best equivocal. The equation of masculinity with rationality comes under further challenge in other realms of life. The issues of embodiment discussed in Chapter 2 cannot be avoided, especially in relation to sexuality – traditionally seen both as an important arena for the definition of masculinity and as a threat to rational control.

The men in this group grew up in a world governed by compulsory heterosexuality, and their interviews document its cultural and personal pressure. Given this, it is notable that homosexual experience is not uncommon – either as an aspect of' childhood sexual explorations, or as an element of adult experience. There is, in fact, impressive diversity in sexual careers in the group. Some have had an active sex life since school days, like Hugh Trelawney, 'Animal of the Year' at his university. Others recall no childhood eroticism and have restricted sex lives now. Some have been set on one course from the start, like Paul Nikolaou and Charles Lawrence. Others, like Peter Streckfuss, have had a change of direction in sexuality that they experience as a pivotal event in their lives.

Though diverse in their practice *of* sex, the men share a cultural experience *about* sex. As boys, most grew up in conventionally patriarchal households with a repressive attitude to sexuality. Most got no sex education from their parents, and at best got prohibitions from their churches. If they had an active sex life in childhood it was a matter of concealed explorations and furtive pleasures.

Sex commonly became a source of tension and anxiety in adolescence and early adulthood. Don Meredith, who lay awake at night listening to his father fucking the housekeeper, during the high school day had crushes on girls but never went beyond sitting beside them on the bus. At college he admired young feminists from a distance, but did not get near them: 'I never felt I really had enough to attract a woman'. A series of nerve-wracking fiascos followed before Don lost his virginity, which Don recounts in hilarious and well-crafted reminiscences. Even then he was not out of the woods: he found he could not ejaculate. He became constantly anxious about this, and contemplated hypnotherapy – though as he noted in passing of his partner, 'it didn't seem to matter to her'.

Sexuality is not inherently a source of emotional disruption, a realm of the irrational, but it can be made so. That is the usual outcome in these life-histories.

The potential for disruption can be handled through different body-reflexive strategies. It can be pre-empted by a course of life that puts sexuality in a well-defined, limited sphere. This is the strategy for Paul Nikolaou, who, as already noted, is about to be married. He is under pressure from his ethnic community to show himself responsible by preserving his and his fiancée's virginity until marriage. It would be 'shameful' to give way to lust. Though he and his fiancée have steamy petting sessions, she always calls a halt before going all the way. Both the dilemma and the resolution are collective practices.

Sexuality can also be managed by negotiation – in effect, talking it into a new shape. Don Meredith, after managing to lose his virginity, worked out a distinct sexual style. He tries to care for his partner, uses lots of fore-play and after-talk, and has some sexual tricks such as finger-fucking.

A sexual etiquette that emphasizes negotiation and the mutual pleasure of man and woman is common among the group. Greg Brook spells it out:

> I always try to please the other party as much as possible. I rarely go hell-for-leather and say, 'Oh well, it's my turn, bugger you . . . this one's mine, you can have yours next week.' Funnily enough, most of the women I've picked are also the same.

In a recently ended relationship Greg felt he had not been communicating, so he now tries to open up more:

> The last relationship I had with a lady was like that. I just decided, well bugger it, if I love the lady, I'll tell her what I feel at the time. Don't wait for a month or a week or even an hour, just say what you feel at the time. And I've felt so much better doing it . . . I think I'm being more honest, so I'm getting much more positive feedback. Because I'm being honest, the other person suddenly becomes honest. And if they don't, I have a tendency to – not ignore them, but just turn off them.

Balance is not easy to reach. The negotiation may involve a serious struggle between partners. Peter Streckfuss, discovering the cornucopia of sexuality in the mid-1970s, demanded an 'open marriage' from his wife Ann. She did not have much choice: he seems to have fucked first and asked permission afterwards. But she did then stand her ground, and 'all hell broke loose'. Some sort of permission having been negotiated, Peter proceeded to fuck Ann's woman friends. 'She was very hurt about that.' All-night talks eventually hammered out some guidelines: keep the affairs away from the house; let the spouse know what's going on. The affairs, in due course, died away. Peter talks of himself now as 'lonely'.

Finally, sexuality can be objectified. Hugh Trelawney, whose self-inflicted wounds and project of reform were mentioned in Chapter 2, now works for a partly pornographic magazine. He is defensive – 'a little bit dicey I suppose' – but also takes pleasure from the attention it gets him. Other people react with fascination to news of his job, and at parties men ask if he fucks the models.

> In the early days I suppose it was semi-exciting. It didn't last long, you just get sick of it.

In his workplace sexuality is defused by routine and by joking. Hugh emphasizes the journalistic quality of his work, trying to assimilate it to regular journalism.

Hugh's obvious unease with his self-justifications suggests limits to the power of instrumental rationality. He has a continuing sense that sexual relations are a realm of human experience that should not be treated this way. Here the process of rationalization is confronted by a moral order which it has not yet fully subdued.[7]

In other areas of life than sexuality we also find limits to rationalization, or even a positive embrace of the irrational. The most striking case is Charles Lawrence. This responsible technical expert in the highly rationalized industry of aviation turns out to be quite superstitious. He quotes a clairvoyant on past lives, attributes his own success firmly to 'luck', buys lottery tickets, and shows at several points a profound fatalism. (Reflecting on this, I was reminded of a recent trip on American Airlines, whose in-flight magazine contained, of all things, a horoscope.) It seems that the embodied rationality of the technology has squeezed out the sense of agency, and left the world controlled by chance or esoteric forces.

There are, of course, broader irrationalist trends in the world of advanced capitalism. Horoscopes are just the beginning of it. The spread of New Age cults and the resurgence of fundamentalist religion are striking features of the contemporary United States. The rebirth of fascism in Europe, and the growing support for racism and chauvinism, are equally striking. The mythopoetic men's movement is part of this spectrum, overlapping with New

Age sensibility, rejecting the claims of reason in order to recapture primitive emotions for men. None of the men in this group have any connection with this movement, which has little presence in Australia. But one can see from their example how it might find an audience in the new middle class in other countries.

Reason and Change

In several areas of these men's lives, then, rationality is limited or disputable. We do not find here a straightforward accommodation between hegemonic masculinity and the rationalized occupational world of advanced capitalism.

At some points, indeed, there is clear resistance to change. Men like Charles Lawrence and Paul Nikolaou set themselves against change in gender relations, affirming a conservative sexual ideology underpinned by conventional divisions of labour and by the institution of marriage. Other men have been forced to renegotiate their masculine place in institutions, and the negotiation has not been smooth. Greg Brook, like Charles and Paul, has a nativist ideology of gender:

> I think the feminist movement's gone too far. Because women are women. They've got to be women. The feminists, as I say – the true, die-hard feminists – have taken it past the extreme, and turned women, those women, into non-entities now. They're not women any more.

Greg professes tolerance on all sides, to (real) women as his equals, and to homosexuals too, 'so long as they're discreet'.

But unlike Charles and Paul, Greg has had to deal with women's authority in the workplace. He worked for his sister's firm and found that she insisted on remaining the boss. She would not follow his 'suggestions' about the direction the business should go. The tension built up and:

> I completely seized up, all my muscles just locked, and I was crazy. I was outside her [his girlfriend's] house, just the usual sitting in the car, it's unbelievable. Suddenly everything just started coming out and all my muscles in my forearms just locked. My hands were stuck to the steering wheel for an hour. I couldn't let go. And she [the girlfriend] was just saying 'Come on, let it out, let it out . . .

cry if you want, do whatever you want, just let it out, say what you
feel, because it's all just built up in there.'

Many things are condensed here: the inscription of masculinity in the body, the gender division of labour in emotion, the displacement of conflict. It is even significant that Greg in his
moment of emotional crisis locks onto the steering wheel of a car.
There is a symbolic link between cars and youthful masculinity,
and his sister had rejected his attempted steering of her business.

Pure economic rationality is incompatible with men's categorical authority over women. This is the contradiction on which
equal opportunity reforms work. In however limited a way, the
instrumental rationality of the marketplace has a power to disrupt
gender. With Greg Brook we see it disrupting hegemonic masculinity in no uncertain way.

All the men in the group have a sense that changes are going
on in gender relations, whether they resist or embrace them.
Some embrace change with ill grace. Peter Streckfuss says he has
taken on more domestic work:

> I do more traditionally female things. I clean, I work, I cook, I wash
> up.

But he criticizes his wife for not taking on 'the equivalent male
tasks' such as chopping the wood and fixing the machinery. And
he lets fly at feminists:

> Now I resent the bleating that goes on among women about how
> they do all these things, how they believe in equality. But they
> wouldn't know where the bloody dipstick was on their engine,
> mate, and they make no attempt to find out. That's what I resent.

In certain circumstances, embracing change in masculinity can
seem the path of rationality. This was clearly true for Hugh
Trelawney. After a physical and emotional crisis of considerable
depth, Hugh felt he needed 'fundamental changes':

> I re-examined the way I related to people, my sort of competition-
> type status-conscious ethos. I looked in particular at the way I
> related to women. I realized I had lost the person who hated the
> automatic consideration of females as inferior and who hated the
> idea of them not getting equal pay. Deep down I was a fucking chau-

vinist, I still treated the love/sex thing as basically a game, as a funny game, something comparable to football.

So Hugh set about changing his personality. He determined to listen to people more, to develop sympathy, to construct relationships, to be more open and vulnerable and to be less competitive.

> I go out of my way to try not to be threatening now. Just me, my persona. People still sort of look for areas of vulnerability in me, and I try to open them up more now too. Sort of be a human being more than a machine. I used to think the goal was to be basically non-human, because to be non-human meant that there were fewer of the ordinary emotional traumas of life that would have to be faced if one could be machine-like.

The project is along the same lines as the reform of masculinity discussed in Chapter 5. But the changes in practice are not as fundamental as Hugh would like to suggest. He still goes in for one-night stands, refusing commitment ('still a runner'), and he calculates he can do this because there is a surplus of women in his age group. He is aware of feminist criticism of men like him, and resents and rejects it. He thinks what he does is OK provided he doesn't lie to his women. He distinguishes sexual revolution from feminism, and discredits radical feminism on the interesting ground that its purpose is to kill off men.

Hugh also puts down Gay Liberation – 'dicks in arseholes' – hastening to add that what gays do is OK by him. He follows that with a long complaint about 'feminine' gays who worry about the colour of their curtains. Yes, he does want to change the way men treat women. No, he does not want to get into a male 'sensitivity competition . . . some people just even become quite boring as a result of that.' Working for a pornographic magazine, whatever his personal intentions, he is involved in commodifying women's sexuality and legitimating a predatory heterosexuality among men.

I have spelt out Hugh's jumble of good intentions, growth-movement jargon ('persona' is Jungian), fear, resentment and bad faith, as he shows with particular clarity the confusions and reactions produced by the attempt to alter an oppressive masculinity without tackling the social structures that give rise to it.

Rationality is, as I noted at the start of the chapter, part of the modern legitimation of patriarchy. It may even be thought a crucially important part. But it is a dangerous legitimation. As the evidence from these life-histories shows, rationality is in certain ways a disturbing element in gender relations. Its social forms (such as market rationality and legal equality) corrode gender hierarchy and support feminist resistance. Its institutionalization in the knowledge-based workplace corrodes authority and sets up tensions within hegemonic masculinity. Technical reason can be mobilized for a project of change, even though it does not address the ultimate goals of change.

Seen close up, hegemonic and complicit masculinities are no more monolithic than are subordinated and marginalized masculinities. In these lives, though they are drawn from only one part of the social spectrum, we see contrasts between domestic patriarchy and sexual adventuring; between generalized and specialized expertise; between egalitarian and hierarchical workplaces; between conciliatory and hostile views of feminism. We even see attempts at reform and modernization, admittedly within well-defined limits. In coming to grips with the politics of change in masculinity, as I will try to do in Part III, it will be important to bear these complexities in mind.

Part III
History and Politics

8

The History of Masculinity

I have stressed that masculinities come into existence at particular times and places, and are always subject to change. Masculinities are, in a word, historical, and this is well documented by the historians whose work was discussed in Chapter 1. But so far the argument has lacked historical depth and an appropriate scale.

To understand the current pattern of masculinities we need to look back over the period in which it came into being. Since masculinity exists only in the context of a whole structure of gender relations, we need to locate it in the formation of the modern gender order as a whole – a process that has taken about four centuries. The local histories of masculinity recently published provide essential detail, but we need an argument of broader scope as well.

It is mainly ethnographic research that has made the scale of the issue, and the vital connections, clear: the unprecedented growth of European and North American power, the creation of global empires and a global capitalist economy, and the unequal encounter of gender orders in the colonized world. I say 'connections' and not 'context', because the fundamental point is that masculinities are not only shaped by the process of imperial expansion, they are active in that process and help to shape it.

Popular culture tells us this without prompting. Exemplars of masculinity, whether legendary or real – from Paul Bunyan in Canada via Davy Crockett in the United States to Lawrence 'of Arabia' in England – have very often been men of the frontier. A game I played as a boy in Australia was, extraordinarily enough, a ritual of imperial expansion in North America, shipped across the Pacific in comic-book and Hollywood images of masculinity: a replay of frontier warfare between 'Cowboys and Indians'. We cannot understand the connection of masculinity and violence at a personal level without understanding that it is also a global connection. European/American masculinities were deeply implicated in the world-wide violence through which European/American culture became dominant.

What follows is, inevitably, only a sketch of a vastly complex history. Yet it seems important to get even rough bearings on a history so charged with significance for our current situation.

The Production of Masculinity in the Formation of the Modern Gender Order

In the period from about 1450 to about 1650 (the 'long' sixteenth century, in the useful phrase of the French historian Fernand Braudel) the modern capitalist economy came into being around the North Atlantic, and the modern gender order also began to take shape in that region. Four developments seem particularly important for the making of those configurations of social practice that we now call 'masculinity'.

First was the cultural change that produced new understandings of sexuality and personhood in metropolitan Europe. When medieval Catholicism, already changing, was disrupted by the spread of Renaissance secular culture and the Protestant reformation, long-established and powerful ideals for men's lives were also disrupted. The monastic system crumbled. The power of religion to control the intellectual world and to regulate everyday life began its slow, contested, but decisive decline.

On the one hand, this opened the way for a growing cultural emphasis on the conjugal household – exemplified by no less a figure than Martin Luther, the married monk. Marital heterosexuality displaced monastic denial as the most honoured form of sexuality. The cultural authority of compulsory heterosexuality clearly followed this shift.

On the other hand, the new emphasis on individuality of expression and on each person's unmediated relationship with God led towards individualism and the concept of an autonomous self. These were cultural prerequisites for the idea of masculinity itself, as defined in Chapter 3, a type of person whose gendered character is the reason for his (or her, in the case of masculine women) actions. Classical philosophy from Descartes to Kant, as Victor Seidler has argued, construed reason and science through oppositions with the natural world and with emotion. With masculinity defined as a character structure marked by rationality, and Western civilization defined as the bearer of reason to a benighted world, a cultural link between the legitimation of patriarchy and the legitimation of empire was forged.[1]

The second development was the creation of overseas empires by the Atlantic seaboard states – Portugal and Spain, then the Netherlands, France and England. (The overland empires of Russia and the United States, and the overseas empires of Germany, Italy and Japan, came in a second round of imperialism.)

Empire was a gendered enterprise from the start, initially an outcome of the segregated men's occupations of soldiering and sea trading. When European women went to the colonies it was mainly as wives and servants within households controlled by men. Apart from a few monarchs (notably Isabella and Elizabeth), the imperial states created to rule the new empires were entirely staffed by men, and developed a statecraft based on the force supplied by the organized bodies of men.

The men who applied force at the colonial frontier, the 'conquistadors' as they were called in the Spanish case, were perhaps the first group to become defined as a masculine cultural type in the modern sense. The conquistador was a figure displaced from customary social relationships, often extremely violent in the search for land, gold and converts, and difficult for the imperial state to control, (The hostility between the royal authorities and Hernan Cortés, the Spanish conqueror of Mexico, was notorious.) Loss of control at the frontier is a recurring theme in the history of empires, and is closely connected with the making of masculine exemplars.

An immediate consequence was a clash over the ethics of conquest, and a demand for controls. Bartolomé de Las Casas's famous denunciation of the bloodbath that resulted from the uncontrolled violence of the Spanish conquerors, in his *Very Brief Relation of the Destruction of the Indies*, is thus a significant moment in the history of masculinity. 'Insatiable greed and ambition, the greatest ever seen in the world, is the cause of their villainies.' Las Casas's rhetoric was literally correct. This was something new in the world, and his own work was the first extended critique of an emerging gender form.[2]

The third key development was the growth of the cities that were the centres of commercial capitalism, notably Antwerp, London and Amsterdam, creating a new setting for everyday life.

This was both more anonymous, and more coherently regulated, than the frontier or the countryside.

The main gender consequences of this change became visible only in the seventeenth and eighteenth centuries, but for brevity I will note them here. The changed conditions of everyday life made a more thoroughgoing individualism possible. In combination with the 'first industrial revolution' and the accumulation of wealth from trade, slaving and colonies, a calculative rationality began to permeate urban culture. This was the development picked up in Max Weber's thesis about the 'Protestant ethic', and it is interesting to notice the gendered character of the 'spirit of capitalism'. Weber's prime exhibit was Benjamin Franklin, and he quoted this passage:

> The most trifling actions that affect a man's credit are to be regarded. The sound of your hammer at five in the morning, or eight at night, heard by a creditor, makes him easy six months longer; but if he sees you at a billiard-table, or hears your voice at a tavern, when you should be at work, he sends for his money the next day . . .

A man, literally, is meant. The entrepreneurial culture and workplaces of commercial capitalism institutionalized a form of masculinity, creating and legitimating new forms of gendered work and power in the counting-house, the warehouse and the exchange.

But this was not the only transformation of gender in the commercial cities. The same period saw the emergence of sexual subcultures. The best documented are the Molly houses of early eighteenth-century London, 'Molly' being a slang term used for effeminate men who met in particular houses and taverns, and whose gender practices included cross-dressing, dancing together and sexual intercourse with each other.

Historians of the period have noted a shift in medical ideologies of gender, from an earlier period when gender anomalies were freely attributed to hermaphroditic bodies, to a later period when a clear-cut dichotomy of bodies was presumed and anomalies therefore became a question of gender deviance. The requirement that one must have a personal identity as a man or a woman, rather than simply a location in the social order as a person with a male or female (or hermaphroditic) body, gradually hardened in European culture. Mary Wollstonecraft's perception of the social bases of women's gendered character, in contrast to that of men, provided the core argument of her *Vindication of the Rights of Woman* at the end of the eighteenth century.[3]

The fourth development was the onset of large-scale European civil war. The sixteenth- and seventeenth-century wars of religion, merging into the dynastic wars of the seventeenth and eighteenth centuries, did more than relocate a few kings and bishops. They disturbed the legitimacy of the gender order. The World Turned Upside Down by revolutionary struggles could be the gender as well as the class order. In the English-speaking countries it was the Quakers, a religious-cum-political sect emerging from the upheavals of the English civil war, who made the first public defence of equality in religion for women. They not only proclaimed the principle, but actually gave women a significant organizing role in practice.

This challenge was turned back (though its memory lingered). The patriarchal order was consolidated by another product of the European civil wars, the strong centralized state. In the era of absolute monarchy the state provided a larger-scale institutionalization of men's power than had been possible before. The professional armies constructed in the religious and dynastic wars, as well as in imperial conquest, became a key part of the modern state. Military prowess as a test of honour was in medieval Europe a class theme of knighthood – the connection mocked in Cervantes' *Don Quixote*. It increasingly became an issue of masculinity and nationalism, a transition visible in Shakespeare's most chauvinistic play:

> On, on, you Noblish English,
> Whose blood is fet from Fathers of Warre-proofe:
> Fathers, that like so many *Alexanders*,
> Have in these parts from Morne till Even fought
> And sheath'd their Swords, for lack of argument.[4]

With the eighteenth century, in seaboard Europe and North America at least, we can speak of a gender order in which masculinity in the modern sense – gendered individual character, defined through an opposition with femininity and institutionalized in economy and state – had been produced and stabilized. For this period we can even define a hegemonic type of masculinity and describe some of its relations to subordinated and marginalized forms.

Though cultural change in the cities has caught the attention of historians, it was the class of hereditary landowners, the gentry, who dominated the North Atlantic world of the eighteenth century. George Washington was a notable example of the class and its hegemonic form of masculinity. Based in land ownership, gentry masculinity was involved in capitalist economic relations (production for the market, extraction of rents) but did not emphasize strict rational calculation in the manner of the merchants.

Nor was it based on a concept of the isolated individual. Land ownership was embedded in kinship; the lineage as much as the individual was the social unit. British politics in the age of Walpole and the Pitts, for instance, generally followed family lines with the state apparatus controlled by great families through patronage. British rule in India and North America was organized on much the same lines.

Gentry masculinity was closely integrated with the state. The gentry provided local administration (through justices of the peace, in the British system) and staffed the military apparatus. The gentry provided army and navy officers, and often recruited the rank and file themselves. At the intersection between this direct involvement in violence and the ethic of family honour was the institution of the duel. Willingness to face an opponent in a potentially lethal one-to-one combat was a key test of gentry masculinity, and it was affronts to honour that provoked such confrontations.

In this sense the masculinity of the gentry was emphatic and violent. Yet the gender order as a whole was not as strongly regulated as it later became. Thus a French gentleman, the Chevalier d'Eon, could be switched from masculine to feminine gender without being socially discredited (though remaining an object of curiosity for the rest of her life). Licence in sexual relationships, especially with women of the lower classes, was a prerogative of rank. It was even to a degree celebrated, by the 'libertines'. It seems that homosexual relationships were being increasingly understood as defining a specific type of men, though in the writings of the Marquis de Sade they are still an aspect of libertinage in general.

Gentry masculinity involved domestic authority over women, though the women were actively involved in making and main-

taining the network of alliances that tied the gentry together –
the strategies lovingly dissected in Jane Austen's novels.

Gentry masculinity involved a much more brutal relationship
with the agricultural workforce, still the bulk of the population.
The social boundary here was marked by the code of honour,
which was not applied outside the gentry. Control was exerted by
evictions, imprisonment, the lash, transportation and hangings.
Applying this violent discipline was not a specialized profession.
It was an ordinary part of local administration, from the English
countryside, and George Washington's slave estate in Virginia, to
the new colony at the Antipodes – where Samuel Marsden, the
'Flogging Parson', became a well-known justice of the peace.[5]

Transformations

The history of European/American masculinity over the last two
hundred years can broadly be understood as the splitting of
gentry masculinity, its gradual displacement by new hegemonic
forms, and the emergence of an array of subordinated and marginalized masculinities. The reasons for these changes are
immensely complex, but I would suggest that three are central:
challenges to the gender order by women, the logic of the gendered accumulation process in industrial capitalism, and the
power relations of empire.

The challenge from women is now well documented. The nineteenth century saw a historic change in gender politics, the emergence of feminism as a form of mass politics – a mobilization for
women's rights, especially the suffrage, in public arenas. This was
closely connected to the growth of the liberal state and its reliance
on concepts of citizenship.

Yet women's challenges to the gender order were not confined
to the suffrage movement, which had a limited reach. Gentry and
middle-class women were active in reforms of morals and domestic customs in the early nineteenth century which sharply challenged the sexual prerogatives of gentry men. Working-class
women contested their economic dependence on men as the
factory system evolved. Middle-class women again challenged
men's prerogatives through the temperance movement of the late
nineteenth century. The conditions for the maintenance of patri-

archy changed with these challenges, and the kind of masculinity which could be hegemonic changed in response.

With the spread of industrial economies and the growth of bureaucratic states (whether liberal or autocratic), the economic and political power of the landowning gentry declined. This was a slow process, and effective rear-guard actions were fought. For instance the Prussian gentry, the Junkers, kept control of the German state into the twentieth century. In the course of the transition, some of the forms of gentry masculinity were handed on to the men of the bourgeoisie. The historian Robert Nye has given us a remarkable example: the transfer of a prickly code of honour, centring on the institution of the duel, to the bourgeoisie in France. The number of duels fought in France actually rose in the later nineteenth century, and a profession of duelling-master developed to induct men into the code and teach the techniques of sword-fighting.[6]

Though some men died in duels, this was basically a symbolic definition of masculinity through violence. Real warfare became increasingly organized. The mass armies of the revolutionary and Napoleonic wars became standing conscript armies with permanent officer corps. Such corps, at first recruited from the gentry, became repositories of gentry codes of masculinity, the Prussian officer corps being the most famous example. (Hitler's generals in the 1940s were still mostly drawn from this background.) But the social context was changed. The new officer corps were professionalized, trained at military schools.

Violence was now combined with rationality, with bureaucratic techniques of organization and constant technological advance in weaponry and transport. Armed forces were reorganized to bring them under the control of a centre of technical knowledge, the General Staff, an institution created by the Prussians and copied in fear by the other Great Powers. If Las Casas's writings can be regarded as a key document of early modern masculinity, perhaps the equivalent for the nineteenth century is Carl von Clausewitz's classic *On War*, proclaiming a social technology of rationalized violence on the largest possible scale. Clausewitz was one of the reformers who created the new Prussian army.[7]

It was the social technique of bureaucratically rationalized violence, as much as sheer superiority of weapons, that made European states and settlers almost invincible in the colonial wars of the nineteenth century. But this technique risked destroying the society that sustained it. The vast destructiveness of the Great War led to revolutionary upheaval in 1917–23. In much of Europe the capitalist order was stabilized, after a decade of further struggle, only by fascist movements.

In gender terms, fascism was a naked reassertion of male supremacy in societies that had been moving towards equality for women. To accomplish this, fascism promoted new images of hegemonic masculinity, glorifying irrationality (the 'triumph of the will', thinking with 'the blood') and the unrestrained violence of the frontline soldier. Its dynamics soon led to a new and even more devastating global war.[8]

The defeat of fascism in the Second World War cut off this turn in hegemonic masculinity. But it certainly did not end the bureaucratic institutionalization of violence. Hitler himself had modernized his armed forces and was an enthusiast for high-technology weapons; in that respect fascism supported rationalization. The Red Army and United States armed forces which triumphed in 1945 continued to multiply their destructive capability, as the nuclear arsenal built up. In China, Pakistan, Indonesia, Argentina, Chile and much of Africa, less technologically advanced armies remain central to the politics of their respective states. There are currently about twenty million in the world's armed forces, the vast majority being men, with their organization modelled on the armies of the North Atlantic powers.

The growing significance of technical expertise in the military paralleled developments in other parts of the economy. The nineteenth century saw the foundation of mass elementary schooling, and the twentieth century has added public secondary and university systems. Research institutes were invented and the research capabilities of corporations and government departments have been hugely expanded. Labour markets have been transformed by the multiplication of professions with claims to expertise. Information industries have expanded geometrically. Currently one of the two richest persons in the United States is a specialist in computer programming, a man whose company designed the operating system for the computer I am using to write this text (plus a few million other computers).[9]

These trends have seen another split in hegemonic masculinity. Practice organized around dominance was increasingly incompatible with practice organized around expertise or technical knowledge. Management was divided from professions, and relations between the two became a chronic problem in corporations and in the state. (The correct use of experts – 'on tap or on top' – is a classic issue in management science; while the idea of 'management science' itself reveals the prestige of expertise.) Factional divisions opened in both capitalist ruling classes and communist elites between those willing to coerce workers (conservatives/hard-liners), and those willing to make concessions on the strength of technological advance and economic growth (liberals/reformers).

A polarity thus developed within hegemonic masculinity between dominance and technical expertise. In this case, however, neither version has succeeded in displacing the other. They currently coexist as gendered practices, sometimes in opposition and sometimes meshing. As alternative versions of hegemonic masculinity they can be called upon by advertising and political campaigns – 'tough on crime' vs. 'information superhighway', to take examples from current United States politics. The new-class life-histories discussed in Chapter 7 show some of the tensions in this situation.[10]

As hegemonic masculinity in the metropole became more subject to rationalization, violence and licence were, symbolically and to some extent actually, pushed out to the colonies. On the frontier of white settlement regulation was ineffective, violence endemic and physical conditions harsh. Industries such as mining offered spectacular profits on a chancy basis. A very imbalanced sex ratio allowed a cultural masculinization of the frontier.

Jock Phillips's study of New Zealand, discussed in Chapter 1, draws the contrast between two groups of men and two cultural accounts of masculinity: the brawling single frontiersman and the settled married pioneer farmer. The distinction is familiar on the Western frontier in North America. It is a striking fact that even before this frontier closed, with military defeat of the native peoples and the spread of white settlement across the continent, frontiersmen were being promoted as exemplars of masculinity.

The novels of James Fenimore Cooper and the Wild West show of Buffalo Bill Cody were early steps in a course that led eventually to the Western as a film genre and its self-conscious cult of inarticulate masculine heroism. The historian John MacKenzie has called attention to the similar cult of the hunter in the late nineteenth-century British empire. Wilderness, hunting and bushcraft were welded into a distinct ideology of manhood by figures such as Robert Baden-Powell, the founder of the scouting movement for boys, and Theodore Roosevelt in the United States.[11]

The scouting movement celebrated the frontier, but it was actually a movement for boys in the metropole. Here it took its place in a long series of attempts to foster particular forms of masculinity among boys. Other moments in this history include the nineteenth-century reform of the British elite public school, in the period after Dr Arnold; the Church of England Boys' Brigade directed at working-class youth; the German youth movement at the turn of the century; the Hitler Youth, turned into a mass institution when the Nazis came to power in Germany; and widespread attempts at military training of secondary school boys through army cadet corps, still operating in Australia when I was in high school in 1960. (I rose to the rank of corporal, and learned to fire the Lee-Enfield rifle, a state-of-the-art weapon during the Boer War.)

The striking thing about these movements was not their success, always limited, but the persistence with which ideologists of patriarchy struggled to control and direct the reproduction of masculinity. It is clear that this had become a significant problem in gender politics.[12]

Why was this a problem? Some turn-of-the-century ideologists, as Jeffrey Hantover noted in a study of the Boy Scouts of America, expressed a fear that boys would be feminized through too much influence by women. This directs us to changes in the organization of domestic life. Pressure from women against gentry masculinity had been part of the historical dynamic that led to a key institution of bourgeois culture, the ideology and practice of 'separate spheres'. This defined a domestic sphere of action for women, contrasted with a sphere of economic and political action for men.

The division was supported by an ideology of natural difference between women and men, which was not only promoted by male ideologists (for instance, it was a theme of the duelling cult in France), but was widely acceptable to nineteenth-century feminists as well. The women's sphere was, in ordinary practice, subordinate to the men's. But within that sphere bourgeois women might act as employers of servants and managers of business (with advisors such as Mrs Beeton), and could often count on considerable autonomy. And it was in that sphere that the rearing of young boys was located.[13]

At much the same time hegemonic masculinity was purged in terms of sexuality. As gay historians have shown, the late nineteenth century was the time when 'the homosexual' as a social type became clearly defined. This involved both a medical and a legal demarcation. At earlier periods of history, sodomy had been officially seen as an act which might be undertaken by any man who gave way to evil. Homosexual desire was now viewed as defining a particular type of man, the 'invert' in the most common medical view. New laws criminalized homosexual contact as such (called 'gross indecency' in the 1885 Labouchère Amendment in England), and routine police surveillance of 'perverts' followed.

From the point of view of hegemonic masculinity, the potential for homoerotic pleasure was expelled from the masculine and located in a deviant group, symbolically assimilated to women or to beasts. There was no mirror-type of 'the heterosexual'. Rather, heterosexuality became a required part of manliness. The contradiction between this purged definition of masculinity, and the actual conditions of emotional life among men in military and paramilitary groups reached crisis level in fascism. It helped to justify, and possibly to motivate, Hitler's murder of Ernst Röhm, the homosexual leader of the Storm-troopers, in 1934.[14]

The gradual displacement of the gentry by businessmen and bureaucrats in the metropolitan countries was paralleled by the transformation of peasant populations into industrial and urban working classes. This change too had its gender dimension. The factory system meant a sharper separation of home from workplace, and the dominance of money wages changed economic relations in the household. The expansion of industrial production saw the emergence of forms of masculinity organized around wage-earning capacity, mechanical skills, domestic patriarchy and combative solidarity among wage earners.

Women were, in fact, a large part of the original workforce in the textile factories of the industrial revolution, and were also present in coal mining, printing and steelmaking. They were involved in industrial militancy, sometimes were leaders of strikes, as Mary Blewett has shown for the weavers of Fall River, Massachusetts. The expulsion of women from heavy industry was thus a key process in the formation of working-class masculinity, connected with the strategy of the family wage and drawing on the bourgeois ideology of separate spheres. The craft union movement can be seen as the key institutionalization of this kind of masculinity.[15]

But only part of the working class was ever unionized, or commanded a family wage. The creation of this respectable, orderly masculinity had, as its dialectical opposite, the development of rough, disorderly masculinities among the marginalized 'dangerous classes'. The fear this aroused even among revolutionary socialists can be felt in Friedrich Engels's savage remarks on the urban poor:

> The *lumpenproletariat,* this scum of depraved elements from all classes, with headquarters in the big cities, is the worst of all the possible allies. This rabble is absolutely venal and absolutely brazen . . . Every leader of the workers who uses these scoundrels as guards or relies on them for support proves himself by this action alone a traitor to the movement.

Such groups have attracted little attention as yet from historians of gender, though their presence is documented by historians of class in studies of 'outcast London', of the 'new unionism' of the late nineteenth century, and of workplaces such as wharves and markets which employed casual labour.[16]

Outside the metropole, the economic logic of empire led to extraordinary population shifts as labour forces were moved from one continent to another. This meant the emigration of 'free' settlers to New Zealand, Australia, Canada and Algeria, but violent enslavement or coercive employment in many other cases. They include the shipping of an African slave workforce to Brazil, the Caribbean and North America; the shipping of indentured labour from India to the Caribbean, parts of Africa, Malaya and Fiji; the shipping of Chinese labour to build North American railroads, and convict labour from England and Ireland to Australia.

The legacy of these population movements has commonly been a racial hierarchy, of considerable importance – both symbolically and practically – for the construction of masculinities. As noted in Chapter 3, black masculinity has commonly been pictured as a sexual and social threat in dominant white cultures. This gender ideology has fuelled harsh policing and political racism in settings ranging from the United States to South Africa to contemporary France.

The realities of masculinity in transplanted labour forces have been shaped by the conditions of settlement, which commonly involved poverty and heavy labour as well as the disruption of families and communities. Some of the resulting complexities can be seen in Chandra Jayawardena's study of sugar workers in

British Guiana in the 1950s, descendants of a labour force transplanted from India in the later nineteenth century. Their beliefs and social practices emphasized equality and social solidarity, 'mati' or mateship. Heavy drinking – always in groups – expressed this solidarity. Disputes about offences to honour arose among these men, called 'eye-pass' disputes; but they had a very different logic from the duelling disputes among the French bourgeoisie. They were not based on claims to individual distinction but on the collective rejection of such claims, which would have broken up the community of poor labourers. Here masculine assertion occurred in the cause of equality, not competition.[17]

In colonies where conquered populations were not displaced or massacred but were made into a subordinated labour force on the spot – most of Latin America, India and South-East Asia and parts of Africa – the gender consequences involved a reshaping of local culture under the pressure of the colonizers. The British in India constructed different images of masculinity for different peoples under their rule, for instance, contrasting effeminate Bengalis with fierce Pathans and Sikhs. Like the ideology of white military masculinity discussed earlier, this imagery probably had a role in recruitment and social control.

It is a familiar suggestion that Latin American machismo was a product of the interplay of cultures under colonialism. The conquistadors provided both provocation and model, Spanish Catholicism provided the ideology of female abnegation, and economic oppression blocked other sources of authority for men. As Walter Williams has shown, Spanish colonialism also involved a violent and sustained assault on the customary homosexuality of native cultures. This has influenced contemporary expressions of masculinity. In Mexico, for instance, the public presentation of masculinity is aggressively heterosexual, though the practice is often bisexual.[18]

The history of masculinity, it should be abundantly clear, is not linear. There is no master line of development to which all else is subordinate, no simple shift from 'traditional' to 'modern'. Rather we see, in the world created by the European empires, complex structures of gender relations in which dominant, subordinated and marginalized masculinities are in constant interaction, changing the conditions for each others' existence and transforming themselves as they do.

With that banal but necessary historical point in mind, let us turn to the current state of play.

The Present Moment

The idea that we live at the moment when a traditional male sex role is softening is as drastically inadequate as the idea that a true, natural masculinity is now being recovered. Both ideas ignore most of the world. To grasp what is going on in this global network of gender institutions and relationships requires a very different perspective.

On a global scale, the most profound change is the export of the European/American gender order to the colonized world. There is every reason to think this trend is accelerating. As the world capitalist order becomes more complete, as more local production systems are linked in to global markets and local labour brought into wage systems, local versions of Western patriarchal institutions are installed. These include corporations, state bureaucracies, armies and mass education systems. I have already indicated the scale of Westernized armies in the contemporary world. Education sectors are somewhat bigger (in the developing countries as a whole there are approximately 140 teachers for every 100 soldiers). Corporate sectors are bigger again.

This provides a solid institutional base for changes in gender ideology and imagery, and changes in everyday practice. The export of European/American gender ideology can be seen in the mass media of the developing world. A notable example is the promotion of Xuxa in Brazil as an icon of femininity – a blonde model who has become remarkably popular, and remarkably rich, through a television programme for children. (In the same country, street children who don't have television sets have been murdered by male death squads.) Gender regimes are also being transformed in everyday practice. For instance, indigenous customs of same-sex eroticism, as far apart as Brazil and Java, are converging on the Western urban model of 'gay identity'.[19]

For the first time in history, there is a prospect of all indigenous gender regimes foundering under this institutional and cultural pressure. Some gender configurations have already gone. One example is the Confucian tradition of male homosexuality in China, the 'passions of the cut sleeve' (so called from the story of an emperor who cut off the sleeve of his robe rather than disturb his sleeping lover). Another is the tradition of heterosexual eroticism and women's sexual freedom in Polynesian Hawaii. To say they are gone is perhaps too mechanical. Both these traditions were deliberately destroyed under the influence of Western homophobia and missionary puritanism.[20]

Replacing the diversity of gender orders is an increasingly coordinated, increasingly visible global gender order. European/ American gender arrangements are hegemonic in this system. A dramatic demonstration is provided by the recent history of Eastern Europe. As the Stalinist regimes collapsed and market economies were installed, Western ideologies of gender were installed with them and state guarantees of equality for women (which were never consistently applied but had some practical force) have been lost.

However, the global gender order is not homogeneous, not just a matter of cloning European/American culture. Feminist research on women workers in the global factory of modern multinational production has shown differentiated positions being constructed: for electronics assembly workers in Malaysia, prostitutes in the Philippines and Thailand, garment workers in Mexico.[21]

The same is certainly true for men, though this has been less studied. In Japan, for instance, the modernization programme of the Meiji regime in the late nineteenth century led to a large expansion of the education system and competition for access to administrative and clerical jobs. This in turn led to the emergence of the 'salaryman', the deferential but competitive servant of the corporate oligarchs who dominate the Japanese economy. (The term dates from the First World War, though it has only been noticed by English-speaking countries in the last two decades.) This is a notable example of a class-specific form of masculinity which is only conceivable in a global capitalist economy but is also culturally and politically specific.[22]

We should also register the strength of reactions against the Western gender order. The most dramatic, in the last two decades, has been in those parts of the Islamic world where political independence has been followed by a reassertion of men's patriarchal authority. Men who have forced women to wear the veil and withdraw from public arenas are pursuing a gender politics through the same gestures as an anti-colonial politics. (This is not a necessary part of Islam; the largest Islamic country in the world, Indonesia, pays no attention to the veil.)[23]

The men of the metropolitan countries are, collectively, the main beneficiaries of the contemporary world order. The most striking feature of their historical situation is the vastly increased power, over the natural world and over the services of other people, that the accumulation and concentration of wealth has delivered to them. The scale of the concentration should be registered. On recent calculations, the richest fifth of the world's population receives 83 per cent of total world income; the poorest fifth receives only 1.4 per cent. (And national-level studies show the distribution of wealth is substantially more unequal than the distribution of income.)[24]

This amplified power is realized in a number of ways. As consumption of resources (such as oil and ores from the rest of the world), it sustains a level of material comfort previously available only to aristocracies. As investment in technology, it has eliminated most heavy labour from production processes in the rich countries and, as noted in Chapter 7, has restructured occupational hierarchies. The material uses and pleasures of male bodies have thus changed dramatically.

At the same time the wealth of the metropolitan countries sustains elaborate service industries. In these industries the symbolic meanings of masculinity are elaborated – notably in mass media, commercial sport and transportation (fast cars and heavy trucks being vehicles of masculinity in every sense). Metropolitan wealth and technology also sustain masculinized armed forces which have reached a terrifying level of destructiveness, from time to time visited on third-world opponents (Vietnam, Cambodia, Afghanistan, Iraq).

Given these circumstances alone, we should not be surprised to find among the men of the rich countries a widespread awareness of change in gender arrangements. This appeared, in different forms, among all the Australian groups discussed in Part II. A sense of profound change can be documented in other countries as well. What is perhaps more surprising is a sense of change out of control, of dislocation in gender relations. This too is evidently widespread.[25]

The enormous growth of the material power of the men in metropolitan countries has been accompanied, I would argue, by an intensification of crisis tendencies in the gender order. In

Chapter 3 I suggested a framework for understanding these crisis tendencies. They have resulted, clearly enough, in a major loss of legitimacy for patriarchy, and different groups of men are now negotiating this loss in very different ways.

The clearest sign of this loss, and the most striking feature of the present moment in the gender order of the rich countries, is the open challenge to men's privileges made by feminism. By virtue of these countries' wealth and control of mass communications, this challenge circulated globally as soon as it was made. It has been pursued in different ways. 'Western' feminism is now engaged in a complex and tense negotiation with 'third-world' feminism about the legacy of colonialism and racism.[26]

As I have suggested already, the challenge to hegemonic heterosexuality from lesbian and gay movements is logically as profound as the challenge to men's power from feminism, but has not been circulated in the same way. Most heterosexual men are able to marginalize this challenge, to regard it as an issue concerning a minority and not affecting them.

The oppositional movements have opened up a range of possibilities for gender relations which is also historically new. Jeffrey Weeks and others have pointed to the recent multiplication of sexual subcultures and sexual identities. As I argued in Chapter 6, the stabilization of gay communities and gay social identity in metropolitan cities means that the gender order now contains a kind of permanent alternative. The very straight gay is at present a loyal opposition, to be sure, but hegemonic heterosexuality cannot now monopolize the imagination in the way it once did.[27]

The expansion of possibilities is not only a question of growing variety in current sexual practice. There has also been a flowering of utopian thinking about gender and sexuality, a sense of expanded historical possibilities for the longer term. A genre such as feminist science fiction may sound exotic, but when one compares it with the male-supremacist 'space westerns' that used to monopolize science fiction (and are still being churned out), the leap of imagination is very clear. Utopian thinking about sexuality and gender is found in other genres too, among them film, painting, poetry, reggae and rock.[28]

The men of the metropolitan countries thus inhabit a paradoxical moment of history. More than any category of people before them, they collectively have the power – the accumulated resources, the physical and social techniques – to shape the future. More possible futures than were ever recognized have been opened up through the work of feminist and sexual liberation movements and through utopian thinking.

But the category 'men' in the rich countries is not a *group* capable of deliberating and choosing a new historical direction. The differences within this category, as we have seen, are profound. To the extent the members of this category share an interest, as a result of the unequal distribution of resources across the world, and between men and women within the rich countries, it would lead them to reject utopian change and defend the status quo.

In this situation their own gender becomes an inescapable issue. The meaning of masculinity, the variety of masculinities, the difficulties of reproducing masculinity, the nature of gender and the extent of gender inequality all come into question and are furiously debated. I suggest that the growth of interest in masculinity at this point in history is not accidental. The issue will not go away, though media attention to such exotic manifestations as the mythopoetic men's movement will doubtless fade.

These circumstances have produced a wider range of politics addressing masculinity, more attempts to define masculinity and influence its reproduction, than have existed before. In the next chapter I will take a closer look at the main forms of this masculinity politics.

9

Masculinity Politics

Men's Politics and Masculinity Politics

Public politics on almost any definition is men's politics. Men predominate in cabinets, general staffs, the senior civil service, political parties and pressure groups as well as in the executive levels of corporations. Leaders are recruited to office through men's networks. The few women who do break through, such as Indira Gandhi and Margaret Thatcher, do so by their exceptional use of men's networks, not women's.

In only one region of the world, Scandinavia, have women arrived as a group in senior political positions. In Finland 39 per cent of parliamentarians are women, in Norway 36 per cent (1993 figures). The more common situation is illustrated by the 1990 figures for Italy, where 15 per cent of members of parliament were women, and tire United States, with 7 per cent. In Japan, the most impenetrable patriarchy among the major powers, 2 per cent of members of parliament were women in the same year. In a recent study of 502 senior bureaucrats in Japan, only three were women – less than 1 per cent.[1]

That is the way the figures are usually presented in 'equal opportunity' discussions. In thinking about masculinity it is better to turn them around, and observe that 98 per cent of the Japanese Diet are men, 93 per cent of the United States Congress are men, etc. It is worth noting that political representation is marginally more patriarchal in the economically developed countries than in the developing countries, averaging 87 per cent as against 86 per cent (1990 figures).

Politics-as-usual is men's politics. Women's attempts to gain a share of power have revealed a defence in depth operated by the men behind the barricades: from legal exclusion, through formal recruitment rules that require experience, qualifications or 'merit' that are harder for women to gain, to a rich variety of informal biases and assumptions that work in favour of men. Behind these barriers to entry, at the upper reaches of power and only dimly visible from outside, are the self-reproducing strategies of power-holding elites. They include traffic in money and influence, the selection of successors, the mentoring of aides and allies, insistently selecting men for power.

The feminist challenge to this structure has certainly not had a sweeping success, outside Scandinavia. Three years after the end of the 1975–85 United Nations Decade for Women, men still made up 85 per cent of elected representatives, world-wide. Five years after that, in 1993, the figure had risen again to 90 per cent.

But the challenge has problematized the situation, has made it a practical and intellectual issue. A theory of the state as a patriarchal institution has been emerging.[2] As I argued at the end of Chapter 8, 'in the last two decades men's position in gender relations, routinely the ground of politics, has also become the object of politics.

I will define as 'masculinity politics' those mobilizations and struggles where the meaning of masculine gender is at issue, and, with it, men's position in gender relations. In such politics masculinity is made a principal theme, not taken for granted as background.

The stake in masculinity politics is the power illustrated by the statistics just quoted – the capacity of certain men to control social resources through gender processes – and the kind of society 'being produced by that power. This is a large stake, larger than is recognized in most current discussions of masculinity. Men's control of resources, and the processes that sustain their control, are of course not the only forces shaping the world. But they are a substantial influence on issues about violence, inequality, technology, pollution and world development. Masculinity politics concerns the making of the gendered power that is deployed in those issues. It is a force in the background of some of the most fateful issues of our time.

As I have emphasized throughout the book, masculinity is not a single pattern. Masculinity politics, accordingly, will take a number of forms; but not an infinite number. In the rich countries at present there are four main forms of masculinity politics, each with a definite relation to the overall structure of gender relations. In this chapter I will discuss them in turn, looking at the kinds of practice in which conceptions of masculinity are embedded, their structural bases in gender relations, and their significance for the overall question of gender justice.[3]

Masculinity Therapy

The kind of masculinity politics that is currently most talked about, especially in the United States, is focused on the healing of wounds done to heterosexual men by gender relations.

Its roots go back to the early 1970s, the waning of the New Left and the growth of counter-cultural therapy. Techniques pioneered by psychiatrists and clinical psychologists moved out of the clinical setting and acquired a popular following. The entrepreneurs of the growth movement created a milieu that embraced a colourful variety of practices and cults: transactional analysis, herbal medicine, 'Eastern' religion, martial arts, bio-energetics, massage, neo-Jungian therapy, and in due course New Age mythologies and 12-step recovery programmes of many kinds. Though centred in the United States, this milieu developed in other rich countries as well. The Australian version was noticed in Chapters 5 and 7.

The main techniques used in the therapeutic milieu are individual counselling by a therapist, merging into individual meditation under guidance, and continuing groups or one-off workshops usually run by a facilitator to whom fees are paid. In such groups and workshops, participants share their emotions and experiences, and get insight and group validation in return.[4]

No sooner had issues about masculinity and the male role been raised by Women's Liberation at the end of the 1960s, than they were reinterpreted as therapeutic issues. During the 1970s there was a small boom in groups, workshops and counsellors concerned with 'men and feminism', 'male sexuality', 'male liberation', and 'men's issues'. In the later 1970s books written by therapists began to roll off the presses, using this therapeutic experience as source material. The titles included *The Hazards of Being Male, Sex and the Liberated Man, Tenderness is Strength, Men in Transition*. Similar articles appeared in the journals of psychotherapy, with titles such as 'Requiem for Superman'.[5]

This activity was at first close to feminism, at least to liberal feminism. Early therapeutic groups for men were called 'consciousness-raising groups'. A critical attitude was taken to the 'traditional male role'. The rationale for therapy was that men needed therapists' help in breaking out of the male role and becoming more sensitive and emotionally expressive. The psychiatrist Kenneth Solomon, for instance, explicitly formulated the goal of 'gender-role therapy' as moving the client towards androgyny.

This was not necessarily easy for therapists. In a perceptive paper in 1979, Sheryl Bear and her colleagues observed that psychotherapists tended to ignore social contexts, to be conservative themselves about gender, and to demand stereotypical behaviour from their clients. Consciousness-raising for therapists was going to be important.

But such warnings were set aside as a fundamental change came over the field. A paper by Jack Kaufman and Richard Timmers published only four years later marks the shift. This described a group of American male therapists, initially pro-feminist but feeling that they lacked something, who went in search of the masculine. They used familiar group-therapy techniques, and unfamiliar images from the poet Robert Bly, to overcome their resistances to encountering 'the hairy man', the deep masculine. Once the deep masculine was found, they helped initiate each other into it.[6]

The main direction taken by masculinity therapy in the 1980s was this attempt to restore a masculinity thought to have been lost or damaged in recent social change. It proved remarkably popular in the United States. Bly's own book *Iron John* was a runaway best-seller in 1990–1 and there has been a rush of publications in its wake. The range of ideas about restoration, and the common ground, can be seen by comparing four recent popular Books About Men based on masculinity therapy.[7]

Warren Farrell's *Why Men Are the Way They Are* is particularly poignant as Farrell wrote one of the original Books About Men, *The Liberated Man*. In the early 1970s he organized a men's support network for NOW, the largest feminist organization in the United States. He helped set up a number of consciousness-raising groups for men, and encouraged public demonstrations in support of feminist causes. He offered a vigorous critique of the masculine value system' and the way men were trapped by the male role. In an early paper Farrell did not hesitate to call men 'a dominant class' who needed to renounce their position of privilege.

A decade later, things were greatly changed. Farrell now argued that too much attention had been given to women's experience of powerlessness and it was time to give attention to men's experience of powerlessness. As this might seem to contradict the facts he had noticed in the early 1970s, Farrell carefully redefined power by shifting from the public world to the inner world of emotion. Men did not *feel* emotionally in control of their lives, therefore they lacked power. Men should not feel guilty about what is wrong with the world since women were equally to blame. If women wanted men to change, *women* had to make that happen by changing their emotional expectations of men. But Farrell held out little hope for this. He now saw men's and women's psychologies as starkly different, revealed in their 'primary fantasies' (men: sex with lots of beautiful women; women: a secure home).

(Since this chapter was written, Farrell has published another book on the subject, *The Myth of Male Power*. It repeats these arguments with greater vehemence, increased bitterness against feminism, more emphasis on the biological base of sex difference, and a new respect for – guess what? – Robert Bly and male rituals.)

Herb Goldberg's *The Inner Male* was also a return performance after a 1970s book, *The Hazards of Being Male*. As the subtitle *Surviving the Myth of Masculine Privilege* indicated, Goldberg in the 1970s was well to the right of Farrell in the 1970s. By the late 1980s they had converged. Goldberg too counselled men that they were not to blame for gender troubles. Liberation had been tried and had failed, leaving men confused and resentful. It failed because it denied the basic emotional differences between women and men, which in Goldberg's view were polarized unconscious characters macho vs. earth-mother. This 'gender undertow' subverted any conscious politics of change. Therapy could help men and women reduce their defensiveness and thus allow them to communicate better. Goldberg was vague about how that would affect the larger problems, apparently hoping for some trickle-down effect from individual therapy with opinion leaders.

But Goldberg was crystal clear about the strategy he rejected. His earlier book had been respectful of feminism as a source of positive change. In *The Inner Male* the gloves came off. Its most striking feature was a series of hostile case studies of 'liberated' women and their male fellow-travellers: Marilyn the Female Macho, Ann the Liberated Ice Queen, Karen the Liberated Engulfer, Alice the Complete-Liberation Crazy-Maker, Benjamin the Totalitarian Humanist, etc. At the end of this parade, Goldberg admitted that they were not real cases at all. He had made them up, to reflect *his* 'perception and belief' that 'liberated' people were defensive and deceptive. This passage is essential reading for anyone curious about the epistemological status of pop psychology.[8]

Robert Bly's *Iron John* has been so widely thought a striking novelty that it is worth noticing how much ground it shared with earlier Books About Men. Like Farrell and Goldberg, Bly thought men have been unjustly accused by feminism; that men should not accept blame; that they should acknowledge and celebrate their difference from women. Like Farrell and Goldberg he rejected a politics of social equality and emphasized the arena of emotions. His blind spots – race, sexuality, cultural difference, class – are much the same. Bly differed in emphasizing men's separation from their fathers as a source of emotional damage, and in emphasizing a need for initiation among men rather than negotiation between men and women.

What this amounted to, nevertheless, was the same kind of answer to the difficulties of gender: a therapy for masculinity. Bly's eclectic symbolism and search for archetypes, and media attention to the oddities of his movement (beating on drums, pretending to be warriors), should not conceal this. The substance of the 'mythopoetic men's movement' is the familiar group technique of the therapeutic milieu. Workshops are set up by therapeutic entrepreneurs; participants contribute accounts of their emotions and experiences and gain group validation in exchange. Popular therapeutic cults of the past two decades have usually combined these techniques with the persona of a leader, and a trade-mark ritual and jargon. Bly had been providing these in workshops and other meetings for about a decade before the publication of *Iron John*.

Sam Keen's *Fire in the Belly* shared Bly's loosely Jungian conception of masculinity as an emotional system rooted in archetypes. Keen, like Farrell, had a background in consciousness-raising groups and psychotherapy, and he shared with Goldberg, Bly and

Farrell a preoccupation with emotional relationships, a speculative method and a satisfaction with snippets of evidence. Keen too
prescribed a therapy for wounded masculinity, a healing journey.
Like Bly's idea of a mythic initiation into masculinity, Keen's
therapy involved a separation from femininity to find a deeper
masculine truth.

Keen, however, saw this as a psychic journey, not a separatist
men's cult. He connected the healing of masculinity with the
healing of the planet and the healing of a society marked by
homophobia, racism and environmental degradation. In short,
Keen saw masculinity therapy as part of a broader project of
reform, however metaphorical his language for it.

Nevertheless the main tendency of masculinity therapy is to
replace a politics of reform rather than support it. The political
context is relevant. Goldberg's venom against 'liberated' women
and men had much in common with Reaganite attacks on 'liberals' of the same date. Farrell's latest book attacks 'political cor-
rectness' and indeed all public policy initiatives for women. But
an internal dynamic is also important. As some of the cases in
Chapters 5 and 7 illustrate, middle-class Western men often
experience feminism as an accusation, and some adopt it as self-
blame. The early Men's Liberation debates quite probably heightened the sense of guilt. The rightward turn in masculinity therapy
in the 1980s offered reassurance in place of stress and a personal
resolution of the guilt – rather than reform of the situation that
produced it.

The structural base of this form of masculinity politics is the
complicit masculinity defined in Chapter 3. The therapists indicate this through their own themes. Their clients are indeed not
to blame, in the sense that they are not themselves the bearers
of hegemonic masculinity. But they are also not the oppressed.
Authors such as Farrell, Goldberg and Bly simply presuppose a
white, heterosexual, middle-class American readership. The men
addressed are those who quietly benefit from patriarchy without
being militant in its defence.

This group is the base of the politics in a quite literal sense.
They pay to attend the therapy sessions, workshops and conferences, and buy the books and journals. The limits of masculinity
therapy are in turn set by their interests. They are prepared to
adjust their relationships with women, but not to reform them in

any fundamental way. Thus the initial commitment of the movement to feminism was shallow, and an anti-feminist shift readily occurred. No alliance with gay men is even on the horizon. (In 1993, when the Clinton administration reneged on explicit guarantees to gay people about employment in the military, no protest was heard from these quarters.) The self-absorption that is an important practical consequence of masculinity therapy, and the translation of social issues about men into questions of pure psychology, are both connected with the profound interest this group has in limiting the revolutionary upheaval in gender relations that was on the agenda in the early 1970s.

To understand the significance of masculinity therapy as a form of masculinity politics, then, we must look beyond its own preoccupation with men's emotional wounds and personal healing. The larger consequence of the popular forms of masculinity therapy is an adaptation of patriarchal structures through the *modernization* of masculinity. For although texts like Bly's are nostalgic and the mythopoetic imagery can be strikingly reactionary, the tendency of therapeutic practice is towards accommodation between men and women, adjustment at the level of personal relations. In this, masculinity therapy is politically distinct from the hard-line masculinity politics discussed in the following section.

We should not leave this topic without noting that masculinity therapy is not the only way in which therapy, and even Jungian ideas, can be used in masculinity politics. The British therapist John Rowan in *The Horned God*, a book also published in the late 1980s, shows other possibilities.

Rowan, like Farrell, started with anti-sexist men's groups, and developed a broad experience in the therapeutic milieu. Rowan, however, searched for resources to support men's continuing commitment to feminism. The image of the 'horned god' within a context of goddess-consciousness is his attempt to find archetypal support for men in a world where women are strong and men remain engaged with them, rather than trying to separate. The goal of his therapeutic work is not the restoration of masculinity, nor the promotion of androgyny (criticized as based on a patriarchal masculine/feminine dichotomy), but revolutionary change in the relations between women and men. The character of this project will be considered in Chapter 10.[9]

The Gun Lobby: Defending Hegemonic Masculinity

In 1987 a particularly frightening multiple murder by a young man in Melbourne led to a public outcry in Australia against automatic weapons, and guns in general. Opinion polls supported tighter gun control. The new Labor Party premier of the neighbouring state of New South Wales, a machine politician who needed a popular mandate, brought in strict gun control legislation and early the next year went into an election. He was defeated. Conventional wisdom attributed this to a vigorous campaign in support of gun ownership that gained wide support, especially in country areas.

This was the first time Australia had experienced such a campaign. The 'gun lobby' is familiar and powerful in the United States. It has become particularly influential since 1977 when a right-wing mobilization threw out the old leadership of the National Rifle Association and converted it to a mass organization actively promoting the ownership and use of guns. In struggles over gun control legislation the NRA routinely outspent the gun control lobby by ten to one. In a remarkable book, *Warrior Dreams*, William Gibson has traced links between the NRA, the gun industry, and a variety of paranoid groups training in violence and promoting 'New War' myths – articulated in fantasy, but with all too real consequences.[10]

It is a cliché that the gun is a penis-symbol as well as a weapon. Gun organizations are conventionally masculine in cultural style; hunting and gun magazines dress their models in check shirts and boots to emphasize their masculinity. The gun lobby hardly has to labour the inference that politicians trying to take away our guns are emasculating us. At both symbolic and practical levels, the defence of gun ownership is a defence of hegemonic masculinity.

Most of the time, defence of the patriarchal order does not require an explicit masculinity politics. Given that heterosexual men socially selected for hegemonic masculinity run the corporations and the state, the routine maintenance of these institutions will normally do the job. This is the core of the collective project of hegemonic masculinity, and the reason why this project most of the time is not visible as a project. Most of the time masculinity need not be thematized at all. What is brought to attention is national security, or corporate profit, or family values, or true religion, or individual freedom, or international competitiveness, or economic efficiency, or the advance of science. Through the everyday working of institutions defended in such terms, the dominance of a particular kind of masculinity is achieved.

Yet crisis tendencies in the gender order do emerge, and in response to them hegemonic masculinity *is* likely to be thematized and a 'gun lobby' type of politics arises. The interplay between routine maintenance and explicit masculinity politics can be followed in different arenas of practice. I will briefly discuss three: masculine violence, the promotion of exemplary masculinities and the management of organizations.

I have already noted the mixture of open violence and low-level harassment involved in straight men's subordination of gay men. It is clear that the men involved in gay-bashing often see themselves as avengers on behalf of society, punishing the betrayers of manhood. Research on domestic violence finds something similar. Husbands who batter wives typically feel that they are exercising a right, maintaining good order in the family and punishing their wives' delinquency – especially wives' failure to keep their proper place (e.g., not doing domestic work to the husband's satisfaction, or answering back).[11]

Violence on the largest possible scale is the purpose of the military; and no arena has been more important for the definition of hegemonic masculinity in European/American culture. The imaginative literature of combat is very clear on this role, from its endorsement in *The Red Badge of Courage* (1895) to its terrible refutation in *All Quiet on the Western Front* (1929). The figure of the hero is central to the Western cultural imagery of the masculine (a point reinforced by the 'warrior' and 'hero' archetypes in the current wave of neo-Jungian books). Armies have freely drawn on this imagery for purposes of recruitment. 'The United States Army builds *MEN*', proclaimed a recruiting poster of 1917, showing an Aryan mesomorph simultaneously as athlete, craftsman, crusader and private soldier.

Yet we would be sadly misled if we believed military operations actually work on the basis of crusading heroism. Another document of the same war shows the distance between image and practice. James McCudden, the greatest British air ace with 57 German aircraft shot down, finished an autobiography shortly before his death in 1918. He started with aircraft as a mechanic. His book reveals an intense interest in technical aspects of flying, a respectful attitude to the Germans, and a cautious, calculative approach to battle. Nothing could be further from the public image of fighter pilots as hyper-masculine knights of the air – the 'fighter jocks' of Tom Wolfe's *The Right Stuff* – an attitude McCudden himself contemptuously dismissed as 'cavalry tactics in the air'. Yet the patriotic publishers of his book called it *Flying Fury*.

McCudden's caution was shared by the troops in the trenches below him. A remarkable piece of research by Tony Ashworth has shown that for much of the war, on many parts of the Western Front, the troops operated a 'live and let live' system, limiting the actual violence. Tacit agreements with enemy troops, and grass-roots social controls, resulted in truces or ritualized aggression that was easily avoided – to the fury of the high command. Paul Fussell's research on American frontline soldiers in the Second World War confirms the gap between media imagery and the daily reality of boredom and petty tyranny (nicely called 'chickenshit' by the troops). For the minority in actual combat the daily reality was extreme fear, chancy outcomes and disgusting deaths – being dismembered by artillery was the commonest way to die. The techniques of industrialized war have almost nothing to do with the conventions of individual heroism.[12]

Yet the imagery of masculine heroism is not *culturally* irrelevant. Something has to glue the army together and keep the men in line, or at least enough in line for the organization to produce its violent effects. Part of the struggle for hegemony in the gender order is the use of culture for such disciplinary purposes: setting standards, claiming popular assent and discrediting those who fall short. The production of exemplary masculinities is thus integral to the politics of hegemonic masculinity.

The importance of exemplary masculinities has probably increased over the last two centuries with the decline of religious legitimations for patriarchy in the West. Some of the major genres of commercial popular culture centre on exemplary masculinities: the pulp Western, the thriller, the sports broadcast (increasingly orchestrated as a spectacle centring on millionaire stars) and the Hollywood movie.

The symbolism of masculinity in these genres is by no means fixed. Joan Mellen, studying American film, traced a narrowing of the emotional range allowed to masculine heroes from early in the century. Hollywood concentrated increasingly on the proof of masculinity by violence. Mellen's book was published in the late 1970s, just as Stallone and Schwarzenegger were becoming major stars: this trend continued. With the gradually increasing pressure for gender equality, it seems, a market was created for representations of power in the arena men could still claim as distinctively their own, plain violence.

There is a sense, too, in which exemplary masculinity became collectivized. The rise of *Playboy* magazine in the 1950s was a striking example. The readership of this magazine was positioned as a corporate sexual hero, consuming an endless supply of desirable 'girls'. The Playboy corporation managed a double commercialization of this fantasy in 1960 with the opening of the first Playboy Clubs. A readership was converted into a membership, with women employees grotesquely subordinated as 'Bunnies'. The growth of the video pornography industry suggests this collectivization is still going on.[13]

The corporate activity behind media celebrities and the commercialization of sex brings us to the third arena of hegemonic masculinity politics, the management of patriarchal organizations. Institutions do not maintain themselves; someone has to practise power for power effects to occur. Historians provide excellent accounts of this. Chapter 1 mentioned Michael Grossberg's research on the formation of the legal profession in the United States; another example is Michael Roper's analysis of the changing character of masculine authority in British manufacturing companies.

The fact that power relations must be practised allows for divergence in *how* they are practised. Chapter 8 discussed the divergence between masculinity strategies emphasizing command and those emphasizing expertise. This is familiar in business and politics as the conflict between line management and professionals, between hard-liners and liberals, between entrepreneurs and bureaucrats. It appears even in the management of armies, between blood-and-guts generals and technocrats.

Such divergences can make it difficult to see the gender politics involved. There is no Patriarch Headquarters, with flags and limousines, where all the strategies are worked out. It is common for different groups of men, each pursuing a project of hegemonic masculinity, to come into conflict with each other. A classic example is the annual fight between police and bikers at the Bathurst motorcycle races in Australia.[14]

It is important, then, to acknowledge that there is an active defence of hegemonic masculinity and the position of economic, ideological and sexual dominance held by heterosexual men. This defence takes a variety of forms and it often has to yield ground or change tactics. But it has formidable resources, and in recent decades, in the face of historic challenges, has been impressively successful.

The consequences of this defence are not just the slowing down or turning back of gender change, as in the cases of parliamentary representation and the breakdown of guarantees for women in Eastern Europe. The consequences are also found in long-term trends in the institutional order that hegemonic masculinity dominates. These trends include the growing destructiveness of military technology (not least the spread of nuclear weapons), the long-term degradation of the environment and the increase of economic inequality on a world scale. The successful maintenance of a competitive and dominance-oriented masculinity, in the central institutions of the world order, makes each of these trends more dangerous and more difficult to reverse.

Gay Liberation

The main alternative to hegemonic masculinity in recent Western history is homosexual masculinity, and the most explicit political opposition among men was articulated by the Gay Liberation movement.

Most forms of political action by homosexual men over the last hundred years have been wary in style and severely limited in their goals. Magnus Hirschfeld's pioneering Scientific-Humanitarian Committee, set up in 1897, relied heavily on Hirschfeld's status as a doctor and on claims to be advancing a scientific discourse. A second generation, working through organizations such as the Mattachine Society in the United States (1950) and the Homosexual Law Reform Society (1958) in Britain, used discreet lobbying tactics to influence the state. Jeffrey Weeks remarked of the latter that it was 'a classical middle-class single-issue pressure group', marked by caution and a desire for respectability.[15]

These were not the only attempts to pursue a politics of homosexuality, but they were characteristic in their restraint. There was even a trend away from gender issues (most of the late nineteenth-century theorists having interpreted homosexual people in some fashion as an intermediate gender) towards an ungendered politics of individual rights.

The Gay Liberation movement sparked by the 1968 Stonewall riot in New York – resistance to police raiding a gay bar – seemed at the time a very dramatic break from the caution of previous decades. Historians have since emphasized the continuities, tracing the gradual growth of the urban gay communities which were electrified by Gay Liberation. Yet there was a major break in the object of politics. Close association with radical feminism, also growing explosively at the time, and the broad 1960s challenge to established power, allowed Gay Liberation to mount an explicit challenge to hegemonic masculinity and the gender order in which it was embedded.

Statement after statement named straight men, patriarchy, the family and heterosexism as the sources of gay oppression. As Dennis Altman put it in *Homosexual: Oppression and Liberation*:

> In many ways we represent the most blatant challenge of all to the mores of a society organized around belief in the nuclear family and sharply differentiated gender differences.[16]

Psychoanalytic ideas prompted certain Gay Liberation theorists, especially in Europe, to argue that gay politics expressed a necessary gender radicalism. Necessary, because homosexuality was the repressed truth of conventional masculinity. Guy Hocquenghem argued in *Homosexual Desire* that the homosexual exists first in the imagination of 'normal' people, and is produced as an alien type when the flux of desire is Oedipalized, i.e., brought under the sway of the patriarchal family. Anally-connected desire is what is left out of the paranoid world of masculine normality, in which women are the only legitimate sexual objects, and possessors-of-phalluses struggle with each other for power and wealth.

Mario Mieli's psychoanalysis was less avant-garde than Hocquenghem's, but his gender doctrine in *Homosexuality and Liberation* was even blunter. Straight men's oppression of homosexual men, he argued, is a direct consequence of the repression of the feminine in men, in the attempt to bolster male supremacy. Violence results from the strength of the repression. Men's homosexuality necessarily contains femininity, and a radical politics of

gay liberation must assert this. Mieli thus celebrated queens, trans-
vestites, glitter, humour and parody as essential parts of a transformative politics. David Fernbach in *The Spiral Path,* less spirited
but more systematic, presented the gender system as the basis of
the situation of homosexual men and women. Fernbach saw the
necessary goal of homosexual politics as the abolition of gender
itself.[17]

This radical challenge to gender did not, however, become the
mainstream of gay community life or politics. Not drag queens
but 'Castro Street clones', equipped with jeans and T-shirts, mous-
taches and cropped hair, became the international leaders of
style in gay communities in the later 1970s. The diversification of
sexual scenes brought leather, SM and rough trade to greater
prominence. There may have been, as some argue, an element of
parody in gay men's adoption of hyper-masculine styles. But there
is little doubt about the cultural shift away from femininity.

At the same time gay community politics was reconfigured.
The alliance with feminism weakened, as liberal feminism gained
a foothold in the establishment and radical feminism moved
towards separatism. A new kind of institutional politics emerged
as gay representatives entered municipal government and gay
businessmen developed a political presence. In urban politics in
the United States, the revolutionary impulse of Gay Liberation
was replaced by something resembling ethnic pressure-group
politics, jockeying for space within the system rather than trying
to overthrow it.

The HIV/AIDS epidemic has, for the most part, reinforced this
trend. Gay organizations have functioned as pressure groups (lobbying for funds and changes in policy) and as service providers
(care, research, education). They have spoken for a constituency
in a range of committees, boards, enquiries and panels. This is
not monolithic. Contestatory politics continued, for instance in
ACT UP and Queer Nation. But pressure-group politics is certainly the main trend. The very straight gay of Chapter 6 expresses
a pattern in public affairs as well as private life.[18]

But if gay communities dropped Gay Liberation theory, homophobic politicians continued to believe it. Lurid abuse of homosexuals accompanied the HIV epidemic in the mid-1980s. The
early 1990s in the United States saw a fresh wave of homophobic
campaigns. Agitators of the religious right picture gay men as an
army of lawbreakers, violating God's commands, threatening first

the family and then the larger social order. Popular homophobia, so far as I have been able to trace its themes, says nothing about God but is graphic about sex. Anal sexuality is a focus of disgust, and receptive anal sex is a mark of feminization. Homophobic humour among straight men still revolves around the limp wrist, the mincing walk and innuendo about castration.[19]

Nor are these themes absent from the gay cultural scene. Drag shows remain popular even if much of the audience is wearing engineer boots, and have been used effectively as vehicles of AIDS education. Camp and 'nellie' personal styles persisted alongside the 'clone' style; Judy Garland has yet to become unpopular. A degree of gender dissidence persists alongside the sexual dissidence, and is now being vigorously revived in 'queer' style and theory.

There is, then, an unavoidable politics of masculinity in and around contemporary men's homosexuality. The structural base of this politics is the main type of subordinated masculinity in the contemporary gender order. The turbulence of the story just outlined shows that the relationship between this politics and its social base is far from simple. We cannot think of the gay community as a homogeneous source of radical gender politics.

Indeed the base is necessarily divided. As I argued in Chapter 6, the social definition of the object of desire through hegemonic masculinity creates a contradiction in and around gay masculinity which no changes of style can erase. The growth of a respectable, ethnic-style politics in gay communities depends on observing convention enough for gay representatives to operate in city halls, bankers' offices and medical committees. Mario Mieli, in his floral gown and silver heels, would not bring home the bacon. Yet full assimilation is impossible, given the overall structure of gender relations. Hegemonic masculinity forbids the receptive pleasures of the anus and opposes assimilation. Gay men get murdered in homophobic attacks regardless of their personal styles.[20]

Plainly a gay community does not automatically generate an oppositional masculinity politics. Yet the presence of a stable alternative to hegemonic masculinity – the irreversible achievement of the last quarter-century – reconfigures the politics of masculinity as a whole, making gender dissidence a permanent possibility. Both practical and theoretical challenges to the gender order will continue to arise, not necessarily from a partly pacified gay community, but certainly from the situation defined by its presence.

Exit Politics

Implicit in the idea of practice is the principle that social action is always creative. No straight man is mechanically committed to defending the gender order, any more than a gay man is mechanically committed to rejecting it. It is possible for straight men to oppose patriarchy and try to exit from the worlds of hegemonic and complicit masculinity.

This was the intention of the radical wing of Men's Liberation in the 1970s. Their strategy was for men to confront and change their masculinity (usually understood as internalized sex role expectations) in order to pursue a politics of social justice. The logic corresponded to the moment of contestation defined in Chapter 5.

The scope and intentions of this politics are well illustrated by the 1980 British document 'A minimum self-definition of the anti-sexist men's movement' presented at a conference in Bristol. This statement expressed support for Women's Liberation and Gay Liberation, and rejected racism and imperialism. It argued that men's power over women also distorted men's lives, and that changing this situation required joint action by men. It required new relationships with children, and change in the relationship between work and domestic life. Change required the creation of an anti-sexist culture as well as reform in personal life.[21]

There was shared ground between this politics and the early phase of masculinity therapy, a sense that men's lives were being damaged and needed repair. But there was also a large difference. Here the focus was on contesting the social inequalities of gender, especially the subordination of women. There was often a flavour of men's-auxiliary-to-the-women's-movement about both action and theory: men running the creches at women's conferences, men being required to read feminist books, men holding discussions under women's supervision.

Being an auxiliary was, indeed, proposed as a strategy by some American authors: in the gaudy *Effeminist Manifesto* composed in New York in 1973, and in more sustained fashion by John

Stoltenberg, whose book *Refusing to Be a Man* was published recently. Stoltenberg's vehement arguments against pornography illustrate the obvious problem of the strategy. To which feminism should men be auxiliary? – since feminists are divided on this issue, as on many others. How can a politics whose main theme is anger towards men serve to mobilize men broadly?[22]

This said, it is striking how persistently attempts have been made to organize anti-sexist politics among men. Jon Snodgrass's anthology *For Men Against Sexism* documents American efforts in the 1970s, and Andrew Tolson's *The Limits of Masculinity* documents British groups of the same period. The British magazine *Achilles Heel* published theoretical and practical discussions of high quality from the late 1970s. German anti-sexist discussions are documented by Georg Brzoska and Gerhard Hafner, Canadian experience by Michael Kaufman in *Cracking the Armour*. There have been groups such as 'Men Opposing Patriarchy' in Australia, and there has been discussion of men and feminism in Sweden. In recent years there has been a growing number of anti-sexist courses on masculinity in universities in the United States.

The most sustained attempt to organize a men's movement is the National Organization for Men Against Sexism in the United States, founded in the early 1980s. This was formerly the National Organization for Changing Men; the 1990 name change was part of an attempt to define a sharper anti-patriarchal politics. The move reflected the tension between masculinity therapy and exit politics that runs through the organization and its associated magazine, *Changing Men*. The magazine is simultaneously an attempt to popularize anti-sexist perspectives, a publicity outlet for therapists and a venue for art and literature exploring 'men's issues'. Building and maintaining this organization in the climate of the 1980s was a formidable task. No broad movement has crystallized around it; NOMAS seems well established in its bases in universities and the therapeutic milieu, but has not grown much beyond them.[23]

Some common features of these efforts (in English-speaking countries at least) are worth noting. The scale of organized counter-sexist projects among men is generally small; there is no mobilization here comparable with feminism or the gay movement. Particular campaigns can pick up wider support. The broadest has been the White Ribbon campaign in Canada, in opposition to violence against women. Commemorating the women murdered in 1989 at the University of Montreal engineering school, this turned into a mass action which gained support from a wide spectrum of men (including prominent men in politics and the media) as well as from women.

Nevertheless the general pattern is of small and not very stable groups. Paul Lichterman's careful research on an anti-sexist group MOVE (Men Overcoming Violence) in the United States, which had worked with batterers and pursued public issues about masculinity and violence, shows how difficult it was for them to sustain a consistently critical stance towards masculinity. The feminist impulse was gradually displaced, and the tone of the group was increasingly set by counselling psychologists engaged in developing a professional specialty in men's problems.[24]

Men's counter-sexist projects commonly involve both heterosexual and gay men, and make little distinction between them. They often develop in the context of other radical politics, such as environmentalism or socialism. These points suggest the lack of a clear-cut social base, a point to which I shall return.

Finally, these projects share the experience of being delegitimated to a marked degree. Feminist commentary, while sometimes welcoming efforts at change, has been generally sceptical of organizing among men and sometimes openly hostile, treating it as a reactionary swindle. The mass media persistently satirize 'the New Sensitive Man', let alone active feminist men. From the point of view of hegemonic masculinity the whole thing is a ludicrous exercise in men trying to turn themselves into women.[25]

This is, of course, the other meaning of 'refusing to be a man' – exiting from the gender, rather than trying to conduct a dissident politics within it. In this limiting case of masculinity politics, practice is turned towards lived masculinity not to modernize or restore it but to dismantle it.

Mario Mieli's arguments about the necessary effeminacy of gay men, and the repressed femininity of straight men, led him to advocate a 'transsexual' strategy for liberation. 'Radical drag', reshuffling elements of gender (for instance, combining a dress with a beard), was a tactic of Gay Liberation in the early 1970s.

As we have seen, the mainstream of gay community life moved decisively away from Mieli's path. The gender-violating exit from masculinity has increasingly been defined not as a political strategy but as a specialized sexual identity: more exactly two, 'transvestite' and 'transsexual'. Medical sexology underpins this definition, creating syndromes out of the flux of practice. Dissidence becomes – in a wonderful expression I found in the *Archives of Sexual Behavior* – 'nonhomosexual gender dysphorias'. The medicalization of gender dissidence makes a surgical procedure the criterion of seriousness. Straight doctors become the arbiters of elegance: it is their gender ideology to which 'transsexuals' must conform to win the prize of surgical castration and genital remodelling. Hegemonic masculinity regulates even the exit from masculinity.[26]

The reassertion of gender dichotomy by surgery has not eliminated gender ambiguity from the culture. Drag is endemic in theatre, for instance. In *Vested Interests* Marjorie Garber has wittily documented cross-dressing as a theme of cultural anxiety in a remarkable variety of arenas, from detective fiction to television to popular music to anthropology journals. The Lacanian theory that underpins her analysis is ahistorical, and Gerber tends to homogenize very different situations. But a much more historically sensitive analysis makes a similar point. Carol Clover's *Men, Women, and Chain Saws* shows how the developing horror movie genre in the 1970s and 1980s responded to the cultural destabilization of masculinity in that period. The films did this both by using ambivalent characters, or characters whose gender meanings shifted within the story, and – more strikingly – by positioning a mostly young male audience in a relation of identification with female characters.[27]

Such treatments of gender ambiguity, not as a syndrome but as a form of cultural politics, jibe with Mieli's model of sexual politics, and together they offer an important clue to the sources of men's counter-sexist politics. This is not a masculinity politics with a base in a major form of masculinity, as are the other three types discussed in this chapter. It is, rather, a politics that arises in relation to the *overall* structure of the gender order.

The point here is that the making of masculinity, in the moment of engagement defined in the case studies of Part II, is structured not only by immediate social relationships but also by the pattern of the gender order as a whole. Masculinity is shaped in relation to an overall structure of power (the subordination of women to men), and in relation to a general symbolism of difference (the opposition of femininity and masculinity). Men's counter-sexist politics is dissidence directed towards the former, gender-violation is dissidence directed towards the latter. They

need not go together – hence some feminists object to transsexualism as a reaffirmation of patriarchy – but they can.

Since exit politics relates to the overall structure of the gender
order, it has no local base. It cannot be understood as the pursuit
of the concrete interest of any group of men, since men in general
benefit from the subordination of women. So exit politics is hard
to articulate and rarely becomes a mass politics.

To resist the integration of personality around the subordination of women or the dichotomy of masculinity/femininity is to
court dis-integration, the gender vertigo discussed in Chapter 5.
This is high on stress, the opposite of masculinity therapy. Exit
politics is therefore likely to be episodic. At the same time, it can
emerge anywhere in the structure. It is impossible to purge from
the gender order.

Currently operating at the fringe of mass sexual politics, as a
flickering realization of radical negations of hegemonic masculinity, it is difficult to see exit politics as the broad path to the
future for heterosexual men. But it is also difficult to see any
future without it. More than any other contemporary form of masculinity politics it represents the potential for change across the
gender order as a whole. In the final chapter I will discuss ways
in which this potential might still be realized.

10

Practice and Utopia

Full fadom five thy Father lies,
　Of his bones are Corrall made:
Those are pearles that were his eies,
　Nothing of him that doth fade,
But doth suffer a Sea-change
Into something rich, & strange
　　　　　Shakespeare, *The Tempest*

This chapter will consider what our current knowledge of masculinity means for the project of social justice in gender relations. That project requires us to think both *in* our current situations and *beyond* them, about current practice and possible utopia.[1]

It has become customary in Books About Men to hang one's hat on an archetype chosen from myth or story. I think this is a fine custom, and what better storyteller than Shakespeare? My quotation is meant to recall no archetype of the distant past, but the utopian dimension of our relation to the future. It is sung by the spirit Ariel to a shipwrecked youth. Like everything in the magnificent pageant of *The Tempest*, the song is illusion. But like all rich fantasy it creates a world of possibility, which remains as a counterpoint when Prospero breaks his staff and drowns his book, and mundane life reasserts itself. We need that counterpoint in our world too. The outcome of a project of social justice in sexual politics will indeed be 'something rich, & strange', not something we have had before.

Historical Consciousness

The case studies of Part II showed a widespread awareness of turbulence and change in gender relations. These Australian men's consciousness of change is not exceptional. Researchers in the United States were documenting men's awareness of change, and ambivalence about it, in the 1970s. Early theorists of the 'male role' were already trying to understand sex role change in the 1950s, despite that decade's reputation for conservatism. There was every reason for this awareness. Massive changes in married women's employment rates had occurred, in industrial countries, before the Women's Liberation movement emerged; change in heterosexual practice was underway, with increasingly reliable contraception; and the structure of families was changing, with rising expectation of life, rising divorce rates and lower fertility.[2]

But other patterns have not changed. Men continue to draw a patriarchal dividend, in the metropole as well as the periphery. In 1990, for instance, men's median income in the United States was 197 per cent of women's median income. In almost all regions of the world in the 1990s, men virtually monopolize the elite levels of corporate and state power. Heterosexual men of all classes are in a position to command sexual services from women, through purchase, custom, force or pressure. Men still virtually monopolize weapons, and mostly control heavy machinery and new technology. It is clear that massive inequalities of resources, and asymmetries in practice, persist. The extension of the European/American pattern of patriarchy across the world, traced in Chapter 8, often erodes local bases of women's authority.[3]

So the 'change' of which there is so much awareness is not the crumbling of the material and institutional structures of patriarchy. What has crumbled, in the industrial countries, is the *legitimation* of patriarchy. In Chapter 4 I quoted a young working-class man with a record of violence, unemployment and imprisonment, briskly endorsing equal rights for women and complaining about 'prejudiced blokes' who do not. The vast change in legitimation over the past century is, for me, summed up in that comment.

No huge crowds of men have become feminists. The green men of Chapter 5 are distinctly a minority. But the underlying terms of discussion have shifted. In all public forums, and increasingly in private forums, it is now the denial of equality for women and the maintenance of homophobia that demand justifications. Such justifications are constantly offered, of course. But the fact that patriarchy has to be excused and defended against a cultural presumption of equality gives a hysterical quality to sociobiology, to gun-lobby ideologists, to the right wing of masculinity therapy and to new-right 'traditional values' religious populism.

In some milieux, such as younger professional and intellectual networks in Western cities, domestic equality and shared household labour is now common sense. How many men actually take on full-time care of babies depends (as Lynne Segal notes in *Slow Motion*) on economic arrangements that make it affordable; the point here is that many households think this is the *right* thing to do. Some institutions also are functioning to extend equality. The education system has tended to equalize access, and its economic weight has grown. Within the patriarchal state particular units work in the interests of women, for instance, equal opportunity programmes, women's services and campaigns to prevent violence against women. Localized institutional change of this kind consolidates the shift in gender ideology.

At the heart of this cultural change, deeper than the liberal concept of 'equal rights' through which it is often expressed, is the emergence of a historical consciousness about gender. The knowledge that gender was a structure of social relations, open to social reform, was slower to emerge than the corresponding knowledge about class. But during the nineteenth and twentieth centuries this did emerge in the metropole, stimulated not only by the gender dynamics of industrial capitalism (as commonly thought) but also by the imperial encounter with the dramatically different gender orders of 'native' peoples. For those 'native' peoples, in turn, the historicity of gender was violently made obvious by conquest, and by the colonial systems under which they had to deal with the gender regimes of the colonizers.

Almost everywhere, the historicity of gender was first registered as an issue about women: the 'woman question' of the late nineteenth century, the 'women's issues' of the twentieth. This follows from the patriarchal structuring of culture itself, as well as from the fact that gender politics first became a mass politics in women's struggles (for property rights, for the vote, for equal pay). The application to men followed, with difficulty. The story of psychoanalysis and sex role theory outlined in Chapter 1 reveals the long struggle to express a developing historical consciousness of masculinity in the language of science.

This consciousness erupted in the Women's Liberation, Gay Liberation and Men's Liberation movements. Millennia of patriarchy could now be brought to an end. The technological conditions existed, the change of consciousness was upon us. In Men's Liberation writing, this sense of a great historical drama unfolding gave resonance to otherwise modest reform proposals and vague rhetorics of change. Most of the 1970s writers implied that masculinity was in crisis and that the crisis itself would drive change forward. The end would be a world where masculinity as we knew it would be annihilated, replaced by some kind of androgyny. The 'exit politics' discussed in Chapter 9 carries forward this sense of an ending, however muted the rhetoric has now become.

The shift in cultural presuppositions about masculinity marked by the liberation movements of the early 1970s is irreversible. The more conservative ideologies that have moved in on the terrain are varieties of historical consciousness about masculinity, not reversions to prehistorical consciousness. They all accept the fact of social transformations of masculinity. Some, including sociobiologists and the neo-conservative theorist George Gilder, decry the fact, thinking that society has moved too far from nature.[4] Others embrace the possibility of transforming gender. For instance, masculinity therapy is all about social techniques for changing masculinity, in the various directions recommended by different therapists and gurus. Gun-lobby politics tries to revive lost manhood, and this too presumes a manhood capable of being lost and regained. None assume, none can assume, that men and masculinity simply are as they are.

This historical consciousness is, I would suggest, the distinctive feature of contemporary masculinity politics, and the horizon of contemporary thought on masculinity. But whereas Men's Liberation believed that apocalyptic awareness of the historicity of masculinity itself defined the political goal – the annihilation of masculinity – we now know that very different politics can be pursued within this horizon. Accordingly, we must examine the purposes of action.

Purposes of Action

The consciousness of historical change in gender, even as it opens up a politics of change, also seems to limit it. With shifting settings and diverse groupings, on what common principles can politics rest?

It is easy to conclude there can be none. Two respectable bodies of opinion say so, liberal pluralism and postmodernism. Liberal pluralism, the mainstream ideology of parliamentary capitalism, recognizes no continuing basis of politics beyond individual interest. The interests of individuals are aggregated in shifting groups whose pushing and tugging constitute the political process. Postmodernism, justifiably sceptical of the idea of a prepolitical individual, also rejects the collectivist alternative and the idea of a 'foundation' for politics. With the 'grand narratives' of modernity discredited, politics in postmodernity becomes a kaleidoscope of assertions and resistances whose end no one can formulate, let alone foresee.

Both positions underestimate the onto-formativity of practice (defined in Chapter 2), the capacity to create social reality. Opposition is not just 'resistance', it brings new social arrangements into being (however partially). Thus feminism is more than contesting the discursive positioning of women; feminism involves building new health services, defining new pay scales, creating peaceable households and cooperative child care, and so on. The labour movement tries to create more democratic workplaces; anti-colonial movements build structures of self-government. All of these movements create new cultural forms and circulate new knowledge.

Implicit in most of these projects, and a condition for the success of others, is the principle of social justice, which in most cases means the pursuit of equality. Pursuing social justice does not mean pursuing uniformity, as anti-egalitarians repeatedly claim. The philosopher Michael Walzer has convincingly shown that some notion of 'complex equality' is a requirement of a contemporary concept of justice. Issues of justice arise in spheres of life which are differently structured and which cannot be reduced to one another.[5] Indeed that is a familiar experience in any kind of political practice that goes beyond a single issue.

In gender relations complex equality concerns the different structures within the gender order, defined in Chapter 3. Pursuing social justice in power relations means contesting men's predominance in the state, professions and management, and ending men's violence against women. It also means changing the institutional structures that make elite power and body-to-body violence possible in the first place. Pursuing social justice in the gender division of labour means ending the patriarchal dividend in the money economy, sharing the burden of domestic work and equalizing access to education and training (still massively unequal on a world scale). Pursuing social justice in the structure of cathexis means ending the stigma of sexual difference and the imposition of compulsory heterosexuality, and reconstructing heterosexuality on the basis of reciprocity not hierarchy. As a condition for this, it means overcoming the socially produced ignorance that makes sexuality an arena of fear and a vector of disease.

Social justice in gender relations, understood in this way, is a generalizable interest but not a demand for uniformity. Complex equality is precisely the condition needed for diversity as a real practice, for open-ended explorations of human possibility. Social justice does not imply the 'terrorism' that postmodernism attributes to statements of universals; indeed, social justice is what is implied in struggle against terror understood as die exercise of force (rather than a form of speech). The pursuit of social justice certainly does not exhaust politics, but it does provide a generalizable baseline for an arena such as the politics of masculinity. This is the basis of the position on the construction of knowledge about masculinity stated in Chapter 1.

The statistics of inequality list men, not masculinities, as the advantaged group. Carole Pateman has remarked that men exercise power not over a gender but over embodied women, and exercise power as a sex.[6] There is an important problem about political purposes here, not just a terminological quibble. Is a politics of social justice directed against the advantages and power of men, or is it directed against the present form of masculinity? If it is basically about the advantages of men, then much of the agonizing over the social construction of masculinity is beside the point. Rather than annihilating masculinity or even mildly diminishing it, we should be getting out the tools and reforming the economic and political machinery. If the problem is basically about masculinity, structural change should follow from a remaking of personality. But in that case the current project of personal change is radically incomplete, because it ignores the masculinity in *women's* personalities (though often recognizing the femininity in men's); the process cannot be confined to therapy or politics among men.

Though most discussion of masculinity is silent about the issue, it follows from both psychoanalytic and social-construction principles that women are bearers of masculinity as well as men. Girls identify with fathers as well as mothers. Girls cathect their mothers as objects of Oedipal desire (a process different from pre-Oedipal bonding, as discussed in Chapter 5). Women's personalities are layered in the same sense (not necessarily on the same pattern) as men's. Girls and women participate in masculinized institutions and practices, from bureaucracies to competitive sports. We attend to spectacular moments of gender separation (like the Olympic figure skating finals) and often miss, as Barrie Thorne points out in *Gender Play*, a background routine of gender integration. This integration, however, is not on equal terms. It occurs in a context of patriarchal institutions where the 'male is norm', or the masculine is authoritative. To root out masculinity as such would require a project of change in women's lives as well as men's. It is not immediately clear that justice would be served by discouraging girls from playing baseball or women from exercising bureaucratic skills.

Yet to focus *only* on dismantling men's advantages over women through a politics of equal rights would be to abandon our knowledge of how those advantages are reproduced and defended. It would, indeed, abandon our understanding of masculinity as practice; presuming there had been some cosmic accident in which bodies-with-penises happened to land in positions of power and proceeded to recruit their friends-with-penises to replace them ever after. This is, pretty much, the view of the matter taken by liberal feminism: an irrational prejudice keeps women out of the US Senate or the Japanese Diet, to the great loss of the nations concerned.

The defenders of patriarchy know better. The defence of injustice in gender relations constantly appeals to difference, to a masculine/feminine opposition defining one place for female bodies and another place for male. But this is never 'difference' in a purely logical sense. As Chapter 2 showed, bodily difference becomes social reality through body-reflexive practices, in which the social relations of gender are experienced in the body (as sexual arousals and turn-offs, as muscular tensions and posture, as comfort and discomfort) and are themselves constituted in bodily action (in sexuality, in sport, in labour, etc.). The social organization of these practices in a patriarchal gender order constitutes difference as dominance, as unavoidably hierarchical. This has been documented in immense detail by two decades of feminist cultural criticism – and it was of course visible long before, to observers of masculinity such as Alfred Adler.

Difference/dominance means not logical separation but intimate supremacy. It involves immediate social relations as well as

broad cultural themes. It can be realized violently in body practices such as rape and domestic assault. In some countries where
subsistence levels are very low it is realized in the elemental form
of boys getting more food than girls. We can trace the problem
of difference/dominance almost endlessly through social settings
where men and women interact: in occupation of space by boys
and men, the many streets where women walk only under threat,
the intrusion by boys on girls' games in playgrounds, the inter-
ruption of women's speech in conversations, and so on.[7] These
are enactments of hegemonic masculinity in everyday life; for it
is of course hegemonic masculinity, not any subordinated or mar-
ginalised form, that occupies the masculine pole of difference in
patriarchal culture.

The pattern of difference/dominance is so deeply embedded
in culture, institutions and body-reflexive practices that it functions as a limit to the rights-based politics of reform. Beyond a
certain point, the critique of dominance is rejected as an attack
on difference – a project that risks gender vertigo and violence.
In Lacanian terms it means attacking the Phallus, the point of
intersection between patriarchal dominance of culture and the
bodily experience of masculinity; in more orthodox Freudian
terms it means reviving the terror of castration. Even if we think
these are only first approximations to a psychology of masculinity, they suggest the depth of resistance likely to be met. The emotional turmoil and guilt feelings described by the environmental
activists in Chapter 5 are a measure of the resistance even in
favourable circumstances. In other circumstances the project will
be rejected out of hand as an attempt to turn men into women.
Violence against gay men, treated in patriarchal ideology as feminized men, indicates the practical hatred that can be aroused.

It follows that a *degendering* strategy, an attempt to dismantle
hegemonic masculinity, is unavoidable; a *degendered* rights-based
politics of social justice cannot proceed without it.

Degendering and Recomposing

The degendering strategy applies not only at the level of culture
and institutions, but also at the level of the body – the ground
chosen by defenders of patriarchy, where the fear of men being
turned into women is most poignant. It is hardly a coincidence

that a surgical procedure for doing just that was created at the same historical moment as the most radical challenge to the gender order. The striking consequence is that *surgery* provides the popular figure of gender change, a procedure performed by authoritative, affluent men on anaesthetized bodies.

A politics of social justice needs to change body-reflexive practice, not by losing agency but by extending it, working through the agency of the body – exactly what is negated by the anaesthetist. Rather than the disembodiment involved in role reform, this requires *re-embodiment* for men, a search for different ways of using, feeling and showing male bodies.

Re-embodiment is involved, for instance, in changing the division of labour in early child care. As well as the institutional changes required, this has an important bodily dimension. Baby work is very tactile, from getting the milk in, to wiping the shit up, to rocking a small person to sleep. To engage with this experience is to develop capacities of male bodies other than those developed in war, sport or industrial labour. It is also to experience other pleasures. I am intrigued to see postcards, posters and even rock videos appearing which show men cuddling babies, images that strongly convey the sensual pleasure involved.

To argue for degendering is to revisit an old feminist debate over equality and difference. It was successfully argued in the late 1970s that a degendering strategy of equality undermined women rather than affirming them, because it demanded they become like men; equality meant sameness, and women's culture would be lost. A strategy based from the start on a critique of masculinity does not face exactly this difficulty, but it faces a related one. Abolishing hegemonic masculinity risks abolishing, along with the violence and hatred, the positive culture produced around hegemonic masculinity. This includes hero stories from the *Ramayana* and the *Iliad* to the *Twilight of the Gods*; participatory pleasures such as neighbourhood baseball; abstract beauty in fields such as pure mathematics; ethics of sacrifice on behalf of others. That is a heritage worth having, for girls and women as well as boys and men. (As the rich heritage of feminine culture is worth having, for boys and men as well as girls and women.)

To claim that heritage while moving towards social justice requires us to break the terms of the old argument and assert difference and degendering at the same time. Such strategies have been proposed from time to time. Mario Mieli's transsexual gay

politics calls on a range of symbols – heterosexual and gay, feminine and masculine – in a constantly changing improvisation. A
very sinmilar strategy is now proposed under the name of 'queer
theory'. Wendy Chapkis's exploration of the politics of appearance among women proposes moving 'toward a more colorful
revolution', with space for pleasure, creativity and diversity.[8] The
idea is to recompose, rather than delete; the cultural elements of
gender. The result would be a kind of gender multiculturalism.

Though the strategy sounds exotic, the everyday practice
underlying it is not. The sex difference research discussed in
Chapter 1 has been showing for a very long time that supposedly
gendered traits are mostly shared between women and men. It is
quite practical to combine symbolically gendered activities: body-
builders can work in kindergartens, lesbians can wear leather
jackets, boys can learn to cook.

Chapkis rightly argues, however, that playing with the elements
of gender can be benign only if the 'package deal' that links
beauty and status is unpacked. A recomposing strategy is intimately linked to the project of social justice. Given that project,
elements of patriarchal culture can not only be recombined but
can be developed in new ways. For instance, heroism is so tightly
bound into the construct of hegemonic masculinity that it is virtually impossible, in contemporary mass culture, to represent gay
men as heroic. The project of social justice makes it possible to
celebrate the heroism of gay men that arises from their homosexuality – resisting pogroms, exploring frontiers of experience,
facing the HIV epidemic or AIDS itself. Heroism need not have
a bad name.

Given the possibilities of recombination, much of a degendered
and regendered world will be familiar. But we should not underestimate the difference between the configuration of that world
and our own. Only glimpses of this configuration are available
today, in what has been called 'prefigurative politics' in Britain,
and in feminist utopian fiction.[9] What we are moving towards is
indeed 'something rich, & strange'; and therefore, necessarily, a
source of fear as well as desire.

Forms of Action

The main model for political action on masculinity in rich countries is the idea of a 'men's movement'. In the 1970s this was called

the 'Men's Liberation Movement' and was straightforwardly imitated from the Women's Liberation Movement, with a little impulse from Gay Liberation. At the base were many small self-managing 'men's consciousness-raising groups', which in time came to be called simply 'men's groups'. These groups came together from time to time at conferences or in campaigns on particular issues; but – in common with other legatees of the 1960s New Left – each group decided its own path and the movement as a whole was markedly decentralized.

This political model has the virtues of flexibility, anti-authoritarianism and inventiveness. The same group can tackle both personal life and public agendas, as shown by the groups mentioned in Chapter 9.[10] Men's groups in Britain, the United States and Australia have sustained a wide range of activities, from exploration of gender issues in their own lives (the bedrock) to publishing magazines, organizing demonstrations, providing child care at feminist conferences, running violence prevention programmes, running play groups, and so on.

Yet the flexibility which allows that inventiveness also allows a shift to a very different kind of politics. The American group studied by Paul Lichterman moved away from the systematic critique of masculinity in search of a 'pro-male' position. Therapeutically tinged men's groups provided the starting-point in the early 1980s for the 'mythopoetic' men's movement in the United States, and the broader masculinity-therapy movement of the last decade, which now operates on a larger scale than Men's Liberation ever did. A decentralized, anti-authoritarian movement proved to be a field that entrepreneurial gurus and psychological professionalism could readily occupy.

The underlying problem was clearly stated by Andrew Tolson in the most thoughtful analysis ever made of the problems of Men's Liberation, based on experience of an anti-sexist men's group in Britain. The model of a liberation movement simply cannot apply to the group that holds the position of power; as Tolson put it, 'in a certain sense, we were imperialists in a rebellion of slaves'.[11] Consciousness-raising for straight men did not lead towards mobilization and group affirmation, as it did for women and for gay men; after initial gains in insight, it led to marginalization and disintegration.

Men's Liberation, as the first form of the exit politics defined in Chapter 9, tried to base its project on the power axis of patriarchy, on the fact of the domination of women, not on any particular form of masculinity. Its structural basis was feminism, not a socially definable group of men. It is not surprising that a tense and convoluted argument about anti-sexist men's relationship to the women's movement resulted (and is still echoing through recent theoretical writing).[12] Nor is it surprising that the movement was unstable, and was readily displaced by the masculinity-therapy movement – which *is* based on a particular form of masculinity, and articulates the interest of a substantial group of men.

The structural problem of counter-sexist politics among men needs to be stated plainly, as it is constantly evaded. The familiar forms of radical politics, rely on mobilizing solidarity around a shared interest. That is common to working-class politics, national liberation movements, feminism and gay liberation. This *cannot* be the main form of counter-sexist politics among men, because the project of social justice in gender relations is directed *against* the interest they share. Broadly speaking, anti-sexist politics must be a source of disunity among men, not a source of solidarity. There is a rigorous logic to the trends of the 1980s: the more men's groups and their gurus emphasized solidarity among men (being 'positive about men', seeking the 'deep masculine', etc.), the more willing they became to abandon issues of social justice.

If this were all that could be said about forms of action, we might as well pack up and go home. But as I noted in Chapter 9, anti-sexist politics has continued, among straight men as well as gay men. In certain settings (e.g., the academic social sciences) it is flourishing. We can understand this by attending to the other strategic possibilities that are opened up by the structure of gender relations, allowing forms of politics that do not depend on the 'movement' model. Two general features of the gender order create these possibilities: the complexities and contradictions of the relationships constructing masculinity; and the interplay of gender with other social structures.

In earlier chapters of this book I have documented the multiple forms of masculinity in culture and social relations, and the contradictory layers and identifications within masculinity at the level of personality. It is useful to recall the way these contradictions are read by existential psychoanalysis (Chapter 1, Chapter 5) as contradictory commitments or projects taken up by the same person. The crisis tendencies in gender relations identified theoretically in Chapter 3, and traced through the case studies in Part II, have foci in particular groups but in broad terms invest all men's lives. In this sense there are multiple bases within gender relations for political projects to transform masculinity (at least in partial ways), and these bases are widely present. The repeated renewal of anti-sexist politics among men is, from this point of view, not surprising. We can rely on resistance, and attempts at change, constantly welling up.

Nevertheless the best prospects for masculinity politics may be found outside pure gender politics, at the intersections of gender with other structures. There are situations where solidarity among men is pursued for other reasons than masculinity, and may support a project of gender justice, especially where there is explicit solidarity with women in the same situation. These situations arise in labour and socialist parties, the unions, the environmental movement, community politics, anti-colonial resistance movements, movements for cultural democracy and movements for racial equality.

The importance of masculinity politics in such contexts has been particularly recognized in Britain – one of the reasons for the impressive quality of British theoretical work on masculinity. The discussion has particularly concerned the labour movement and class. One does not expect to find a brave new world directly prefigured in working-class life. Class deprivation generates ugly expressions of masculine supremacy, as the British experience of football crowd violence and skinhead racism goes to show. Yet class deprivation leads to other things besides alienated violence.

Strikes and lockouts have often been the occasion for progressive gender politics, from the Fall River labour struggles of nineteenth-century Massachusetts to the bitter 1984 coal miner's strike in Britain, where women's militancy began gender change in a heavily masculinized industry. Labor Party men in Australia provided key political support for feminist initiatives in the bureaucracy and for the growth of women's services. A recent period of Labor Party control of the federal government, for instance, produced a unique national strategy about violence against women. In 1979–80 the United Steelworkers of America successfully pressed for women to be hired at the Hamilton Steelworks in Canada. Some years earlier the Builders Labourers Federation in New South Wales sponsored the entry of women workers on totally masculinized building sites.[13]

I list these cases, not to suggest that official labour is the great white hope of women (another list could be compiled of unions that fought to keep women out of their industries, plus Labor Party patriarchs of the deepest dye), but to show the range of possibilities where class and gender politics interact. The masculinity politics that arises from such interactions, and therefore develops in a great variety of class, ethnic and social movement contexts, will not be a unified 'men's movement'. For one thing, almost every step involves joint action with women. For another, social struggles in workplaces, institutions, communities and regions inevitably have divergent logics, and often bring to light the conflicting interests of different groups of men.

What is involved here, rather than a men's movement, is *alliance politics*. Here the project of social justice depends on the overlapping of interests between different groups (rather than mobilization of one group around its common interest). The overlapping may be temporary, but need not be. There is nothing that rules out long-term alliances, perfectly familiar in politics.

There is a widespread belief that a politics of alliances means pluralism, compromise and therefore containment. It is a familiar militant gesture to denounce such compromises and insist on revolutionary purity; this gesture is not unknown in men's anti-sexist politics, for instance, from anti-pornography activists.[14] I would argue that the pluralism is necessary but the containment is not. If patriarchy is understood as a historical structure, rather than a timeless dichotomy of men abusing women, then it will be ended by a historical process. The strategic problem is to generate pressures that will cumulate towards a transformation of the whole structure; the structural mutation is the end of the process, not the beginning. In earlier stages, any initiative that sets up pressure towards that historical change is worth having.

Education

Though schools have been a rich site for studying the reproduction of masculinities (from *Learning to Labour* to *Gender Play*), and though most of the people doing research on masculinity work in the education industry (as academics or students), there is surprisingly little discussion of the role of education in the transformation of masculinity. Discussions of 'gender and education' overwhelmingly concentrate on the education of girls and issues about femininity. There has been some debate about the introduction of 'men's studies' in American universities. There is of course a literature on the education of boys going back to Dr Arnold. But there is little discussion, informed by research on masculinity, about education for boys in modern mass school systems; let alone about the principles that would include girls as well as boys in an educational process addressing masculinity.[15]

I would argue that these are questions of major importance, and that education is a key site of alliance politics. Any significant work on these issues done by men must be done in alliance with women, who have been opening up the issues about gender in education and have the practical know-how. Any curriculum must address the diversity of masculinities, and the intersections of gender with race, class and nationality, if it is not to fall into a sterile choice between celebration and negation of masculinity in general.

The importance of education for masculinity politics follows from the onto-formativity of gender practices, the fact that our enactments of masculinity and femininity bring a social reality into being. Education is often discussed as if it involved only information, teachers tipping measured doses of facts into the pupils' heads; but that is just part of the process. At a deeper level, education is the formation of capacities for practice.[16] A social justice agenda in education must concern the full range of capacities for practice, the justice of the way those capacities are developed and distributed and the ways they are put into effect.

Therefore the educational strategy must be centrally concerned with curriculum. Curricular justice, as I have argued in *Schools and Social Justice*, means organizing knowledge from the point of view of the least advantaged.[17] This reverses the current social practice of organizing knowledge from the point of view of the privileged. We do not abandon existing knowledge, but reconfigure it, to open up the possibilities that current social inequalities conceal.

One step in this direction is taken when we pluralize the sources of curriculum content. This is the logic of multicultural curriculum, developed in the idea of a gender-inclusive curriculum put forward by Jean Blackburn.[18] A second step is taken when an inclusive curriculum inverts the hegemony that characterized the old dominant curriculum. For instance, instead of requiring working-class students to participate in learning organized around the interests of the middle class, middle-class students are required to participate in learning organized around working-class interests.

Taking this second step in gender relations is both decisive and delicate. Requiring boys to participate in curriculum organized around the interests of girls, and straight students to participate in curriculum organized around the interests of lesbians and gays, demands a capacity for empathy, for taking the viewpoint of the other, which is systematically denied in hegemonic masculinity. Everything we know about gender relations in schools and colleges suggests this will be difficult to do. (Witness the teasing of boys in elementary school playgrounds who show any interest in girls' games; witness the scarcity of men in college courses about gender.) Yet this step pursues classic goals of education – to broaden experience, to pursue justice, to participate fully in culture – applied to one of the most important areas of the students' lives. Interest is likely to be high, even if support is not. And many teachers take this step in everyday practice in classrooms, with limited resources, and little in the way of theoretical or political support. Providing the resources and support is one of the more useful things academic researchers concerned with masculinity might do.

To speak of knowledge organized from the point of view of the least advantaged does not mean building the curriculum only on the experiences of the least advantaged. (Indeed, curriculum cannot simply reflect any group's experience; it always involves a critique of experience, a selection from culture.) A curriculum for social justice needs to examine the experience of the advantaged also. In practical terms, this is often the best point of entry to gender issues for straight men and boys – sometimes the only possible point of entry.

Here the social science research on masculinity is an essential resource, allowing a range of situations to be discussed, and providing models for the exploration of local realities. For instance, the moments of engagement with hegemonic masculinity, of distancing, and of separation explored in Chapter 5, can be found in many other contexts and many other lives. For instance, the Canadian high school boys interviewed by Blye Frank show how separation is accomplished in the face of intimidation:

> I make sure that I don't walk too feminine. I have done some modelling before, so if I were to walk that way around, school people would notice. I have been harassed. They do make fun of me by saying, 'Do you think you're a fruit?'[19]

When it is safe for him to answer 'Yes', we will have made some progress.

Prospects

It is one thing to define a political strategy, entirely another to put it into effect. The means have to be considered. In the first moment of Men's Liberation, activists could believe themselves borne forward on a tidal wave of historical change. The wave broke, and no means of further progress was left on the beach. We now speak of a 'men's movement' partly from politeness, and partly because certain activities have the form of a social movement. But taking a cool look around the political scenery of the industrial capitalist world, we must conclude that the project of transforming masculinity has almost no political weight at all – no leverage on public policy, no organizational resources, no popular base and no presence in mass culture (except as a footnote to feminism and a critique of the excesses of masculinity therapy). By comparison, Gay Liberation mutated into new forms of gay community politics that confronted the HIV/AIDS epidemic, founded a range of new institutions, achieved major changes in social practice (through the community-based Safe Sex strategy) and gained a voice in a range of policy debates.[20]

The simple calculus of interest would predict that any men's movement against hegemonic masculinity would be weak. The general interest of men in patriarchy is formidable. It was badly underestimated by sex role reformers[21] and it is easily underestimated still; that is why I have been at pains to spell it out in this book.

Men's interest in patriarchy is condensed in hegemonic masculinity and is defended by all the cultural machinery that exalts hegemonic masculinity. It is institutionalized in the state; enforced by violence, intimidation and ridicule in the lives of straight men – the high school experience of the Canadian teenagers just mentioned is all too familiar; and enforced by violence against women and gay men. The European/American pattern of men's investment in patriarchy is being extended across the world by the globalization of culture and economic relations. Its grip in the metropole is strengthened by the commodification of exemplary masculinities such as sports stars, and by the collusion between gun-lobby politics and commercial media to celebrate violence. Men's interest in patriarchy is further sustained by *women's* invest-ment in patriarchy, as expressed in loyalty to patriarchal religions, in narratives of romance, in enforcing difference/dominance in the lives of children, not to mention women's activism against abortion rights and homosexuality.

Yet this interest, formidable as it may be, is fissured by all the complexities in the social construction of masculinity mapped in this book. There are differences and tensions between hegemonic and complicit masculinities; oppositions between hegemonic masculinity and subordinated and marginalized mas-culinities. Each of these configurations of practice is internally divided, not least by the layering of personality described by psy-choanalysis, the contradictions in gender at the level of personal-ity. Their realization in social life differs, as we have seen again and again, according to the interplay of gender with class relations, race relations and the forces of globalization. (Globalization, con-trary to most metropolitan theorists of cultural change, constructs very different situations in the metropole and the periphery.)

Men's interest in patriarchy, then, does not act as a unified force in a homogeneous structure. Recognizing this, we can move decisively beyond the one-dimensional strategic thinking that flowed from earlier models of patriarchy.[22] In the context of the broad delegitimation of patriarchy, men's relational interests in the welfare of women and girls can displace the same men's gender-specific interests in supremacy. A heterosexual sensibility can be formed without homophobia, so alliances of straight men with gay politics become possible. The pattern of change in patri-archy in the metropolitan countries, discussed at the start of this chapter, means that the familiar array of masculinities will con-tinue to be produced and institutionalized, but a cultural recon-figuration of their elements has become possible. Thus the paradox of masculinity politics in the 1980s: reactionary gender politics in the state and mass media (in the leading capitalist powers), and displacement of the pro-feminist Men's Liberation impulse by masculinity-therapy; but at the same time progressive shifts in many relationships outside state control, and critical analysis of hegemonic masculinity reaching new levels of preci-sion and sophistication.

The decade of the 1990s is not producing a unified movement of men opposing patriarchy, any more than previous decades did.

Men continue to be detached from the defence of patriarchy by the contradictions and intersections of gender relations; new possibilities open for reconfiguration and transformation of masculinities. Developing a politics to take up these openings – without the myth of liberation, in full knowledge of men's shared interest in patriarchy, and therefore expecting little from the model of a 'men's movement' – requires fresh invention as well as accurate knowledge.

I think a fresh politics of masculinity will develop in new arenas: for instance, the politics of the curriculum, work around AIDS/ HIV and anti-racist politics. I think it will require new forms, involving both men and women, and centring on alliance work rather than 'men's groups'. I think it will be far more internationalist than masculinity politics has been so far, contesting globalization-from-above as other democratic movements do.[23] And in some sense it must be a politics beyond interests, a politics of pure possibility. Though that is, perhaps, another way of expressing the interest all people on this planet share in social justice, peace and balance with the natural world.

Afterword: The Contemporary Politics of Masculinity

Some time ago, the US sociologist Goode (1982) published an important essay 'Why men resist', reflecting on men's responses to the Women's Liberation movement. Men resisted change, Goode argued, because they were the privileged group in gender relations. But this privilege was offset in a number of ways, and was cross-cut by the interests men shared with particular women (e.g. wives and daughters).

Challenging the idea of a 'backlash', Goode offered evidence that men's attitudes (in the USA at least) had become increasingly favourable to gender equality. However this was not put into practice evenly. Men were losing their cultural centrality, but in relation to jobs and housework, were successfully resisting change. Ultimately an economic dynamic prevailed: 'the underlying shift is towards the decreasing marginal utility of males'. This accounted both for men's resistance to gender equality, and for the futility of this resistance. The socio-economic forces now in play would continue to push modern society towards gender equality.

Twenty years later the Swiss sociologist Godenzi (2000) published another notable essay on men and gender inequality, also emphasizing the economic dimension. His essay is darker – perhaps reflecting the intervening history, also reflecting his concern with men's violence. Reviewing international statistics, Godenzi documents gender inequalities in relation to work time, organizational power, income, freedom from housework, etc. He shows that at the end of the twentieth century, a massive system of material privilege still exists globally. Men's violence, Godenzi argues, is not an individual pathology but a logical consequence of men's collective privilege. Violence grows out of inequality, sustains inequality, and is also a response to the contemporary challenge to inequality.

In this Afterword I will extend the discussion of politics in Chapters 9 and 10, pursuing Goode's and Godenzi's investigation of men's interests in relation to gender equality. I will consider the role of men and masculinities in the politics of violence, and discuss the global dimension in masculinity politics.

Men's Interests in Contemporary Patriarchy: A Draft Balance Sheet

Godenzi's statistical appraisal of men's economic advantage builds on a prior literature which looked at economic statistics the other way up – as measures of the disadvantage of women. That continues to be the usual way of looking at gender inequality. There are now many sources of information about women's under-representation in elite occupations and top management, women's economic disadvantages, educational exclusion and literacy rates, legal disadvantages, more restricted sexual life, etc. A selection of such statistics is now routinely incorporated by the United Nations Development Programme into its annual *Human Development Report*, as an index of women's social progress.

Another literature has now appeared that contests the idea of women's disadvantage. Disregarding for the moment the bitter polemical tone of most of this literature (e.g. Farrell 1993, Sommers 2000), it has identified certain areas of life, in the rich countries, where statistical comparisons show a disadvantage to men and boys. These are, most notably, the outcomes of secondary education, death rates, many forms of injury, some diseases, some forms of violence, and imprisonment.

Treating 'men' and 'women' as undifferentiated categories (as most of these statistical exercises do), it is possible to draw up a collective balance sheet for men showing both the gains and losses, or benefits and costs, from contemporary gender arrangements.

Since the topics of the existing statistical comparisons are very diverse, we need a way of sorting the information. The UNDP's approach, combining a number of measures into a single 'index', produces a dramatic outcome – a list of countries ranked in terms of gender equity. But that seems to me intellectually misleading. There are a number of dimensions in gender relations, and the patterns of inequality in these different dimensions may be qualitatively different.

The brief presentation below follows the model in *Gender* (Connell 2002), where sources of information are documented. The model distinguishes four major dimensions (or structures) in gender relations. This discussion focuses on the current state of play in the rich Western countries (the European community, north America and Australasia).

(a) Power

Advantages: Men hold predominant authority in business and the state, with a near-monopoly of top positions. Men and boys tend to control public spaces such as streets and playgrounds. Men hold authority in many families and institutions of civil society. Men have near total control of coercive institutions (military, police) and control of the means of violence (weapons, military training). Men are relatively free from rape and serious domestic violence.

Disadvantages: Men are the overwhelming majority of people arrested and imprisoned, including those executed. Men are the main targets of military violence and criminal assault. Men are more likely to be the targets of economic competition and organizational rivalry.

(b) Division of labour

Advantages: Men have approximately twice the average income of women, and control most of the major concentrations of wealth. Men have higher levels of economic participation, and better access to future opportunities e.g. promotions. Men, especially husbands, receive benefits from the unpaid labour of women. Men control most of the machinery (e.g. transport, power generation, computers) that is the basis of a modern economy and specifically multiplies the economic value of labour.

Disadvantages: Men predominate in dangerous and highly toxic occupations. Men include a higher proportion of sole earners ('breadwinners') with social compulsion to remain employed. Because of the occupational division of labour, men's skills are subject to rapid obsolescence. Men pay a higher average rate of taxation, with income disproportionately redistributed to women, through the welfare state.

(c) Cathexis

Advantages: Men receive much emotional support from women without social obligation to reciprocate. Heterosexuality is socially organized to prioritize men's pleasure, in personal relationships as well as sexualized mass media. A double standard legitimates men's sexual freedom and a commercial sex industry services it.

Disadvantages: Men's sexuality is more alienated, and more sharply constrained by homophobia. A taboo on free expression of emotions, especially vulnerability, continues (this is perhaps now changing). Men are substantially excluded from relationships with very young children.

(d) Symbolism

Advantages: Men control most cultural institutions (churches, universities, media). Religion generally, and sometimes specifically, defines men as superordinate to women. Men have higher levels of recognition, i.e. they and their activities are regarded as more important, newsworthy, and appropriate to resource. (Example: sport.) Boys and men predominate in high-return and highly resourced areas of education. (Examples: MBA, biotechnology, IT.)

Disadvantages: Boys and men are losing ground in general education. They are under-represented in important learning experiences, e.g. humanistic studies. Mothers' legitimacy in child-care tends to over-ride fathers' interests in marital separation disputes.

Gender centrally involves social embodiment, based on body-reflexive practices where the body is both agent and object of practice. The gender order therefore has important effects at the level of the body as well as in social relations.

The bodily effects of the current gender order on men collectively include: higher levels of injury (including industrial accidents, road injuries), higher exposure to many forms of toxicity and stress, higher levels of drug dependency (most commonly, alcoholism), higher levels of participation in sport and other outdoor activities. Men are much less likely than women to wear restrictive or fragile clothing, and to commit time and money to beautifying the body (this connects both to men's greater freedom of movement and control of space, and to men's greater economic resources, making them less dependent on being 'attractive').

Now to complicate matters. This 'balance sheet' is not like a corporate accounting exercise where there is a bottom line, subtracting costs from income. That is the error made by backlash polemicists who try to refute feminism by reciting men's disadvantages. As Cox (1995) shows, a rhetoric of 'competing victims' leads nowhere. We cannot even understand the balance by seeing the disadvantages as 'the costs of being on top', though that is a better starting point – it suggests that there is a connection between the up-side and the down-side.

A fully relational approach to gender sees the connection as substantive. The disadvantages listed above are, broadly speaking, the *conditions* of the advantages. Men cannot hold state power without having become, collectively, the agents of violence. Men cannot be the beneficiaries of domestic labour and emotion work without losing intimate connections, for instance with young children. Men cannot predominate in the capitalist economy without being subject to economic stress and paying for most of the social services. And so on.

But the men who benefit most, and the men who pay most, are not necessarily the same people. Here it is easy to fall into logical fallacy by ignoring diversity within the category 'men'. The men who are targets of disproportionate violence, for instance, are not the same men as those who hold military and political leadership positions. 'Men' pay more tax, but the bulk of tax transfers come from wage-earners, not from the corporate elite. The men who benefit from recognition and hold social authority are not, by and large, those who do toxic and dangerous work or who have high rates of imprisonment.

Class, race and generational differences, to recall a familiar argument, cross-cut the category 'men', spreading the gains and costs of gender relations very unevenly among men. The different situations defined by these structures are among the important bases of diversity in gender practices and consciousness, that is to say, among patterns of masculinity.

Should we therefore abandon the category 'men' altogether? That would be as much a mistake as reifying it. The *overall* gender relation between women and men is a powerful basis of consciousness and practice too. For instance, those who enforce by extreme violence the marginality of gay men – that is to say, homophobic killers – are mostly young and economically disadvantaged men. Yet to themselves they are proving their manhood and defending the honour of men (Tomsen 2002). Those teenagers who engage in violence against girlfriends are, predominantly, at the bottom of the economic order. Often they have suffered the toxicity of the gender order directly, by violence at the hands of fathers or stepfathers. Yet they too think of themselves as defending the legitimate rights of men and putting women in their proper place (Totten 2000).

'Backlash' Politics: Mobilizing Men's Interests Against Change?

It is a familiar thesis that underlying interests take effect in history when they are brought to consciousness and made the basis of group mobilization. On that thesis hang much-debated questions about class – the significance of 'false consciousness', the role of a class 'vanguard', etc. Frustrated by the convolutions of those debates, some theorists have concluded that interests exist only discursively, only as articulated by social movements. The movements themselves, however, continue to stress material inequalities and to act as if interests were real.

It is easy to see gender reform in this light – up to a point. Gender inequalities (such as women's lower incomes, higher rates of casual employment, exclusion from arenas of power and authority) define the underlying interest. Feminism is the mobilization, which articulates women's interest in change and seeks to turn it into a practical program. The fact that some women oppose feminism is a practical but not a conceptual problem. Cross-cutting interests, uneven mobilization, or the grip of conservative ideology, can explain that.

The position of men, however, has caused problems from the start. Early theorists of women's liberation simply defined men as the ruling class in patriarchy, and expected men to oppose women's advancement on all fronts, whatever their principles. Morgan (1970: xxxi) summed it up with edged wit:

> So we know that a male-dominated socialist revolution in economic and even cultural terms, were it to occur tomorrow, would be *no* revolution, but only another coup d'état among men.

But in the same year came the first calls for 'men's liberation', which assumed that men would *benefit* from women's liberation, and that women and men *shared* a fundamental interest in ending sex roles. For about five years, an anti-sexist men's movement in the USA attempted to mobilize men *in alliance* with women's organizations and in support of women's movement actions (Pleck and Sawyer 1974, Farrell 1974). These ideas were widespread. No less a figure than Olof Palme, the social-democratic prime minister of Sweden, expounded the idea of the joint emancipation of men and women from traditional sex roles (Palme 1972).

The alliance was prised apart, in the later 1970s and early 1980s, from both sides. This period saw the rise of distinctly anti-feminist 'men's rights' groups, and also saw Western feminism's focus on male violence and shift towards separatist strategies. Both tendencies reinforced the sense of opposite sides and fundamentally incompatible interests. A point was reached where the principle of alliance between women and men became difficult to articulate (Segal 1987), and consciously 'pro-feminist' men's groups found the going very much harder (Lichterman 1989).

I recall this almost-forgotten debate as it shows with particular clarity the difficulty of defining a univocal men's interest in relation to gender reform. The concept of a 'backlash' against feminism and women, of which Goode was an early critic, often presupposes a univocal interest. Goode, in fact, was so early a critic (his text dates from a lecture series in 1979) that the full force of new-right anti-feminism only developed after he wrote, in the era of Reagan, Thatcher and Kohl.

The gender politics that unfolded then – including attacks on abortion rights and abortion providers, the demolition of affirmative action programs, the demonizing of 'welfare mothers', the winding back of social welfare measures, the attacks on 'permissiveness' and 'homosexual lifestyles', and glorification of 'the traditional family' – certainly slowed the pace of gender reform. But many of these campaigns were led by women, not by men, and were presented as being in the interests of women. Around 'permissiveness', indeed, a remarkable alliance developed between feminist anti-pornography campaigners and right-wing authoritarians in attempts to criminalize the commercial sex industry.

Reflecting on this development, McIntosh (1993) postulated inherent contradictions in sexual politics, and thought that feminism had to break out in an entirely new direction. When he came to survey the landscape of masculinity politics in the United States, Messner (1997) was able to locate no less than eight 'men's movements', or movements in masculinity politics, with different agendas for change.

Gender complexities continue in the new conservatism. George W. Bush was the first US president to place a woman in the very heart of the state power structure, as National Security Advisor to the president. Condoleezza Rice has, on press accounts, been one of the Bush administration's hawks, urging violent intervention in the Middle East and an expansion of US military forces. Yet the US state, and the right wing of the Republican Party in that country, remain overwhelmingly the province of men – and men of a particular character, power-oriented, ruthless and brutal, restrained by little more than calculations of likely opposition. What they do, when they think they can get away with it, is shown by the appalling concentration camp they run at Guantanamo Bay. Similarly, the character of the men running the neo-conservative Australian government is shown by the desert and island concentration camps for refugees seeking entry to this country.

Goode was right that there has been a historic shift of popular attitudes towards formal gender equality. Evidence of a generational move in this direction continues to accumulate, from Germany and other European countries as well as the USA (e.g.

Zulehner and Volz, 1998). But popular attitudes are not the whole story. Major institutions, including two of the three main cultural institutions of contemporary Western society, the church and the mass media (education is a different story), continue to be not only male-dominated but active producers of a male-centred gender culture.

This is not a monolithic process. The Catholic church, with a strong impulse from the centre, has become more conservative on gender issues. This church totally excludes women from authority and remains the most spectacular patriarchy in the world today. The major Protestant churches have become on the whole more progressive, in particular opening the ministry to women. But a gulf is widening between these reforming churches and an intransigently conservative wing of Protestantism which is close to the Catholic position on gender issues. These neo-conservative sects seem to be where the growth in Protestant numbers is occurring (e.g. in Brazil), and they provide a key political base for the neo-conservative leaders such as President Bush.

The media construct a rather different version of gender ideology. The mass-circulation press and tabloid TV depend heavily on a double agenda of titillation and reassurance. A staple diet of sexualized images of women, celebrity gossip and erotically tinged advertising constructs gender and sexuality as an arena of 'freedom'. This arena centres on a model of men choosing women (and women therefore needing to make themselves desirable). At the same time heterosexuality, masculine authority and feminine nurturance are made normative by the dominant media story-lines and entertainment genres, providing reassurance both for the alienated wage-earner and the bored housewife with children. Exceptions and alternatives – homosexuality, transsexuality, incest, female domination, and so on – are perversely celebrated by being made into a running freak show for mass entertainment (Jerry Springer serves as an example). What conservative religion denounces, commercial media make money from.

Though the churches and the conventional media generate patriarchal ideology, neither functions as a mobilizer of *men* specifically. Indeed most of the church's following is made up of women, and women are also prominent in the television audience.

A much more specific address to men, together with the most vehement public expressions of contempt for women anywhere in contemporary society, are found in the growing institutional, media and business complex of commercial sports. The large-scale injection of corporate money into sports within the last generation has fuelled an impressive growth of visibility and political importance. With its overwhelming focus on male athletes, its celebration of force, domination and competitive success, its valorization of male commentators and executives, its marginalization and frequent ridicule of women, the sports/business complex has become an increasingly important site for representing and defining gender.

This is not traditional patriarchy. It is something new, welding exemplary bodies to entrepreneurial culture. In traditional domestic patriarchy, women's participation is essential to the construction and maintenance of masculinity. In the sports/business complex the participation of women is not essential – male stars' 'girlfriends' are as close as women usually get to the main action. The US sociologist Messner (2002), one of the leading analysts of contemporary sports, formulates it well by saying that commercial sports define the renewed *centrality* of men, and of a particular version of masculinity.

There is, then, a backlash, but it has been more powerful culturally than politically. It has not mobilized men as a sex class for political warfare, defending a collective interest. To the extent it has mobilized men, it is as consumers, through genres such as the 'new lad' magazines, hyper-masculine computer games, and the culture of sports fans. Men's benefits from an unequal gender order are defended diffusely, by conservative churches, by media ridicule of gender reform movements, and by deeply entrenched resistance to change in institutions such as the military and the courts.

Neoliberalism and Men's Interests

Of the many political and cultural initiatives launched by the Women's Liberation impulse in the 1960s and 1970s, 'equal opportunity' is one that has survived best. As a principle of organizational reform, EEO (equal employment opportunity) is now almost universally accepted in Western societies. Politicians, public servants and businessmen will almost always endorse this principle; it is embedded in law and actually enforced by courts.

But it is important to look at the specific shape of this reform. EEO has been adopted as a de-gendering principle. Procedures and regulations explicitly favouring men have been deleted from the organizational rule-book, with some fanfare. The modern manager says, when describing appointments and promotions, 'I look at the person' – i.e. explicitly *not* taking into account whether that person is man or woman, black or white, able-bodied or disabled.

That is to say, EEO has become an *individualizing* principle rather than a principle of group advancement. The same politicians, public servants and businessmen almost universally reject 'affirmative action' programs for under-represented groups – commonly giving the reason that such programs are discriminatory and violate equal opportunity principles.

EEO has been re-shaped this way mainly because the organizational reforms triggered by the new feminism occurred at the same time as, and interacted with, the organizational reform agenda of neo-liberalism (Yeatman 1990). The new public sector management, privatization, de-regulation, the shift to 'flatter' management structures, the generic manager model, user-pays principles, and emphasis on entrepreneurial activity form a complex, not entirely consistent but very powerful agenda. Reforms based on this agenda have swept through both public and private sector organizations in the last twenty years.

Together with the neo-liberal market agenda in public politics, which has hammered the remains of the postwar welfare state and re-drawn the boundaries of the public and private sectors, this has created an environment in which individualism as an ideology has performed an astonishing comeback. Regarded thirty years ago as intellectually obsolete, a celebration of the entrepreneurial individual is currently the centrepiece of Western political culture. An individualized version of 'equal opportunity' not only fits with this celebration, it helps to give individualism its current legitimacy. Individualized EEO can be seen as realizing the aspirations of formerly excluded groups through the 'achievements' of their most energetic members.

Neo-liberalism is rhetorically gender-neutral. The individual has no gender, and the market delivers advantage to the smartest entrepreneur, not to men or women as such. There is a large difference, then, between neo-liberal ideology and the gendered ideologies of the churches, the mass media, and the sports/

business complex. Neo-liberalism is inconsistent with traditional patriarchy. This inconsistency sometimes erupts in the form of factional tensions within conservative parties, between their family-values wing and their economic-rationalist wing.

But if neo-liberalism is post-patriarchal, that is not to say it favours social justice in relation to gender. Neo-liberal politics has no interest in justice at all. Neo-liberal regimes have been associated with a worsening in the position of women in most respects. The most dramatic case is eastern Europe, where the restoration of capitalism and the arrival of neo-liberal politics has accompanied a sharp deterioration in the position of women. In rich Western countries, neo-liberalism has attacked the welfare state, on which far more women than men depend; supported deregulation of labour markets, resulting in increased casualization of women workers; shrunk public sector employment, the sector of the economy where women predominate; lowered rates of personal taxation, the main basis of tax transfers to women; and squeezed public education, the key pathway to labour market advancement for women.

Indirectly, therefore, neo-liberalism has acted in ways that degrade the position of the majority of women, at the same time as it celebrates the entry of a minority of women into the officially de-gendered heaven of professional success.

The crucial point is the relation between neo-liberalism, the position of men, and the reconstruction of bourgeois masculinity. Neo-liberalism similarly degrades the economic and social position of some men, but not all. Many men are relatively advantaged by the shift of social resources from the state to the market, and by the de-regulation of markets. And there is a particular group who are the intended beneficiaries of the whole neo-liberal policy package – entrepreneurs.

The 'individual' may be formally gender-neutral, but one cannot say the same about the 'entrepreneur'. The desired attributes of managers and capitalists as entrepreneurs (thrusting competitiveness, ruthlessness, focus on the bottom line, etc.) are coded masculine in gender ideology, and in cold fact the people who fulfil these functions overwhelmingly are men.

The new entrepreneurialism deletes some items from the older package of bourgeois masculinity: religious commitment, rigid personal probity and marital loyalty. These are regarded as outdated, even slightly comic, in big businessmen now. Forms of amusement and patronage have also changed. Stodgy corporations in search of prestige may still give money to the opera, but new entrepreneurs are more likely to have a corporate box at the football or even to buy a football or baseball team.

There is an interplay between the new entrepreneurial capitalism and the commercialization of sport, in which the influence is not all one way. Sport has become a vital public metaphor of capitalism and market society, with its mesmerizing, endless spectacle of competition and upheaval resulting always in the same kind of hierarchy as before. This metaphor could not work if it had to bridge a gender gap. It works because the champion sportsman and the successful entrepreneur are both men bearing related kinds of masculinity.

The new entrepreneurial management cannot be understood without reference to the new configuration of capitalism: the re-emergence of finance capital, the deregulation of markets, and above all, the growth of global markets, global communications and transnational corporations. These global arenas are now a crucially important feature of modern society and, as I suggested in the Introduction, play a growing part in contemporary constructions of masculinity.

I would argue, therefore, that the rise of new groups of managers and owners to unprecedented global power is associated with new patterns of business masculinity and, by implication, new patterns of hegemony in gender relations. For instance this type of entrepreneurialism, increasingly detached from local gender orders, does not valorize the family or the husband/father position for men. It is therefore not surprising that the homophobia so prominent in older hegemonic masculinities is reduced, even absent. It is now possible for gay men to be 'out' and still function as multi-national managers, in a way inconceivable in big business one or two generations ago. On the other hand, the 'generic manager' model has eroded commitments to particular firms, industries or trades. With a decline in those commitments, capitalism has lost an important basis for solidarity between managers and working-class men. This is clearly shown in Roper's (1994) excellent history of managers in British engineering firms.

There is also a reorganization of male managers' relations with women. Older 'service' relationships are in decline. The boss-and-secretary couple is disappearing, while the businessman married to a full-time wife-mother-hostess, though surviving, is becoming less the standard pattern. Women are becoming more marginal, more transient, in the lives of managers, unless they are there on the same terms as the men, i.e. as entrepreneurial individuals. In which case they have to 'manage like a man', as Wajcman (1999) aptly puts it.

But the same is true for men. Increasingly the test of membership in the hegemonic group is the willingness to discard other ties and generate a particular kind of performance – the life-denying labour of entrepreneurial management. The interwoven class and gender dynamic of neo-liberal globalization, taking shape in the masculinity of entrepreneurial management, may be shifting resources towards men but at the same time it is widening material divisions among men. This may help explain the energy going into new models of exemplary masculinity located in the realm of consumption, especially in sport. It further suggests these trends are unlikely to reach a stable solution to the current tensions around gender and gender reform.

The Problem of Violence – Personal and International

The most urgent problem facing human society now, as it has been for half a century, is to prevent the recurrence of nuclear war. There has been only one episode of nuclear war so far – the atomic bombs dropped on Japan in 1945, at a time when the killing power of a nuclear weapon was no greater than that of a heavy conventional air raid. The nuclear arsenal now has the capacity to wipe out human life. It is only likely to be used in war.

War itself is complex and its character and conditions change. Internationally, the end of the Cold War was followed by some reduction of military forces. But that has been followed by more nuclear proliferation, military confrontations such as the Gulf Wars, and the diverse forms of violence labelled 'terrorism' (Onwudiwe 2000). In Western societies, violence remains a prominent theme in mass culture, from action movies to sport (Messner 2002). Violence remains a chronic problem in interpersonal relations, from bar brawls to sexual abuse.

A connection between violence and masculine gender at the personal level is indicated by statistics (men account for about 90 per cent of homicides, assaults and prison inmates in countries such as the USA and Australia), by studies of crimes such as homicide (Polk 1994), and by close-focus studies of offenders (Messerschmidt 2000). A link also exists for organizational violence: most soldiers, air-force pilots, suicide bombers, police and prison guards are men.

These well-known facts have gradually been recognized as a problem. What roles do dominant forms of masculinity play in legitimating violence, whether in families or in military confrontations such as the Gulf War? What part does gender play in cultures of violence and institutions that use force? What patterns of personal development lead boys and men towards violent actions? There is now active debate about these issues and their implications for peace-keeping (Breines et al. 2000). Recognizing masculinities as a link between social conflict and violence has opened up new perspectives in violence prevention (Kaufman 1999, 2001). But how we should understand the connection is sharply debated, with psychosocial, structural and discursive interpretations all being advanced (Jefferson 2002).

Clearly, gender does not provide a simple key to understanding violence. Violence is known to have multiple causes and varies socially, cross-nationally and over time (Archer and Gartner 1984); an important case being the connection between homicide rates and regional poverty (Pridemore 2002). Above all, masculinity cannot be interpreted as a fixed propensity to violence. As the research reviewed in this book shows, masculinities are diverse, and change historically. Comparative studies, such as Kersten's (1993) work on Australia, Germany and Japan, indicate that varying rates of violent crime may be linked to the specific histories of masculinities in different cultures. Therefore we must explore specific masculinities to understand how social tensions are expressed as violence by specific agents. Tomsen's (1998) exploration of 'heterosexual panic' in cases of homophobic homicide by young men indicates one such mechanism.

Further, interpersonal violence is not the same thing as the deployment of masculinities in the public realm in violent confrontations such as the Gulf Wars. War, including nuclear war, involves the action of institutions and groups – armies, governments, weapons industries, guerilla movements, etc. To understand the gender dimension of war we need to understand such issues as the institutionalization of masculinities in military forces, as studied by Barrett (1996). A documentary case-study approach to masculinities and conflict was pioneered by Messerschmidt

(1997) in a study of the 'Challenger' space shuttle disaster, and this also has potential for understanding war.

We now have studies of the organizational construction of masculinities in the armed forces of Germany (Seifert 1993), Britain (Morgan 1994), the United States (Barrett 1996), Australia (Agostino 1998), Israel (Klein 2000), and Turkey (Sinclair-Webb 2000). We also have illuminating accounts of the shaping of masculinities in armed or partly armed resistance movements, in Palestine (Peteet 2000) and in South Africa (Xaba 2001).

The studies of state military forces show an organizational effort to produce and make hegemonic a narrowly defined masculinity which will make its bearers efficient in producing the organization's effects of violence. As Barrett in particular demonstrates, the requirements may be different in different branches of the armed forces. The studies of resistance movements show less obvious institutionalization, but a powerful informal group process that tends to produce masculinities oriented to personal violence.

We now have a unique study of masculinities in the aftermath of war, and the gendered process of international peace-keeping, in the case of Bosnia (Cockburn and Zarkov 2002). We also have some very illuminating studies of the gendered cultural processes that usually support – but sometimes undermine – war. In a complex study of Soviet cultural and political history Novikova (2000) traces the gender imagery that sustained military morale in earlier periods, but which unravelled during the Afghanistan intervention, and resulted in a sharp reversal in gender politics after the collapse of the USSR. In a study of Gulf War I, Niva (1998) shows how the imagery of the US intervention in 1990-1 attempted to reconcile the military toughness and aggression with the themes of tenderness and compassion among men. Those themes had emerged in the recent re-working of US masculinities, and were important in gaining legitimacy for the military action.

It seems that by 2003 this direction was largely abandoned. The Bush administration, in the aftermath of the World Trade Centre massacre, made an attempt to gain international support for its 'war on terror'. But for the attack on Iraq, the US government effectively abandoned this search for international legitimacy and relied on force alone. The US government and media did succeed in gaining domestic legitimacy for the attack on Iraq, largely by convincing a majority of the American public that the Iraqi government was linked with the WTC attack. This was known in the rest of the world to be untrue.

How a reliance on naked force became a credible political option is, perhaps, suggested by another cultural study. Gibson (1994) traced the rise of a hypermasculine 'paramilitary culture' in the USA in the period after the defeat in Vietnam. Though the current US government does not directly come from the paramilitary fringe it comes from a political culture more influenced by ideas of direct violent action than any previous administration.

A deeper understanding of these links, both at the personal and the institutional level, may make a great deal of difference to practice, as well as to research. Policies against violence may be ineffective, or even counter-productive, unless the gender dynamics involved are understood.

For instance, confrontational policing in some situations creates a masculine challenge that generates, rather than reduces, violence (cf. Tomsen 1997). This seems very close to the dynamic produced by the Israeli occupation in Palestine, and is likely to be reproduced by the current Western offensives against Islamic societies.

Some violence prevention programs began in the 1990s to use ideas from masculinity research, both in broad public campaigns (Kaufman 1999) and to develop strategies for difficult groups such as adolescent youth (Denborough 1996) and prison inmates (Sabo, Kupers and London 2001).

It is important that this strategy should spread, but it is essential that it should be informed by up-to-date understandings of masculinities. Keys to this work will be the capacity to grasp the situational specificity of masculinities, violence and violence prevention, and the capacity to move from the individual level to the level of institutions and nations. The continued development of our understanding of masculinities is an important part of the knowledge we need to build a more peaceful, survivable world.

Masculinity Politics on a World Scale

The world gender order mostly privileges men over women. Though there are many local exceptions, there is a patriarchal dividend for men collectively, arising from higher incomes, higher labour force participation, unequal property ownership, greater access to institutional power, as well as cultural and sexual privilege. This has been documented by international research on women's situation (Taylor 1985, Valdés and Gomáriz 1995), though its implications for men have mostly been ignored. The conditions thus exist for the production of a hegemonic masculinity on a world scale – that is to say, a dominant form of masculinity that embodies, organizes and legitimates men's domination in the world gender order as a whole.

The inequalities of the world gender order, like the inequalities of local gender orders, produce resistance. The main pressure for change has come from an international feminist movement (Bulbeck 1998). International cooperation among feminist groups goes back at least a century, though it is only in recent decades that a women's movement has established a strong presence in international forums. Mechanisms such as the 1979 Convention on the Elimination of all forms of Discrimination Against Women, and the 1975–85 United Nations Decade for Women, placed gender inequality on the diplomatic agenda. The follow-up 1995 Beijing Conference agreed on a detailed 'Platform for Action', providing for international action on issues ranging from economic exclusion, women's health, and violence against women, to girls' education.

Equally important is the circulation of ideas, methods and examples of action. The presence of a worldwide feminist movement, and the undeniable fact of a worldwide debate about gender issues, has intensified cultural pressure for change. In Japan, for instance, a range of women's organizations existed before 1970, but a new activism was sparked by the international Women's Liberation movement (Tanaka 1977). This was reflected in cultural genres such as girls' fiction and comic books with images of powerful women. Men, and men's cultural genres, gradually responded – sometimes with marked hostility. Ito (1992), tracing these changes, argues that the older patterns of Japanese 'men's culture' have collapsed, amid intensified debate about the situation of men. However no new model of masculinity has become dominant.

With local variations, a similar course of events has occurred in many developed countries. Challenge and resistance, plus the disruptions involved in the creation of a world gender order, have meant many local instabilities in gender arrangements. They include:

- contestation of all-male networks and sexist organizational culture as women move into political office, the bureaucracy and higher education (Eisenstein 1991),
- the disruption of sexual identities that produced 'queer' politics and other challenges to gay identities in metropolitan countries (Seidman 1996),
- the shifts in the urban intelligentsia that produced pro-feminist politics among heterosexual men (Pease 1997),
- media images of 'the new sensitive man', the shoulder-padded businesswoman, and other icons of gender change.

One response to such instabilities, on the part of groups whose power or identity is challenged, is to reaffirm local gender hierarchies. A masculine fundamentalism is, accordingly, an identifiable pattern in gender politics – the 'gun lobby' discussed in Chapter 9. Swart (2001) documents a striking case in South Africa, the paramilitary Afrikaner Weerstandsbeweging (AWB) movement led by Eugene Terre Blanche. This attempts to mobilize Afrikaner men against the post-apartheid regime. A cult of masculine toughness is interwoven with open racism; weapons are celebrated and women are explicitly excluded from authority. There are obvious similarities to the militia movement in the United States documented by Gibson (1994) and more recently discussed by Kimmel (2004). Tillner (2000), discussing masculinity and racism in central Europe, notes evidence that it is not underprivileged youth as such who are recruited to racism. Rather, it is young men oriented to dominance, an orientation that plays out in gender as well as race.

These fundamentalist reactions against gender change are spectacular, but are not, I consider, the majority response among men. As I noted in the Introduction, there is considerable survey evidence for acceptance of gender change, i.e. a swing of popular attitudes towards gender equality. This change of attitudes, however, need not result in changed practices. For instance, Fuller remarks that despite changes of opinion among Peruvian men,

> the realms in which masculine solidarity networks are constructed that guarantee access to networks of influence, alliances, and

support are reproduced through a masculine culture of sports, alcohol consumption, visits to whorehouses, or stories about sexual conquests. These mechanisms assure a monopoly of, or, at least, differential access by men to the public sphere and are a key part of the system of power in which masculinity is forged. (Fuller 2001: 325)

I would argue that this practical recuperation of gender change is a more widespread, and more successful, form of reaction among men than masculine fundamentalism is. Such recuperation is supported by neo-liberalism. Through the market agenda, the patriarchal dividend to men is defended or restored, without an explicit masculinity politics in the form of a mobilization of men.

Within the global arena of international relations, the international state, multi-national corporations and global markets, there is nevertheless a deployment of masculinities. Two models of the state of play in this arena have recently been offered.

One is the model of transnational business masculinity described in the Introduction. This has replaced older local models of bourgeois masculinity, which were more embedded in local organizations and local conservative cultures. In global arenas, transnational business masculinity has had only one major contender for hegemony in recent decades, the rigid, control-oriented masculinity of the military, and its variant in the military-style bureaucratic dictatorships of Stalinism. With the collapse of Stalinism and the end of the Cold War, the more flexible, calculative, egocentric masculinity of the new capitalist entrepreneur holds the world stage. The political leadership of the major powers, through such figures as Clinton, Schröder and Blair, for a while conformed to this model of masculinity, working out a non-threatening accommodation with feminism.

Transnational business masculinity is not homogeneous. A Confucian variant, based in East Asia, has a stronger commitment to hierarchy and social consensus. A secularized-Christian variant, based in North America, has more hedonism and individualism, and greater tolerance for social conflict. In certain arenas there is already conflict between the business and political leaderships embodying these forms of masculinity. Such conflicts have arisen over 'human rights' versus 'Asian values', and over the extent of trade and investment liberalization.

Focusing more on international politics than on business, Hooper (1998) suggests a somewhat different pattern of hegemony in the masculinities of global arenas. A tough, power-oriented masculinity predominates in the arena of diplomacy, war and power politics – distanced from the feminized world of domesticity, but also distinguished from other masculinities, such as those of working-class men, subordinated ethnic groups, wimps and homosexuals. This is not just a matter of pre-existing masculinity being expressed in international politics. Hooper argues that international politics is a primary site for the construction of masculinities, for instance in war, or through continuing security threats.

Hooper further argues that recent globalization trends have 'softened' hegemonic masculinity in several ways. Ties with the military have been loosened, with a world trend towards demilitarization – the total numbers of men in world armies have fallen significantly since the Cold War. Men are now more often positioned as consumers, and contemporary management gives more emphasis to traditionally 'feminine' qualities such as interpersonal skills and teamwork. Hooper also comments on the interplay of North American with Japanese corporate culture, noting some borrowing in both directions in the context of global re-structuring.

Though the softening of hegemonic masculinity described by Hooper (1998), Niva (1998) and Messner (1993) is real enough, it does not mean the obliteration of 'harder' masculinities. The election of George W. Bush to the presidency, the political aftermath of the attack on the World Trade Centre in New York, and the re-mobilization of nationalism and military force in the United States culminating in the attack on Iraq in 2003, show that hard-line political leadership is still possible in the remaining superpower. It has never gone away in China. Bush's distinctive combination of US nationalism, religiosity, support for corporate interests and rejection of alternative points of view is not, perhaps, an easily exported model of masculinity. But local equivalents can be forged elsewhere.

If these are the contenders for hegemony, they are not the only articulations of masculinity in global forums. The international circulation of 'gay' identities is an important indication that non-hegemonic masculinities may operate in global arenas. They can find political expression, for instance around human rights and AIDS prevention (Altman 2001).

Another political alternative is provided by counter-hegemonic movements opposed to the current world gender order and the groups dominant in it. They are sometimes associated with the promotion of new masculinities, but also address masculinity as an obstacle to the reform of gender relations. The largest and best known are the pro-feminist men's groups in the USA, with their umbrella group NOMAS (National Organization of Men Against Sexism) which has been active since the early 1980s (Cohen 1991). More globally oriented is the 'White Ribbon' campaign, originating in Canada as a remarkably successful mobilization to oppose men's violence against women, and now working internationally (Kaufman 1999).

Such movements, groups or reform agendas exist in many countries, including Germany (*Widersprüche* 1995), Britain (Seidler 1991), Australia (Pease 1997), Mexico (Zingoni 1998), Russia (Sinelnikov 2000), India (Kulkarni 2001) and the Nordic countries (Oftung 2000). The spectrum of issues they address is well illustrated by the conference of the Japanese men's movement in Kyoto in 1996. This conference included sessions on youth, gay issues, work, child rearing, bodies, and communications with women, as well as addressing the topic of the globalization of the men's movement (Menzu Senta 1997).

Most of these movements and groups are small and some are short-lived. They have, however, been a presence in gender politics since the 1970s, and have built up a body of experience and ideas. These are circulated internationally by translations and re-publications of writings, travel by activists and researchers, and through intergovernmental agencies.

Recently some international agencies, including the Council of Europe (Olafsdóttir 2000), FLACSO (Valdés and Olavarría 1998) and UNESCO (Breines et al. 2000), sponsored the first conferences to discuss the implications for public policy of the new perspectives on masculinity.

The United Nations has now become the focus of international discussions about men and gender reform. The role of men in achieving gender equality emerged as an issue in the Program for Action adopted at the 1995 Beijing world conference on women. A number of other international conferences during the last ten years have touched on the matter. The issue came to a focus in the 2004 meeting of the UN Commission on the Status of Women, which had 'the role of men and boys in achieving gender equality' as one of its two main themes. Building on year-long preparations involving a range of activists and researchers from all continents (UN Division for the Advancement of Women 2004), this meeting adopted a set of 'Agreed Conclusions' on the role of men and boys, the first broad international policy statement in the field.

It seems that issues about changing men and masculinities have arrived on the international agenda. They have arrived, however, at a moment when neo-conservative politics is riding high and is certain to oppose any widespread moves towards gender equality. It seems that the politics of masculinity will continue to be contested. The issues explored in this book continue to be difficult, but important, questions for the future of human society.

Notes

Part I Knowledge and its Problems

CHAPTER 1 THE SCIENCE OF MASCULINITY

1 Freud 1953 [1905]: 219–220.
2 *The Glebe and Western Weekly* (Sydney), 7 July 1993.
3 A useful collection of these claims is K. Thompson 1991.
4 A painfully mythologized version of these locally famous exchanges has now been published by the publican: Elliott 1992.
5 Mannheim 1985 [1929] is the classic of the sociology of knowledge. For an example of field studies of scientists, see Charlesworth et al. 1989. Foucault 1977 is a superb historical study of the practical context of knowledge.
6 Kessler and McKenna 1978; West and Zimmerman 1987.
7 For warrior DNA, see Bly 1990: 150. For the now rich literature on gender and science, see Keller 1985, Harding 1991; for masculinity specifically, see Easlea 1983.
8 The connection of evolutionary science with social critique is made clear in the biography of Darwin by Desmond and Moore 1992. A classic statement of the constantly reconstructive character of science is Lakatos 1970.
9 Lyotard 1984 for grand narratives, Pusey 1991 for economic rationalism.
10 As argued by Marcuse 1955, Mitchell 1975.
11 Freud 1953 [1900], 1955 [1909a], 1955 [1909b].
12 Freud 1955 [1905], 1955 [1917]. Anyone inspired to read this case should also read an astonishing document, the Wolf Man's account of Freud: Pankejeff 1971.
13 Freud 1961 [1930]. Laplanche and Pontalis 1973: 435–8 summarize the theory of the super-ego; for application to masculinity, see Silverman 1986.

14 For accounts of the debate on femininity, see Chodorow 1978 and Garrison 1981. The original papers on masculinity are Klein 1928, Boehm 1930, Horney 1932.

15 Reik 1967 [1957]; Bieber et al. 1962; for an example of normalization as cure, see Dolto 1974.

16 Lewes 1988.

17 Jung 1953 [1928]: 187. The themes stated here were elaborated without much basic change in a range of essays and books, e.g., Jung 1982. On Jung's break from Freud, see Wehr 1987.

18 Jung 1953: 199–208.

19 Bethal 1985, Bly 1990, and others too numerous to mention.

20 For examples, Kaufman and Timmers 1983, K. Thompson 1991.

21 Erikson 1950.

22 For core gender identity, Stoller 1968, 1976. On child development, Tyson 1986; on homosexuality, Friedman 1988; for anthropological application, Stoller and Herdt 1982. On the invention of the transsexual, see King 1981, and for a remarkable community study, Bolin 1988.

23 May 1986. May's own work on gender (1980) emphasizes fantasy, but is based on a curiously rigid dichotomy.

24 Adler 1956: 55; 1992 [1927]; 1928. Adler is much neglected in the recent revival of interest in psychoanalysis. An outline of his story is given by Ellenberger 1970. The most detailed account of his relations with Freud is given by Stepansky 1983, whose view of the split I have followed. Stepansky, however, takes the astonishing view that Adler's observations on gender constitute neither 'political' nor 'social' analysis, and that Adler's considerable writings on social issues are mere 'pretexts' for advancing psychological ideas. Stepansky's complete neglect of feminism in Adler's environment betrays the narrowness of his perspective.

25 Reich 1970 [1933], 1972.

26 Horkheimer 1936, Fromm 1942, Adorno et al. 1950. For the US controversy over *The Authoritarian Personality*, see Christie and Jahoda 1954.

27 Malinowski 1927; for later support, Parsons 1964.

28 Sartre 1958, de Beauvoir 1972 [1949].

29 Laing 1960: 73; Laing 1961, Laing and Esterson 1964.

30 As seen in the later work of Sartre 1968, 1976. On its relevance to gender, see Connell 1982.

31 This is a drastic summary of a complex group of positions. For the history of the Lacanian school, see Roudinesco 1990. For its feminist uses, see Mitchell 1975, Irigaray 1985, and Grosz 1990.

32 Deleuze and Guattari 1977, Hocquenghem 1978.

33 Chodorow 1978, 1985; Dinnerstein 1976. Craib 1987 applies the object-relations approach with a clearer appreciation of the institu-

tional bases of masculine dominance, but breaks off. For critique of this approach to theorizing masculinity, see McMahon 1993.

34 Rosenberg 1982.

35 Epstein 1988. The vast compilation by Maccoby and Jacklin 1975 established the general pattern of sex difference findings. In the meta-analytic literature, e.g., Eagly 1987, there is a conscious attempt to supersede this position. Stretching every point, Eagly is still unable to establish sex difference as a strong determinant of traits.

36 Among them Florian Znaniecki, Talcott Parsons, Ralph Linton, Siegfried Nadel, Bruce Biddle. I have described this history in Connell 1979.

37 Komarovsky 1964; Parsons and Bales 1956. For a more detailed account of this history, see Carrigan et al. 1985.

38 Hacker 1957; compare Hartley 1959.

39 Schools Commission 1975. One of the most popular models of sex role reform was 'androgyny': see Bem 1974, Lenney 1979.

40 Pleck and Sawyer 1974, Farrell 1974 and Nichols 1975 were early theorizations of Men's Liberation. Farrell's later turn to the right is discussed in Chapter 9 below. The papers mentioned are Balswick and Peek 1971, Harrison 1978.

41 Pleck 1976, 1977; Snodgrass 1977. For beginnings of the turn against feminism, see the Berkeley Men's Center statement of 1973 printed in Pleck and Sawyer 1974: 174; and Goldberg 1976.

42 Pleck 1981: 160.

43 For the role concept in general, see Urry 1970, Coulson 1972, and Connell 1979. For sex role theory, see Edwards 1983, Stacey and Thorne 1985. For critiques of its use in masculinity research, see Carrigan et al. 1985, Kimmel 1987.

44 Stearns 1979, Pleck and Pleck 1980, are literate examples. There were others much worse, which in charity I forbear to cite.

45 For the sweeping survey approach, see Rotundo 1993; for local studies, Carnes and Griffen 1990, Roper and Tosh 1991, and specifically Heward 1988, Grossberg 1990.

46 Seccombe 1986. This argument about the political character of the family wage is reinforced by detailed regional studies such as Metcalfe 1988 on Australian miners, Rose 1992 on British weavers.

47 Gilding 1991.

48 Phillips 1980, 1984, 1987.

49 Mead 1963 [1935]. Her later theorizing on gender became more conservative: Mead 1950.

50 Herzfeld 1985; for an example of the discussion of machismo, see Bolton 1979.

51 Herdt 1981, 1982, 1984. Modjeska 1990 questions the scope of 'ritualized homosexuality'.

52 Gilmore 1990.

53 Strathern 1978, 1981.
54 Schieffelin 1982.
55 Clifford and Marcus 1986, Strathern 1991.
56 On interaction and gender, West and Zimmerman 1987; on masculinities, Messner 1992, Klein 1993.
57 Gruneau and Whitson 1993, Fine 1987.
58 Donaldson 1991.
59 Collinson, Knights and Collinson 1990, Tolson 1977, Messerschmidt 1993, Staples 1982.
60 Willis 1977, Kessler et al. 1985.
61 Carrigan, Connell and Lee 1985 define hegemonic masculinity; for a critique of the concept, see Donaldson 1993.
62 Walker 1988.
63 On the dialectic in schools, Connell 1989; in the gym, Klein 1993.
64 Cockburn 1983: 171–2. Her later work heightens the emphasis on the political character of the process: Cockburn 1991. On the steelworkers, Corman, Luxton, Livingstone and Seccombe 1993.
65 Hearn 1987, Seidler 1989. Others on the British left have pursued similar themes, e.g., Brittan 1989, Hearn and Morgan 1990, and Segal 1990 (discussed in the next section).
66 This is best seen in movement magazines, such as *Achilles Heel* (Britain), *Changing Men* (United States) and *XY* (Australia). For fundamentalist writing from a 'ministry to men' ('Jesus was maximizing Bill's manhood'), see Cole 1974.
67 Weinberg 1973, Herek 1986.
68 Mieli 1980 on secret desire; Connell, Davis and Dowsett 1993 on sexualization,
69 Altman 1972, Watney 1980.
70 Morgan 1970, Mitchell 1971. For a useful recent survey of the concept see Walhy 1989.
71 Comer 1974; Dalla Costa and James 1972. Segal 1983 documents British debates about reconstructing family relationships.
72 For a survey of this turn in feminist thought, see Segal 1987. For evidence of its continued relevance, Smith 1989.
73 Ehrenreich 1983. For feminist scepticism about the academic men's movement, see Canaan and Griffin 1990.
74 Chesler 1978; Segal 1990.
75 Badinter 1992. Kemper 1990 has looked into the research on testosterone and shows the complexity of the social/biological causal links.
76 My argument here draws on the 'critical theory' of the Frankfurt School, yet I want to emphasize the importance of empirical knowledge in critique. Critical knowledge should be more scientific than positivism, not less: more respectful of facts, more profound in its exploration social reality. Useful models have been developed in education studies: Giroux 1983, Sullivan 1984, Wexler 1992.

CHAPTER 2 MEN'S BODIES

1 For early sociobiology, see Tiger 1969, Tiger and Fox 1971 (men's clubs); for later development, Wilson 1978. Goldberg 1993 is a champion of hormones.
2 *San Francisco Chronicle,* 3 February 1994.
3 Kemper 1990: 221. For an excellent critique of the logic of sociobiological arguments, see Rose, Kamin and Lewontin 1984: ch. 6.
4 Imperato-McGinley et al. 1979.
5 For recent examples of feminist visual semiotics, see *Feminist Review* 1994, no. 46. For fashion and beauty, Wilson 1987, Chapkis 1986. For theories of regulation, Foucault 1977, Turner 1984. For sport, Theberge 1991; for reconstructive surgery and gender, Dull and West 1991, Tiefer 1986.
6 Easthope 1986; Jeffords 1989; Garber 1992.
7 Vance 1989: 21.
8 Pringle 1992.
9 Harrison 1978. For the latest example of this preoccupation in Books About Men, see Farrell 1993: chs 4–7.
10 Rossi 1985: 161.
11 For multiple genders, see Williams 1986, Trumbach 1991. For the history of scientific perceptions of sex, Laqueur 1990.
12 It is specifically men's bodies that form the mass spectacle of sport, women's sports being marginalized by the media: Duncan et al. 1990. My argument here draws on the research collected in Messner and Sabo 1990.
13 Gerschick and Miller 1993.
14 Donaldson 1991: 18. On South Africa, see Nattrass 1992; on 'new class' and education, Gouldner 1979.
15 'Byzantium', in Yeats 1950: 280–1.
16 Connell 1983: 19.
17 Messner 1992, Curry 1992.
18 Hocquenghem 1978.
19 Cummings 1992 speaks for herself; D'Eon from the grave via Kates 1991. For David, see Laing 1960: 73.
20 Turner 1984. Rhode 1990 presents recent US feminist thinking on difference.
21 Morin 1986 has helpful technical detail for those who would like to try. Hocquenghem 1978 enthusiastically develops the cultural meaning; Connell and Kippax 1990 have sobering details on practice.
22 Kosík 1976.

CHAPTER 3 THE SOCIAL ORGANIZATION OF MASCULINITY

1 Bloch 1978 outlines the argument for the Protestant middle classes of England and North America. Laqueur 1999 offers a more sweeping argument on similar lines about views of the body.
2 Tiger 1969: 211. Tiger goes on to suggest that war may be part of 'the masculine aesthetic', like driving a racing car at high speed . . . The passage is still worth reading; like Bly's *Iron John*, a stunning example of the muddled thinking that the question of masculinity seems to provoke, in this case flavoured by what C. Wright Mills once called 'crackpot realtsm'.
3 The deeply confused logic of M/F scales was laid bare in a classic paper by Constantinople 1973. Ethnographic positivism on masculinity reaches a nadir in Gilmore 1990, who swings between normative theory and positivist practice.
4 Kessler and McKenna 1978 develop the important argument about the 'primacy of gender attribution'. For an illuminating discussion of masculine women, see Devor 1989.
5 Eastliope 1986; Brannon 1976.
6 A strictly semiotic approach in the literature on masculinity is not common; this approach is found mostly in more general treatments of gender. However, Saco 1992 offers a very clear defence of the approach, and its potential is shown by the collection in which her paper appears, Craig 1992.
7 Sartre 1968: 159–60.
8 Hollway 1984.
9 Franzway et al. 1989, Grant and Tancred 1992.
10 Mitchell 1971, Rubin 1975. The three-fold model is spelt out in Connell 1987.
11 Hunt 1980. Feminist political economy is, however, under way, and these notes draw on Mies 1986, Waring 1988, Armstrong and Armstrong 1990.
12 Some of the best writing on the politics of heterosexuality comes from Canada: Valverde 1985, Buchbinder et al. 1987. The conceptual approach here is developed in Connell and Dowsett 1992.
13 Interview with Ice-T in *City on a Hilt Press* (Santa Cruz, CA), 21 Jan 1993; Hoch 1979.
14 Rose 1992, ch. 6 especially.
15 I would emphasize the dynamic character of Gramsci's concept of hegemony, which is not the functionalist theory of cultural reproduction often portrayed. Gramsci always had in mind a social struggle for leadership in historical change.
16 Wotherspoon 1991 (chapter 3) describes this climate, and discreetly does not mention individuals.

17 Altman 1972; Anti-Discrimination Board 1982. Quotation from Connell, Davis and Dowsett 1993: 122.

18 See, for instance, the white US families described by Rubin 1976.

19 Staples 1982. The more recent United States literature on black masculinity, e.g., Majors and Gordon 1994, has made a worrying retreat from Staples's structural analysis towards sex role theory; its favoured political strategy, not surprisingly, is counselling programs to resocialize black youth.

20 Ellmann 1987.

21 For patterns of wealth, see the survey of US millionaires by *Forbes* magazine, 19 October 1992. On parliaments, see 1993 survey by Inter-Parliamentary Union reported in *San Francisco Chronicle* 12 September 1993, and United Nations Development Programme 1992: 145. The results of time-budget studies may surprise some readers; see Bittman 1991.

22 The argument here draws on Russell 1982, Connell 1985, Ptacek 1988, Smith 1989.

23 Messerschmidt 1993: 105–17.

24 For the general concept of crisis tendencies, see Habermas 1976, O'Connor 1987; for its relevance to gender, Connell 1987: 158–63.

25 Kimmel 1987; Theweleit 1987; Gibson 1994.

26 A response documented in great detail by Kimmel and Mosmiller 1992.

Part II Four Studies of the Dynamics of Masculinity

INTRODUCTION

1 For defences of life-history method, see Plummer 1983, McCall and Wittner 1990. For social change, Thomas and Znaniecki 1927, Blauner 1989. Sartre's discussion of the 'progressive-regressive method', the most important theorization of life-history method but not much known in social science, is in Sartre 1968. I am conscious that Sartre's approach to the subject is itself gendered; and in using it I have taken account of post-structuralist writings tin subjectivity and gender such as Weedon 1987.

2 This might be called a strategic rather than a representative sample. The approach is usual in oral history. In sociology it is familiar as theoretical sampling' in the account of 'grounded theory' by Glaser *and* Strauss 1967.

3 Further details: the histories were collected in New South Wales, most hut not all in Sydney, in 1985–6. Some fell outside the four groups discussed here. Interviews lasted between one and two hours,

and were tape-recorded. Participants were told our research objective, to explore changes in masculinity and men's lives, We used a 'focused interview' format, with a definite agenda of topics but complete flexibility for the interviewer about how to enter those topics, and what answers to follow up. Three interviewers were involved, one woman and two men. (I was one – though I did the fewest interviews.) The recordings were fully transcribed. In preparing the case studies I used both the transcriptions and the tapes, to get a fuller sense of meaning and emotion. Thirty-six case studies were completed; writing them took me to the end of 1988. The four group studies, and some papers focusing on specific themes, were written from 1989 to 1992. In writing the group studies I had as exemplars not only social scientists using life-history material, such as David Riesman's *Faces in the Crowd* (1952), but also novelists writing about the interplay of life stories, notably Heinrich Böll's wonderful *Group Portrait with Lady* (1973).

CHAPTER 4   LIVE FAST AND DIE YOUNG

1 Stacey 1990; Segal 1990: 294–319.
2 Tolson 1977: 58–81; Willis 1979; Donaldson 1991.
3 Walker 1989.
4 Marx 1969 [1849]: 171.
5 Wilson and Wyn 1987.
6 Hopper and Moore 1990.
7 Walker 1989, Fine 1991.
8 Rubin 1975, Rich 1980.
9 Connell, Davis and Dowsett 1993.
10 Cunneen and Lynch 1988; Hopper and Moore 1983 on the United States.
11 Willis 1978.
12 Messerschmidt 1993, ch. 4.
13 Stoller 1968; see the critique in Chapter 1 above.
14 Sennett and Cobb 1973.
15 Congdon 1975, Willis 1978.
16 As defined, for instance, in the group studied by Bolin 1988.
17 Corman, Luxton, Livingstone and Seccombe 1993, Burgmann 1980.

CHAPTER 5   A WHOLE NEW WORLD

1 For background on the counter-culture in Australia, see Smith and Crossley 1975.
2 The Franklin Dam action is documented in Wilderness Society 1983.

The Australian environmental movement is described in Hutton 1987; for an excellent study of strategy and grass-roots reality, see Watson 1990.

3 For the history of the movement, see Curthoys 1988.

4 Kristeva 1984.

5 Freud 1961 [1930]: 65–8.

6 Horney 1932, Dinnerstein 1976.

7 Not a rhetorical flourish. For wages and conditions in the international garment industry, see Fuentes and Ehrenreich 1983, Enloe 1990.

8 Set forth in the 'Effeminist Manifesto'; Dansky, Knoebel and Pitchford 1977.

9 As documented for Australian hospitals in Game and Pringle 1983. For an excellent discussion of men working in such situations, see Williams 1989.

CHAPTER 6 A VERY STRAIGHT GAY

1 For the countries listed, see: Weeks 1977, D'Emilio 1983, Kinsman 1987, Wotherspoon 1991.

2 On identity, see Troiden 1989, Cass 1990; on subculture, see Epstein 1987, Herdt 1992.

3 Blachford 1981, Weeks 1986.

4 Krafft-Ebing 1965 [1886]. Bieber et al. 1962 and Friedman 1988 show shifting psychoanalytic views. The San Francisco study is Bell et al. 1981.

5 As defined by interviews with other groups in the research, and historical studies such as Game and Pringle 1979, Gilding 1991.

6 For other evidence of mixed early sexuality, see Kinsey et al. 1948: 168, Schofield 1965: 58. For recent survey research, see Turner 1989. Freud's phrase is from the *Three Essays*, 1905.

7 Connell and Kippax 1990.

8 See the discussions in Sargent 1983, Weeks 1986.

9 See the classic discussion of this issue by Williams 1986.

10 My thinking about violence against gays is influenced by McMaster 1991, whose description of the injuries in this murder I have paraphrased. For local youth culture, see Walker 1988.

11 Lynch 1992.

12 Connell, Davis and Dowsett 1993.

13 See Mieli 1980.

14 Altman 1982.

15 For a detailed account of this example of a further moment, the creation of leathermen, see M. Thompson 1991.

16 I owe this observation to Sue Kippax; some evidence for it is provided in Connell and Kippax 1990.

CHAPTER 7 MEN OF REASON

1 On rationality, masculinity and European philosophy, see Seidler 1989. On instrumental/expressive, Parsons and Bales 1956. On the cultural masculinization of science and technology, Easlea 1981, 1983.
2 Winter and Robert 1980: 270.
3 There is an enormous literature on the new middle class. I have found particularly useful Gouldner 1979, emphasizing the cultural significance of higher education, and Sharp 1983.
4 Cockburn 1985.
5 Habermas 1976, Part II, ch. 7.
6 For Apple Computer, see Roszak 1986; for the junk bond office, see Vise and Coll 1991.
7 An excellent analysis of these themes is made by Poole 1991.

Part III   History and Politics

CHAPTER 8 THE HISTORY OF MASCULINITY

1 On reason, masculinity and classical philosophy, see Seidler 1989, ch. 2. Fromm 1942 opened up some of the themes sketched here.
2 Las Casas 1992 [1552]: 31. This is not to say his critique was couched in gender terms; it was phrased in the language of Catholic evangelism and political morality.
3 For the quotation from Franklin, Weber 1976 [1904–5]: 49. For the Molly houses, Bray 1982, ch. 4. On bodies and genders, Trumbach 1991; on fixed identity, Foucault 1980b; and on the formation of gendered character, Wollstonecraft 1975 [1792].
4 *Henry V*, Act III, scene i. Henry's speech is class-stratified; this is the part addressed to the nobility. Hence 'noblish', usually corrected to 'noblest', may contain an echo of 'noblesse'. Shakespeare, like Cervantes, was also adept at deflating the ideology of valour:

> Can Honour set too a legge? No: or an arme? No: Or take away the greefe of a wound? No. Honour hath no skill in Surgerie, then? No. What is Honour? A word. What is that word Honour? Ayre: a trim reckoning *(Henry IV,* Part I, Act V, scene i.)

For the Quaker story, see Bacon 1986, ch. 1.

5 This sketch of gentry masculinity is put together from a wide range of sources, principally British, American and Australian. For d'Eon, see Kates 1991; on the duel, Kiernan 1988. For gentry relations with the agricultural workforce in the Antipodes, Connell and Irving 1992, ch. 2. Curiously the most famous theorist of libertinage, a member of this class, took what was already an old-fashioned view of sodomy as an expression of generalized enthusiasm for evil: de Sade 1966 [1785].

6 Nyc 1993.

7 Clausewitz 1976 [1832]. On the Prussian officer corps, see Wheeler-Bennett 1953, and on the General Staff concept, Dupuy 1977.

8 On masculine imagery in the origins of German fascism, see Theweleit 1987; for its development by the Nazi leadership, see, for example, Manvell and Fraenkel 1960.

9 Bill Gates, part-owner of Microsoft Corporation and estimated by *Forbes* magazine (19 October 1992) to be worth 6.3 billion dollars.

10 These factional divisions are discussed in many places; a well-known example is Galbraith 1967.

11 Phillips 1987; for similar themes in the United States, see Stein 1984. On the 'hunter', see MacKenzie 1987, Marsh 1990 cautions that this imagery could be very remote from the reality of metropolitan life.

12 Several of these movements are documented in Mangan and Walvin 1987.

13 Hantover 1978. This sketch of the ideology and practice of 'separate spheres' is of course an enormous oversimplification; for the complex details, in middle-class England, see the wonderful study by Davidoff and Hall 1987.

14 Weeks 1977, D'Emilio and Freedman 1988. The sexual politics of the Röhm purge is noted in Orlow 1969, 1973, ch. 3.

15 Blewett 1990. On the family wage and expulsions of women from industry, see Seccombe 1986, Cockburn 1983.

16 Engels 1969 [1870]: 163. A classic of class-analytic research on the urban poor is Stedman Jones 1971, who notes a softening of Engels's attitude to the poor when they looked like candidates for being organized.

17 Jayawardena 1963.

18 For British constructions of Bengali masculinity, see Sinha 1987. For 'machismo', see the discussion in Chapter 1 above, and for the Spanish colonial assault on the berdache and its long-term consequences, Williams 1986: ch. 7.

19 For the remarkable story of Xuxa, see Simpson 1993. On the emergence of gay identity in Brazil, see Parker 1985, in Java, see Oetomo 1990.

20 Hinsch 1990; Ortner 1981.

21 Fuentes and Ehrenreich 1983.
22 Kinmonth 1981.
23 For this dynamic in Algeria, see Knauss 1987.
24 For these estimates, see United Nations Development Programme 1992.
25 For all its flakiness as research, Hite 1981 at least documents this; as, in another way, does the whole genre of Books About Men discussed in Chapter 1, and the masculinity therapy discussed in Chapter 9.
26 For an account of this negotiation, see Bulbeck 1988.
27 Weeks 1986. Further evidence of the stabilization of the alternative is in Herdt 1992.
28 I have in mind work such as Le Guin 1973, Piercy 1976.

CHAPTER 9   MASCULINITY POLITICS

1 Parliamentary representation figures from Inter-Parliamentary Union, reported in *San Francisco Chronicle* 12 September 1993; and United Nations Development Programme 1992: 191. Figures on Japanese senior civil servants from Kim 1988.
2 I have summarized this in Connell 1990.
3 As this paragraph specifies, I am concerned in this chapter only with masculinity politics among men. 'There is also a masculinity politics among women; I touched on feminist versions of this in Chapter 1.
4 This description is derived partly from interviews discussed in Chapters 5 and 7, partly from published material in the United States. My best informant, a therapeutic entrepreneur interviewed in the life-history project, is not quoted here as he would be individually identifiable.
5 Goldberg 1976, Ellis 1976, Lyon 1977, Solomon and Levy 1982 (whose book marks the connection with official psychiatry, as well as the beginning of the reaction), Silverberg 1984.
6 Bear et al. 1979; Kaufman and Timmers 1983.
7 Farrell 1986 and 1993, Goldberg 1988, Bly 1990, Keen 1991. Comparisons: Farrell 1971–2, Farrell 1974, Goldberg 1976. I have made a longer critique of Bly elsewhere, Connell 1992.
8 Goldberg 1988:186–7.
9 Rowan 1987. There is of course a range of positions among therapists. A concern with liberalizing masculinity is often carried forward, e.g., Silverberg 1984, alongside celebrations of the masculine, or eclectically mixed with it, as in Keen 1991.
10 Leddy 1987, telling the story of the NRA from a pro-gun position, incidentally revealing it as one of the success stories of new right politics; Gibson 1994.

11 The connection of hegemonic masculinity with violence is an important theme in the critical literature on masculinity, distinguishing it
   from sex role literature. See Fasteau 1974, Patton and Poole 1985,
   Kaufman 1993. Russell 1982 (on rape in marriage) and Ptacek 1988
   (on domestic violence) document the rationalizations mentioned in
   the text.

12 Crane 1925 [1895], Remarque 1929, McCudden 1973 [?1918], Wolfe
   1980, Ashworth 1980, Fussell 1989.

13 Mellen 1978, an unpretentious account more sensitive to nuance
   than Easthope 1986. On Playboy Corporation, see Miller 1984.
   Ehrenreich 1983 interprets this story as part of a 'flight from commitment' on the part of American men, which tends to confuse
   ideology with reality and misses the corporate reconstitution of
   masculinity.

14 Cunneen and Lynch 1988.

15 Weeks 1977:171. On this history in the United States, see D'Emilio
   1983; in Canada, Kinsman 1987; in Australia, Wotherspoon 1991.
   Wolff 1986 on Hirschfeld is poor historiography but has useful
   material.

16 Altman 1972: 56.

17 Hocquenghem 1978, Mieli 1980, Fernbach 1981.

18 The meaning of the masculine turn among gay men was sharply
   debated; see Humphries 1985. The parallel with ethnic politics is
   developed by Altman 1982 and Epstein 1987.

19 Bryant 1977 gives an autobiographical account of homophobic cam-
   paigning; Altman 1986 surveys homophobe politics in the HIV epidemic. For popular homophobia I have drawn on the interviews for
   the study in Part II; Bersani 1987 suggests these themes resonate in
   North America.

20 For the gown and heels, Mieli 1980: 197. The murders include one
   of the first elected representatives, Harvey Milk in San Francisco.

21 Bristol Anti-Sexist Men's Conference 1980.

22 Dansky et al. 1977, Stoltenberg 1990. For feminist critiques of the
   anti-pornography movement, see Segal and McIntosh 1993.

23 Snodgrass 1977, Tolson 1977, Seidler 1991 (a collection of *Achilles
   Heel* material), Brzoska and Hafner 1988, Kaufman 1993, Bengtsson
   and Frykman 1988.

24 Lichterman 1989.

25 An early and completely hostile feminist response to Men's Liberation is Hanisch 1975. A more complex appraisal is in Segal 1990, ch.
   10, who examines the issues of strategy involved.

26 Blanchard 1989 is the author of the fine phrase. Bolin's 1988 excellent study refutes the more lurid claims of Raymond 1979, but
   Raymond's observations on the sexual politics of the medical pro-

fession are well supported. Millot 1990 from a Lacanian perspective points to the imperfect resolution provided by surgery.

27 Garber 1992, Clover 1992. On the various forms of drag, see Kirk and Heath 1984, who along with glitzy photos have very interesting oral-history evidence of the blurred gay/transvestite milieu in London in the 1940s and 1950s, before the syndrome-marking process kicked in.

CHAPTER 10   PRACTICE AND UTOPIA

1 I mean 'utopia' in the sense of Mannheim 1985 [1929], a frame of thought that transcends the existing social situation, grounded in the interest an oppressed group has in that transcendence.

2 For American men in the 1970s, Komarovsky 1973, Shostak 1977. For 1950s concern with male sex role change, Hacker 1957.

3 For inequalities of income, see United States Bureau 'of the Census 1990. The figures used are for median incomes of those, 15 years and older, who have incomes. A classic demonstration of the pressure on local gender regimes and women's authority is Pearlman's (1984) study of the Mazatec people in Mexico.

4 Gilder 1975. This idea is widespread; it is the simplest formula of gender conservatism under the hegemony of science discussed in Chapter 1.

5 Walzer 1983.

6 See the discussion of this remark by Pringle 1992.

7 For the gender patterning of domestic violence, see Dobash et al. 1992. For gender bias in development, Elson 1991; evidence on malnutrition in Bangladesh, Nepal and Botswana is cited by Taylor 1985. For a recent study of interactions, Thorne 1993.

8 Mieli 1980, Chapkis 1986. I have outlined the conceptual background to this strategy in Connell 1987, ch. 13.

9 For 'prefigurative politics', see Rowbotham, Segal and Wainwright 1979: 71–8. Piercy 1976 is a notable example of utopian fiction.

10 The best account of such a group is Lichterman 1989.

11 Tolson 1977: 143.

12 For the early stages, see Tolson's account and Snodgrass 1977. For recent echoes, the super-convoluted debate (overlaid with poststructuralism and literary snobbery) in Jardine and Smith 1987; and (more respectful of readers) Hearn and Morgan 1990.

13 Robins 1984 on football violence (from the young men's point of view); Barnsley Women Against Pit Closures 1984, on gender in the coal strike; Corman et al. 1993 on steelworkers; Burgmann 1980 on builders labourers. For the Australian strategy, see National Committee on Violence Against Women 1992.

14 Perhaps the best-known recent example is Stoltenberg 1990.
15 Yates 1993 ends an excellent review of the education of girls by remarking how little attention has been paid to addressing the education of boys and its contribution to sexual inequality. For attempts to do that, see Inner City Education Centre 1985, Askew and Ross 1988. For the debate on 'men's studies', see Farrant and Brod 1986, Hearn and Morgan 1990.
16 Connell 1994.
17 Connell 1993.
18 See Yates 1993: 89; Blackburn called it the 'sexually inclusive curriculum'.
19 Frank 1993: 56.
20 For gay community action and its effect on practice, see Kippax et al. 1993.
21 Even the most politically sophisticated: Goode 1982, who recognizes the complexities of change in gender relations, but misses violence, homophobia, institutional power and the state.
22 And, one must acknowledge, is still found in some versions of feminism – e.g., MacKinnon 1989. Contrast Walby 1989, Nicholson 1990.
23 To give some rationale for some of these predictions: the politics of the curriculum is discussed above. The HIV epidemic is mainly a heterosexual epidemic on a world scale (Mann et al. 1992); the politics of masculine sexuality involved in its spread includes both straight and gay men. Gibson 1994 notes the intersection of hegemonic masculinity and racism in what he calls 'paramilitary culture' in the United States – to contest one requires contesting the other. The suggestion about alliances of women and men follows from the earlier discussion of masculinity-women as well as femininity-in-men, and women's investment in patriarchy. For globalization-from-below, see Brecher et al. 1993.

References

Adler, Alfred. 1928. 'Psychologie der Macht'. pp. 41–6 in *Gewalt und Gewaltlosigkeit,* ed. F. Kobler. Zürich: Rotapfelverlag.
——. 1956. *The Individual Psychology of Alfred Adler: A Systematic Presentation in Selections from his Writings.* New York: Basic Books.
——. 1992 [1927]. *Understanding Human Nature,* trans. Colin Brett. Oxford: Oneworld.
Adorno, Theodor W., Else Frenkel-Brunswik, Daniel J. Levinson and R. Nevitt Sanford. 1950. *The Authoritarian Personality.* New York: Harper.
Agostino, Katerina. 1998. 'The making of warriors: men, identity and military culture'. *Journal of Interdisciplinary Gender Studies* 3: 58–75.
Altman, Dennis. 1972. *Homosexual: Oppression and Liberation.* Sydney: Angus & Robertson.
——. 1982. *The Homosexualization of America, the Americanization of the Homosexual.* New York: St Martin's Press.
——. 1986. *AIDS in the Mind of America.* New York: Anchor/Doubleday.
——. 2001. *Global Sex.* Chicago: University of Chicago Press.
Anti-Discrimination Board, New South Wales. 1982. *Discrimination and Homosexuality.* Sydney: Anti-Discrimination Board.
Archer, D. & R. Gartner. 1984. *Violence & Crime in Cross-National Perspective.* New Haven: Yale University Press.
Arilha, Margareth, Sandra G. Unbehaum Ridenti and Benedito Medrado, eds. 1998. *Homens e Masculinidades: Outras Palavras.* Sao Paulo: ECOS/Editora 34.
Armstrong, Pat and Hugh Armstrong. 1990. *Theorizing Women's Work.* Toronto: Garamond Press.
Ashworth, Tony. 1980. *Trench Warfare 1914–1918: The Live and Let Live System.* New York: Holmes & Meier.
Askew, Sue and Carol Ross. 1988. *Boys Don't Cry: Boys and* Sexism *in Education.* Milton Keynes: Open University Press.
Bacon, Margaret Hope. 1986. *Mothers of Feminism: The Story of Quaker Women in America.* San Francisco: Harper & Row.
Badinter, Elisabeth. 1992. *XY: de l'identité masculine.* Paris: Odile Jacob.

Balswick, Jack O. and Charles Peek. 1971. 'The inexpressive male: a tragedy of American society'. *The Family Co-ordinator* 20: 363–8.

Barnsley Women Against Pit Closures. 1984. *Women Against Pit Closures.* Barnsley.

Barrett, Frank J. 1996. 'The organizational construction of hegemonic masculinity: The case of the U.S. Navy'. *Gender, Work and Organization* 3: 129–42.

Bauman, Zygmunt. 1998. *Globalization: The Human Consequences.* Cambridge: Polity Press.

Bear, Sheryl, Michael Berger and Larry Wright. 1979. 'Even cowboys sing the blues: difficulties experienced by men trying to adopt non-traditional sex roles and how clinicians can be helpful to them'. *Sex Roles* 5: 191–8.

Beauvoir, Simone de. 1972 [1949]. *The Second Sex.* Harmondsworth: Penguin.

Bell, Alan P., Martin S. Weinberg and Sue Kiefer Hammersmith. 1981. *Sexual Preference: Its Development in Men and Women.* Bloomington: Indiana University Press.

Bem, Sandra L. 1974. 'The measurement of psychological androgyny'. *Journal of Consulting and Clinical Psychology* 42: 155–62.

Bengtsson, Margot and Jonas Frykman. 1988. *Om Maskulinitet: Mannen som Forskningsprojekt.* Stockholm: Delegationen för Jämställdhetsforskning.

Bersani, Leo. 1987, December. 'Is the rectum a grave?' *October* 197–222.

Bethal, Marshall. 1985. 'The mythic male: spectrum of masculinity'. *Colorado Institute of Transpersonal Psychology Journal* 2: 9ff.

Bieber, Irving et al. 1962. *Homosexuality: A Psychoanalytic Study.* New York: Basic Books.

Birrell, Susan and Cheryl L. Cole. 1990. 'Double fault: Renee Richards and the construction and naturalization of difference'. *Sociology of Sport Journal* 7: 1–21.

Bittman, Michael. 1991. *Juggling Time: How Australian Families Use Time.* Canberra: Commonwealth of Australia, Office of the Status of Women.

Blachford, Gregg. 1981. 'Male dominance and the gay world'. pp. 184–210 in *The Making of the Modern Homosexual,* ed. Kenneth Plummer. London: Hutchinson.

Blanchard, Ray. 1989. 'The classification and labeling of non-homosexual gender dysphorias'. *Archives of Sexual Behavior* 18: 315–34.

Blauner, Bob. 1989. *Black Lives, White Lives: Three Decades of Race Relations in America.* Berkeley: University of California Press.

Blewett, Mary H. 1990. 'Masculinity and mobility: the dilemma of Lancashire weavers and spinners in late-nineteenth-century Fall River, Massachusetts'. pp. 164–77 in *Meanings for Manhood: Constructions of Masculinity in Victorian America,* ed. Mark C. Carnes and Clyde Griffen. Chicago: University of Chicago Press.

Bloch, Ruth H. 1978. 'Untangling the roots of modern sex roles: a survey of four centuries of change'. *Signs* 4: 237–52.

Bly, Robert. 1990. *Iron John: A Book About Men.* Reading, MA: Addison-Wesley.

Boehm, Felix. 1930. 'The femininity complex in men'. *International Journal of Psycho-analysis* 11: 444–69.

Bolin, Anne. 1988. *In Search of Eve: Transsexual Rites of Passage.* South Hadley, MA: Bergin & Garvey.

Böll, Heinrich. 1973. *Group Portrait with Lady.* New York: McGraw-Hill.

Bolton, Ralph. 1979. 'Machismo in motion: the ethos of Peruvian truckers'. *Ethos* 7: 312–42.

Bosse, Hans and Vera King, eds. 2000. *Männlichkeitsentwürfe.* Frankfurt: Campus Verlag.

Brandes, Holger and Hermann Bullinger, eds. 1996. *Handbuch Männerarbeit.* Weinheim: Psychologie Verlags Union.

Brannon, Robert. 1976. 'The male sex role: our culture's blueprint of manhood, and what it's done for us lately'. pp. 1–45 in *The Forty-Nine Percent Majority: The Male Sex Role,* ed. Deborah S. David and Robert Brannon. Reading, MA: Addison-Wesley.

Bray, Alan. 1982. *Homosexuality in Renaissance England.* London: Gay Men's Press.

Brecher, Jeremy, John Brown Childs and Jill Cutler, eds. 1993. *Global Visions: Beyond the New World Order.* Boston: South End Press.

Breines, Ingeborg, Robert Connell and Ingrid Eide, eds. 2000. *Male Roles, Masculinities and Violence: A Culture of Peace Perspective.* Paris: UNESCO Publishing.

Bristol Anti-Sexist Men's Conference. 1980. 'A minimum self-definition of the anti-sexist men's movement'. *Achilles Heel* 2–3.

Brittan, Arthur. 1989. *Masculinity and Power.* Oxford: Blackwell.

Bryant, Anita. 1977. *The Anita Bryant Story: The Survival of our Nation's Families and the Threat of Militant Homosexuality.* Old Tappan, NJ: Revell.

Brzoska, Georg and Gerhard Hafner. 1988. *Möglichkeiten und Perspektiven der Veränderung der Männer.* Bonn: BMJFFG.

Buchbinder, David. 1998. *Performance Anxieties: Re-producing Masculinity.* Sydney: Allen & Unwin.

Buchbinder, Howard, Varda Burstyn, Dinah Forbes and Mercedes Steedman. 1987. *Who's On Top? The Politics of Heterosexuality.* Toronto: Garamond Press.

Bulbeck, Chilla. 1988. *One World Women's Movement.* London: Pluto Press.

———. 1998. *Re-Orienting Western Feminisms: Women's Diversity in a Postcolonial World.* Cambridge: Cambridge University Press.

Burgmann, Meredith. 1980. 'Revolution and machismo'. *In Women, Class and History,* ed. Elizabeth Windschuttle. Australia: Fontana.

Campbell, Hugh and Michael Mayerfeld Bell. 2000. 'The question of rural masculinities'. *Rural Sociology* 65: 532–46.

Canaan, Joyce E. and Christine Griffin. 1990. 'The new men's studies: part of the problem or part of the solution?' pp. 206–14 in *Men, Masculinities and Social Theory*, ed. Jeff Hearn and David Morgan. London: Unwin Hyman.

Carnes, Mark C. and Clyde Griffen, eds. 1990. *Meanings for Manhood: Constructions of Masculinity in Victorian America*. Chicago: University of Chicago Press.

Carrigan, Tim, R. W. Connell and John Lee. 1985. 'Toward a new sociology of masculinity'. *Theory and Society* 14: 551–604.

Cass, Vivienne C. 1990. 'The implications of homosexual identity formation for the Kinsey model and scale of sexual preference'. pp. 239–66 in *Homosexuality/Heterosexuality: Concepts of Sexual Orientation*, ed. D. P. McWhirter et al. New York: Oxford University Press.

Chang, Kimberly A. and L. H. M. Ling. 2000. 'Globalization and its intimate other: Filipina domestic workers in Hong Kong'. pp. 27–43 in *Gender and Global Restructuring*, ed. Marianne H. Marchand and Anne Sisson Runyan. London: Routledge.

Chapkis, Wendy. 1986. *Beauty Secrets: Women and the Politics of Appearance*. Boston: South End Press.

Charlesworth, M., L. Farrall, T. Stokes and D. Turnbull. 1989. *Life Among the Scientists: An Anthropological Study' of an Australian Scientific Community*. Melbourne: Oxford University Press.

Chesler, Phyllis. 1978. *About Men*. London: Women's Press.

Chodorow, Nancy. 1978. *The Reproduction of Mothering: Psychoanalysis and the Sociology of Gender*. Berkeley: University of California Press.

——. 1985. 'Beyond drive theory: object relations and the limits of radical individualism'. *Theory and Society* 14: 271–319.

——. 1994. *Femininities, Masculinities, Sexualities: Freud and Beyond*. Lexington: University Press of Kentucky.

Christie, Richard and Marie Jahoda, eds. 1954. *Studies in the Scope and Method of "The Authoritarian Personality"*. Glencoe, IL: Free Press.

Clausewitz, Carl von. 1976 [1832]. *On War*. Princeton: Princeton University Press.

Clifford, James and George E. Marcus, eds. 1986. *Writing Culture: The Poetics and Politics of Ethnography*. Berkeley: University of California Press.

Clover, Carol J. 1992. *Men, Women, and Chain Saws: Gender in the Modern Horror Film*. Princeton: Princeton University Press.

Cockburn, Cynthia. 1983. *Brothers: Male Dominance and Technological Change*. London: Pluto Press.

——. 1985. *Machinery of Dominance: Women, Men, and Technological Know-How*. London: Pluto Press.

——. 1991. *In the Way of Women: Men's Resistance to Sex Equality in Organizations*. London: Macmillan.

Cockburn, Cynthia and Dubravka Zarkov. 2002. *The Postwar Moment*. London: Lawrence and Wishart.

Cohen, Jon. 1991. 'NOMAS: Challenging male supremacy'. *Changing Men*, 10th Anniversary Issue, Winter/Spring: 45–6.

Cole, Edwin Louis. 1974. *Maximized Manhood: A Guide to Family Survival*. Springdale, PA: Whitaker House.

Collier, Richard. 1998. *Masculinities, Crime and Criminology*. London: Sage.

Collinson, David, David Knights and Margaret Collinson. 1990. *Managing to Discriminate*. London: Routledge.

Comer, Lee. 1974. *Wedlocked Women*. Leeds: Feminist Books.

Congdon, Kirby. 1975. *Chain Drive*. Llanfynydd: Unicorn.

Connell, R. W. 1979. 'The concept of role and what to do with it'. *Australian and New Zealand Journal of Sociology* 15: 7–17.

——. 1982. 'Class, patriarchy, and Sartre's theory of practice'. *Theory and Society* 11: 305–20.

——. 1983. *Which Way is Up? Essays on Sex, Class and Culture*. Sydney: Allen & Unwin.

——. 1985. 'Masculinity, violence and war', pp. 4–10 in *War/Masculinity*, ed. Paul Patton and Ross Poole. Sydney: Intervention.

——. 1987. *Gender and Power: Society, the Person and Sexual Politics*. Cambridge: Polity Press.

——. 1989. 'Cool guys, swots and wimps: the interplay of masculinity and education'. *Oxford Review of Education* 15: 291–303.

——. 1990. 'The state, gender, and sexual politics: theory and appraisal'. *Theory and Society* 19: 507–44.

——. 1992. 'Drumming up the wrong tree. *Tikkun* 7: 31–6.

——. 1992a. 'A very straight gay: masculinity, homosexual experience and the dynamics of gender'. *American Sociological Review* 57: 735–51.

——. 1993. *Schools and Social Justice*. Philadelphia: Temple University Press.

——. 1994. 'Transformative labour: theorizing the politics of teachers' work'. *In The Politics of Educators' Work and Lives*, ed. Mark B. Ginsburg. New York: Garland.

——. 1998. 'Masculinities and globalization'. *Men and Masculinities* 1: 3–23.

——. 2000. *The Men and the Boys*. Sydney, Allen & Unwin; Cambridge, Polity Press; Berkeley: University of California Press.

——. 2002. *Gender*. Cambridge: Polity Press.

Connell, R. W., M. Davis and G. W. Dowsett. 1993. 'A bastard of a life: homosexual desire and practice among men in working-class milieux'. *Australian and New Zealand Journal of Sociology* 29: 112–35.

Connell, R. W. and G. W. Dowsett, eds. 1992. *Rethinking Sex: Social Theory and Sexuality Research.* Melbourne: Melbourne University Press.

Connell, R. W. and T. H. Irving. 1992. *Class Structure in Australian History,* 2nd edn. Melbourne: Longman Cheshire.

Connell, R. W. and Susan Kippax. 1990. 'Sexuality in the AIDS crisis: patterns of sexual practice and pleasure in a sample of Australian gay and bisexual men'. *Journal of Sex Research* 27: 167–98.

Connell, R. W. and Julian Wood. 2004. 'Globalization and business masculinities'. *Men and Masculinities,* in press.

Constantinople, Anne. 1973. 'Masculinity-femininity: an exception to a famous dictum?' *Psychological Bulletin* 80: 389–407.

Corman, June, Meg Luxton, David Livingstone and Wally Seccombe. 1993. *Recasting Steel Labour: The Stelco Story.* Halifax: Fernwood.

Coulson, Margaret A. 1972. 'Role: a redundant concept in sociology? Sonic educational considerations'; pp. 107–28 in *Role,* ed. J. A. Jackson. Cambridge: Cambridge University Press.

Cox, Eva. 1995. 'Boys and girls and the costs of gendered behaviour'. *Proceedings of the Promoting Gender Equity Conference,* Ministerial Council for Education, Employment, Training and Youth Affairs, Canberra.

Craib, Ian. 1987. 'Masculinity and male dominance'. *Sociological Review* 34: 721–43.

Craig, Steve, ed. 1992. *Men, Masculinity and the Media.* Newbury Park, CA: Sage.

Crane, Stephen. 1975 [1895]. *The Red Badge of Courage.* Charlottesville: University Press of Virginia.

Cummings, Katherine. 1992. *Katherine's Diary: The Story of a Transsexual.* Melbourne: Heinemann.

Cunneen, Chris and Julie Stubbs. 2000. 'Male violence, male fantasy and the commodification of women through the internet'. *International Review of Victimology* 7: 5–28.

Cunneen, Chris and Rob Lynch. 1988. 'The social-historical roots of conflict in riots at the Bathurst bike races'. *Australian and New Zealand Journal of Sociology* 24: 5–31.

Curry, Timothy John. 'A little pain never hurt anyone: athletic career socialization and the normalization of sport injury'. *Gregory Stone Symposium,* Las Vegas, 1992, February 9.

Curthoys, Ann. 1988. *For and Against Feminism: A Personal Journey into Feminist Theory and History.* Sydney: Allen & Unwin.

Dalla Costa, Mariarosa and Selma James. 1972. *The Power of Women and the Subversion of the Community.* Bristol: Falling Wall Press.

Dansky, Steven, John Knoebel and Kenneth Pitchford. 1977. 'The effeminist manifesto'. pp. 116–20 in *For Men Against Sexism,* ed. Jon Snodgrass. Albion, CA: Times Change Press.

Davidoff, Leonore and Catherine Hall. 1987. *Family Fortunes: Men and Women of the English Middle Class.* London: Hutchinson.

Deleuze, Gilles and Felix Guattari. 1977. *Anti-Oedipus: Capitalism and Schizophrenia.* New York: Viking.

Demetriou, D. Z. 2001. 'Connell's concept of hegemonic masculinity'. *Theory & Society* 30: 337–61.

D'Emilio, John. 1983. *Sexual Politics, Sexual Communities: The Making of a Homosexual Minority in the United States 1940–1970.* Chicago: University of Chicago Press.

D'Emilio, John and Estelle B. Freedman. 1988. *Intimate Matters: A History of Sexuality in America.* New York: Harper & Row.

Denborough, David. 1996. 'Step by Step: Developing Respectful and Effective Ways of Working with Young Men to Reduce Violence'. pp. 91–115 in *Men's Ways of Being,* ed. McLean, Chris, Maggie Carey and Cheryle White. Boulder: Westview Press.

Desmond, Adrian and James Moore. 1992. *Darwin.* Harmondsworth: Penguin.

Devor, Holly. 1989. *Gender Blending: Confronting the Limits of Duality.* Bloomington and Indianapolis: Indiana University Press.

Dinnerstein, Dorothy. 1976. *The Mermaid and the Minotaur: Sexual Arrangements and Human Malaise.* New York: Harper & Row.

Dobash, R. Emerson and Russell P. Dobash. 1992. *Women, Violence and Social Change.* London: Routledge.

Dolto, Françoise. 1974. *Dominique: Analysis of an Adolescent.* London: Souvenir Press.

Donaldson, Mike. 1991. *Time of our Lives: Labour and Love in the Working Class.* Sydney: Allen & Unwin.

——. 1993. 'What is hegemonic masculinity?' *Theory and Society* 22: 643–57.

——. 2003. 'Studying up: the masculinity of the hegemonic'. In *Male Trouble: Studying Australian Masculinities,* ed. Stephen Tomsen and Mike Donaldson. Melbourne: Pluto Press.

Dull, Diana and Candace West. 1991. 'Accounting for cosmetic surgery: the accomplishment of gender'. *Social Problems* 38: 54–70.

Duncan, Margaret Carlisle, Michael A. Messner, Linda Williams and Kerry Jensen. 1990. *Gender Stereotyping in Televised Sports.* Los Angeles: Amateur Athletic Foundation of Los Angeles.

Dupuy, T. N. 1977. *A Genius for War: The German Army and General Staff, 1807–1945.* London: Macdonald & Jane's.

Eagly, Alice H. 1987. *Sex Differences in Social Behavior: A Social-Role Interpretation.* Hillsdale, NJ: Lawrence Erlbaum.

Easlea, Brian. 1981. *Science and Sexual Oppression: Patriarchy's Confrontation with Woman and Nature.* London: Weidenfeld & Nicolson.

——. 1983. *Fathering the Unthinkable: Masculinity, Scientists and the Nuclear Arms Race.* London: Pluto Press.

Easthope, Anthony. 1986. *What a Man's Gotta Do: The Masculine Myth in Popular Culture*. London: Paladin.

Edwards, Anne R. 1983. 'Sex roles: a problem for sociology and for women'. *Australian and New Zealand Journal of Sociology* 19: 385–412.

Ehrenreich, Barbara. 1983. *The Hearts of Men: American Dreams and the Flight from Commitment*. London: Pluto Press.

Eisenstein, Hester. 1991. *Gender Shock: Practising Feminism on Two Continents*. Sydney: Allen & Unwin.

Ellenberger, Henri F. 1970. *The Discovery of the Unconscious: The History and Evolution of Dynamic Psychiatry*. New York: Basic Books.

Elliott, Arthur J. 1992. *The Publican and the Priest*. Sydney: Artway Productions.

Ellis, Albert. 1976. *Sex and the Liberated Man*. Secaucus, NJ: Lyle Stuart.

Ellmann, Richard. 1987. *Oscar Wilde*. London: Hamish Hamilton.

Elson, Diane, ed. 1991. *Male Bias in the Development Process*. Manchester: Manchester University Press.

Engels, Friedrich. 1969 [1870]. Preface to 'The Peasant War in Germany'. pp. 158–65 in Karl Marx and Friedrich Engels, *Selected Works*, vol. 2. Moscow: Progress.

Enloe, Cynthia. 1990. *Bananas, Beaches and Bases: Making Feminist Sense of International Politics*. Berkeley: University of California Press.

Epstein, Cynthia Fuchs. 1988. *Deceptive Distinctions: Sex, Gender and the Social Order*. New Haven: Yale University Press.

Epstein, Steven. 1987. 'Gay politics, ethnic identity: the limits of social constructionism'. *Socialist Review* 9–54.

Erikson, Erik H. 1950. *Childhood and Society*. London: Imago.

——. 1951. 'Sex differences in the play configurations of pre-adolescents'. *American Journal of Orthopsychiatry* 21: 667–92.

——. 1968. *Identity, Youth and Crisis*. New York: Norton.

Farrant, Patricia and Harry Brod, eds. 1986. 'Men's studies'. Special Issue of *Journal of the National Association for Women Deans, Administrators and Counselors* 49: 4.

Farrell, Warren. 1971–2. 'Male consciousness-raising, from a sociological and political perspective'. *Sociological Focus* 5: 19–28.

——. 1974. *The Liberated Man, Beyond Masculinity: Freeing Men and their Relationships with Women*. New York: Random House.

——. 1986. *Why Men Are the Way They Are: The Male–Female Dynamic*. New York: McGraw-Hill.

——. 1993. *The Myth of Male Power: Why Men are the Disposable Sex*. New York: Simon & Schuster.

Fasteau, Marc Feigen. 1974. *The Male Machine*. New York: McGraw-Hill.

Feminism and Psychology, 2001, vol. 11, no. 1, special issue on 'Men and masculinities: discursive approaches'.

Fernbach, David. 1981. *The Spiral Path: A Gay Contribution to Human Survival*. London: Gay Men's Press.

Fine, Gary Alan. 1987. *With the Boys: Little League Baseball and Preadolescent Culture.* Chicago: University of Chicago Press.

Fine, Michelle. 1991. *Framing Dropouts: Notes on the Politics of an Urban Public High School.* Albany: State University of New York Press.

Foucault, Michel. 1977. *Discipline and Punish: The Birth of the Prison.* New York: Pantheon.

——. 1980a. *The History of Sexuality,* vol. I: *An Introduction.* New York: Vintage.

——. 1980b. *Introduction to Herculine Barbin: Being the Recently Discovered Memoirs of a Nineteenth-Century French Hermaphrodite.* New York: Pantheon.

Frank, Blye. 1993. 'Straight/strait jackets for masculinity: educating for "real" men'. *Atlantis* 18: 47–59.

Franzway, Suzanne, Dianne Court and R. W. Connell. 1989. *Staking a Claim: Feminism, Bureaucracy and the State.* Sydney: Allen & Unwin; Cambridge: Polity Press.

Freud, Sigmund. 1953 [1900]. *The Interpretation of Dreams. Complete Psychological Works, Standard Edition,* vols 4–5. London: Hogarth.

——. 1953 [1905]. *Three Essays on the Theory of Sexuality. Complete Psychological Works, Standard Edition,* vol. 7. London: Hogarth.

——. 1955 [1909a]. *Analysis of a Phobia in a Five-Year-Old Boy. Complete Psychological Works, Standard Edition,* vol. 10, 1–149. London: Hogarth.

——. 1955 [1909b]. *Notes Upon a Case of Obsessional Neurosis. Complete Psychological Works, Standard Edition,* vol. '10, 151–249. London: Hogarth.

——. 1955 [1917]. *From the History of an Infantile Neurosis. Complete Psychological Works, Standard Edition,* vol. 17. London: Hogarth.

Freud, Sigmund. 1961 [1930]. *Civilization and its Discontents. Complete Psychological Works, Standard Edition,* vol. 21. London: Hogarth.

Friedman, Richard C. 1988. *Male Homosexuality: A Contemporary Psychoanalytic Perspective.* New Haven: Yale University Press.

Fromm, Erich. 1942. *The Fear of Freedom.* London: Routledge & Kegan Paul.

Fronesis. 2001. 'Mannen' (special issue on men), no. 8.

Fuentes, Annette and Barbara Ehrenreich. 1983. *Women in the Global Factory.* Boston: South End Press.

Fuller, Norma. 2001. 'The social construction of gender identity among Peruvian men'. *Men and Masculinities* 3: 316–31.

Fussell, Paul. 1989. *Wartime: Understanding and Behavior in the Second World War.* New York: Oxford University Press.

Galbraith, John K. 1967. *The New Industrial State.* Boston: Houghton Mifflin.

Game, Anne and Rosemary Pringle. 1979. 'The making of the Australian family'. *Intervention* 12: 63–83.

——. 1983. *Gender at Work.* Sydney: Allen & Unwin.

Garber, Marjorie. 1992. *Vested Interests: Cross-Dressing and Cultural Anxiety.* New York: Routledge.

Garrison, Dee. 1981. 'Karen Horney and feminism'. *Signs* 6: 672–91.

Gee, James Paul, Glynda Hull and Colin Lankshear. 1996. *The New Work Order: Behind the Language of the New Capitalism.* Sydney: Allen & Unwin.

Gerschick, Thomas J. and Adam Stephen Miller. 1993. 'Coming to terms: masculinity and physical disability'. *American Sociological Association Annual Meeting*, Miami.

Ghoussoub, Mai and Emma Sinclair-Webb, eds. 2000. *Imagined Masculinities: Male Identity and Culture in the Modern Middle East.* London: Saqi Books.

Gibson, James William. 1994. *Warrior Dreams: Paramilitary Culture in Post-Vietnam American.* New York: Hill & Wang.

Gierycz, Dorota. 1999. 'Women in decision making: can we change the status quo?'. In *Towards a Woman's Agenda for a Culture of Peace*, ed. I. Breines, D. Gierycz and B. A. Reardon. Paris: UNESCO.

Gilder, George. 1975. *Sexual Suicide.* New York: Bantam.

Gilding, Michael. 1991. *The Making and Breaking of the Australian Family.* Sydney: Allen & Unwin.

Gilmore, David D. 1990. *Manhood in the Making: Cultural Concepts of Masculinity.* New Haven: Yale University Press.

Giroux, Henry A. 1983. *Theory and Resistance in Education: A Pedagogy for the Opposition.* New York: Bergin & Garvey.

Gittings, C. E., ed. 1996. *Imperialism and Gender: Constructions of Masculinity.* United Kingdom: Dangaroo Press.

Glaser, Barney G. and Anselm L. Strauss. 1967. *The Discovery of Grounded Theory: Strategies for Qualitative Research.* New York: Aldine.

Godenzi, Alberto. 2000. 'Determinants of culture: men and economic power'. pp. 35–51 in *Male Roles, Masculinities and Violence*, ed. Ingeborg Breines, Robert Connell and Ingrid Eide. Paris: UNESCO Publishing.

Goldberg, Herb. 1976. *The Hazards of Being Male: Surviving the Myth of Masculine Privilege.* New York: Nash.

——. 1988. *The Inner Male: Overcoming Roadblocks to Intimacy.* New York: Signet.

Goldberg, Steven. 1993. *Why Men Rule: A Theory of Male Dominance.* Chicago: Open Court.

Goode, William J. 1982. 'Why men resist'. pp. 131–50 in *Rethinking the Family*, ed. Barrie Thorne and Marilyn Yalom. New York: Longman.

Gouldner, Alvin W. 1979. *The Future of Intellectuals and the Rise of the New Class.* New York: Continuum.

Grant, Judith and Peta Tancred. 1992. 'A feminist perspective on state bureaucracy'. pp. 112–28 in *Gendering Organizational Analysis*, ed. Albert J. Mills and Peta Tancred. Newbury Park, CA: Sage.

Grossberg, Michael. 1990. 'Institutionalizing masculinity: the law as a masculine profession'. pp. 133–51 in *Meanings for Manhood: Constructions of Masculinity in Victorian America*, ed. Mark C. Carnes and Clyde Griffen. Chicago: University of Chicago Press.

Grosz, Elizabeth A. 1990. *Jacques Lacan: A Feminist Introduction*. London: Routledge.

Gruneau, Richard and David Whitson. 1993. *Hockey Night in Canada: Sport, Identities and Cultural Politics*. Toronto: Garamond Press.

Gutmann, Matthew. 1996. *The Meanings of Macho: Being a Man in Mexico City*. Berkeley: University of California Press.

——. 2001. 'Men and masculinities in Latin America'. *Men & Masculinities* 3, no. 3, special issue.

——. 2002. *The Romance of Democracy: Compliant Defiance in Contemporary Mexico*. Berkeley: University of California Press.

Habermas, Jürgen. 1976. *Legitimation Crisis*. London: Heinemann.

Hacker, Helen Mayer. 1957. 'The new burdens of masculinity'. *Marriage and Family Living* 19: 227–33.

Hanisch, Carol. 1975. 'Men's liberation'. pp. 60–4 in *Feminist Revolution*, Redstockings. New York: Redstockings.

Hantover, Jeffrey P. 1978. 'The boy scouts and the validation of masculinity'. *Journal of Social Issues* 34: 184–95.

Harding, Sandra. 1991. *Whose Science? Whose Knowledge? Thinking from Women's Lives*. Ithaca, NY: Cornell University Press.

Harrison, James. 1978. 'Warning: the male sex role may be dangerous to your health'. *Journal of Social Issues* 34: 65–86.

Hartley, Ruth E. 1959. 'Sex-role pressures and the socialization of the male child'. *Psychological Reports* 5: 457–68.

Hayslett-McCall, K. L. & T. J. Bernard. 2002. 'Attachment, masculinity, & self-control'. *Theor. Criminol.* 6: 5–33.

Hearn, Jeff. 1987. *The Gender of Oppression: Men, Masculinity, and the Critique of Marxism*. Brighton: Wheatsheaf.

——. 1998. *The Violences of Men: How Press Talk About and How Agencies Respond to Men's Violence to Women*. Sage: London.

Hearn, Jeff and David Morgan, eds. 1990. *Men, Masculinities and Social Theory*. London: Unwin Hyman.

Hearn, Jeff, Keith Pringle, Ursula Müller, Elzbeieta Oleksy, Emmi Lattu, Janna Chernova, Harry Ferguson, Øystein Holter, Voldemar Kolga, Irina Novikova, Carmine Ventimiglia, Eivind Olsvik and Teemu Tallberg, 2002a. 'Critical studies on men in ten European countries: (1) The state of academic research'. *Men and Masculinities* 4: 380–408.

——. 2002b. 'Critical studies on men in ten European countries: (2) The state of statistical information'. *Men and Masculinities* 5: 5–31.

Herdt, Gilbert H. 1981. *Guardians of the Flutes: Idioms of Masculinity*. New York: McGraw-Hill.

——, ed. 1982. *Rituals of Manhood: Male Initiation in Papua New Guinea.* Berkeley: University of California Press.

——, ed. 1984. *Ritualized Homosexuality in Melanesia.* Berkeley: University of California Press.

——, ed. 1992. *Gay Culture in America: Essays from the Field.* Boston: Beacon Press.

Herek, Gregory M. 1986. 'On heterosexual masculinity: some psychical consequences of the social construction of gender and sexuality'. *American Behavioral Scientist* 29: 563–77.

Herzfeld, Michael. 1985. *The Poetics of Manhood: Contest and Identity in a Cretan Mountain Village.* Princeton: Princeton University Press.

Heward, Christine. 1988. *Making a Man of Him: Parents and their Sons' Education at an English Public School 1929–50.* London: Routledge.

Hinsch, Bret. 1990. *Passions of the Cut Sleeve: The Male Homosexual Tradition in China.* Berkeley: University of California Press.

Hirst, Paul, and Grahame Thompson. 1996. *Globalization in Question: The International Economy and the Possibilities of Governance.* Cambridge: Polity Press.

Hite, Shere. 1981. *The Hite Report on Male Sexuality.* New York: Knopf.

Hoch, Paul. 1979. *White Hero, Black Beast: Racism, Sexism and the Mask of Masculinity.* London: Pluto Press.

Hocquenghem, Guy. 1978 [1972]. *Homosexual Desire.* London: Allison & Busby.

Hollway, Wendy. 1984. 'Gender difference and the production of subjectivity'. pp. 227–63 in *Changing the Subject,* ed. J. Henriques et al. London: Methuen.

Holter, Øystein G. 1989. *Menn.* Oslo: Aschehoug.

Holter, Øystein G. and Helen Aarseth. 1993. *Menns Livssammenheng* [Men's Life Patterns]. Oslo.

Hooper, Charlotte. 1998. 'Masculinist practices and gender politics: the operation of multiple masculinities in international relations'. pp. 28–53 in *The 'Man' Question in International Relations,* ed. Marysia Zalewski and Jane Parpart. Boulder: Westview.

——. 2000. 'Masculinities in transition: The case of globalization'. In *Gender and Global Restructuring,* ed. Marchand, Marianne and Runyan, Anne Sisson. London: Routledge, 59–73.

Hopper, Columbus B. and Johnny Moore. 1983. 'Hell on wheels: the outlaw motorcycle gangs'. *Journal of American Culture* 6: 58–64.

——. 1990. 'Women in outlaw motorcycle gangs'. *Journal of Contemporary Ethnography* 18: 363–87.

Horkheimer, Max, ed. 1936. *Studien über Autorität und Familie.* Paris: Alcan.

Horney, Karen. 1932. 'The dread of woman: observations on a specific difference in the dread felt by men and by women respectively for the opposite sex'. *International Journal of Psycho-analysis* 13: 348–60.

Humphries, Martin. 1985. 'Gay machismo'. pp. 70–85 in *The Sexuality of Men*, ed. Andy Metcalf and Martin Humphries. London: Pluto Press.

Hunt, Pauline. 1980. *Gender and Class Consciousness*. London: Macmillan.

Hurrelmann, Klaus and Petra Kolip, eds. 2002. *Geschlecht, Gesundheit und Krankheit: Männer und Frauen im Vergleich*. Bern: Verlag Hans Huber.

Hutton, D., ed. 1987. *Green Politics in Australia*. Sydney: Angus & Robertson.

Imperato-McGinley, Julianne, Ralph E. Peterson, Teofilo Gautier and Erasmo Sturla. 1979. 'Androgens and the evolution of male-gender identity among male pseudohermaphrodites with 5-alpha-reductase deficiency'. *New England Journal of Medicine* 300: 1233–7.

Inner City Education Centre. 1985. *Boys Own: Boys, Sexism and Change*. Sydney: Inner City Education Centre.

Irigaray, Luce. 1985. *This Sex Which Is Not One*. Ithaca, NY: Cornell University Press.

Ito, Kimio, 1992. 'Cultural change and gender identity trends in the 1970s and 1980s'. *International Journal of Japanese Sociology* 1: 79–98.

Jardine, Alice and Paul Smith, eds. 1987. *Men in Feminism*. New York: Methuen.

Jayawardena, Chandra. 1963. *Conflict and Solidarity in a Guianese Plantation*. London: Athlone Press.

Jefferson, T. 2002. 'Subordinating hegemonic masculinity'. *Theoretical Criminology* 6: 63–88.

Jeffords, Susan. 1989. *The Remasculinization of America: Gender and the Vietnam War*. Bloomington: Indiana University Press.

Jones, Ernest, ed. 1924. *Social Aspects of Psycho-Analysis*. London: Williams & Norgate.

Jung, Carl G. 1953 [1928]. 'The relations between the ego and the unconscious'. *Collected Works*, volume 7: *Two Essays on Analytical Psychology*. London: Routledge & Kegan Paul.

——. 1982. *Aspects of the Feminine*. Princeton: Princeton University Press.

Kates, Gary. 1991. 'D'Eon returns to France: gender and power in 1777'. pp. 167–94 in *Body Guards: The Cultural Politics of Gender Ambiguity*, ed. Julia Epstein and Kristina Straub. New York: Routledge.

Kaufman, Jack and Richard L. Timmers. 1983: 'Searching for the hairy man'. *Social Work with Groups* 6: 163–75.

Kaufman, Michael. 1993. *Cracking the Armour: Power, Pain and the Lives of Men*. Toronto: Viking.

——, ed. 1999. 'Men & violence'. *International Association for Studies of Men Newsletter* 6, special issue.

——. 2001. 'The White Ribbon campaign: involving men and boys in ending global violence against women'. In *A Man's World? Changing*

Men's Practices in a Globalized World, ed. Pease, Bob and Pringle, Keith. London: Zed Books, 38–51.

Keen, Sam. 1991. *Fire in the Belly: On Being a Man*. New York: Bantam.

Keller, Evelyn Fox. 1985. *Reflections on Gender and Science*. New Haven: Yale University Press.

Kemper, Theodore D. 1990. *Social Structure and Testosterone: Explorations of the Socio-bio-social Chain*. New Brunswick, NJ: Rutgers University Press.

Kersten, J. 1993. 'Crime & masculinities in Australia, Germany & Japan'. *International Sociology* 8: 461–78.

Kessler, S., D. J. Ashenden, R. W. Connell and G. W. Dowsett. 1985. 'Gender relations in secondary schooling'. *Sociology of Education* 58: 34–48.

Kessler, Suzanne J. and Wendy McKenna. 1978. *Gender: An Ethnomethodological Approach*. New York: Wiley.

Kiernan, V. G. 1988. *The Duel in European History: Honour and the Reign of Aristocracy*. Oxford: Oxford University Press.

Kim, Paul S. 1988. *Japan's Civil Service System: Its Structure, Personnel and Politics*. New York: Greenwood Press.

Kimmel, Michael S. 1987. 'Rethinking "masculinity": new directions in research', pp. 9–24 in *Changing Men: New Directions in Research on Men and Masculinity*, ed. Michael S. Kimmel. Newbury Park, CA: Sage.

———. 2004. 'Globalization and its mal(e)contents: the gendered moral and political economy of terrorism'. In *Handbook of Research on Men and Masculinities*, ed. M. Kimmel, J. Hearn and R. W. Connell. Thousand Oaks: Sage.

Kimmel, Michael S. and Michael A. Messner, eds. 2001. *Men's Lives*. 5th edn. Boston: Allyn and Bacon.

Kimmel, Michael S. and Thomas E. Mosmiller, eds. 1992. *Against the Tide: Pro-Feminist Men in the United States, 1776–1990, a Documentary History*. Boston: Beacon Press.

Kindler, Heinz. 2002. *Väter und Kinder*. Juventa: Weinheim and München.

King, Dave. 1981. 'Gender confusions: psychological and psychiatric conceptions of transvestism and transsexualism'. pp. 155–83 in *The Making of the Modern Homosexual*, ed. Kenneth Plummer. London: Hutchinson.

Kinmonth, Earl H. 1981. *The Self-Made Man in Maiji Japanese Thought: From Samurai to Salary Man*. Berkeley: University of California Press.

Kinsey, Alfred C., Wardell B. Pomeroy and Clyde E. Martin. 1948. *Sexual Behavior in the Human Male*. Philadelphia: Saunders.

Kinsman, Gary. 1987. *The Regulation of Desire: Sexuality in Canada*. Montreal: Black Rose Books.

Kippax, Susan, R. W. Connell, G. W. Dowsett and June Crawford. 1993. *Sustaining Safe Sex: Gay Communities Respond to AIDS.* London: Falmer Press.

Kirk, Kris and Ed Heath. 1984. *Men in Frocks.* London: GMP.

Klein, Alan M. 1993. *Little Big Men: Bodybuilding Subculture and Gender Construction.* Albany: State University of New York Press.

Klein, Melanie. 1928. 'Early stages of the Oedipus conflict'. *International Journal of Psycho-analysis* 9: 167–80.

Klein, Uta. 2000. ' "Our best boys": the making of masculinity in Israeli society'. In *Male Roles, Masculinities and Violence: A Culture of Peace Perspective,* ed. Breines, Ingeborg, R. W. Connell and Ingrid Eide. Paris: UNESCO Publishing.

Knauss, Peter R. 1987. *The Persistence of Patriarchy: Class, Gender and Ideology in Twentieth Century Algeria.* New York: Praeger.

Komarovsky, Mirra. 1964. *Blue Collar Marriage.* New York: Vintage.

——. 1973. 'Cultural contradictions and sex roles: the masculine case'. *American Journal of Sociology* 78: 873–84.

Kosík, Karel. 1976. *Dialectics of the Concrete: A Study on Problems of Man and the World.* Dordrecht: D. Reidel.

Krafft-Ebing, R. von. 1965 [1886]. *Psychopathia Sexualis.* New York: Paperback Library.

Kristeva, Julia. 1984. *Revolution in Poetic Language.* New York: Columbia University Press.

Kulkarni, Mangesh. 2001. 'Reconstructing Indian masculinities'. *Gentleman* (Mumbai), May 2001.

Kupers, Terry. 1993. *Revisioning Men's Lives: Gender, Intimacy, and Power.* New York: Guilford Press.

Kvinder Kon & Forskning. 1999. 'Maskuliniteter' (special issue on masculinities), vol. 8, no. 3.

Laing, R. D. 1960. *The Divided Self: An Existential Study in Sanity and Madness.* London: Tavistock.

——. 1961. *Self and Others.* London: Tavistock.

Laing, R. D. and A. Esterson. 1964. *Sanity, Madness and the Family: Families of Schizaphrenics.* London: Tavistock.

Lakatos, Imre. 1970. 'Falsification and the methodology of scientific research programmes'. pp. 91–196 in *Criticism and the Growth of Knowledge,* ed. Imre Lakatos and Alan Musgrave. Cambridge: Cambridge University Press.

Laplanche, J. and J. B. Pontalis. 1973. *The Language of Psycho-Analysis.* New York: Norton.

Laqueur, Thomas W. 1990. *Making Sex: Body and Gender from the Greeks to Freud.* Cambridge, MA: Harvard University Press.

Las Casas, Bartolomé de. 1992 [1552]. *The Devastation of the Indies: A Brief Account.* Baltimore: Johns Hopkins University Press.

Law, Robin, Hugh Campbell and John Dolan, eds. 1999. *Masculinities in Aotearoa/New Zealand.* Palmerston North: Dunmore Press.

Leddy, Edward F. 1987. *Magnum Force Lobby: The National Rifle Association Fights Gun Control.* Lanham, MD: University Press of America.

Le Guin, Ursula. 1973. *The Left Hand of Darkness.* London: Panther.

Lenney, Ellen. 1979. 'Androgyny: some audacious assertions towards its coming of age. *Sex Roles* 5: 703–19.

Lewes, Kenneth. 1988. *The Psychoanalytic Theory of Male Homosexuality.* New York: Simon & Schuster.

Lichterman, Paul. 1989. 'Making a politics of masculinity'. *Comparative Social Research* 11: 185–208.

Lingard, Bob and Peter Douglas. 1999. *Men Engaging Feminisms: Profeminism, Backlashes and Schooling.* Philadelphia: Open University Press.

Livingstone, David W. and Meg Luxton. 1989. 'Gender consciousness at work: modification of the male breadwinner norm among steelworkers and their spouses'. *Canadian Review of Sociology and Anthropology* 26: 240–75.

Lynch, Frederick R. 1992. 'Nonghetto gays: an ethnography of suburban homosexuals'. pp. 165–201 in *Gay Culture in America*, ed. Gilbert H. Herdt. Boston: Beacon Press.

Lyon, Harold C. Jr. 1977. *Tenderness is Strength.* New York: Harper & Row.

Lyotard, Jean-François. 1984. *The Postmodern Condition: A Report on Knowledge.* Minneapolis: University of Minnesota Press.

McCall, Michal M. and Judith Wittner. 1990. 'The good news about life history'. pp. 46–89 in *Symbolic Interaction and Cultural Studies*, ed. Howard S. Becker and Michal M. McCall. Chicago: University of Chicago Press.

Maccoby, Eleanor Emmons and Carol Nagy Jacklin. 1975. *The Psychology of Sex Differences.* Stanford, CA: Stanford University Press.

McCudden, James T. B. 1973 [?1918]. *Flying Fury: Five Years in the Royal Flying Corps.* Folkestone: Bailey Brothers & Swinfen.

McIntosh, Mary. 1993. 'Liberalism and the contradictions of sexual politics'. pp. 155–68 in *Sex Exposed: Sexuality and the Pornography Debate*, ed. Lynne Segal and Mary McIntosh. New Brunswick: Rutgers University Press.

MacKenzie, John M. 1987. 'The imperial pioneer and hunter and the British masculine stereotype in late Victorian and Edwardian times'. pp. 176–98 in *Manliness and Morality: Middle-Class Masculinity in Britain and America, 1800–1940*, ed. J. A. Mangan and James Walvin. Manchester: Manchester University Press.

McKeown, Kieran, Harry Ferguson and Dermot Rooney. 1999. *Changing Fathers?*, Dublin: Collins Press.

MacKinnon, Catharine A. 1989. *Toward a Feminist Theory of the State.* Cambridge, MA: Harvard University Press.

McMahon, Anthony. 1993. 'Male readings of feminist theory: the psychologization of sexual politics in the masculinity literature. *Theory and Society* 22: 675–95.

McMaster, David. 1991. 'One does not stir without the "other": homophobia, masculinity and intention'. BA Honours Research Essay. Sydney: Macquarie University, Sociology Discipline.

Majors, Richard G. and Jacob U. Gordon. 1994. *The American Black Male: His Present Status and his Future.* Chicago: Nelson-Hall.

Malinowski, Bronislaw. 1927. *Sex and Repression in Savage Society.* London: Routledge & Kegan Paul.

——. 1932. *The Sexual Life of Savages in North-Western Melanesia.* London: Routledge & Kegan Paul.

Mangan, J. A. and James Walvin, eds. 1987. *Manliness and Morality: Middle-Class Masculinity in Britain and America, 1800–1940.* Manchester: Manchester University Press.

Mann, Jonathan M., Daniel J. M. Tarantola and Thomas W. Netter, eds. 1992. *AIDS in the World.* Cambridge, MA: Harvard University Press.

Mannheim, Karl, 1985 [1929]. *Ideology and Utopia: An Introduction to the Sociology of Knowledge.* San Diego: Harcourt Brace Jovanovich.

Manvell, Roger and Heinrich Fraenkel. 1960. *Doctor Goebbels: His Life and Death.* London: Heinemann.

Marchand, Marianne H. and Anne Sisson Runyan, eds. 2000. *Gender & Global Restructuring: Sightings, Sites and Resistances.* London: Routledge.

Marcuse, Herbert. 1955. *Eros and Civilization: A Philosophical Inquiry into Freud.* Boston: Beacon Press.

Marsh, Margaret. 1990. 'Suburban men and masculine domesticity, 1870–1915'. pp. 111–27 in *Meanings for Manhood: Constructions of Masculinity in Victorian America,* ed. Mark C. Carnes and Clyde Griffen. Chicago: University of Chicago Press.

Martino, Wayne and Pallota-Chiarolli. 2003. *So What's a Boy? Addressing Issue of Masculinity and Schooling.* Sydney: Allen and Unwin.

Marx, Karl. 1969 [1849]. 'Wage labour and capital'. pp. 142–74 in Karl Marx and Frederick Engels, *Selected Works,* vol. 1. Moscow: Progress.

May, Robert. 1980. *Sex and Fantasy: Patterns of Male and Female Development.* New York: Norton.

——. 1986. 'Concerning a psychoanalytic view of maleness'. *Psychoanalytic Review* 73: 579–97.

Mead, Margaret. 1950. *Male and Female: A Study of the Sexes in a Changing World.* London: Gollancz.

——. 1963 [1935]. *Sex and Temperament in Three Primitive Societies.* New York: William Morrow.

Mellen, Joan. 1978. *Big Bad Wolves: Masculinity in the American Film.* London: Elm Tree Books.

Menzu Senta [Men's Centre Japan]. 1997. *Otokotachi no watashisagashi* [How are men seeking their new selves?]. Kyoto: Kamogawa.

Messerschmidt, James W. 1993. *Masculinities and Crime: Critique and Reconceptualization of Theory.* Lanham, MD: Rowman & Littlefield.

——. 1997. *Crime as Structured Action: Gender, Race, Class, and Crime in the Making.* Thousand Oaks: Sage.

——. 2000. *Nine Lives: Adolescent Masculinities, The Body, and Violence.* Boulder: Westview Press.

Messner, Michael A. 1992. *Power at Play: Sports and the Problem of Masculinity.* Boston: Beacon Press.

——. 1993. ' "Changing men" and feminist politics in the United States'. *Theory and Society* 22: 723–37.

——. 1997. *The Politics of Masculinities: Men in Movements.* Thousand Oaks: Sage.

——. 2002. *Taking the Field: Women, Men, and Sports.* Minneapolis: University of Minnesota Press.

Messner, Michael A. and Don Sabo, eds. 1990. *Sport, Men and the Gender Order: Critical Feminist Perspectives.* Champaign, IL: Human Kinetics Books.

Metcalfe, Andrew W. 1988. *For Freedom and Dignity: Historical Agency and Class Structures in the Coalfields of NSW.* Sydney: Allen & Unwin.

Metz-Göckel, Sigrid and Ursula Müller. 1985. *Der Mann: Die Brigitte-Studie.* Hamburg: Beltz.

Mieli, Mario. 1980 [1977]. *Homosexuality and Liberation: Elements of a Gay Critique.* London: Gay Men's Press.

Mies, Maria. 1986. *Patriarchy and Accumulation on a World Scale: Women in the International Division of Labour.* London: Zed Books.

Miller, Russell. 1984. *Bunny: The Real Story of Playboy.* London: Michael Joseph.

Millot, Catherine. 1990. *Horsexe: Essay on Transsexuality.* Brooklyn: Autonomedia.

Mitchell, Juliet. 1971. *Woman's Estate.* Harmondsworth: Penguin.

——. 1975. *Psychoanalysis and Feminism.* New York: Vintage.

Modjeska, Nicholas. 1990. 'The Duna PALENA NANE and the sociology of bachelor cults', Macquarie University School of Behavioural Sciences.

Morgan, David. 1994. 'Theater of war: combat, the military and masculinity'. In *Theorizing Masculinities*, ed. H. Brod and M. Kaufman. Thousand Oaks: Sage.

Morgan, Robin. 1970. 'Introduction' to *Sisterhood is Powerful: An Anthology of Writings from the Women's Liberation Movement.* New York: Vintage.

Morin, Jack. 1986. *Anal Pleasure and Health: A Guide for Men and Women.* Burlingame, CA: Yes Press.

Morrell, Robert. 2001a. *From Boys to Gentlemen: Settler Masculinity in Colonial Natal, 1880–1920.* Pretoria: University of South Africa Press.

——, ed. 2001b. *Changing Men in Southern Africa.* London, Zed Books.

Nagel, Joane. 1998. 'Masculinity and nationalism: gender and sexuality in the making of nations'. *Ethnic and Racial Studies* 21: 242–69.

National Committee on Violence Against Women. 1992. *The National Strategy on Violence Against Women.* Canberra: Australian Government Publishing Service.

Nattrass, Nicoli. 1992. *Profits and Wages: The South African Economic Challenge.* Harmondsworth: Penguin.

Nichols, Jack. 1975. *Men's Liberation: A New Definition of Masculinity.* New York: Penguin.

Nicholson, Linda J., ed. 1990. *Feminism/Postmodernism.* New York: Routledge.

Niva, Steve. 1998. 'Tough and tender: new world order masculinity and the Gulf War'. pp. 109–28 in *The 'Man' Question in International Relations,* ed. Zalewski, Marysia and Jane Parpart. Boulder: Westview Press.

Novikova, Irina. 2000. 'Soviet and post-Soviet masculinities: after men's wars in women's memories'. In *Male Roles, Masculinities and Violence: A Culture of Peace Perspective,* ed. Breines, Ingeborg, R. W. Connell and Ingrid Eide. Paris: UNESCO Publishing, 117–29.

Nye, Robert A. 1993. *Masculinity and Male Codes of Honor in Modern France.* New York: Oxford University Press.

O'Connor, James. 1987. *The Meaning of Crisis: A Theoretical Introduction.* Oxford: Blackwell.

Oetomo, Dede. 1990. 'Patterns of bisexuality in Indonesia'. Universitas Airlangga, Faculty of Social and Political Sciences.

Oftung, Knut. 2000. 'Men and gender equality in the Nordic countries'. pp. 143–62 in *Male Roles, Masculinities and Violence: A Culture of Peace Perspective,* ed. Ingeborg Breines, Robert Connell and Ingrid Eide. Paris: UNESCO Publishing.

Ólafsdóttir, Olöf. 2000. 'Statement'. pp. 281–3 in *Male Roles, Masculinities and Violence: A Culture of Peace Perspective,* ed. Ingeborg Breines, Robert Connell and Ingrid Eide. Paris: UNESCO Publishing.

Olavarría, José. 2001. *Y Todos Querian Ser (buenos) Padres: Varones de Santiago de Chile en conflicto.* Santiago: FLACSO-Chile.

Olavarría, José and Enrique Moletto. 2002. *Hombres: Identidad/es y Sexualidad/es: III Eucuentro de Estudios de Masculinidades.* Santiago: FLACSO-Chile.

Onwudiwe, I. D. 2000. *The Globalization of Terrorism.* Ashgate.

Orlow, Dietrich. 1969, 1973. *The History of the Nazi Party,* 2 vols. Pittsburgh: University of Pittsburgh Press.

Ortner, Sherry B. 1981. 'Gender and sexuality in hierarchical societies: the case of Polynesia and some comparative implications'. pp. 360–409 in *Sexual Meanings: The Cultural Construction of Sexuality,* ed. S. B. Ortner and H. Whitehead. Cambridge: Cambridge University Press.

Ouzgane, Lahoucine and Daniel Coleman. 1998. *Jouvert: A Journal of Postcolonial Studies* Vol. 2, no. 1. Special Issue on Postcolonial Masculinities. Electronic journal at http//social.chass.ncsu.edu/jouvert.

Palme, Olof. 1972. 'The emancipation of man'. *Journal of Social Issues* 28: 2, 237–46.

Pankejeff, Sergius. 1971. *The Wolf-Man, By the Wolf-Man.* New York: Basic Books.

Parker, Richard. 1985. Masculinity, femininity, and homosexuality: on the anthropological interpretation of sexual meanings in Brazil'. *Journal of Homosexuality* 11: 155–63.

Parsons, Anne. 1964. 'Is the Oedipus complex universal? The Jones-Malinowski debate revisited and a South Italian "nuclear complex"'. *The Psychoanalytic Study of Society* 3: 278–326.

Parsons, Talcott and Robert F. Bales. 1956. *Family, Socialization and Interaction Process.* London: Routledge & Kegan Paul.

Patton, Paul and Ross Poole, eds. 1985. *War/Masculinity.* Sydney: Intervention Publications.

Pearlman, Cynthia L. 1984. 'Machismo, Marianismo and change in indigenous Mexico: a case study from Oaxaca'. *Quarterly Journal of Ideology* 8: 53–9.

Pease, Bob. 1997. *Men and Sexual Politics: Towards a Profeminist Practice.* Adelaide: Dulwich Centre.

——. 2000. *Recreating Men: Postmodern Masculinity Politics.* London: Sage.

Pease, Bob and Keith Pringle, eds. 2001. *A Man's World? Changing Men's Practices in a Globalized World.* London: Zed Books.

Perkins, Roberta. 1983. *The 'Drag Queen' Scene: Transsexuals in King's Cross.* Sydney: Allen & Unwin.

Peteet, Julie. 2000. 'Male gender and rituals of resistance in the Palestinian Intifada: A cultural politics of violence'. In *Imagined Masculinities: Male Identity and Culture in the Modern Middle East,* ed. Ghoussoub, Mai and Emma Sinclair-Webb. London: Saqi Books.

Petersen, A. 1998. *Unmasking the Masculine: 'Men' and 'Identity' in a Sceptical Age.* London: Sage.

Phillips, J. O. C. 1980. 'Mumny's boys: Pakeha men and male culture in New Zealand'. pp. 217–43 in *Women in New Zealand Society,* ed. Phillida Bunkle and Beryl Hughes. Allen & Unwin.

——. 1984. 'Rugby, war and the mythology of the New Zealand male'. *New Zealand Journal of History* 18: 83–103.

——. 1987. *A Man's Country? The Image of the Pakeha Male, A History.* Auckland: Penguin.

Piercy, Marge. 1976. *Woman on the Edge of Time.* New York: Knopf.

Pleck, Elizabeth H. and Joseph H. Pleck, eds. 1980. *The American Man.* Englewood Cliffs, NJ: Prentice-Hall.

Pleck, Joseph H. 1976. 'The male sex role: definitions, problems, and sources of change'. *Journal of Social Issues* 32: 155–64.

——. 1977. 'Men's power with women, other men, and society: a men's movement analysis'. *Women and Men: The Consequences of Power*, ed. D. Hiller and R. Sheets. Cincinnati: University of Cincinnati, Office of Women's Studies.

——. 1981. *The Myth of Masculinity*. Cambridge, MA: MIT Press.

Pleck, Joseph H. and Jack Sawyer, eds. 1974. *Men and Masculinity*. Englewood Cliffs, NJ: Prentice-Hall.

Plummer, Ken, 1983. *Documents of Life: An Introduction to the Problems and Literature of a Humanistic Method*. London: Allen & Unwin.

Polk, K. 1994. *When Men Kill: Scenarios of Masculine Violence*. Cambridge: Cambridge University Press.

Poole, Ross. 1991. *Morality and Modernity*. London: Routledge.

Poynting, Scott, Greg Noble and Paul Tabar. 1998. ' "If anybody called me a wog they wouldn't be speaking to me alone": protest masculinity and Lebanese youth in Western Sydney'. *Journal of Interdisciplinary Gender Studies* 3: 76–94.

Pridemore, W. A. 2002. 'What we know about social structure and homicide'. *Violence & Victims* 17: 127–56.

Pringle, Rosemary. 1992. 'Absolute sex? Unpacking the sexuality/gender relationship'. pp. 76–101 in *Rethinking Sex: Social Theory and Sexuality Research*, ed. R. W. Connell and G. W. Dowsett. Melbourne: Melbourne University Press.

Ptacek, James. 1988. 'Why do men batter their wives?' pp. 133–57 in *Feminist Perspectives on Wife Abuse*, ed. Kersti Yllö and Michele Bograd. Newbury Park, CA: Sage.

Pusey, Michael. 1991. *Economic Rationalism in Canberra: A Nation-Building State Changes its Mind*. London: Cambridge University Press.

Raymond, Janice G. 1979. *The Transsexual Empire*. Boston: Beacon Press.

Reich, Wilhelm. 1970 [1933]. *The Mass Psychology of Fascism*. New York: Farrar, Strauss & Giroux.

——. 1972. *Sex-pol: Essays, 1929–1934*. New York: Vintage.

Reik, Theodor. 1967 [1957]. Of *Love and Lust: On the Psychoanalysis of Romantic and Sexual Emotions*. New York: Farrar, Strauss.

Remarque, Erich Maria. 1929. *All Quiet on the Western Front*. Boston: Little, Brown & Co.

Rhode, Deborah L., ed. 1990. *Theoretical Perspectives on Sexual Difference*. New Haven: Yale University Press.

Rich, Adrienne. 1980. 'Compulsory heterosexuality and lesbian existence'. *Signs* 5: 631–60.

Riesman, David. 1952. *Faces in the Crowd: Individual Studies in Character and Politics*. New Haven: Yale University Press.

Roberson, J. E. and N. Suzuki, eds. 2003. *Men & Masculinities in Contemporary Japan*. London: Routledge.

Robins, David. 1984. *We Hate Humans*. Harmondsworth: Penguin.

Roper, Michael. 1994. *Masculinity and the British Organization Man Since 1945*. Oxford: Oxford University Press.

Roper, Michael and John Tosh, eds. 1991. *Manful Assertions: Masculinities in Britain since 1800*. London: Routledge.

Rose, Sonya O. 1992. *Limited Livelihoods: Gender and Class in Nineteenth-Century England*. Berkeley: University of California Press.

Rose, Steven, Leon J. Kamin and R. C. Lewontin. 1984, *Not in our Genes: Biology, Ideology and Human Nature*. Harmondsworth: Penguin.

Rosenberg, Rosalind. 1982. *Beyond Separate Spheres: The Intellectual Roots of Modern Feminism*. New Haven: Yale University Press.

Rossi, Alice S. 1985. 'Gender and parenthood'. pp. 161–91 in *Gender and the Life Course*, ed. Alice S. Rossi. New York: Aldine.

Roszak, Theodore. 1986. *The Cult of Information: The Folklore of Computers and the True Art of Thinking*. New York: Pantheon.

Rotundo, E. Anthony. 1993. *American Manhood: Transformations of Masculinity from the Revolution to the Modern Era*. New York: Basic Books.

Roudinesco, Elisabeth. 1990. *Jacques Lacan & Co.: A History of Psychoanalysis in France, 1925–1985*. Chicago: University of Chicago Press.

Rowan, John. 1987. *The Horned God: Feminism and Men as Wounding and Healing*. London: Routledge & Kegan Paul.

Rowbotham, Sheila, Lynne Segal and Hilary Wainwright. 1979. *Beyond the Fragments: Feminism and the Making of Socialism*. London: Islington Community Press.

Rubin, Gayle. 1975. 'The traffic in women: notes on the "political economy" of sex'. pp. 157–210 in *Toward an Anthropology of Women*, ed. Rayna R. Reiter. New York: Monthly Review Press.

Rubin, Lillian B. 1976. *Worlds of Pain: Life in the Working-Class Family*. New York: Basic Books.

Russell, Diana E. H. 1982. *Rape in Marriage*. New York: Macmillan.

Sabo, D., T. A. Kupers and W. London, eds. 2001. *Prison Masculinities*. Philadelphia: Temple University Press.

Saco, Diana. 1992. 'Masculinity as signs: poststructuralist feminist approaches to the study of gender'. pp. 23–39 in *Men, Masculinity and the Media*, ed. Steve Craig. Newbury Park, CA: Sage.

Sade, Donatien Alphonse-Françoise, Marquis de. 1966 [1785]. *The 120 Days of Sodom, and Other Writings*. New York: Grove Press.

Sargent, Dave. 1983. 'Reformulating (homo) sexual politics'. pp. 163–82 in *Beyond Marxism*, ed. Judith Allen and Paul Patton. Sydney: Intervention.

Sartre, Jean Paul. 1958 [1943]. *Being and Nothingness: An Essay on Phenomenological Ontology*. London: Methuen.

———. 1968 [1960]. *Search for a Method*. New York: Vintage.

———. 1976 [1960]. *Critique of Diatectical Reason, I: Theory of Practical Ensembles*. London: NLB.

Schieffelin, E. L. 1982. 'The Bau A ceremonial hunting lodge: an alternative to initiation'. pp. 155–200 in *Rituals of Manhood: Male Initiation in Papua New Guinea*, ed. Gilbert H. Herdt. Berkeley: University of California Press.

Schofield, Michael. 1965, *The Sexual Behavior of Young People*. Boston: Little, Brown & Co.

Schofield, Toni, R. W. Connell, Linley Walker, Julian Wood and Dianne Butland. 2000. 'Understanding men's health: a gender-relations approach to masculinity, health and illness'. *Journal of American College Health* 48: 247–56.

Schools Commission. 1975. *Girls, School and Society*. Canberra: Schools Commission.

Seccombe, Wally. 1986. 'Patriarchy stabilized: the construction of the male breadwinner wage norm in nineteenth-century Britain'. *Social History* 2: 53–75.

Segal, Lynne. 1987. *Is the Future Female? Troubled Thoughts on Contemporary Feminism*. London: Virago.

——. 1990. *Slow Motion: Changing Masculinities, Changing Men*. London: Virago.

——. 1997. *Slow Motion: Changing Masculinities, Changing Men*. 2nd edn. London, Virago.

——, ed. 1983. *What Is To Be Done About the Family?* London: Penguin Books & Socialist Society.

Segal, Lynne and Mat McIntosh, eds. 1993. *Sex Exposed: Sexuality and the Pornography Debate*. New Brunswick, NJ: Rutgers University Press.

Seidler, Victor J. 1989. *Rediscovering Masculinity: Reason, Language and Sexuality*. London: Routledge.

——, ed. 1991. *Achilles Heel Reader: Men, Sexual Politics and Socialism*. London: Routledge.

Seidman, Steven, ed. 1996. *Queer Theory/Sociology*. Oxford: Blackwell.

Seifert, Ruth. 1993. *Individualisierungsprozesse, Geschlechterverhältnisse und die soziale Konstruktion des Soldaten*. Munich: Sozialwissenschaftliches Institut der Bundeswehr.

Sennett, Richard and Jonathan Cobb. 1973. *The Hidden injuries of Class*. New York: Vintage.

Sharp, Geoff. 1983. 'Intellectuals in transition'. *Arena* 65: 84–95.

Shostak, *Arthur* B. 1977. 'The women's liberation movement and its various impacts on American men'. *Journal of Sociology and Social Welfare* 4: 897–907.

Silverberg, Robert Allen. 1984. 'Requiem for Superman: men in psychotherapy'. *Arete* 9: 21–35.

Silverman, Martin. 1986. 'The male superego'. *Psychoanalytic Review* 73: 427–44.

Simpson. Amelia. 1993. *Xuxa: The Mega-Marketing of Gender, Race and Modernity*. Philadelphia: Temple University Press.

Sinclair-Webb, Emma. 2000. ' "Our Bülent is now a commando": military service and manhood in Turkey'. In *Imagined Masculinities: Male Identity and Culture in the Modern Middle East*, ed. Ghoussoub, Mai and Emma Sinclair-Webb. London: Saqi Books.

Sinelnikov, Andrei. 2000. 'Masculinity *à la russe*: gender issues in the Russian federation today'. pp. 201–9 in *Male Roles, Masculinities and Violence: A Culture of Peace Perspective*, ed. Ingeborg Breines, Robert Connell and Ingrid Eide. Paris: UNESCO Publishing.

Sinha, Mrinalini. 1987. 'Gender and imperialism: colonial policy and the ideology of moral imperialism in late nineteenth-century Bengal'. pp. 217–31 in *Changing Men: New Directions in Research on Men and Masculinity*, ed. Michael S. Kimmel. Newbury Park, CA: Sage.

Sklair, L. 1995. *Sociology of the Global System*. 2nd edn. Baltimore, Johns Hopkins University Press.

Smith, Joan. 1989. *Misogynies*. London: Faber & Faber.

Smith, Margaret and David Crossley. 1975. *The Way Out*. Melbourne: Lansdowne Press.

Smith, Steve. 1998. 'Unacceptable conclusions and the "man" question: masculinity, gender and international relations'. In *The 'Man' Question in International Relations*, ed. Zalewski, Marysia and Jane Parpart. Boulder: Westview, 54–72.

Snodgrass, Jon, ed. 1977. *For Men Against Sexism: A Book of Readings*. Albion, CA: Times Change Press.

Solomon, Kenneth and Norman B. Levy, eds. 1982. *Men in Transition: Theory and Therapy*. New York: Plenum Press.

Sommers, Christina Hoff. 2000. *The War Against Boys: How Misguided Feminism is Harming Our Young Men*. New York: Simon & Schuster.

Stacey, Judith. 1990. *Brave New Families: Stories of Domestic Upheaval in Late Twentieth Century America*. New York: Basic Books.

Stacey, Judith and Barrie Thorne. 1985. 'The missing feminist revolution in sociology'. *Social Problems* 32: 301–16.

Staples, Robert. 1982. *Black Masculinity: The Black Male's Role in American Society*. San Francisco: Black Scholar Press.

Stearns, Peter N. 1979. *Be a Man! Males in Modern Society*. New York: Holmes & Meier.

Stedman Jones, Gareth. 1971. *Outcast London: A Study in the Relationship between Classes in Victorian Society*. Oxford: Clarendon Press.

Stein, Howard F. 1984. 'Sittin' tight and bustin' loose: contradiction and conflict in mid-western masculinity and the psycho-history of America'. *Journal of Psychohistory* 11: 501–12.

Stepansky, Paul E. 1983. In *Freud's Shadow: Adler in Context*. Hillsdale, NJ: Analytic Press & Lawrence Erlbaum.

Stoller, Robert J. 1968. *Sex and Gender: On the Development of Masculinity and Femininity.* New York: Science House.

——. 1976. *Sex and Gender,* vol. 2: *The Transsexual Experiment.* New York: Jason Aronson.

Stoller, Robert J. and Gilbert H. Herdt. 1982. 'The development of masculinity: a cross-cultural contribution', *American Psychoanalytical Association Journal* 30: 29–59.

Stoltenberg, John. 1990. *Refusing to Be a Man.* London: Fontana.

Strathern, Marilyn. 1978. 'The achievement of sex: paradoxes in Hagen gender-thinking'. pp. 171–202 in *The Yearbook of Symbolic Anthropology,* ed. E. Schwimmer. London: Hurst.

——. 1981. 'Self-interest and the social good: some implications of Hagen gender imagery'. pp. 166–91 in *Sexual Meanings: The Cultural Construction of Gender and Sexuality,* ed. S. B. Ortner and H. Whitehead. Cambridge: Cambridge University Press.

——. 1991. *Partial Connections.* Savage, MD: Rowman & Littlefield.

Sullivan, Edmund V. 1984. *A Critical Psychology: Interpretation of the Personal World.* New York: Plenum.

Swart, Sandra. 2001. ' "Man, gun and horse": hard right Afrikaner masculine identity in post-apartheid South Africa'. pp. 75–89 in *Changing Men in Southern Africa,* ed. Robert Morrell. Pietermaritzburg: University of Natal Press.

Tacey, David J. 1990. 'Reconstructing masculinity: a post-Jungian response to contemporary men's issues'. *Meanjin* 49: 781–92.

Tanaka Kazuko. 1977. *A Short History of the Women's Movement in Modern Japan.* 3rd edn. Japan: Femintern Press.

Taylor, Debbie. 1985. 'Women, an analysis'. pp. 1–98 in *Women, A World Report,* New Internationalist. London: Methuen.

Theberge, Nancy. 1991. 'Reflections on the body in the sociology of sport'. *Quest* 43: 123–34.

Theweleit Klaus. 1987. *Male Fantasies.* Cambridge: Polity Press.

Thomas, William I. and Florian Znaniecki. 1927. *The Polish Peasant in Europe and America.* New York: Knopf.

Thompson, Keith, ed. 1991. *To Be a Man: In Search of the Deep Masculine.* Los Angeles: Tarcher/Perigee.

Thompson, Mark, ed. 1991. *Leatherfolk: Radical Sex, People, Politics, and Practice.* Boston: Alyson Publications.

Thorne, Barrie. 1993. *Gender Play: Girls and Boys in School.* New Brunswick: Rutgers University Press.

Tiefer, Leonore. 1986. 'In pursuit of the perfect penis'. *American Behavioral Scientist* 29: 579–99.

Tiger, Lionel. 1969. *Men in Groups.* New York: Random House.

Tiger, Lionel and Robin Fox. 1971. *The Imperial Animal.* New York: Holt, Rinehart & Winston.

Tillner, Georg. 2000. 'The identity of dominance: masculinity and xeno-phobia'. pp. 53–9 in *Male Roles, Masculinities and Violence: A Culture of Peace Perspective*, ed. Ingeborg Breines, Robert Connell and Ingrid Eide. Paris: UNESCO Publishing.

Tolson, Andrew. 1977. *The Limits of Masculinity*. London: Tavistock.

Tomsen, Stephen. 1997. 'A top night: Social protest, masculinity and the culture of drinking violence'. *British Journal of Criminology* 37: 90–103.

——. 1998. '"He had to be a poofter or something": violence, male honour and heterosexual panic'. *Journal of Interdisciplinary Gender Studies* 3: 44–57.

——. 2002. *Hatred, Murder and Male Honour: Anti-homosexual Homicides in New South Wales, 1980–2000*. Canberra: Australian Institute of Criminology (Research and Public Policy Series, no. 43).

Tomsen, Stephen and Mike Donaldson, eds. 2003. *Male Trouble: Looking at Australian Masculinities*, Melbourne: Pluto Press.

Totten, Mark D. 2000. *Guys, Gangs and Girlfriend Abuse*. Peterborough: Broadview Press.

Troiden, Richard R. 1989. 'The formation of homosexual identities'. *Journal of Homosexuality* 17: 43–73.

Trumbach, Randolph. 1991. 'London's Sapphists: from three sexes to four genders in the making of modern culture', pp. 112–41 in *Body Guards: The Cultural Politics of Gender Ambiguity*, ed. Julia Epstein and Kristina Straub. New York: Routledge.

Turner, Bryan S. 1984. *The Body and Society*. Oxford: Blackwell.

Turner, Charles F. 1989. 'Research on sexual behaviors that transmit HIV: progress and problems'. *AIDS* 3: S63–9.

Tyson, Phyllis. 1986. 'Male gender identity: early developmental roots'. *Psychoanalytic Review* 73: 405–25.

United Nations Development Programme. 1992. *Human Development Report*. New York: Oxford University Press.

United Nations Division for the Advancement of Women. 2004. *The Role of Men and Boys in Achieving Gender Equality: Report of the Expert Group Meeting, Brasilia, Brazil, 21 to 24 October 2003*. New York: United Nations Organization.

United States Bureau of the Census. 1990. *Census of Population, Social and Economic Characteristics, United States, 1990*. CP-2-1.

Urry, John. 1970. 'Role analysis and the sociological enterprise'. *Sociological Review* 18: 351–64.

Valdés, Teresa and Enrique Gomáriz. 1995. *Latin American Women: Compared Figures*. Santiago: Instituto de la Mujer and FLACSO.

Valdés, Teresa and José Olavarría. 1998. 'Ser hombre en Santiago de Chile: A pesar de todo, un mismo modelo'. pp. 12–36 in *Masculin-idades y Equidad de Género en América Latina*, ed. Teresa Valdés and José Olavarría. Santiago: FLACSO/UNFPA.

Valverde, Mariana. 1985. *Sex, Power and Pleasure*, Toronto: Women's Press.

Vance, Carole S. 1989. 'Social construction theory: problems in the history of sexuality'. pp. 13–34 in *Homosexuality, Which Homosexuality?*, ed. Dennis Altman et al. Amsterdam and London: Uitgeverij An Dekker/Schorer & GMP.

Vise, David A. and Steve Coll. 1991. *Eagle on the Street*. New York: Charles Scribner's Sons.

Wajcman, Judy. 1999. *Managing Like a Man: Women and Men in Corporate Management*. Sydney: Allen & Unwin.

Walby, Sylvia. 1989. 'Theorising patriarchy'. *Sociology* 23: 213–34.

Walker, James C. 1988. *Louts and Legends: Male Youth Culture in an Inner-City School*. Sydney: Allen & Unwin.

Walker, Linley. 1989. 'Australian maid'. Doctoral Dissertation. Sydney: Macquarie University, School of Behavioural Sciences.

Walzer, Michael. 1983. *Spheres of Justice: A Defense of Pluralism and Equality*. New York: Basic Books.

Waring, Marilyn. 1988. *Counting for Nothing: What Men Value and What Women are Worth*. Wellington: Allen & Unwin and Port Nicholson Press.

Watney, Simon. 1980. 'The ideology of GLF'. pp. 64–76 in *Homosexuality: Power and Politics*, ed. Gay Left Collective. London: Allison & Busby.

Watson, Ian. 1990. *Fighting Over the Forests*. Sydney: Allen & Unwin.

Weber, Max. 1976 [1904–5]. *The Protestant Ethic and the Spirit of Capitalism*. New York: Scribner.

Weedon, Chris. 1987. *Feminist Practice and Poststructuralist Theory*. Oxford: Blackwell.

Weeks, Jeffrey. 1977. *Coming Out: Homosexual Politics in Britain, from the Nineteenth Century to the Present*. London: Quartet.

——. 1986. *Sexuality*. London: Horwood & Tavistock.

Wehr, Gerhard. 1987. *Jung: A Biography*. Boston: Shambhala.

Weinberg, George H. 1973. *Society and the Healthy Homosexual*. New York: Anchor.

Welzer-Lang, Daniel. 2000. *Nouvelles approaches des hommes et du masculin*. Toulouse: Presses Universitaries du Mirail.

West, Candace and Don H. Zimmerman. 1987. 'Doing gender'. *Gender and Society* 1: 125–51.

Wetherell, Margaret and Nigel Edley. 1999. 'Negotiating hegemonic masculinity: imaginary positions and psycho-discursive practices'. *Feminism and Psychology* 9: 335–56.

Wexler, Philip. 1992. *Becoming Somebody: Toward a Social Psychology of School*. London: Palmer.

Wheeler-Bennett, John. 1953. *Nemesis of Power: The German Army in Politics, 1918–1945*. London: Macmillan.

White, Sara. 2000. ' "Did the earth move?" The hazards of bringing men and masculinities into gender and development'. *IDS Bulletin* 31: 33–41.

Whitehead, Stephen M. and Frank J. Barrett. 2001. *The Masculinities Reader*. Cambridge: Polity Press.

Widersprüche. 1995. Special issue: 'Männlichkeiten', no. 56/7.

——. 1998. Special issue: 'Multioptionale Männlichkeiten?', no. 67.

Wilderness Society. 1983. *Franklin Blockade, by the Blockaders*. Hobart: Wilderness Society.

Williams, Christine L. 1989. *Gender Differences at Work: Women and Men in Nontraditional Occupations*. Berkeley: University of California Press.

Williams, Walter L. 1986. *The Spirit and the Flesh: Sexual Diversity in American Indian Culture*. Boston: Beacon Press.

Willis, Paul. 1977. *Learning to Labour: Low Working Class Kids get Working Class Jobs*. Farnborough: Saxon House.

——. 1978. *Profane Culture*. London: Routledge & Kegan Paul.

——. 1979. 'Shop floor culture, masculinity and the wage form'. pp. 185–98 in *Working Class Culture*, ed. J. Clarke, C. Chritcher and R. Johnson. London: Hutchinson.

Wilson, Bruce and Johanna Wyn. 1987. *Shaping Futures: Youth Action for Livelihood*. Sydney: Allen & Unwin.

Wilson, Edward O. 1978. *On Human Nature*. Cambridge, MA: Harvard University Press.

Wilson, Elizabeth. 1987. *Adorned in Dreams: Fashion and Modernity*. Berkeley: University of California Press.

Winter, Michael F. and Ellen R. Robert. 1980. 'Male dominance, late capitalism, and the growth of instrumental reason'. *Berkeley Journal of Sociology* 249–80.

Wölfl, Edith 2001. *Gewaltbereite Jungen – was kann Erziehung leisten? Anregungen für eine gender-orientierte Pädogogik*. München, Ernst Reinhardt Verlag.

Wolfe, Tom. 1980. *The Right Stuff*. New York: Bantam.

Wolff, Charlotte. 1986. *Magnus Hirschfeld: A Portrait of a Pioneer in Sexology*. London: Quartet.

Wollstonecraft, Mary. 1975 [1792]. *Vindication of the Rights of Woman*. Harmondsworth: Penguin.

Worth, Heather, Anna Paris and Lousia Allen. 2002. *The Life of Brian*. Dunedin: University of Otago Press.

Wotherspoon, Gary. 1991. *City of the Plain: History of a Gay Sub-culture*. Sydney: Hale & Iremonger.

Xaba, Thokozani. 2001. 'Masculinity and its malcontents: the confrontation between "struggle masculinity" and "post-struggle masculinity" (1990–1997)'. In *Changing Men in Southern Africa*, ed. Morrell, Robert. London: Zed Books.

Yates, Lyn. 1993. *The Education of Girls: Policy, Research and the Question of Gender.* Hawthorn, Victoria: Australian Council for Educational Research.

Yeatman, Anna. 1990. *Bureaucrats, Technocrats, Femocrats: Essays on the Contemporary Australian State.* Sydney: Allen & Unwin.

Yeats, William Butler. 1950. *Collected Poems.* London: Macmillan.

Zalewski, Marysia and Jane Parpart, eds. 1998. *The 'Man' Question in International Relations.* Boulder: Westview Press.

Zingoni, Eduardo Liendro. 1998. 'Masculinidades y violencia desde un programa de acción en México'. pp. 130–6 in *Masculinidades y Equidad de Género en América Latina,* ed. Teresa Valdés and José Olavarría. Santiago: FLACSO/UNFPA.

Zulehner, Paul M., and Rainer Volz. 1998. *Männer im Aufbruch: Wie Deutschlands Männer sich selbst und wie Frauen sie sehen.* Ostfildern: Schwabenverlag.

Index